Keto Cookbook for Beginners

1000 Recipes for Low-Carb Lovers | The Complete
Beginner's Guide with 28 Days Keto Meal Plan to
Help You Enjoy Keto Diet Lifestyle

Andrew Callahan

Content

INTRODUCTION

I was unable to figure out the most effective way to manage my eating habits due to my hectic schedule. Every week, my weight monitoring was never a tad off with all my efforts to find a solution, so I realized it was necessary to find an effective diet-management strategy soon, or things will not be good for my health and well-being. Furthermore, I would be in a poor position of fitting into the costly clothes I had planned to wear for my 20th wedding anniversary dinner! It was a surprise to me that my health was so poor and I didn't realize it until my last annual check-up, which had me stunned!

"So how do I get from here?" I thought to myself. I have not been able to find an effective method before. I am too busy to focus on diets that require food to be measured and weighted. In all likelihood, I've gone through many diets that I want to keep track of, and nothing has changed in my life.

Depressed, I went to visit my friends whom I had not visited for a long time. I was stunned by the drastic change in the appearance of my friends. Not only had they shed significant weight, but also they had changed their attitude towards life to be more positive.

I met a friend who had tried various diets and was then taken on the ketogenic eating program like me. Since we have implemented the ketogenic diet, we're happy to see a significant improvement in our weight loss, health and our lifestyle. It certainly shows! As soon as I found this ketogenic diet plan to be awesome, I started learning more about it. At first, I wanted to know what I could get out of the keto diet and whether it would fit into my very busy life.

As a mom with a full-time job and four kids who participate in numerous extracurricular activities, I'm always finding myself unable to make time for food preparation. Plus, having to balance my small business that I run from home and my family's demands keeps me constantly on my toes.

This keto-based diet opened my eyes. Not only am I able to keep my children happy by implementing a new meal plan, but I've gained more support when it comes to meal preparation. Additionally, we all have been feeling better since we began keto. I've observed a significant decrease in my weight and I'm sleeping better and feeling more rested!

I believed that the advantages of the keto diet to my family and myself have been enlightening. And I am convinced that sharing our eating plan will help many individuals who are struggling to find a way of keeping their health and well-being.

Without further delay, let's dive into the fundamentals of keto and how it works for all of us.

Chapter 1 A Complete Guide for Beginners

What Is a Keto Diet?

Dietary ketogenic is a low-carb, high-fat diet. It's the process that drastically reduces your intake of carbohydrates and substitutes the calories with fat. A reduction in carbs places your body into a metabolic state, also known to be ketosis.

When this happens, it creates a body that is extremely efficient when it comes to utilizing fat to create energy. It also transforms calories into ketones in the liver. These ketones are utilized to supply an energy source to your brain.

Ketogenic diets can cause significant reductions on blood sugar levels as well as amounts of insulin. This, when combined with the increase in ketones can provide some health benefits.

There are several ketogenic diets like:

Standard Ketogenic Diet (SKD)

It is a diet that is low in carbohydrates, moderate in protein, and very high in fat. It typically contains 70 percent protein, 20 percent fat and only 10% carbohydrates.

Acyclic Ketogenic Diet (CKD)

The diet is characterized by periods of higher carbohydrate and refeeds. For instance, five ketogenic days, which are then followed by two days of carbohydrate highs.

Targeted Ketogenic Diet (TKD)

The TKD diet permits you to incorporate carbs into your workout.

High Protein Ketogenic diet (HPKD)

The ketogenic diet is high-protein. The ratio is typically 40 percent fats, 60 percent protein, and 5% carbohydrates.

However, only the traditional ketogenic diets have been extensively studied. Targeted ketogenic diets or cyclical ketogenic ones are more sophisticated methods that are mostly used by bodybuilders and athletes.

How to Get Into Ketosis

Eat Less Than 20 Grams of Net Carbs Per Day

The low-carb diet is the primary aspect to achieve ketosis. Cells usually make use of sugar or sucrose as their primary energy source. But, they also utilize other sources of energy such as fatty acids and ketones.

The body stores glycogen as glucose in your liver and muscle. If your intake of carbohydrates is very low, glycogen stores decrease and levels of hormone insulin decline. This allows fat acid to be released from the fat stores in your body. The amount of carbs that trigger ketosis differs with each individual and is influenced by various factors like the type of exercise you do.

Certain individuals should limit their net carbohydrate consume to 20 grams daily. Everyone will require various amounts of carbs to ensure they stay ketosis-like and maintain it according to the calories consumed and level of activity. In general, eating between 5 to 10 percent of calories from carbohydrates could trigger ketosis.

· ·

Avoid Eating out

Do not eat at restaurants. Although there are plenty of keto-friendly eateries, dining out can make it difficult to monitor your carbs.

Measure Ketones

As with many other aspects of nutrition, the process of achieving and maintaining ketosis is highly individual.

Thus, it's beneficial to check your levels of ketone to make sure that you're meeting your goals. The three ketones, namely beta-hydroxybutyrate, acetone and acetoacetate can be detected in breath, urine or blood. Utilizing one or all of these methods to measure ketones, you can determine whether you need any changes in order to be in ketosis.

The Best Way to Test Ketones

Testing Ketones in Blood

Additionally, ketones can be measured using an instrument for measuring blood ketones. Like how the glucose meter functions. It is a tiny sample of blood put on a strip and then put into the device.

It determines what amount of beta-hydroxybutyrate is found in blood, and has been proven as a valid indicator of ketosis condition. The disadvantage of the ketones test within blood samples is the fact that strips cost a lot of money.

Testing Ketones in Breath

Acetone can be found in your breath. Research has proven that the presence of acetone in breath is a reliable method to test the ketosis level of people taking ketogenic diets.

The Ketonix Meter analyzes acetone levels in the air you breathe. After you breathe in the Ketonix meter, light flashes to tell if you're in a high level of ketosis.

Testing Ketones in Urine

The ketone found by urine test is Acetoacetate. The strips of urine containing Ketone are dipped into urine, and they change to various shades of pink or purple depending on the quantity of ketones present in them. A darker shade indicates more ketones. These urine tests are straightforward to use and are fairly cheap. Although their long-term accuracy usage has been questioned, they can first determine if

you're experiencing ketosis. A study found that ketones in urine tend to be higher in the early morning hours and following dinner when following ketogenic diets.

How Does Keto Diet Benefit You?

Weight Loss Without Hunger

A keto diet is considered to be helpful in losing weight and preventing other health related diseases. The research has proven that ketogenic diets can be as effective at losing weight as a low-fat eating plan. Furthermore, it is full of nutrients that you'll lose weight without having to track calories or the quantity of food you eat.

Research showed that following an extremely low-carb, ketogenic diet is proved to be slightly more effective in weight loss over the low-fat diet. People with dietary ketosis lost an average of two pounds (0.9 kilogram) more than those who adhered to a low-fat diet. The keto diet also resulted in reductions of diastolic blood pressure and the levels of triglycerides. Another study found that those who ate the ketogenic diet for eight weeks lost nearly five times as much weight as people who ate the low-fat diet. The higher ketones, the decreased blood sugar along with improved insulin sensitivity could be a factor.

Control or Reverse Type 2 Diabetes

The term "diabetes" refers to changes in metabolism, including elevated blood sugar levels and diminished performance of the insulin. The ketogenic diet can aid in the elimination of excess fat. It also is linked with type 2 disease, prediabetes and metabolic syndrome. An investigation of females with type 2 diabetes found that a ketogenic diet over 90 days significantly reduced amounts of hemoglobin A1C, which can be a test for the long-term control of blood sugar levels.

Improve Metabolic Health & Blood Pressure

Even a small amount of weight through the keto diet could aid in reducing cardiovascular risk factors like excessive weight, high blood pressure. In addition, according to a study, it will result in lower levels of LDL ("bad") cholesterol levels and greater HDL cholesterol. This helps in preventing heart disease. The keto diet may also reduce blood sugar levels that are linked to inflammation that damages arteries.

Potential Risks of a Keto Diet

Like all diets, there are dangers associated with the keto diet. Here are three dangers associated with the keto diet you must be aware of before embarking on the keto diet.

The Keto Flu

The lower intake of carbs can be a shock for the body. In the process of switching your body between fats and carbs for energy, you could suffer from flu-like symptoms. There is the possibility of experiencing dizziness, nausea, headaches and constipation.

Many people experience relief after several weeks. It is vital to be aware of your symptoms and consume electrolyte-rich, sodium and potassium-rich foods.

The Stress to Your Kidneys

High-fat foods are the norm in your ketogenic diet. Consuming foods such as eggs, cheese, and meat can result in the possibility of developing kidney stones. These food items can cause your urine and blood to become more acidic, which can lead to calcium excretion through your urine. Research suggests that keto decreases citrate levels which is a chemical that bonds to calcium. Drink plenty of fluids and keep your weight in check.

Nutrient Deficiencies

Due to the numerous restrictions on what types of foods you can consume in the diet, you're missing the most important minerals and vitamins. The diet isn't providing sufficient vitamin D calcium, magnesium, and Phosphorus. In time, you may be deficient in vitamins and might need to take supplements to treat them.

Keto Macros: Carbs, Protein, and Fat

Ketosis can be achieved by cutting down on carbohydrates for a period of time to drain glycogen stores in the body, in addition to eating plenty of high-quality fat-rich foods.

Since the ketogenic diet concentrates on macronutrients (proteins as well as carbs and fats), you must be aware of how to calculate keto macros to determine the nutrients your body requires in order to reach ketosis.

Carbohydrates

When people think of energy, people think about carbs. The reason is that carbohydrates break down into glucose, which your body makes to provide fuel for yourself unless you're in ketosis of course.

Carbs are present in the fruits, vegetables and starches, grains and a variety of processed foods.

Protein

Protein is broken into amino acids which are utilized by the body to build muscles, hair, fingernails and hair and many more. Protein is fundamental in the creation of hormones, enzymes and other bodily chemicals.

Protein sources that are approved by Keto include things similar to animal products such as eggs, beef, and fish as well as dairy products.

Fat

Fat is essential for keeping your nervous system and brain well-maintained. Fat is a significant portion of ketogenic diets, approximately 70 percent.

The concept is to eat large quantities of high-quality fats and limiting your carb intake puts your body in ketosis which means that you burn fat as the main fuel source.

Foods to Eat on Keto Diet

Here's an overview of the keto-friendly and low-carb food items that you can consume when following keto.

Fish and Seafood

Fish is high in vitamin B as well as potassium and selenium. It's also a great source of protein. Mackerel, salmon and sardines, albacore tuna, mackerel, and other fish that are fat contain plenty of omega-3 fats which have been shown to reduce blood sugar levels and increase insulin sensitivity. Regular fish consumption can reduce the risk of chronic diseases and also improve mental health related.

Low-Carb Veggies

Non-starchy vegetables aren't low in carbs. However, they are rich in numerous minerals, like vitamin C and diverse minerals. They also contain antioxidants that assist in protecting cells from damage caused by free radicals. Select non-starchy vegetables with lower than eight grams of net carbs per cup. Net carbs are the total of all carbs less fiber. Cauliflower or broccoli bell peppers and green beans, bell peppers and all are suitable to fill the bill.

Meat and Poultry

Meat is a fantastic source of protein and is high in fat and considered as a primary ingredient in a ketogenic diet. Fresh meat and poultry contain no carbs and are rich in B vitamins, as well as various minerals, including selenium along with potassium, zinc and selenium. Although processed meats such as bacon and sausage are permitted in ketosis, they're not great for heart health and can increase the risk of developing certain forms of cancer when you consume an excessive amount of.

Dark Chocolate and Cocoa Powder

Find the label on these products, as the amount of carbohydrates in them will depend on the type and quantity of food you consume. Cocoa is dubbed a "superfruit" because of the abundance of antioxidants. In addition dark chocolate is brimming with flavanols that can reduce the chance of developing heart disease by lowering blood pressure and helping to maintain the health of blood vessels.

Foods You Will Eliminate on Keto Diet

Grains and Starches

Cereal cruncher, cereal bread, rice pasta, as well as cereals, are packed with carbs. Whole wheat pasta and the latest bean-based pastas are high in carbs. Consider alternatives such as spiralized vegetables, which are low in carbs and healthier. Healthy breakfast cereals that contain whole-grain and sugar are high in carbohydrates and should be avoided or cut down on.

Starchy Vegetables

While they are good sources of potassium, vitamin C and the dietary fiber, but they are not recommended when following the keto diet due to their high levels of carbs. Reduce consumption of some healthy but high-carbohydrate foods, including peas and corn.

Starchy vegetables with slightly less carbohydrates per serving include the carrot and beets. It is possible to have small amounts of them if they meet your daily carbohydrate allowance. If you're looking for starchy veggies, try adding them lightly to a bowl or salad instead of making them the centerpiece of the dish.

Most Fruit, Except Berries and Melon

Fruits like mangoes and grapes, and bananas are naturally rich in carbohydrates. While they're delicious and nutritious, they may prevent your body from reaching or keeping ketosis.

Beans, Chickpeas, Lentils, Peas and Edamame

Keto-friendly people are aiming to consume upwards of 70% of the calories that they need from fat. They'll also consume very little carbs. Therefore, for the major part, you'll skimp in the form of fruit, beans and legumes (like lentils and beans), most dairy, starchy vegetables and whole grains.

Although you don't require only beans or fruit for health, if you combine and remove various foods, you may be left with a less-than-nutritious diet. Roasted chickpeas could be one of the most popular snacks but they're unlikely to work with keto. Also the legume edamame bean is a type that is generally not part of keto diets.

Common Mistakes When Following a Keto Diet

Going Overboard With Fat

The keto diet is rich in fat, and many people are scared to eat excessive amounts of fat due to the belief that fat can make you overweight. Since you're limiting your intake of carbohydrates, it is essential to consume more fat. Insufficient intake of fat can affect the functioning of your hormones and your metabolism. Even after eating a balanced diet, you'll feel fatigued due to a deficiency of macro and micronutrients. It is equally vital to choose the right type of fat. Include animal fats and olive oil, as well as monounsaturated oils in your diet.

Fear of Too Much Protein

It's a popular belief that eating excessive protein can cause a metabolic reaction which increases blood sugar levels and takes the ketosis process. It's known as the process of gluconeogenesis and, contrary to many beliefs, you don't have to be concerned about protein excess when you're on ketogenic diets. Here's why:

1. The process is constantly occurring in ketosis.

No matter how much protein you consume in the keto diet it is already taking place since your body requires small levels of glucose to perform.

2. Gluconeogenesis occurs only in tiny quantities.

Don't worry even on a protein-rich diet, as it's likely that you're using ketones for the primary fuel source.

3. Gluconeogenesis can be beneficial to your health.

Like too much glucose is harmful but too little could be fatal to you. Gluconeogenesis helps prevent hypoglycemia. It also helps the tissues to produce energy that isn't capable of metabolizing ketones. This includes red blood cells, which are part of your kidney, as well as testicles.

It's likely that you're not receiving sufficient protein. Protein's amino acids aid in strengthening and repairing muscles as well as other tissues. Protein is also helpful in keeping your body full and helps you lose weight.

Chasing Higher Ketone Levels

It's gratifying to get the high ketone levels even when you're only beginning your journey. Ketones are an excellent indicator that all the efforts are paying off.

But, seeing ketones with high levels within the urinary strips or on your blood ketone meters isn't your primary goal when you are on a ketogenic diet, especially in the long run. A long-lasting high reading on ketone levels isn't always a positive thing. It's normal to have higher levels of ketones when first beginning to use keto. It's likely that you have an increased amount of fat that needs to be burned, and your body isn't accustomed to burning ketones to fuel. This causes a higher level of ketones.

As time passes the body becomes more efficient in burning ketones, meaning they're no longer circulating in your bloodstream, or being eliminated through urine. This means you'll have lower blood levels however MORE ketones are being burned up for fuel.

FAQs

Is Keto Safe?

Since the diet is not a balanced diet , and eliminates so many healthy foods, there's plenty of reason to think that sticking on this diet for a substantial period of time will not be healthy.

It's feasible that extreme diets such as keto may have long-term consequences on your metabolism and capacity to shed pounds even if you adhere to them for a brief period of time. Diets that are restrictive like keto can result in social isolation and disordered eating habits. Keto is not recommended for people with any condition related to their liver, pancreas thyroid or gallbladder.

How Much Weight Can I Expect to Lose on Keto?

Based on the size of your body and the amount of water weight you're carrying around, this weight loss could be different. In general, people report losing in the first week that range between 1 one pound (0.5 kilograms) up to 10 pounds or more (5 kilograms). The more weight you have the more water weight you're likely to lose when following the keto diet.

You can check the ketones level in your body to determine if your body is in ketosis. In this phase of burning fat it is possible to shed 1 to 2 pounds per week. Also, you'll notice that you're feeling less hungry since the fat you're taking in can make you feel more satisfied.

What Is The Difference Between Keto and Low Carb?

When choosing between keto and low carb eating plans, you have a variety of aspects to take into consideration.

The major difference between the two diets is the amount of carbohydrate consumed. When you're following the low-carb diet generally, you consume between 50 and 150 grams of carbohydrates daily, whereas those on keto diets have a daily intake of carbohydrates that is restricted to less than 50 grams. Another significant distinction is the amount of protein consumed. If you're on a low-carb diet, the intake of protein is often quite excessive; however, in ketogenic diets, consumption of protein must be moderate, about 20% of calories.

Furthermore, fat consumption tends to be greater on keto diets since fats substitute for protein and carbs. The keto diet is too restrictive for a majority of people, leading to inadequate long-term compliance. Additionally the keto diet is more likely to trigger undesirable side effects. So, a low-carb diet is probably an ideal choice for the majority of people.

28 Days Keto Diet Meal Plan

DAYS	BREAKFAST	LUNCH	DINNER	SNACK/DESSERT
1	Indian Masala Omelet	Marjoram Beef Ribs	Super Cheesy Salmon Zoodles	EL Presidente Guac
2	Sticky Wrapped Eggs	Halibut Curry	Chicken Enchilada Bowl	Trail Mix with Dried Coconut and Strawberries
3	Breakfast Roll-Ups	Green Bean Casserole	Low-Carb Chili	Cheesecake Balls
4	French Toast	Chilean Sea Bass with Olive Relish	Zoodle, Bacon, Spinach, and Halloumi Gratin	Hearty Crème Brûlée
5	Counterfeit Bagels	Zucchini and Daikon Fritters	Trout Casserole	Almond Sesame Crackers
6	Traditional Porridge	Lemon-Rosemary Spatchcock Chicken	Bacon Mac 'n' Cheese	Angel Food Mug Cake with Strawberries
7	Prosciutto Baked Eggs with Spinach	Salmon Steaks with Garlicky Yogurt	Oregano Beef	Easy Baked Zucchini Chips
8	Primal Omelet	Zesty Grilled Chicken	Mayo-Less Tuna Salad	Pumpkin Walnut Cheesecake
9	Keto English Muffins	Cheesy Cauliflower Gratin	Stewed Chicken and Sausage	Stuffed Party Shrooms
10	Chocolate Chip Pancake	Lamb Koobideh	Keto Greek Avgolemono	Berry Cheesecake Fat Bomb
11	Christmas Soufflé	Chicken Pesto Pizzas	Chicken and Mixed Greens Salad	Burrata Caprese Stack

DAYS	BREAKFAST	LUNCH	DINNER	SNACK/DESSERT
12	Biscuits and Gravy	Beef and Eggplant Tagine	Stuffed Mushrooms with Chicken	Pumpkin Pie Spice Pots De Crème
13	Indian Masala Omelet	Parmesan Salmon Loaf	Brazilian Tempero Baiano Chicken Drumsticks	Greens Chips with Curried Yogurt Sauce
14	Radish Hash Browns	Beef Chili	Chilean Sea Bass with Olive Relish	Lemon Vanilla Cheesecake
15	French Toast	Italian Beef Burgers	Braised Chicken Legs with Olives and Artichokes	Crispy Bacon Wrapped Onion Rings
16	Sticky Wrapped Eggs	Fried Red Snapper	Barbacoa Beef Roast	Chocolate Cake with Walnuts
17	Breakfast Roll-Ups	Cheesy Zucchini Gratin	Rib Eye with Chimichurri Sauce	Easy Peasy Peanut Butter Cookies
18	Classic Cinnamon Roll Coffee Cake	Chicken Alfredo with Bacon	Salmon Steaks with Garlicky Yogurt	Toasted Coconut Marshmallows
19	Savory Zucchini Cheddar Waffles	Beef Cheeseburger Pie	Friday Night Fish Fry	Marinated Cheese
20	Traditional Porridge	Trout Casserole	Rubbed Whole Chicken	Nutty Shortbread Cookies
21	Primal Omelet	Beef and Mushroom Stew	Seared-Salmon Shirataki Rice Bowls	Vanilla Ice Cream
22	Coconut Flour Macadamia Pancakes	Southern Pulled Pork "Spaghetti"	Spicy Shrimp Fried Rice	Cauliflower Popcorn
23	Protein Waffles	Mayo-Less Tuna Salad	Chicken Pot Pie Crumble	Lemon Drops
24	Keto Cabbage Hash Browns	Thanksgiving Turkey Breast	South Indian Fried Fish	Crunchy Jicama Fries
25	Bacon Cheese Egg with Avocado	Grilled Paprika Chicken with Steamed Broccoli	Korean Ground Beef Bowl	Fruit Pizza
26	Cheesy Egg and Spinach Nest	Baked Coconut Haddock	Cheesy Zucchini Gratin	Citrus-Marinated Olives
27	No-Bake Keto Power Bars	Broccoli and Mushroom Bake	Juicy No-Fail Burger	Fast Chocolate Mousse
28	Nutty "Oatmeal"	Muffin Top Tuna Pops	Southern Pulled Pork "Spaghetti"	Coconut Cajun Shrimp

Golden Gate Granola

Prep time: 10 minutes | Cook time: 1 hour | Makes 4 cups

¼ cup (½ stick) unsalted butter
¼ cup powdered erythritol
¼ teaspoon plus 10 drops of liquid stevia
1 teaspoon ground cinnamon
½ teaspoon vanilla extract
1 cup raw almonds
1 cup raw hazelnuts
1 cup unsweetened coconut flakes
½ cup raw pumpkin seeds
¼ cup hemp hearts

1. Preheat the oven to 275°F and line a rimmed baking sheet with parchment paper or a silicone baking mat. 2. In a small saucepan over medium heat, combine the butter, erythritol, stevia, cinnamon, and vanilla extract. Stirring occasionally, heat until the butter and erythritol are melted and dissolved. Remove from the heat and set aside. 3. In a large bowl, combine the nuts, coconut flakes, pumpkin seeds, and hemp hearts. Pour the melted butter mixture over the nut mixture and toss using a rubber spatula, making sure that everything is well coated. 4. Pour the granola onto the lined baking sheet and spread it out into an even layer. Bake for 1 hour, stirring every 15 minutes or so, until dark golden brown. 5. Let the granola cool in the pan for at least 1 hour to allow it to harden and form clumps. Store in a sealed jar or zip-top plastic bag for up to 3 weeks. It does not need to be refrigerated.
Per Serving
Calories: 200 | fat: 18g | protein: 5g | carbs: 5g | net carbs: 2g | fiber: 3g

Cheese Ciabatta with Pepperoni

Prep time: 10 minutes | Cook time: 10 minutes | Serves 6

10 ounces (283 g) cream cheese, melted
2½ cups mozzarella cheese, shredded
4 large eggs, beaten
3 tablespoons Romano
cheese, grated
½ cup pork rinds, crushed
2½ teaspoons baking powder
½ cup tomato puree
12 large slices pepperoni

1. Combine eggs, mozzarella cheese and cream cheese. Place in baking powder, pork rinds, and Romano cheese. Form into 6 chiabatta shapes. Set a nonstick pan over medium heat. Cook each ciabatta for 2 minutes per side. Sprinkle tomato puree over each one and top with pepperoni slices to serve.
Per Serving
Calories: 466 | fat: 41g | protein: 20g | carbs: 6g | net carbs: 6g | fiber: 0g

Bacon-Jalapeño Egg Cups

Prep time: 5 minutes | Cook time: 25 minutes | Makes 6 egg cups

For the Bacon:
6 bacon slices
1 tablespoon butter
For the Eggs:
2 jalapeño peppers
4 large eggs
2 ounces (57 g) cream cheese, at room temperature
Pink Himalayan salt
Freshly ground black pepper
¼ cup shredded Mexican blend cheese

To Make the Bacon: 1. Preheat the oven to 375°F. **2.** While the oven is warming up, heat a large skillet over medium-high heat. Add the bacon slices and cook partially, about 4 minutes. Transfer the bacon to a paper towel–lined plate. **3.** Coat six cups of a standard muffin tin with the butter. Place a partially cooked bacon strip in each cup to line the sides. **To Make the Eggs: 1.** Cut one jalapeño lengthwise, seed it, and mince it. Cut the remaining jalapeño into rings, discarding the seeds. Set aside. **2.** In a medium bowl, beat the eggs with a hand mixer until well beaten. Add the cream cheese and diced jalapeño, season with pink Himalayan salt and pepper, and beat again to combine. **3.** Pour the egg mixture into the prepared muffin tin, filling each cup about two-thirds of the way up so they have room to rise. **4.** Top each cup with some of the shredded cheese and a ring of jalapeño, and bake for 20 minutes. **5.** Cool for 10 minutes, and serve hot.
Per Serving
Calories: 159 | fat: 13g | protein: 9g | carbs: 1g | net carbs: 1g | fiber: 0g

Heart-Healthy Hazelnut-Collagen Shake

Prep time: 5 minutes | Cook time: 0 minutes | Serves 1

1½ cups unsweetened almond milk
2 tablespoons hazelnut butter
2 tablespoons grass-fed collagen powder
½-1 teaspoon cinnamon
⅛ teaspoon LoSalt or pink Himalayan salt
⅛ teaspoon sugar-free almond extract
1 tablespoon macadamia oil or hazelnut oil

1. Place all of the ingredients in a blender and pulse until smooth and frothy. Serve immediately.
Per Serving
Calories: 507 | fat: 41g | protein: 3g | carbs: 35g | fiber: 12g | sodium: 569mg

Bacon Lovers' Quiche

Prep time: 20 minutes | Cook time: 45 minutes | Serves 8

Crust:
2 cups blanched almond flour
1 large egg
2 tablespoons melted lard, plus more for the pans
⅛ teaspoon finely ground gray sea salt
Filling:
6 strips bacon (about 6 ounces/170 g)
1⅓ cups full-fat coconut milk

4 large eggs
¼ cup plus 2 tablespoons nutritional yeast
¼ teaspoon finely ground gray sea salt
¼ teaspoon ground black pepper
⅛ teaspoon ground nutmeg
For Garnish (Optional):
Cooked chopped bacon (reserved from above)
Sliced fresh chives

1. Preheat the oven to 350°F (177°C) and lightly grease four 4-inch (10-cm) tart pans with lard. 2. **Make the Crusts:** Mix the almond flour, egg, lard, and salt until completely incorporated. 3. Divide the dough into 4 pieces and place in a tart pan. Press the dough into the pans, about ⅛ inch (3 mm) thick. 4. Par-bake the tart pans for 13 to 15 minutes, until the crusts are lightly golden. 5. **Prepare the Filling:** Cook the bacon in a frying pan over medium heat until crispy, then roughly chop it; reserve the bacon grease. Mix and whisk the coconut milk, eggs, nutritional yeast, salt, pepper, nutmeg bacon pieces and still-warm reserved bacon grease in a bowl. 6. Remove the par-baked crusts from the oven and reduce the temperature to 325°F (163°C). Leaving the crusts on the baking sheet, fill them with the egg filling. 7. Return the quiches to the oven and bake for 30 minutes until the tops are lightly golden. Cool for 30 minutes before serving and garnish as you like.
Per Serving
Calories: 404 | fat: 31g | protein: 23g | carbs: 9g | net carbs: 4g | fiber: 5g

Egg Muffins in Ham Cups

Prep time: 5 minutes | Cook time: 18 minutes | Serves 6

1 tablespoon coconut oil, melted
6 slices ham (thin-sliced is better)

6 large eggs
Salt and pepper, to taste
3 tablespoons shredded Cheddar cheese (optional)

1. Preheat the oven to 400ºF (205ºC). Brush six cups of a muffin tin with the melted coconut oil. 2. Line each cup with 1 slice of ham. Crack 1 egg into each cup. Season with salt and pepper, then sprinkle ½ tablespoon of Cheddar cheese on each egg. 3. Bake for 13 to 18 minutes depending on how you like your egg yolks set. 4. Remove from the oven and let cool for a few minutes before carefully removing the "muffins." Refrigerate in a glass or plastic container so they don't get smushed or dried out.

Per Serving
Calories: 178 | fat: 13g | protein: 14g | carbs: 1g | net carbs: 1g | fiber: 0g

Cheesy Cauliflower Grits

Prep time: 5 minutes | Cook time: 15 minutes | Serves 4

¼ cup heavy cream
4 tablespoons unsalted butter, divided
1 teaspoon salt
½ teaspoon garlic powder
¼ teaspoon freshly ground

black pepper
2 cups riced cauliflower
¾ cup shredded Cheddar cheese
¼ cup shredded Parmesan cheese

1. In a medium saucepan over high heat, combine the heavy cream, 2 tablespoons of butter, salt, garlic powder, and pepper and bring to just below a boil. Add the riced cauliflower and reduce heat to low. 2. Simmer, stirring occasionally, for 8 to 10 minutes, until the cauliflower is tender, most of the water from the vegetable has evaporated, and the mixture is thick and creamy. 3. Remove from the heat and stir in the shredded cheeses and remaining 2 tablespoons of butter. Serve warm.
Per Serving
Calories: 280 | fat: 26g | protein: 8g | carbs: 5g | net carbs: 4g | fiber: 1g

Cross-Country Scrambler

Prep time: 5 minutes | Cook time: 28 minutes | Serves 2

8 strips bacon (about 8 ounces/227 g)
1 packed cup spiral-sliced butternut squash (about 5¼ ounces/150 g)
½ green bell pepper, diced

6 large eggs, beaten
½ cup sliced green onions (green parts only)
¼ teaspoon ground black pepper

1. Cook the bacon in a large frying pan over medium heat until crispy, about 15 minutes. Remove the bacon from the pan, leaving the grease in the pan. When the bacon has cooled, crumble it. 2. Add the squash and bell pepper to the pan with the bacon grease. Cover and cook over medium-low heat for 8 minutes, or until the vegetables are fork-tender. 3. Add the beaten eggs, green onions, and black pepper. Mix with a large spoon until fully incorporated. 4. Cook, uncovered, for 5 minutes, stirring every minute, or until the eggs are cooked to your liking. Once complete, fold in half of the crumbled bacon. 5. Divide evenly between 2 plates, top with remaining crumbled bacon, and dig in!
Per Serving
Calories: 395 | fat: 27g | protein: 26g | carbs: 12g | net carbs: 9g | fiber: 3g

PB&J Overnight Hemp

Prep time: 5 minutes | Cook time: 0 minutes | serves 6

3 cups unsweetened almond milk, plus more for serving
1 tablespoon sugar-free peanut butter
4 drops liquid stevia or sugar-free sweetener of choice

1½ cups hemp hearts
2 tablespoons chia seeds
¼ cup cacao nibs
⅛ cup unsweetened coconut flakes
¼ cup freeze-dried raspberries

1. In a large mixing bowl, whisk together the almond milk, peanut butter, and stevia. 2. Once well combined, add the hemp hearts, chia seeds, cacao nibs, coconut, and raspberries, and stir together. 3. Pour the mixture into a lidded storage container and place in the refrigerator for at least 8 hours. 4. Divide the mixture among 6 small serving bowls and top with a splash of almond milk.

Per Serving
Calories: 324 | fat: 24g | protein: 16g | carbs: 10g | net carbs: 2g | fiber: 8g

Waffles with Sausage Gravy

Prep time: 5 minutes | Cook time: 15 minutes | Serves 4

Sausage Gravy:
1 pound (454 g) ground pork (or ground beef or turkey)
1 teaspoon dried sage
½ teaspoon dried thyme
½ teaspoon garlic powder
¼ teaspoon kosher salt
¼ teaspoon black pepper
About 1¼ cups full-fat coconut milk

Waffles:
2 large eggs
1 tablespoon melted coconut oil
½ cup full-fat coconut milk
¾ cup almond flour or nut pulp
¼ teaspoon salt
½ teaspoon baking soda
1½ teaspoons arrowroot powder

1. Heat a large skillet over medium heat and add the ground pork. Break up with a fork as it cooks. 2. When the pork is mostly cooked, in about 5 minutes, add the spices and stir well. Cook until fully browned, another 2 to 3 minutes. Add the coconut milk and allow to come to a simmer, then turn the heat to low. 3. In a medium bowl, whisk the eggs with the coconut oil and coconut milk. Add the pulp, salt, baking soda, and arrowroot powder, and mix well. The waffle batter will be thicker than a traditional batter; if needed, add a little water a tablespoon at a time until it is pourable. 4. Pour some batter into a waffle maker set on medium-low heat. (Alternatively, use a lightly greased pan or griddle and make pancakes.) Remove the waffle from the waffle maker when cooked through and continue to make waffles with the remaining batter. 5. Serve the waffles with the gravy on top.

Per Serving
Calories: 644 | fat: 56g | protein: 28g | carbs: 7g | net carbs: 3g | fiber: 4g

No-Crust Spinach Quiche

Prep time: 10 minutes | Cook time: 35 minutes | Serves 6

4 tablespoons butter, divided
1 onion, diced
2 garlic cloves, minced
2 cups fresh spinach, chopped
Salt and freshly ground

black pepper, to taste
10 eggs
1 cup heavy (whipping) cream
2 cups shredded cheese (Colby-Monterey Jack is good), divided

1. Preheat the oven to 375ºF (190ºC). 2. Grease a large round baking dish with 2 tablespoons of butter. 3. In a medium skillet over medium heat, combine the onion, garlic, spinach, and remaining 2 tablespoons of butter. Season with salt and pepper. Sauté for 4 to 5 minutes and remove from the heat. 4. In a large bowl, whisk the eggs and cream. Add the spinach and 1 cup of cheese and mix to combine. Pour the mixture into the prepared baking dish and season with more salt and pepper. Top with the remaining 1 cup of cheese. Bake for about 30 minutes or until the eggs are set. Cool slightly, slice, and serve. Refrigerate leftovers in an airtight container for up to 1 week.

Per Serving
Calories: 483 | fat: 43g | protein: 21g | carbs: 4g | net carbs: 4g | fiber: 0g

Grain-Free Granola

Prep time: 5 minutes | Cook time: 30 minutes | Makes 3 cups

1 cup chopped raw pecans
1 cup roasted and salted shelled sunflower seeds
1 cup unsweetened coconut flakes
¼ cup finely ground blanched almond flour

1 large egg white
¼ cup granular erythritol
2 tablespoons salted butter, melted
1 teaspoon vanilla extract
⅛ teaspoon liquid stevia

1. Preheat the oven to 325°F. Line a sheet pan with parchment paper. 2. In a medium-sized bowl, stir together the pecans, sunflower seeds, coconut flakes, and almond flour. 3. In a small bowl, whisk the egg white, then stir in the erythritol, melted butter, vanilla extract, and stevia. Pour over the pecan mixture and stir until the pecan mixture is completely coated with the egg white mixture. 4. Spread the granola evenly on the sheet pan. Bake for 25 to 30 minutes, stirring every 10 minutes, until light golden brown. Allow to cool completely before serving. Leftovers can be stored in an airtight container for up to 2 weeks.

Per Serving
Calories: 186 | fat: 18g | protein: 4g | carbs: 5g | net carbs: 2g | fiber: 3g

Cheesy Sausage and Egg Muffins

Prep time: 10 minutes | Cook time: 30 minutes | Makes 12 muffins

Nonstick cooking spray (optional)
8 large eggs
6 ounces (170 g) cream cheese
2 tablespoons butter
½ teaspoon freshly ground black pepper
½ teaspoon garlic powder
4 ounces (113 g) cooked breakfast sausage
½ cup grated Cheddar cheese

1. Preheat the oven to 350ºF (180ºC). Prepare a 12-cup muffin pan with cooking spray or cupcake liners and set aside. 2. In a blender or with a hand mixer, mix the eggs, cream cheese, butter, pepper, and garlic powder until fluffy. 3. Divide the mixture evenly between the prepared muffin cups. 4. Sprinkle each cup evenly with the sausage and cheese. 5. Bake for 30 minutes. Serve warm.

Per Serving 1 muffin
Calories: 168 | fat: 15g | protein: 7g | carbs: 1g | net carbs: 1g | fiber: 0g

Cheesy Sausage Quiche

Prep time: 5 minutes | Cook time: 40 minutes | Serves 6

6 eggs
12 ounces (340 g) raw sausage roll
10 cherry tomatoes, halved
2 tablespoons heavy cream
2 tablespoons Parmesan cheese
¼ teaspoon salt
A pinch of black pepper
2 tablespoons chopped parsley
5 eggplant slices

1. Preheat your oven to 370ºF. 2. Grease a pie dish with cooking spray. Press the sausage roll at the bottom of a pie dish. Arrange the eggplant slices on top of the sausage. Top with cherry tomatoes. 3. Whisk the eggs along with the heavy cream, salt, Parmesan cheese, and black pepper. Spoon the mixture over the sausage. Bake for about 40 minutes until browned around the edges. Serve warm, sprinkled with parsley.

Per Serving
Calories: 340 | fat: 28g | protein: 17g | carbs: 4g | net carbs: 3g | fiber: 1g

Chorizo Cotija Morning Muffins

Prep time: 15 minutes | Cook time: 27 minutes | Makes 1 dozen muffins

6 ounces (170 g) fresh (raw) chorizo
½ cup (1 stick) unsalted butter, melted (but not hot)
4 large eggs
¼ cup water
1 cup golden flax meal
¼ cup coconut flour
1 cup shredded Cotija cheese (about 4 ounces/113 g), plus extra for garnish (optional)
1 teaspoon baking powder
½ teaspoon pink Himalayan salt
½ teaspoon garlic powder
½ teaspoon dried oregano leaves
¼ teaspoon chili powder
¼ teaspoon paprika

1. Preheat the oven to 350°F and line a 12-well muffin tin with paper liners. 2. Heat the sausage over medium-high heat in a medium-sized skillet . Flatten and break apart the sausage with a spatula. Cook for 5 to 7 minutes until cooked through. Remove the chorizo and set aside on a paper towel-lined plate. 3. Put the melted butter, eggs, and water in a large bowl and combine using a whisk. Add the flax meal, coconut flour, Cotija cheese, baking powder, and seasonings and combine with a rubber spatula. 4. Add the cooked chorizo and stir to combine. Scoop the mixture evenly into the 12 cupcake liners with a spoon, filling them nearly to the top. 5. Bake for 20 minutes, or until a toothpick inserted in the center of a muffin comes out clean. Allow to cool in the pan for at least 10 minutes before removing and serving. Garnish with extra Cotija, if desired. 6. Store leftovers in a sealed container or zip-top plastic bag for up to a week. To reheat, microwave for 30 to 45 seconds. Unfortunately, these muffins do not freeze well.

Per Serving
Calories: 246 | fat: 20g | protein: 12g | carbs: 5g | net carbs: 1g | fiber: 4g

Breakfast Roll-Ups

Prep time: 5 minutes | Cook time: 11 minutes | Makes 3 roll-ups

4 large eggs
¼ cup heavy whipping cream
½ teaspoon pink Himalayan salt
6 ounces (170 g) fresh spinach
6 slices bacon, cooked
2 ounces (57 g) fresh (soft) goat cheese

1. Heat a 12-inch skillet over low heat and grease with coconut oil spray. 2. Put the eggs, cream, and salt in a medium-sized bowl and whisk to combine. 3. Scoop out some of the egg mixture in the center of the hot skillet and coats the entire flat surface by tilting the pan . Cover with a lid and cook for 2 to 3 minutes, until cooked through. Repeat with the rest of the egg mixture to make a total of 3 egg wraps. 4. Place the spinach in the skillet coated with coconut oil spray over medium heat. Cover with the lid and cook for 1 to 2 minutes, until the spinach has wilted and cooked down. Remove from the skillet. 5. Divide the cooked spinach among the 3 egg wraps, placing it along the edge of each wrap. Place 2 slices of bacon on top of the spinach in each wrap and divide the goat cheese evenly among the wraps. 6. Starting at the edge with the fillings, roll each egg wrap into a burrito, folding in the ends, or simply roll it up like crepe. Serve warm.

Per Serving
Calories: 299 | fat: 24g | protein: 20g | carbs: 4g | net carbs: 2g | fiber: 2g

Chocolate Chip Waffle

Prep time: 5 minutes | Cook time: 5 minutes | Serves 1

⅓ cup blanched almond flour
½ tablespoon coconut flour
¼ teaspoon baking powder
2 large eggs
¼ teaspoon vanilla extract
4 drops liquid stevia
1 tablespoon stevia-

sweetened chocolate chips
For Topping: (Optional)
Swerve confectioners'-style
sweetener
Sugar-free syrup
Salted butter

1. Preheat a waffle maker to medium-high heat. 2. Place all the ingredients except the chocolate chips in a large bowl and blend until smooth. Fold in the chocolate chips. 3. Spray the hot waffle maker with nonstick cooking spray. 4. Pour the batter into the hot waffle iron and cook for 3 to 5 minutes, until light golden brown. 5. Serve dusted with Swerve confectioners'-style sweetener and topped with sugar-free syrup and butter, if desired.
Per Serving 1 waffle
Calories: 398 | fat: 31g | protein: 23g | carbs: 14g | net carbs: 6g | fiber: 8g

Smoked Sausage and Mushroom Breakfast Skillet

Prep time: 15 minutes | Cook time: 35 minutes | serves 6

8 large eggs
¼ cup heavy whipping
cream
1 cup shredded cheddar
cheese
Pinch of salt
Pinch of ground black

pepper
12 ounces (340 g) smoked
sausage, sliced
1 cup diced white mushrooms
¼ cup sliced green onions,
plus extra for garnish if
desired

1. In a medium-sized bowl, whisk together the eggs and cream, then stir in the cheese, salt, and pepper. Set aside. 2. Preheat the oven to 400°F. 3. Heat a 12-inch cast-iron skillet or other ovenproof skillet over medium heat. Cook the sausage slices until browned on both sides, 5 to 6 minutes. Add the mushrooms and green onions and continue cooking until the mushrooms are tender, about 5 minutes. Turn off the heat. 4. Pour the egg mixture evenly over the sausage and vegetables in the skillet. Bake for 25 minutes or until the eggs are set. 5. Run a knife around the edge of the skillet before slicing. Garnish with more green onions, if desired, and serve immediately. Leftovers can be stored in the refrigerator for up to 5 days. Reheat just until warmed; be careful not to overheat or the eggs will become rubbery.
Per Serving
Calories: 281 | fat: 23g | protein: 16g | carbs: 3g | net carbs: 2g | fiber: 0g

Double-Berry Smoothie

Prep time: 5 minutes | Cook time: 0 minutes | Serves 5

2 cups unsweetened vanilla
almond milk
2 cups (9 ounces/255 g)
raspberries, fresh or frozen
1 cup (3½ ounces/99 g)
blueberries, fresh or frozen
½ cup monk fruit/erythritol

sweetener blend (1:1 sugar
replacement)
½ cup almond butter, no
sugar added
½ cup lemon juice
¼ cup chia seeds

1. In a blender, combine all the ingredients and blend until smooth. If using fresh berries, chill the smoothie for 30 minutes.
Per Serving
Calories: 256 | fat: 18g | protein: 8g | carbs: 39g | net carbs: 11g | fiber: 28g

Rosti with Bacon, Mushrooms, and Green Onions

Prep time: 10 minutes | Cook time: 25 minutes | Serves 2

2 slices bacon, diced
2 tablespoons coconut oil
or lard
1 cup mushrooms, thinly
sliced
¼ cup chopped green
onions, plus more for

garnish (optional)
¼ teaspoon minced garlic
1 cup shredded cabbage
1 large egg
½ teaspoon fine sea salt
⅛ teaspoon freshly ground
black pepper

1. Place the bacon in a large skillet over medium heat and fry until cooked and crispy. Reserve a little bit of the cooked bacon for garnish, if desired. Add the coconut oil, mushrooms, green onions, and garlic. Sauté for 5 minutes, or until the mushrooms are golden. 2. In a large bowl, mix the shredded cabbage, egg, salt, and pepper. Transfer to the skillet with the bacon mixture. Spread out the cabbage mixture in the pan and press it down to form a large pancake. Cook over medium heat until the bottom is crispy and golden brown, about 5 minutes. Flip with a large spatula and cook for another 10 minutes, or until the cabbage softens. 3. Remove from the heat and serve. Store extras in an airtight container in the fridge for up to 4 days. To reheat, fry in a skillet with a tablespoon of Paleo fat or coconut oil on both sides until crispy, about 3 minutes a side. Garnish with green onions and/or reserved bacon, if desired.
Per Serving
Calories: 275 | fat: 24g | protein: 10g | carbs: 5g | net carbs: 3g | fiber: 2g

Tuscan "Quiche" Bites

Prep time: 15 minutes | Cook time: 45 minutes | serves 4

2 tablespoons cold-pressed olive oil
½ cup sliced cremini mushrooms
⅓ cup chopped onion
¼ cup sliced cherry tomatoes
1 teaspoon garlic powder
1 cup coarsely chopped fresh spinach
¼ cup sliced black olives
1 (14 ounces/397 g) block organic firm sprouted tofu,

drained
¼ cup water
2 tablespoons tahini
2 tablespoons nutritional yeast
1 teaspoon dried basil
1 teaspoon dried oregano
¼ teaspoon ground cumin
⅛ teaspoon turmeric powder
½ teaspoon kala namak salt (optional)
Nonstick cooking spray

1. Preheat the oven to 350°F. 2. Heat the olive oil in a large skillet over medium heat. Add the mushrooms, onion, tomatoes, and garlic powder, and sauté for about 5 minutes. Once the mushrooms start to sweat and the tomatoes start to blister, turn off the heat. 3. Stir in the spinach and olives and set aside. 4. In a blender, combine the tofu with the water, tahini, nutritional yeast, basil, oregano, cumin, turmeric, and salt (if using). Blend until a fluffy, egglike consistency is obtained, adding a little more water if needed. 5. Transfer the mixture to a large mixing bowl and fold in the sautéed vegetables. 6. Coat a six-cup muffin pan with cooking spray. Divide the batter equally among the muffin cups. 7. Bake in the preheated oven for 45 minutes until a toothpick inserted into the center of a quiche comes out clean. 8. Allow the quiches to cool for 10 minutes before serving, because the centers will be very hot.
Per Serving
Calories: 241 | fat: 18g | protein: 14g | carbs: 7g | net carbs: 4g | fiber: 3g

Chocolate Raspberry Smoothie

Prep time: 5 minutes | Cook time: 0 minutes | Serves 1

¾ cup water
½ packed cup frozen raspberries
4 large ice cubes (approximately ½ cup)
¼ cup full-fat coconut, nut, or dairy milk
¼ medium avocado, peeled
2 tablespoons cacao powder
2 tablespoons ground chia or flax seeds
2 scoops grass-fed collagen

peptides
¼ teaspoon pure vanilla extract
⅛ teaspoon green stevia, or 2 or 3 drops stevia extract (optional)
Pinch of sea salt
Cacao nibs, for garnish (optional)
Whole fresh raspberries, for garnish (optional)

1. Place all the ingredients in a blender and blend until smooth. If you prefer a thinner smoothie, add more water or milk to your liking. 2. Garnish with cacao nibs and fresh raspberries, if desired.
Per Serving
Calories: 444 | fat: 27g | protein: 28g | carbs: 27g | net carbs: 8g | fiber: 19g

Quick Low-Carb Avocado Toasts

Prep time: 10 minutes | Cook time: 10 minutes | Makes 4 toasts

Quick Bread Base:
¼ cup (28 g/1 ounce) flax meal
2 tablespoons (16 g/0.6 ounce) coconut flour
2 teaspoons (2 g) psyllium powder
⅛ teaspoon baking soda
½ teaspoon dried herbs, ¼ teaspoon paprika or ground turmeric (optional)
Salt and black pepper, to taste
¼ teaspoon apple cider vinegar
1 teaspoon extra-virgin olive oil or ghee, plus more for greasing

1 large egg
2 tablespoons water
Avocado Topping:
1 large ripe avocado
¼ small red onion or 1 spring onion, minced
1 tablespoon extra-virgin olive oil
1 tablespoon fresh lemon juice
Salt, black pepper, and/or chile flakes, to taste
2 teaspoons chopped fresh herbs, such as parsley or chives
2 ounces (57 g) smoked salmon and/or poached egg (optional)

Make The Bread Base: Combine all the dry ingredients in a bowl. Add the wet ingredients. Combine and set aside for 5 minutes. Divide the mixture between two wide ramekins lightly greased with the olive oil and microwave on high for about 2 minutes, checking every 30 to 60 seconds to avoid overcooking. (If the bread ends up too dry, you can "rehydrate" it: Pour 1 tablespoon [15 ml] of water evenly over it, then return it to the microwave for 30 seconds.) Let it cool slightly, then cut widthwise. Place on a dry nonstick pan and toast for 1 to 2 minutes per side. Set aside. **Make the Topping:** In a bowl, mash the avocado with the onion, oil, lemon juice, salt, pepper, and chile flakes. To serve, spread the avocado mixture on top of the sliced bread and add fresh herbs. Optionally, top with smoked salmon. Store the bread separately from the topping at room temperature in a sealed container for 1 day, in the fridge for up to 5 days, or freeze for up to 3 months. Refrigerate the topping in a sealed jar for up to 3 days.
Per Serving
Calories: 112 | fat: 10g | protein: 3g | carbs: 4g | fiber: 3g | sodium: 71mg

Blender Cinnamon Pancakes with Cacao Cream Topping

Prep time: 10 minutes | Cook time: 10 minutes | Serves 4

Cinnamon Pancakes:
2 cups pecans
4 large eggs
1 tablespoon cinnamon
½ teaspoon baking soda
1 teaspoon fresh lemon juice or apple cider vinegar
1 tablespoon virgin coconut oil or ghee

Cacao Cream Topping:
1 cup coconut cream
1½ tablespoons raw cacao powder
Low-carb sweetener, to taste (optional)

To Serve:
9 medium strawberries, sliced
1 tablespoon unsweetened shredded coconut

To Make the Pancakes: 1. Place the pecans in a blender and process until powdered. Add all of the remaining ingredients apart from the ghee. Blend again until smooth. 2. Place a nonstick pan greased with 1 teaspoon of the coconut oil over low heat. Using a ¼-cup (60 ml) measure per pancake, cook in batches of 2 to 3 small pancakes over low heat until bubbles begin to form on the pancakes. Use a spatula to flip over, then cook for 30 to 40 seconds and place on a plate. Grease the pan with more coconut oil between batches. Transfer the pancakes to a plate. **To Make the Cacao Cream Topping:** 1. Place the coconut cream in a bowl. Add the cacao powder and sweetener, if using. Whisk until well combined and creamy. 2. Serve the pancakes with the cacao cream, sliced strawberries and a sprinkle of shredded coconut. You can enhance the flavor of the shredded coconut by toasting it in a dry pan for about 1 minute.
Per Serving
Calories: 665 | fat: 65g | protein: 14g | carbs: 17g | fiber: 9g | sodium: 232mg

Creamy Almond Coffee Smoothie

Prep time: 5 minutes | Cook time: 0 minutes | Serves 2

2 cups unsweetened strong-brewed coffee
1 cup unsweetened almond milk
1 cup unsweetened coconut milk

2 tablespoons chia seeds
2 tablespoons flaxseed meal
2 tablespoons coconut oil
⅛ teaspoon ground cinnamon
Monk fruit sweetener, granulated, to taste

1. Make coffee ice cubes. Pour the coffee into an ice cube tray and freeze for 4 hours minimum. 2. Blend the smoothie. Put all of the coffee ice cubes (2 cups worth), almond milk, coconut milk, chia seeds, flaxseed meal, coconut oil, and cinnamon in a blender and blend until smooth and creamy. 3. Add a sweetener. Add in as much (or as little) sweetener as you like and blend again. 4.

Serve. Pour into two tall glasses and serve immediately.
Per Serving
Calories: 444 | fat: 44g | protein: 6g | carbs: 6g | net carbs: 2g | fiber: 4g

Allspice Muffins

Prep time: 15 minutes | Cook time: 25 minutes | Makes 12 muffins

Dry Ingredients:
1½ cups blanched almond flour
½ cup roughly ground flax seeds
½ cup confectioners'-style erythritol
2 teaspoons baking powder
1 tablespoon plus 1 teaspoon ground allspice
½ teaspoon finely ground

gray sea salt
Wet Ingredients:
6 large eggs
½ cup melted (but not hot) coconut oil
½ cup full-fat coconut milk
Grated zest of 1 lemon
1 teaspoon vanilla extract
Topping:
¼ cup raw walnut pieces

1. Preheat the oven to 350°F (177°C) and line a muffin pan with 12 paper liners, or have on hand a 12-cavity silicone muffin pan. 2. Place the dry ingredients in a medium-sized bowl and mix until fully blended. 3. In a large bowl, whisk the eggs, coconut oil, coconut milk, lemon zest, and vanilla. Once combined, add the dry mixture to the wet. Stir with a spatula just until incorporated. 4. Pour the batter into the prepared muffin cups, filling each about three-quarters full. Sprinkle the tops with the walnuts. 5. Bake for 22 to 25 minutes, until the tops are golden and a toothpick inserted in the middle comes out clean. 6. Allow the muffins to cool in the pan for 30 minutes before removing and serving.
Per Serving
Calories: 273 | fat: 24g | protein: 8g | carbs: 6g | net carbs: 2g | fiber: 4g

Baked Eggs in Avocados

Prep time: 10 minutes | Cook time: 10 minutes | Serves 4

2 large avocados, halved and pitted
4 small eggs

Salt and black pepper to season
Chopped parsley to garnish

1. Preheat the oven to 400ºF. 2. Crack each egg into each avocado half and place them on a greased baking sheet. Bake the filled avocados in the oven for 8 or 10 minutes or until eggs are cooked. Season with salt and pepper, and garnish with parsley.
Per Serving
Calories: 220 | fat: 18g | protein: 7g | carbs: 10g | net carbs: 3g | fiber: 7g

Bacon & Cheese Zucchini Balls

Prep time: 15 minutes | Cook time: 10 minutes | Serves 6

4 cups zoodles
½ pound (227 g) bacon, chopped
6 ounces (170 g) cottage cheese, curds
6 ounces (170 g) cream cheese
1 cup fontina cheese
½ cup dill pickles, chopped, squeezed
2 cloves garlic, crushed
1 cup grated Parmesan cheese
½ teaspoon caraway seeds
¼ teaspoon dried dill weed
½ teaspoon onion powder
Salt and black pepper, to taste
1 cup crushed pork rinds
Cooking oil

1. Thoroughly mix zoodles, cottage cheese, dill pickles, ½ cup of Parmesan cheese, garlic, cream cheese, bacon, and fontina cheese until well combined. Shape the mixture into balls. Refrigerate for 3 hours. 2. In a mixing bowl, mix the remaining ½ cup of Parmesan cheese, crushed pork rinds, dill, black pepper, onion powder, caraway seeds, and salt. Roll cheese ball in Parmesan mixture to coat. 3. Set a skillet over medium heat and warm 1-inch of oil. Fry cheeseballs until browned on all sides. Set on a paper towel to soak up any excess oil.

Per Serving
Calories: 427 | fat: 33g | protein: 25g | carbs: 9g | net carbs: 7g | fiber: 2g

Super Breakfast Combo

Prep time: 10 minutes | Cook time: 0 minutes | Serves 1

Chocolate Fat Bombs:
1 tablespoon coconut butter
2 teaspoons coconut oil
1 teaspoon cocoa powder
½ teaspoon confectioners'-style erythritol, or 1 drop liquid stevia
Matcha Latte:
1 cup boiling water
2 tablespoons collagen peptides or protein powder
1 tablespoon coconut butter, coconut oil, or nut butter
1 teaspoon erythritol, or 2 drops liquid stevia
1 teaspoon matcha powder
½ teaspoon maca powder (optional)
¼ teaspoon chaga powder or ashwagandha powder (optional)
1¼ cups full-fat coconut milk, hot

1. To prepare the fat bomb, place all the ingredients in a bowl and either set out in the sun to melt or microwave for 20 to 30 seconds. Once the coconut butter has melted, whisk thoroughly and transfer to a paper muffin liner, a silicone mold, a plastic container—anything will do. Place in the freezer for 5 minutes, or until hardened. 2. Meanwhile, place the boiling water, collagen, coconut butter, sweetener, matcha, and maca and chaga, if using, in a 20 ounces (600 ml) or larger mug. Whisk until the ingredients are incorporated and the lumps are gone, about 1 minute. Stir in the hot coconut milk. 3. Serve the latte with the chilled fat bomb.

Per Serving
Calories: 740 | fat: 65g | protein: 26g | carbs: 12g | net carbs: 2g | fiber: 9g

Dreamy Matcha Latte

Prep time: 2 minutes | Cook time: 0 minutes | Serves 1

1 cup hot water
⅓ cup full-fat coconut, nut, or dairy milk
1 tablespoon cacao butter
1 scoop grass-fed collagen peptides
½ to 1 teaspoon matcha powder
2 or 3 drops stevia extract (optional)

1. Place all the ingredients in a blender and blend until smooth.

Per Serving
Calories: 261 | fat: 23g | protein: 13g | carbs: 2g | net carbs: 2g | fiber: 0g

Waffles

Prep time: 5 minutes | Cook time: 30 minutes | Makes 6 waffles

1 (8 ounces/227 g) package cream cheese, cubed
6 large eggs
2 tablespoons granular erythritol
1 tablespoon baking powder
2 teaspoons ground cinnamon
1 teaspoon vanilla extract
Pinch of salt
Serving Suggestions:
Sugar-free pancake syrup
Fresh blueberries
Butter

1. Preheat a waffle iron according to the manufacturer's directions. 2. Place all the ingredients in a blender and blend until very smooth. Allow the batter to rest for 10 minutes. 3. Grease the hot waffle iron with oil. Pour enough of the batter into the waffle iron to make one waffle. (Check the manufacturer's instructions for the exact amount of batter to use.) Be careful to not overfill the waffle iron because these waffles will expand; if you overfill the iron, the batter will overflow. Cook the waffle until it's golden brown. 4. Carefully remove the waffle and repeat the cooking process with the rest of the batter. Serve with syrup, blueberries, and/or butter, if desired. Leftovers can be stored in an airtight container in the refrigerator for up to 5 days. Reheat in the toaster.

Per Serving
Calories: 343 | fat: 26g | protein: 18g | carbs: 4g | net carbs: 3g | fiber: 1g

Biscuits and Gravy

Prep time: 20 minutes | Cook time: 20 minutes | Serves 4

Biscuits:
1 cup almond flour
1½ teaspoons baking powder
½ teaspoon salt
2 tablespoons cold unsalted butter, diced
2 tablespoons heavy cream
½ cup shredded Mozzarella or Cheddar cheese
1 large egg

Gravy:
8 ounces (227 g) ground Italian pork sausage (not sweet)
4 ounces (113 g) cream cheese, room temperature
½ cup heavy cream
½ cup chicken or beef bone broth
1 teaspoon onion powder
1 teaspoon salt
¼ teaspoon freshly ground black pepper

To Make the Biscuits: 1. Preheat the oven to 375ºF (190ºC) and line a large baking sheet with parchment paper. 2. In a large bowl, combine the almond flour, baking powder, and salt and mix well. Add the butter, and use a fork to crumble into the flour mixture until it resembles coarse pebbles. 3. Use the fork to whisk in the heavy cream, 1 tablespoon at a time. Whisk in the cheese and egg until a smooth dough forms. 4. Cut the dough into four equal pieces and form each into a ball. Place on the prepared baking sheet, pressing down slightly with the heel of your palm to flatten a bit, and bake for 16 to 18 minutes, or until golden brown. **To Make the Gravy:** 1. While the biscuits bake, brown the sausage in a medium saucepan over medium heat until cooked through, 3 to 4 minutes. Do not drain the rendered fat. 2. Add the cream cheese, heavy cream, bone broth, onion powder, salt, and pepper to the sausage and reduce heat to low. Stirring constantly, simmer until thickened, another 6 to 8 minutes. Halve the biscuits horizontally and serve topped with gravy.

Per Serving
Calories: 674 | fat: 63g | protein: 20g | carbs: 9g | net carbs: 6g | fiber: 3g

Scrambled Egg Cups

Prep time: 10 minutes | Cook time: 18 minutes | Serves 4

Coconut oil cooking spray
4 large eggs
1 tablespoon heavy (whipping) cream
Pink Himalayan sea salt
Freshly ground black pepper
¼ cup sliced fresh

mushrooms
¼ cup chopped fresh spinach
2 bacon slices, cooked until crisp and crumbled
2 tablespoons chopped onion
¼ cup shredded Cheddar cheese

1. Preheat the oven to 350ºF (180ºC). Spray 4 cups of a muffin pan with the cooking spray. 2. In a medium bowl, whisk the eggs and cream, then season with salt and pepper. 3. In another medium bowl, mix the mushrooms, spinach, bacon, and onion. 4. Spoon the egg mixture evenly into the 4 muffin cups. 5. Top each with some of the bacon mixture. Finally, top the cups with an even sprinkling of Cheddar cheese. 6. Bake for 16 to 18 minutes, until the eggs are set.

Per Serving 1 egg muffin
Calories: 146 | fat: 11g | protein: 10g | carbs: 1g | net carbs: 1g | fiber: 0g

Nori Rolls with Almond Dipping Sauce

Prep time: 30 minutes | Cook time: 5 minutes | Serves 8

Nori Rolls:
8 nori sheets
2 large Hass avocados, skinned, cored, and sliced (about 12 ounces/340 g flesh)
½ English cucumber, sliced thin
3 tablespoons roasted sesame seeds
½ packed cup fresh cilantro leaves, roughly chopped
Almond Dipping Sauce:
1 teaspoon toasted sesame oil

2 small cloves garlic, minced
½ cup unsweetened smooth almond butter
⅓ cup MCT oil
1 tablespoon fresh lime juice
1 tablespoon fish sauce
2 teaspoons coconut aminos
1 teaspoon Sriracha sauce
2 drops liquid stevia
1 tablespoon apple cider vinegar

1. Place a nori sheet on a sushi mat and lightly dampen the bottom three-quarters of the sheet. 1 inch (2. 5 cm) from the end, place ⅛ avocado, then ⅛ cucumber, followed by a sprinkle of sesame seeds and chopped cilantro. 2. Roll from the edge of the sushi mat, over the fillings, not to push the ingredients up the nori sheet. Continue to roll until the last ¼ section is dry. Dampen that area, then roll onto it, pressing down to seal. Rotate the roll in the mat for a couple of seconds to secure the sheet. Place the roll on a clean plate. If dry, dampen it all over. 3. Repeat with the remaining nori roll ingredients. Cut each roll into 6 pieces. 4. **Prepare the Almond Sauce:** Place the sesame oil and minced garlic in a small saucepan. Heat on low just until fragrant, about 2 minutes. 5. Add the almond butter, MCT oil, lime juice, fish sauce, aminos, Sriracha, and stevia. Cook, whisking occasionally, until the mixture is smooth and only lightly simmering. 6. Stir in the vinegar and let the sauce sit for 2 minutes. Drizzle the sauce over the rolls and serve extra on the side for dipping.

Per Serving
Calories: 321 | fat: 29g | protein: 6g | carbs: 9g | net carbs: 3g | fiber: 6g

Mushroom Frittata

Prep time: 10 minutes | Cook time: 15 minutes | Serves 6

2 tablespoons olive oil
1 cup sliced fresh mushrooms
1 cup shredded spinach
6 bacon slices, cooked and chopped

10 large eggs, beaten
½ cup crumbled goat cheese
Sea salt
Freshly ground black pepper

1. Preheat the oven to 350°F. 2. Place a large ovenproof skillet over medium-high heat and add the olive oil. 3. Sauté the mushrooms until lightly browned, about 3 minutes. 4. Add the spinach and bacon and sauté until the greens are wilted, about 1 minute. 5. Add the eggs and cook, lifting the edges of the frittata with a spatula so uncooked egg flows underneath, for 3 to 4 minutes. 6. Sprinkle the top with the crumbled goat cheese and season lightly with salt and pepper. 7. Bake until set and lightly browned, about 15 minutes. 8. Remove the frittata from the oven, and let it stand for 5 minutes. 9. Cut into 6 wedges and serve immediately.
Per Serving
Calories: 379 | fat: 27g | protein: 16g | carbs: 1g | net carbs: 1g | fiber: 0g

Sausage and Greens Hash Bowl

Prep time: 25 minutes | Cook time: 25 minutes | Serves 2

Hash:
⅔ cup peeled and ½-inch-cubed rutabaga
2 tablespoons lard
2 precooked sausages (about 4 ounces/113 g), cut into ½-inch cubes
¼ cup chopped green

onions, green parts only
For the Bowls:
2 cups fresh spinach
½ large Hass avocado, sliced
2 strips bacon, cooked and cut into bite-sized pieces
1 teaspoon finely chopped fresh parsley

1. Steam the rutabaga for 8 to 10 minutes, until fork-tender. 2. Melt the lard in a medium-sized frying pan over medium heat. Add the steamed rutabaga and cook for 7 to 10 minutes, until the rutabaga begins to brown. 3. Add the sausages and green onions and cook for 3 to 5 minutes, until the sausages begin to brown. 4. Meanwhile, **assemble the bowls:** Divide the spinach equally between 2 5. medium-sized serving bowls. When the hash is ready, divide it equally between 6. the bowls, laying it on top of the bed of spinach. Place equal amounts of the sliced avocado, bacon pieces, and parsley on top.
Per Serving
Calories: 560 | fat: 50g | protein: 17g | carbs: 12g | net carbs: 6g | fiber: 6g

Double-Pork Frittata

Prep time: 5 minutes | Cook time: 25 minutes | Serves 4

1 tablespoon butter or pork lard
8 large eggs
1 cup heavy (whipping) cream
Pink Himalayan salt
Freshly ground black pepper

4 ounces (113 g) pancetta, chopped
2 ounces (57 g) prosciutto, thinly sliced
1 tablespoon chopped fresh dill

1. Preheat the oven to 375°F. Coat a 9-by-13-inch baking pan with the butter. 2. In a large bowl, whisk the eggs and cream together. Season with pink Himalayan salt and pepper, and whisk to blend. 3. Pour the egg mixture into the prepared pan. Sprinkle the pancetta in and distribute evenly throughout. 4. Tear off pieces of the prosciutto and place on top, then sprinkle with the dill. 5. Bake for about 25 minutes, or until the edges are golden and the eggs are just set. 6. Transfer to a rack to cool for 5 minutes. 7. Cut into 4 portions and serve hot.
Per Serving
Calories: 437 | fat: 39g | protein: 21g | carbs: 3g | net carbs: 3g | fiber: 0g

Bacon, Spinach, and Avocado Egg Wrap

Prep time: 10 minutes | Cook time: 10 minutes | Serves 2

6 bacon slices
2 large eggs
2 tablespoons heavy (whipping) cream
Pink Himalayan salt

Freshly ground black pepper
1 tablespoon butter, if needed
1 cup fresh spinach (or other greens of your choice)
½ avocado, sliced

1. In a medium skillet over medium-high heat, cook the bacon on both sides until crispy, about 8 minutes. Transfer the bacon to a paper towel–lined plate. 2. In a medium bowl, whisk the eggs and cream, and season with pink Himalayan salt and pepper. Whisk again to combine. 3. Add half the egg mixture to the skillet with the bacon grease. 4. Cook the egg mixture for about 1 minute, or until set, then flip with a spatula and cook the other side for 1 minute. 5. Transfer the cooked-egg mixture to a paper towel–lined plate to soak up extra grease. 6. Repeat steps 4 and 5 for the other half of the egg mixture. If the pan gets dry, add the butter. 7. Place a cooked egg mixture on each of two warmed plates. Top each with half of the spinach, bacon, and avocado slices. 8. Season with pink Himalayan salt and pepper, and roll the wraps. Serve hot.
Per Serving
Calories: 336 | fat: 29g | protein: 17g | carbs: 5g | net carbs: 2g | fiber: 3g

Fontina Cheese and Chorizo Waffles

Prep time: 10 minutes | Cook time: 5 minutes | Serves 6

6 eggs
6 tablespoons almond milk
1 teaspoon Spanish spice mix or allspice
Sea salt and black pepper, to taste
3 chorizo sausages, cooked, chopped
1 cup fontina cheese, shredded

1. Using a mixing bowl, beat the eggs, Spanish spice mix, black pepper, salt, and almond milk. Add in shredded cheese and chopped sausage. Use a nonstick cooking spray to spray a waffle iron. 2. Cook the egg mixture for 5 minutes. Serve alongside homemade sugar-free tomato ketchup.

Per Serving

Calories: 337 | fat: 28g | protein: 18g | carbs: 2g | net carbs: 2g | fiber: 0g

French Toast

Prep time: 10 minutes | Cook time: 12 to 30 minutes | Serves 3

Bread:
1 tablespoon coconut oil or butter, for greasing
1 (7 ounces/198 g) package cauliflower rice
2 eggs
6 tablespoons coconut flour
French Toast:
¼ cup coconut or almond milk
1 teaspoon ground cinnamon
1 teaspoon nutmeg
2 tablespoons erythritol
1 egg
½ scoop Primal Kitchen Collagen Fuel Coconut-Vanilla protein powder
½ teaspoon vanilla extract
2 tablespoons butter-flavored coconut oil or butter
½ cup sugar-free syrup (optional, but highly recommended)

Make the Bread: 1. Preheat the oven to 400°F (205°C). Grease a bread loaf pan with oil or butter. 2. In a bowl, mix the cauliflower rice, eggs, and flour. 3. Pour the mixture into the prepared loaf pan and bake for 15 to 20 minutes. 4. Remove the bread from the oven. Let cool in the pan for 20 to 30 minutes and remove from the pan (this bread is not going to rise), and cut into three equal pieces. **Make the French Toast:** 1. In a bowl, mix the milk, cinnamon, nutmeg, erythritol, egg, protein powder, and vanilla. 2. Heat the coconut oil or butter in a shallow sauté pan over medium heat. 3. Dredge a slice of the bread in the milk mixture, and place it in the warm sauté pan. Repeat with the remaining 2 slices of bread. 4. Cook on one side for about 6 minutes (make sure it isn't burning) and flip to cook on the other side for another 6 minutes or so. 5. Transfer it to plates, and drizzle sugar-free syrup over the top, if desired.

Per Serving

Calories: 506 | fat: 34g | protein: 24g | carbs: 26g | net carbs: 17g | fiber: 9g

Chia Parfait

Prep time: 5 minutes | Cook time: 0 minutes | serves 4

2½ cups unsweetened almond milk
½ cup coconut cream
1 teaspoon ground cinnamon
¼ teaspoon ground cardamom
⅛ teaspoon ground nutmeg
1 teaspoon vanilla extract
¼ cup chia seeds

1. Pour the almond milk and coconut cream into a 32-ounce mason jar. 2. Add the cinnamon, cardamom, nutmeg, vanilla, and chia seeds. 3. Close the lid tightly and shake the jar vigorously. 4. Place the jar in the refrigerator to set for at least 20 minutes or overnight.

Per Serving

Calories: 150 | fat: 11g | protein: 4g | carbs: 8g | net carbs: 2g | fiber: 6g

Breakfast Bake

Prep time: 10 minutes | Cook time: 50 minutes | Serves 8

1 tablespoon olive oil, plus extra for greasing the casserole dish
1 pound (454 g) preservative-free or homemade sausage
8 large eggs
2 cups cooked spaghetti squash
1 tablespoon chopped fresh oregano
Sea salt
Freshly ground black pepper
½ cup shredded Cheddar cheese

1. Preheat the oven to 375°F. Lightly grease a 9-by-13-inch casserole dish with olive oil and set aside. 2. Place a large ovenproof skillet over medium-high heat and add the olive oil. 3. Brown the sausage until cooked through, about 5 minutes. While the sausage is cooking, whisk together the eggs, squash, and oregano in a medium bowl. Season lightly with salt and pepper and set aside. 4. Add the cooked sausage to the egg mixture, stir until just combined, and pour the mixture into the casserole dish. 5. Sprinkle the top of the casserole with the cheese and cover the casserole loosely with aluminum foil. 6. Bake the casserole for 30 minutes, and then remove the foil and bake for an additional 15 minutes. 7. Let the casserole stand for 10 minutes before serving.

Per Serving

Calories: 303 | fat: 24g | protein: 17g | carbs: 4g | net carbs: 3g | fiber: 1g

Cheesy Turkey Sausage Egg Muffins

Prep time: 10 minutes | Cook time: 15 minutes | Serves 3

1 teaspoon butter
6 eggs
Salt and black pepper, to taste
½ teaspoon dried rosemary
1 cup pecorino romano cheese, grated
3 turkey sausages, chopped

1. Preheat oven to 400°F and grease muffin cups with cooking spray. 2. In a skillet over medium heat add the butter and cook the turkey sausages for 4-5 minutes. 3. Beat 3 eggs with a fork. Add in sausages, cheese, and seasonings. Divide between the muffin cups and bake for 4 minutes. Crack in an egg to each of the cups. Bake for an additional 4 minutes. Allow cooling before serving.
Per Serving
Calories: 329 | fat: 21g | protein: 30g | carbs: 2g | net carbs: 2g | fiber: 0g

Market Veggie Tofu Scramble

Prep time: 10 minutes | Cook time: 10 minutes | serves 4

1 (14 ounces/397 g) block firm sprouted organic tofu, pressed and drained
2 tablespoons tahini
2 tablespoons nutritional yeast
1 tablespoon chia seeds
¼ teaspoon turmeric powder
⅛ teaspoon kala namak salt
2 tablespoons cold-pressed
coconut oil
⅓ cup diced yellow onion
⅓ cup diced green bell pepper
¼ teaspoon garlic powder
¼ cup olives
2 cups coarsely chopped fresh spinach
1 teaspoon hot sauce (optional)

1. Blot the tofu with a paper towel to remove as much water as possible, then crumble it by hand into a large mixing bowl. 2. Add the tahini, nutritional yeast, chia seeds, turmeric, and kala namak salt to the bowl. Toss the ingredients together and set aside. 3. Heat the coconut oil in a large skillet over medium heat. 4. Add the onion, bell pepper, and garlic powder to the skillet. 5. Once the vegetables are tender and caramelized, toss in the olives and tofu mixture. 6. Allow the tofu to cook undisturbed for about 4 minutes to create a toasted, hash-like texture, then toss once to toast it a bit more. 7. Once the tofu is toasty, remove the skillet from the heat and stir in the spinach until it wilts. 8. Serve with your favorite hot sauce (if using).
Per Serving
Calories: 253 | fat: 18g | protein: 15g | carbs: 11g | net carbs: 7g | fiber: 4g

Sausage, Egg, and Cheese Breakfast Bake

Prep time: 15 minutes | Cook time: 35 minutes | Serves 6

1 tablespoon unsalted butter
⅓ cup chopped yellow onions
1 pound (454 g) bulk breakfast sausage
8 large eggs
⅓ cup heavy whipping
cream
1 clove garlic, pressed
1 teaspoon salt
½ teaspoon ground black pepper
1 cup shredded cheddar cheese

1. Preheat the oven to 350°F. Lightly coat an 8-inch deep-dish pie dish or baking dish with coconut oil or nonstick cooking spray. 2. Heat the butter in a large skillet over medium heat. Add the onions and sauté until soft, 3 to 4 minutes. 3. Add the sausage and cook until evenly browned, 4 to 5 minutes. Drain and set aside. 4. In a large bowl, whisk the eggs, cream, garlic, salt, and pepper. 5. Spread the sausage evenly on the bottom of the prepared dish and top with the cheese. Pour the egg mixture over the cheese. 6. Bake for 35 minutes, until the eggs are set and the top is lightly golden brown. 7. Allow to cool for 3 to 5 minutes before serving. Leftovers can be covered and stored in the refrigerator for up to 4 days.
Per Serving
Calories: 394 | fat: 33g | protein: 22g | carbs: 3g | net carbs: 3g | fiber: 0g

No Oat–Meal

Prep time: 5 minutes | Cook time: 5 minutes | Serves 2

2 cups water
¼ cup ground flaxseed
¼ cup protein powder, any flavor
2 tablespoons chia seeds
Pinch of pink Himalayan
sea salt
2 tablespoons butter
2 tablespoons heavy (whipping) cream
1 tablespoon granulated erythritol

1. In a medium saucepan, bring the water to a gentle boil. 2. Using a whisk, stir in the flaxseed, protein powder, chia seeds, and salt. 3. Continue to simmer and stir until the mixture reaches the consistency of pudding. 4. Add the butter, cream, and erythritol. 5. Stir until the butter is melted. 6. Remove the saucepan from the heat, and split the cereal between 2 bowls. 7. Add any desired toppings and enjoy!
Per Serving
Calories: 330 | fat: 25g | protein: 15g | carbs: 10g | net carbs: 3g | fiber: 7g

Smoked Ham and Egg Muffins

Prep time: 5 minutes | Cook time: 25 minutes | Serves 9

2 cups chopped smoked ham
⅓ cup grated Parmesan cheese
¼ cup almond flour
9 eggs
⅓ cup mayonnaise, sugar-free
¼ teaspoon garlic powder
¼ cup chopped onion
Sea salt to taste

1. Preheat your oven to 370ºF. 2. Lightly grease nine muffin pans with cooking spray and set aside. Place the onion, ham, garlic powder, and salt, in a food processor, and pulse until ground. Stir in the mayonnaise, almond flour, and Parmesan cheese. Press this mixture into the muffin cups. 3. Make sure it goes all the way up the muffin sides so that there will be room for the egg. Bake for 5 minutes. Crack an egg into each muffin cup. Return to the oven and bake for 20 more minutes or until the tops are firm to the touch and eggs are cooked. Leave to cool slightly before serving.
Per Serving
Calories: 165 | fat: 11g | protein: 14g | carbs: 2g | net carbs: 1g | fiber: 1g

Sawdust Oatmeal

Prep time: 5 minutes | Cook time: 0 minutes | Serves 1

⅓ cup boiling water
2 tablespoons chia seeds
2 tablespoons flaxseed meal
2 tablespoons heavy
whipping cream
1 (1 g) packet 0g net carb sweetener

1. Add all ingredients to a small glass or porcelain bowl. Stir to mix. Be careful as water is very hot. 2. Stir every couple of minutes as it cools to ensure even cooling. The chia seeds soften and expand as they absorb liquid. 3. When it's cool, it's ready to eat.
Per Serving
Calories: 189 | fat: 22g | protein: 8g | carbs: 15g | net carbs: 4g | fiber: 11g

Spicy Egg Muffins with Bacon & Cheese

Prep time: 10 minutes | Cook time: 20 minutes | Serves 6

12 eggs
¼ cup coconut milk
Salt and black pepper to taste
1 cup grated cheddar cheese
12 slices bacon
4 jalapeño peppers, seeded and minced

1. Preheat oven to 370ºF. 2. Crack the eggs into a bowl and whisk with coconut milk until combined. Season salt and pepper, and evenly stir in the cheddar cheese. 3. Line each hole of a muffin tin with a slice of bacon and fill each with the egg mixture twothirds way up. Top with the jalapeno peppers and bake in the oven for 18 to 20 minutes or until puffed and golden. 4.Remove, allow cooling for a few minutes, and serve with arugula salad.
Per Serving
Calories: 440 | fat: 38g | protein: 22g | carbs: 2g | net carbs: 1g | fiber: 1g

Greek Yogurt Parfait

Prep time: 5 minutes | Cook time: 0 minutes | Serves 1

½ cup plain whole-milk Greek yogurt
2 tablespoons heavy whipping cream
¼ cup frozen berries, thawed with juices
½ teaspoon vanilla or
almond extract (optional)
¼ teaspoon ground cinnamon (optional)
1 tablespoon ground flaxseed
2 tablespoons chopped nuts (walnuts or pecans)

1. In a small bowl or glass, combine the yogurt, heavy whipping cream, thawed berries in their juice, vanilla or almond extract (if using), cinnamon (if using), and flaxseed and stir well until smooth. Top with chopped nuts and enjoy.
Per Serving
Calories: 333 | fat: 27g | protein: 10g | carbs: 15g | fiber: 4g | sodium: 71mg

Kale Pâté

Prep time: 10 minutes | Cook time: 0 minutes | Makes 2 cups

2 tablespoons refined avocado oil, for the pan
4 cups chopped kale
½ cup sesame seeds
½ cup refined avocado oil or extra-virgin olive oil
8 green onions, green parts only, roughly chopped
3 tablespoons apple cider vinegar
1¼ teaspoons finely ground gray sea salt

1. Place 2 tablespoons of avocado oil and the chopped kale in a large frying pan over medium heat. Cover and cook until the kale is slightly crispy, stirring occasionally, 3 to 6 minutes. 2. Meanwhile, place the remaining ingredients in a blender or food processor.
Per Serving
Calories: 228 | fat: 22g | protein: 3g | carbs: 6g | net carbs: 4g | fiber: 2g

Chaffles

Prep time: 5 minutes | Cook time: 10 to 15 minutes | Serves 1

Nonstick cooking spray, butter, or oil for greasing the waffle maker

1 large egg
⅓ cup grated Cheddar cheese, divided

1. Grease and preheat a waffle maker. 2. In a small bowl, whisk together the egg and a third of the cheese. 3. Sprinkle some grated cheese right onto the waffle maker and add half the egg and cheese mixture. Sprinkle a little more cheese on the mixture and close the lid on the waffle maker. 4. Let the waffle cook for 4 to 5 minutes. If it's not as crispy as you'd like, flip and cook for 1 to 2 minutes more. Repeat the process with the remaining egg mixture and cheese.

Per Serving
Calories: 222 | fat: 17g | protein: 16g | carbs: 1g | net carbs: 1g | fiber: 0g

Pizza Pâté

Prep time: 10 minutes | Cook time: 0 minutes | Makes 2½ cups

1 cup chopped pepperoni
¾ cup raw almonds, soaked for 12 hours, then drained and rinsed ½ cup (120 ml) melted coconut oil
⅓ cup tomato sauce
¼ cup nutritional yeast
2 teaspoons apple cider

vinegar
2 teaspoons onion powder
1 teaspoon garlic powder
¼ teaspoon finely ground gray sea salt
1 tablespoon finely chopped fresh basil

1. Place all the ingredients except the basil in a high-powered blender or food processor. Blend or pulse until smooth, about 1 minute. 2. Add the basil and pulse until just mixed in.

Per Serving
Calories: 144 | fat: 13g | protein: 5g | carbs: 3g | net carbs: 1g | fiber: 1g

Frozen Keto Coffee

Prep time: 5 minutes | Cook time: 0 minutes | Serves 1

12 ounces (340 g) coffee, chilled
1 scoop MCT powder (or 1 tablespoon MCT oil)
1 tablespoon heavy

(whipping) cream
Pinch ground cinnamon
Dash sweetener (optional)
½ cup ice

1. In a blender, combine the coffee, MCT powder, cream, cinnamon, sweetener (if using), and ice. Blend until smooth.

Per Serving
Calories: 127 | fat: 13g | protein: 1g | carbs: 2g | net carbs: 1g | fiber: 1g

Quick Keto Blender Muffins

Prep time: 5 minutes | Cook time: 25 minutes | Makes 12 muffins

Butter, ghee, or coconut oil for greasing the pan
6 eggs
8 ounces (227 g) cream cheese, at room temperature
2 scoops flavored collagen

powder
1 teaspoon ground cinnamon
1 teaspoon baking powder
Few drops or dash sweetener (optional)

1. Preheat the oven to 350ºF (180ºC). Grease a 12-cup muffin pan very well with butter, ghee, or coconut oil. Alternatively, you can use silicone cups or paper muffin liners. 2. In a blender, combine the eggs, cream cheese, collagen powder, cinnamon, baking powder, and sweetener (if using). Blend until well combined and pour the mixture into the muffin cups, dividing equally. 3. Bake for 22 to 25 minutes until the muffins are golden brown on top and firm. 4. Let cool then store in a glass container or plastic bag in the refrigerator for up to 2 weeks or in the freezer for up to 3 months. 5. To serve refrigerated muffins, heat in the microwave for 30 seconds. To serve from frozen, thaw in the refrigerator overnight and then microwave for 30 seconds, or microwave straight from the freezer for 45 to 60 seconds or until heated through.

Per Serving 1 muffin
Calories: 120 | fat: 10g | protein: 6g | carbs: 1g | net carbs: 1g | fiber: 0g

Turmeric Scrambled Eggs

Prep time: 5 minutes | Cook time: 5 minutes | Serves 2

3 large eggs
2 tablespoons heavy cream (optional)
1 teaspoon ground turmeric

Salt, to taste
Freshly ground black pepper, to taste
1 tablespoon butter

1. In a small bowl, lightly beat the eggs with the cream. Add the turmeric, salt, and pepper. 2. Melt the butter in a skillet over medium heat. When it just starts to bubble, gently pour in the egg mixture. Stir frequently as eggs begin to set, and cook for 2 to 3 minutes. 3. Remove from the heat, taste and add more pepper and salt if needed, and serve.

Per Serving
Calories: 213 | fat: 18g | protein: 10g | carbs: 2g | net carbs: 2g | fiber: 0g

Starbucks Egg Bites

Prep time: 5 minutes | Cook time: 30 minutes | Serves 6

5 large eggs, whisked
1 cup shredded Swiss cheese
1 cup full-fat cottage cheese

⅛ teaspoon salt
⅛ teaspoon black pepper
2 strips no-sugar-added bacon, cooked and crumbled

1. Preheat oven to 350°F. 2. In a large bowl, whisk together eggs, Swiss cheese, cottage cheese, salt, and pepper. 3. Pour six equal amounts of mixture into well-greased muffin tins (or use cupcake liners). 4. Top with bacon bits. 5. Bake 30 minutes until eggs are completely cooked. 6. Remove Starbucks Egg Bites from oven and serve warm.

Per Serving

Calories: 182 | fat: 11g | protein: 16g | carbs: 3g | net carbs: 3g | fiber: 0g

Cheesy Keto Hash Browns with Avocado Mayo

Prep time: 15 minutes | Cook time: 20 minutes | Serves 4

2 cups riced cauliflower, fresh or frozen
2 ounces (57 g) cream cheese, room temperature
2 tablespoons ground flaxseed or flax meal
2 tablespoons almond flour
½ teaspoon garlic powder
1 teaspoon baking powder
1 teaspoon salt, divided
1 large egg, lightly beaten

2 tablespoons minced scallions, green and white parts
6 tablespoons extra-virgin olive oil, divided
1 small very ripe avocado, peeled, pitted, and mashed
1 teaspoon white wine vinegar or lemon juice
¼ teaspoon freshly ground black pepper

1. Steam or microwave the riced cauliflower, covered, until tender. For frozen, cook 2-3 minutes in the microwave or 4-5 minutes on the stovetop. For fresh, cook 1-2 minutes in the microwave or 3-4 minutes on the stovetop. Set aside until completely cooled. 2. Mix the cream cheese in a bowl until smooth. Add the flaxseed, almond flour, garlic powder, baking powder, salt, and the beaten egg and whisk to combine well. 3. When the cauliflower reaches room temperature, cover with a paper towel. Press it continuously until the cauliflower is mostly dried and drained of excess liquid. 4. Stir the cauliflower and scallions into the cream cheese mixture. 5. Heat 2 tablespoons of olive oil in a large skillet over medium heat. Drop heaping tablespoonfuls of the cauliflower batter onto the skillet, and press down with a spatula to form 4 to 6 small patties. Cook for 2 to 4 minutes, until the bottom is browned, then flip and cook another 2 to 4 minutes. Repeat with another 2 tablespoons of olive oil and the remaining batter. 6. To prepare the avocado mayo, blend the remaining 2 tablespoons of olive oil and ½ teaspoon of salt , mashed avocado , vinegar or lemon juice, and pepper and whisk until smooth and creamy. 7. Serve the hash browns warm with avocado mayo.

Per Serving

Calories: 379 | fat: 37g | protein: 6g | carbs: 10g | net carbs: 4g | fiber: 6g

Hardboiled Eggs with Everything Bagel Seasoning

Prep time: 5 minutes | Cook time: 15 minutes | Serves 2

For the Seasoning:
3 tablespoons sesame seeds
1 tablespoon black sesame seeds
1 tablespoon onion flakes

2 teaspoons poppy seeds
1 teaspoon garlic flakes
1 teaspoon coarse sea salt
4 eggs

Make the Seasoning: 1. Mix the seasonings. In a small jar with a lid, stir together the sesame seeds, black sesame seeds, onion flakes, poppy seeds, garlic flakes, and salt until everything is well combined. Store in the sealed jar for up to six months. **Make the Eggs:** 1. Boil the eggs. In a medium saucepan, carefully place the eggs in a single layer. Add enough water to cover the eggs by about 1 inch. Cover the pan and bring the water to a boil over medium-high heat. Boil for 1 minute, then remove the pan from the heat and let it stand, covered, for 10 minutes. 2. Cool and peel the eggs. Remove the eggs from the water with a slotted spoon and run them under cold water to cool them. To peel, tap each egg a few times on a hard surface and carefully pull the shells off the eggs. Give the eggs a quick rinse under cool water to remove any remaining bits of shell. 3. Season and serve. Sprinkle the eggs with some seasoning and divide the eggs between two plates.

Per Serving

Calories: 235 | fat: 17g | protein: 15g | carbs: 6g | net carbs: 4g | fiber: 2g

Overnight "Noats"

Prep time: 5 minutes | Cook time: 0 minutes | Serves 1

2 tablespoons hulled hemp seeds
1 tablespoon chia seeds
½ scoop collagen powder

½ cup unsweetened nut or seed milk (hemp, almond, coconut, cashew)

1. In a small mason jar or glass container, combine the hemp seeds, chia seeds, collagen, and milk. 2. Secure tightly with a lid, shake well, and refrigerate overnight.

Per Serving

Calories: 263 | fat: 19g | protein: 16g | carbs: 7g | net carbs: 2g | fiber: 5g

Bacon Spinach Dip

Prep time: 10 minutes | Cook time: 8 minutes | Makes 2 cups

6 strips bacon (about 6 ounces/170 g)	1 teaspoon finely ground gray sea salt
1 cup raw cashews, soaked for 4 hours, then drained and rinsed ⅔ cup (160 ml) full-fat coconut milk	1 teaspoon onion powder
	½ teaspoon garlic powder
	½ teaspoon ground mustard
¼ cup nutritional yeast	¼ teaspoon ground black pepper
3 tablespoons apple cider vinegar	1 cup spinach, chopped

1. Place the bacon in a large frying pan over medium heat and cook until crisp. Remove from the pan and, when cool enough to handle, crumble and set aside. Transfer the bacon grease in the frying pan to a food processor or blender. (Don't clean the pan; you will use it again shortly.) 2. To the food processor or blender, add the soaked cashews, coconut milk, nutritional yeast, vinegar, salt, and spices. Blend until smooth. 3. Meanwhile, sauté the spinach in the frying pan over medium-low heat just until wilted, about 30 seconds. 4. Add the crumbled bacon and sautéed spinach to the food processor or blender. Pulse just until mixed. 5. Transfer to a serving bowl and dig in!
Per Serving
Calories: 132 | fat: 11g | protein: 4g | carbs: 5g | net carbs: 4g | fiber: 1g

Mug Biscuit

Prep time: 2 minutes | Cook time: 2 minutes | Serves 4

¼ cup blanched almond flour	1 large egg
1 tablespoon coconut flour	1 tablespoon softened coconut oil or ghee, plus more for serving if desired
½ teaspoon baking powder	
¼ teaspoon finely ground sea salt	1 teaspoon apple cider vinegar

1. Place all the ingredients in a microwave-safe mug with a base at least 2 inches (5 cm) in diameter. Mix until fully incorporated, then flatten with the back of a spoon. 2. Place the mug in the microwave and cook on high for 1 minute 30 seconds. 3. Remove the mug from the microwave and insert a toothpick. It should come out clean. If batter is clinging to the toothpick, microwave the biscuit for an additional 15 to 30 seconds. 4. Flip the mug over a clean plate and shake it a bit until the biscuit releases from the mug. If desired, slather the biscuit with the fat of your choice while still warm.

Per Serving
Calories: 399 | fat: 34g | protein: 14g | carbs: 11g | net carbs: 5g | fiber: 6g

Sticky Wrapped Eggs

Prep time: 10 minutes | Cook time: 30 minutes | Makes 12 wrapped eggs

¼ cup coconut aminos	12 strips bacon (about 12 ounces/340 g)
2 tablespoons hot sauce	
12 hard-boiled eggs	6 cups arugula

1. Preheat the oven to 400°F (205°C). Line a standard-size 12-well muffin pan with muffin liners, or use a silicone muffin pan, which won't require liners. 2. Place the coconut aminos and hot sauce in a small bowl and whisk to combine. Set the bowl close to the muffin pan. 3. Peel the hard-boiled eggs. One at a time, wrap each egg in a strip of bacon, then dunk it in the hot sauce mixture and place it in a well of the muffin pan. 4. Bake for 30 minutes, flipping the eggs over halfway through. 5. Divide the arugula evenly among 6 small serving plates. Top each with 2 sticky eggs and the sauce from their muffin liners.
Per Serving
Calories: 438 | fat: 33g | protein: 33g | carbs: 4g | net carbs: 4g | fiber: 0g

Ham & Egg Broccoli Bake

Prep time: 15 minutes | Cook time: 20 minutes | Serves 4

2 heads broccoli, cut into small florets	2 teaspoons ghee
	1 teaspoon dried oregano + extra to garnish
2 red bell peppers, seeded and chopped	Salt and black pepper to taste
¼ cup chopped ham	8 fresh eggs

1. Preheat oven to 425ºF. 2. Melt the ghee in a frying pan over medium heat; brown the ham, stirring frequently, about 3 minutes. 3. Arrange the broccoli, bell peppers, and ham on a foil-lined baking sheet in a single layer, toss to combine; season with salt, oregano, and black pepper. Bake for 10 minutes until the vegetables have softened. 4. Remove, create eight indentations with a spoon, and crack an egg into each. Return to the oven and continue to bake for an additional 5 to 7 minutes until the egg whites are firm. 5. Season with salt, black pepper, and extra oregano, share the bake into four plates and serve with strawberry lemonade (optional).
Per Serving
Calories: 240 | fat: 12g | protein: 22g | carbs: 13g | net carbs: 4g | fiber: 9g

Pumpkin Coconut Flour Pancakes

Prep time: 5 minutes | Cook time: 10 minutes | Serves 6

6 large eggs
½ cup canned unsweetened pumpkin purée
6 tablespoons (1½ ounces/43 g) coconut flour
¼ cup unsweetened coconut milk

⅓ cup avocado oil
½ cup erythritol
1½ tablespoons pumpkin pie spice
1 teaspoon baking powder
1 teaspoon vanilla extract

1. In a blender, combine all the ingredients and purée until smooth. 2. Let the batter sit for 15 to 20 minutes to thicken and stabilize. (This will help with consistency and make the pancakes easier to flip.) 3. Heat an oiled skillet over medium heat. Working in batches, add 2 tablespoons (⅛ cup) batter for each pancake. Don't make them larger than 3 inches across, otherwise they will be hard to flip. Cover with a lid and when bubbles form on the edges, 1 to 2 minutes, flip and cook on the second side for 1 to 2 minutes. 4. Repeat with the remaining batter.
Per Serving
Calories: 234 | fat: 18g | protein: 8g | carbs: 12g | net carbs: 4g | fiber: 8g

Protein Waffles

Prep time: 5 minutes | Cook time: 13 minutes | Makes 3 medium-sized waffles

Waffles:
4 large eggs
¼ cup natural peanut butter
¼ cup mascarpone cheese
¼ cup unsweetened almond milk 1 scoop unflavored whey protein powder

2 tablespoons unsalted butter, melted
Toppings (Optional):
Sugar-free maple syrup
Natural peanut butter
Whipped cream

1. Preheat a waffle iron on the medium setting. 2. Put all the waffle ingredients in a large mixing bowl and combine using a whisk or an electric hand mixer. 3. Open the waffle iron and grease the top and bottom with coconut oil spray. 4. Using a ½-cup measuring cup, scoop up some of the batter and pour it into the center of the waffle iron. Close the lid and allow the waffle to cook for 4 to 4½ minutes, until golden brown. 5. Repeat with the remaining batter, making a total of 3 waffles. 6. Serve the waffles with maple syrup, peanut butter, and/or whipped cream, if desired.
Per Serving
Calories: 409 | fat: 33g | protein: 24g | carbs: 5g | net carbs: 3g | fiber: 2g

Pepper Sausage Fry

Prep time: 5 minutes | Cook time: 20 minutes | Serves 4

¼ cup avocado oil, or ¼ cup coconut oil
12 ounces (340 g) smoked sausages, thinly sliced
1 small green bell pepper, thinly sliced
1 small red bell pepper, thinly sliced
1½ teaspoons garlic powder

1 teaspoon dried oregano leaves
1 teaspoon paprika
¼ teaspoon finely ground sea salt
¼ teaspoon ground black pepper
¼ cup chopped fresh parsley

1. Heat the oil in a large frying pan over medium-low heat until it shimmers. 2. When the oil is shimmering, add the rest of the ingredients, except the parsley. Cover and cook for 15 minutes, until the bell peppers are fork-tender. 3. Remove the lid and continue to cook for 5 to 6 minutes, until the liquid evaporates. 4. Remove from the heat, stir in the parsley, and serve.
Per Serving
Calories: 411 | fat: 38g | protein: 11g | carbs: 6g | net carbs: 5g | fiber: 2g

Primal Omelet

Prep time: 5 minutes | Cook time: 15 minutes | Serves 1

1 tablespoon salted butter
1 ounce (28 g) chopped mushrooms
1 ounce (28 g) chopped onions
1 ounce (28 g) chopped red bell peppers

4 medium eggs
1 ounce (28 g) cream
¼ teaspoon salt
⅛ teaspoon freshly ground pepper
½ ounce (14 g) shredded Cheddar cheese (optional)

1. Melt half the butter in a medium skillet over medium heat. Add vegetables and sauté until soft, 5 to 7 minutes. Remove vegetables from pan. 2. In the same pan, melt the remaining butter. In a small bowl, whisk together eggs, cream, salt, and pepper. Tilt and swirl the pan so the butter coats the entire bottom. Add the egg mixture and tilt and swirl the pan in the same manner. 3. Cook without stirring. As the egg around the edge sets, use a silicone spatula to gently push the egg away from the sides of the pan, and tilt the pan so that the egg mixture in the center can get to the edge. 4. When the entire egg mixture is set, add the vegetables on top of one half of the omelet. Sprinkle half of the cheese (if using) over the vegetables, then gently fold the omelet in half to cover the vegetables. Slide the omelet onto a plate and sprinkle with the remaining cheese. Serve immediately.
Per Serving
Calories: 610 | fat: 49g | protein: 30g | carbs: 12g | net carbs: 8g | fiber: 4g

Hearty Spinach and Bacon Breakfast Bowl

Prep time: 10 minutes | Cook time: 10 minutes | Serves 2

1 tablespoon coconut oil
2 red bell peppers, chopped
½ cup sliced white mushrooms
1 teaspoon minced garlic
½ teaspoon red pepper flakes

4 cups chopped spinach, thoroughly washed
8 cooked uncured bacon slices, chopped
½ cup grated Asiago cheese
½ avocado, sliced

1. Sauté the vegetables. In a large skillet over medium-high heat, melt the coconut oil. Add the red bell peppers, mushrooms, garlic, and red pepper flakes and sauté them until they've softened, about 3 minutes. Add the spinach and cook until it has wilted, about 4 minutes. 2. Finish cooking. Stir in the bacon and Asiago and cook for 2 minutes more. 3. Serve. Divide the mixture between four bowls and top with the avocado slices.

Per Serving
Calories: 445 | fat: 32g | protein: 26g | carbs: 14g | net carbs: 8g | fiber: 6g

Spiced Antioxidant Granola Clusters

Prep time: 10 minutes | Cook time: 1 hour 10 minutes | Serves 10

1 cup unsweetened fine coconut flakes
1 cup unsweetened large coconut flakes
¼ cup packed flax meal
¼ cup chia seeds
½ cup pecans, chopped
1 cup blanched almonds, roughly chopped, or flaked almonds
2 teaspoons cinnamon
1 teaspoon ground anise seed

½ teaspoon ground nutmeg
½ teaspoon ground cloves
1 tablespoon fresh lemon zest
¼ teaspoon black pepper
¼ teaspoon salt
⅓ cup light tahini
¼ cup virgin coconut oil
2 large egg whites
Optional: unsweetened almond milk, coconut cream, coconut yogurt, or full-fat goat's yogurt, to serve

1. Preheat the oven to 265°F (130°C) conventional or 230°F (110°C) fan assisted convection. Line a baking tray with parchment paper. 2. Place all of the dry ingredients, including the lemon zest, in a large bowl. Stir to combine. In a small bowl, mix the tahini with the coconut oil, then add to the dry ingredients. Add the egg whites and mix to combine. 3. Spoon onto the lined baking tray and crumble all over. Bake for 1 hour and 10 minutes to 1 hour and 20 minutes, until golden. Remove from the oven and let cool completely; it will crisp up as it cools. Serve on its own or with almond milk, coconut cream or coconut yogurt, or full-fat goat's yogurt. Store in a jar at room temperature for up to 2 weeks or freeze for up to 3 months.

Per Serving
Calories: 291 | fat: 25g | protein: 6g | carbs: 15g | fiber: 6g | sodium: 128mg

Bacon-Wrapped Western Quiche Tarts

Prep time: 10 minutes | Cook time: 20 minutes | Makes 12 quiche tarts

12 bacon slices
8 eggs
⅓ cup heavy (whipping) cream
1 cup shredded Cheddar cheese

¼ cup finely diced red bell pepper
¼ cup finely diced green bell pepper
¼ cup finely diced yellow onion

1. Preheat the oven to 375°F (190°C). 2. Line each cup of a 12-cup muffin tin with a slice of bacon around the edges and then bake for about 10 minutes until browned but not crisp. 3. In a large bowl, whisk together the eggs and cream. Add the Cheddar, red and green bell peppers, and onion and mix well. 4. Pour the egg mixture into the bacon-lined muffin cups, filling each about three-quarters full. 5. Bake for about 20 minutes until the muffins are golden brown and fully cooked. They should be spongy but not soft in the middle. Use a spoon to lift them from the pan. 6. Store in an airtight container in the refrigerator for up to 1 week.

Per Serving 1 quiche tart
Calories: 154 | fat: 12g | protein: 10g | carbs: 2g | net carbs: 2g | fiber: 0g

Rocket Fuel Hot Chocolate

Prep time: 5 minutes | Cook time: 0 minutes | Makes 2

2 cups milk (nondairy or regular), hot
2 tablespoons cocoa powder
2 tablespoons collagen peptides or protein powder
2 tablespoons coconut oil, MCT oil, unflavored MCT

oil powder, or ghee
1 tablespoon coconut butter
1 tablespoon erythritol, or 4 drops liquid stevia
Pinch of ground cinnamon (optional)

1. Place all the ingredients in a blender and blend for 10 seconds, or until the ingredients are fully incorporated. 2. Divide between 2 mugs, sprinkle with cinnamon if you'd like, and enjoy!

Per Serving
Calories: 357 | fat: 29g | protein: 13g | carbs: 11g | net carbs: 7g | fiber: 4g

Pancakes

Prep time: 10 minutes | Cook time: 40 minutes | Makes 4 pancakes

Pancakes:
2.8 ounces (80 g) unseasoned pork rinds
2 teaspoons ground cinnamon, plus more for garnish (optional)
½ teaspoon baking powder
4 large eggs
½ cup full-fat coconut milk

¼ scant teaspoon liquid stevia
2 tablespoons coconut oil, divided, for the pan
Sauce:
2 tablespoons coconut oil
2 tablespoons unsweetened smooth almond butter

1. Grind the pork rinds in a spice grinder or blender to a very fine but clumping powder. 2. Transfer the ground pork rinds to a small bowl and add the cinnamon and baking powder. Stir to combine. 3. Whisk together the eggs, coconut milk, stevia and add the pork rind mixture and stir. 4. Melt ½ tablespoon of coconut oil over medium-low heat in a nonstick frying pan. 5. Preheat your oven to the lowest temperature possible. 6. Pour a quarter of the batter into the hot oiled pan and spread the batter evenly into a circle. Cook for 4-5 minutes per side, until bubbles form all over. 7. Transfer the pancake on a plate in the preheated oven. 8. Repeat with the remaining coconut oil and batter. 9. While the last pancake is cooking, **prepare the sauce:** Melt the 2 tablespoons of coconut oil and put it in a small bowl along with the almond butter. Stir to combine. 10. When the pancakes are ready, divide between 2 plates and drizzle with the almond butter sauce. Sprinkle with additional cinnamon, if desired.

Per Serving
Calories: 885 | fat: 71g | protein: 53g | carbs: 8g | net carbs: 5g | fiber: 3g

Cinnamon Crunch Cereal

Prep time: 5 minutes | Cook time: 12 minutes | Serves 6

3½ cups (14 ounces/397 g) blanched almond flour
½ cup erythritol
2 teaspoons ground cinnamon
½ teaspoon sea salt
2 large eggs, beaten

1 teaspoon vanilla extract
Cinnamon Coating:
½ cup erythritol
1 tablespoon ground cinnamon
2 tablespoons coconut oil, melted

1. Preheat the oven to 350°F (180°C). 2. Stir together the almond flour, erythritol, cinnamon, sea salt, the eggs and vanilla until a dough forms. 3. Roll the dough out into a very thin rectangle in two large greased pieces of parchment paper (cut to form a rectangle). 4. Place the bottom piece of parchment paper onto an extra-large baking sheet. 5. Cut the dough into ½-inch-wide strips. Rotate the pan 90 degrees and cut the dough strips into ½-inch-wide strips again, so you are left with ½-inch squares. 6. Transfer the pan(s) to the oven and bake for 8 to 12 minutes, until golden brown and crispy. 7. Meanwhile, **make the cinnamon coating:** In a large zip-seal bag, combine the erythritol and cinnamon and shake to mix. 8. When the cereal is finished baking, remove from the oven and cool at room temperature to crisp up. 9. Brush the cereal on both sides with melted coconut oil. Then break apart the squares and add to the bag with the cinnamon-erythritol mixture. Shake to coat. Store in an airtight container in the pantry.

Per Serving
Calories: 446 | fat: 39g | protein: 16g | carbs: 26g | net carbs: 7g | fiber: 19g

Crustless Quiche Lorraine

Prep time: 10 minutes | Cook time: 50 minutes | Serves 6

6 slices bacon
½ cup half-moon sliced onion
6 large eggs
½ cup heavy cream
½ teaspoon sea salt
⅛ teaspoon cayenne pepper
2 tablespoons finely

chopped fresh chives
1 cup (4 ounces/113 g) shredded Swiss cheese, divided into ¾ cup and ¼ cup
1 cup (4 ounces/113 g) shredded Gruyère cheese, divided into ¾ cup and ¼ cup

1. In a large sauté pan, fry the bacon over medium heat until crispy on both sides. Set aside to drain on paper towels, leaving the bacon grease in the pan. 2. Add the onion to the pan with the bacon grease and sauté over medium heat for about 10 minutes, until translucent and starting to brown. Set aside to cool slightly. 3. Preheat the oven to 350°F (180°C). Grease a 9-inch pie pan. 4. In a large bowl, whisk together the eggs, cream, sea salt, cayenne pepper, and chives. Stir in ¾ cup each of the Swiss and Gruyère cheeses. 5. Pour the egg mixture into the prepared pie pan. Sprinkle with the cooked onion. Cut the bacon into small pieces and sprinkle over the eggs. Push the onion and bacon into the eggs. Sprinkle with the remaining ¼ cup each of the Swiss and Gruyère cheeses. 6. Bake for 30 to 40 minutes, until a knife inserted in the center comes out clean.

Per Serving
Calories: 405 | fat: 33g | protein: 22g | carbs: 3g | net carbs: 3g | fiber: 0g

Lemon–Olive Oil Breakfast Cakes with Berry Syrup

Prep time: 5 minutes | Cook time: 10 minutes | Serves 4

For the Pancakes:
1 cup almond flour
1 teaspoon baking powder
¼ teaspoon salt
6 tablespoon extra-virgin olive oil, divided
2 large eggs
Zest and juice of 1 lemon

½ teaspoon almond or vanilla extract
For the Berry Sauce:
1 cup frozen mixed berries
1 tablespoon water or lemon juice, plus more if needed
½ teaspoon vanilla extract

Make the Pancakes: 1. In a large bowl, combine the almond flour, baking powder, and salt and whisk to break up any clumps. 2. Add the 4 tablespoons olive oil, eggs, lemon zest and juice, and almond extract and whisk to combine well. 3. In a large skillet, heat 1 tablespoon of olive oil and spoon about 2 tablespoons of batter for each of 4 pancakes. Cook until bubbles begin to form, 4 to 5 minutes, and flip. Cook another 2 to 3 minutes on second side. Repeat with remaining 1 tablespoon olive oil and batter. **Make the Berry Sauce:** 1. In a small saucepan, heat the frozen berries, water, and vanilla extract over medium-high for 3 to 4 minutes, until bubbly, adding more water if mixture is too thick. Using the back of a spoon or fork, mash the berries and whisk until smooth.
Per Serving
Calories: 381 | fat: 35g | protein: 8g | carbs: 12g | fiber: 4g | sodium: 183mg

Matcha Chia N'Oatmeal

Prep time: 5 minutes | Cook time: 0 minutes | Serves 3

1 cup full-fat coconut milk
1 cup water
2 teaspoons matcha powder
2 scoops collagen peptides
5 drops stevia extract

¼ cup whole chia seeds
1 tablespoon ground chia seeds (optional)
Shredded coconut or coconut flakes, for garnish

1. Put all the ingredients except the whole and ground chia seeds and the shredded coconut in a blender and blend until smooth. Taste and add more stevia if desired. 2. Pour the mixture into a large glass mason jar, add the whole chia seeds, cover, and shake well to combine. Refrigerate for 8 hours or overnight to allow the chia seeds to gel. 3. After it sets, whisk the mixture vigorously to break up the gelled seeds so that they're evenly distributed and the mixture is smooth and thick. 4. Add the ground chia seeds (if using), cover, and shake to combine. Place in the refrigerator to set for up to 1 hour, until thickened a bit more. If you prefer a thinner consistency, you can omit the ground chia seeds. 5. Garnish with shredded coconut before serving.
Per Serving
Calories: 291 | fat: 23g | protein: 12g | carbs: 12g | net carbs: 3g | fiber: 9g

Almond Flour Pancakes

Prep time: 5 minutes | Cook time: 10 minutes | Serves 6

2 cups (8 ounces/227 g) blanched almond flour
¼ cup erythritol
1 tablespoon baking powder
¼ teaspoon sea salt
4 large eggs

⅔ cup unsweetened almond milk
¼ cup avocado oil, plus more for frying
2 teaspoons vanilla extract

1. In a blender, combine all ingredients and blend until smooth. Let the batter rest for 5 to 10 minutes. 2. Preheat a large, very lightly oiled skillet over medium-low heat. (Keep oil very minimal for perfectly round pancakes.) Working in batches, pour circles of batter onto the pan, 2 tablespoons (⅛ cup) at a time for 3-inch pancakes. Cook 1½ to 2 minutes, until bubbles start to form on the edges. Flip and cook another minute or two, until browned on the other side. 3. Repeat with the remaining batter.
Per Serving
Calories: 355 | fat: 31g | protein: 12g | carbs: 12g | net carbs: 5g | fiber: 7g

Smoked Salmon and Cream Cheese Roll-Ups

Prep time: 25 minutes | Cook time: 0 minutes | Serves 2

4 ounces (113 g) cream cheese, at room temperature
1 teaspoon grated lemon zest
1 teaspoon Dijon mustard
2 tablespoons chopped scallions, white and green

parts
Pink Himalayan salt
Freshly ground black pepper
1 (4 ounces/113 g) package cold-smoked salmon (about 12 slices)

1. Put the cream cheese, lemon zest, mustard, and scallions in a food processor (or blender), and season with pink Himalayan salt and pepper. Process until fully mixed and smooth. 2. Spread the cream-cheese mixture on each slice of smoked salmon, and roll it up. Place the rolls on a plate seam-side down. 3. Serve immediately or refrigerate, covered in plastic wrap or in a lidded container, for up to 3 days.
Per Serving
Calories: 268 | fat: 22g | protein: 14g | carbs: 4g | net carbs: 3g | fiber: 1g

Chocoholic Granola

Prep time: 5 minutes | Cook time: 10 minutes | Makes 3½ cups

⅓ cup erythritol
2 tablespoons water
1 teaspoon vanilla extract
⅓ cup cocoa powder
1 teaspoon ground cinnamon

¾ teaspoon finely ground sea salt
3 cups unsweetened coconut flakes

1. Cover a cutting board or baking sheet with a piece of parchment paper and set aside. 2. Place the erythritol, water, and vanilla in a large saucepan over medium-low heat. Bring to a light simmer, stirring every 30 seconds. Continue to Step 3 if using confectioners'-style erythritol; if using granulated erythritol, continue to simmer until the granules can no longer be felt on the back of the spoon. 3. Reduce the heat to low and add the cocoa powder, cinnamon, and salt; mix until fully incorporated. 4. Add the coconut flakes and continue to stir frequently, keeping the temperature low to prevent burning. Cook for 6 to 7 minutes, until the bottom of the pan gets sticky. 5. Remove from the heat and transfer the granola to the parchment paper. Allow to cool completely, about 20 minutes, before enjoying, or transfer to a 1-quart (950-ml) or larger airtight container for storage.
Per Serving
Calories: 106 | fat: 9g | protein: 1g | carbs: 5g | net carbs: 2g | fiber: 3g

Bacon-Artichoke Omelet

Prep time: 10 minutes | Cook time: 10 minutes | Serves 4

6 eggs, beaten
2 tablespoons heavy (whipping) cream
8 bacon slices, cooked and chopped
1 tablespoon olive oil

¼ cup chopped onion
½ cup chopped artichoke hearts (canned, packed in water)
Sea salt
Freshly ground black pepper

1. In a small bowl, whisk together the eggs, heavy cream, and bacon until well blended, and set aside. 2. Place a large skillet over medium-high heat and add the olive oil. 3. Sauté the onion until tender, about 3 minutes. 4. Pour the egg mixture into the skillet, swirling it for 1 minute. 5. Cook the omelet, lifting the edges with a spatula to let the uncooked egg flow underneath, for 2 minutes. 6. Sprinkle the artichoke hearts on top and flip the omelet. Cook for 4 minutes more, until the egg is firm. Flip the omelet over again so the artichoke hearts are on top. 7. Remove from the heat, cut the omelet into quarters, and season with salt and black pepper. Transfer the omelet to plates and serve.
Per Serving
Calories: 435 | fat: 39g | protein: 17g | carbs: 5g | net carbs: 3g | fiber: 2g

Something Different Breakfast Sammy

Prep time: 5 minutes | Cook time: 10 minutes | Serves 1

1 medium Hass avocado, peeled and pitted (about 4 ounces/110 g of flesh)
1 lettuce leaf, torn in half
1 tablespoon mayonnaise
2 strips bacon (about 2 ounces/57 g), cooked until crispy

1 red onion ring
1 tomato slice
Pinch of finely ground sea salt
Pinch of ground black pepper
Pinch of sesame seeds or poppy seeds (optional)

1. Cook the bacon in a medium-sized frying pan over medium heat until crispy, about 10 minutes. 2. Place the avocado halves cut side up on a plate. 3. Lay the lettuce pieces on top of one of the avocado halves, then slather the mayonnaise on the lettuce. Top the lettuce with the bacon, onion, and tomato, then sprinkle with the salt and pepper. 4. Cover the stack with the other avocado half and sprinkle with the seeds, if using. Enjoy immediately!
Per Serving
Calories: 545 | fat: 43g | protein: 19g | carbs: 20g | net carbs: 11g | fiber: 9g

Brussels Sprouts, Bacon, and Eggs

Prep time: 5 minutes | Cook time: 20 minutes | Serves 2

½ pound (227 g) Brussels sprouts, cleaned, trimmed, and halved
1 tablespoon olive oil
Pink Himalayan salt
Freshly ground black pepper

Nonstick cooking spray
6 bacon slices, diced
4 large eggs
Pinch red pepper flakes
2 tablespoons grated Parmesan cheese

1. Preheat the oven to 400°F. 2. In a medium bowl, toss the halved Brussels sprouts in the olive oil, and season with pink Himalayan salt and pepper. 3. Coat a 9-by-13-inch baking pan with cooking spray. 4. Put the Brussels sprouts and bacon in the pan, and roast for 12 minutes. 5. Take the pan out of the oven, and stir the Brussels sprouts and bacon. Using a spoon, create 4 wells in the mixture. 6. Carefully crack an egg into each well. 7. Season the eggs with pink Himalayan salt, black pepper, and red pepper flakes. 8. Sprinkle the Parmesan cheese over the Brussels sprouts and eggs. 9. Cook in the oven for 8 more minutes, or until the eggs are cooked to your preference, and serve.
Per Serving
Calories: 401 | fat: 29g | protein: 27g | carbs: 12g | net carbs: 7g | fiber: 5g

No-Beans Hummus

Prep time: 5 minutes | Cook time: 0 minutes | Makes 2 cups

1 medium head cauliflower, cored and separated into florets (about 15½ ounces/445 g florets)
¼ cup tahini
6 tablespoons extra-virgin olive oil, divided
¼ cup fresh lemon juice

2 small cloves garlic, minced
¾ teaspoon finely ground gray sea salt
½ teaspoon ground cumin
Pinch of paprika, for garnish
Pinch of dried parsley, for garnish

1. Place the cauliflower florets, tahini, 4 tablespoons of the olive oil, lemon juice, garlic, salt, and cumin in a food processor or blender. Pulse until somewhat smooth, or until it reaches the desired hummus-like consistency. 2. Transfer the mixture to a serving bowl. Drizzle with the remaining olive oil and sprinkle with the paprika and parsley.
Per Serving
Calories: 162 | fat: 14g | protein: 2g | carbs: 5g | net carbs: 3g | fiber: 2g

Quick and Easy Capicola Egg Cups

Prep time: 5 minutes | Cook time: 14 minutes | Serves 6

6 slices capicola (regular or spicy)
¾ cup shredded cheddar cheese or other cheese of
choice (optional) 6 large eggs
Salt and pepper
Thinly sliced fresh basil, for garnish (optional)

1. Preheat the oven to 400°F. Spray 6 wells of a standard-size muffin pan with nonstick cooking spray. 2. Place a slice of capicola in each of the 6 greased wells, forming a bowl shape. If using cheese, sprinkle 2 tablespoons into each of the cups formed by the capicola. 3. Crack an egg into each cup and season with salt and pepper. 4. Bake for 12 to 14 minutes, until the egg whites are set. Serve hot, garnished with basil, if desired. **Notes:** You can use prepackaged or deli capicola, or substitute other meats, like ham or bacon. This recipe can easily be doubled or tripled for meal prep. Store the egg cups in airtight containers in the refrigerator for up to 4 days or in the freezer for up to 3 months.
Per Serving
Calories: 260 | fat: 20g | protein: 23g | carbs: 2g | net carbs: 2g | fiber: 0g

Mushroom & Cheese Lettuce Wraps

Prep time: 10 minutes | Cook time: 10 minutes | Serves 4

For the Wraps:
6 eggs
2 tablespoons almond milk
1 tablespoon olive oil
Sea salt, to taste
For the Filling:
1 teaspoon olive oil

1 cup mushrooms, chopped
Salt and black pepper, to taste
½ teaspoon cayenne pepper
8 fresh lettuce leaves
4 slices gruyere cheese
2 tomatoes, sliced

1. Mix all the ingredients for the wraps thoroughly. 2. Set a frying pan over medium heat. Add in ¼ of the mixture and cook for 4 minutes on both sides. Do the same thrice and set the wraps aside, they should be kept warm. 3. In a separate pan over medium heat, warm 1 teaspoon of olive oil. Cook the mushrooms for 5 minutes until soft; add cayenne pepper, black pepper, and salt. Set 1-2 lettuce leaves onto every wrap, split the mushrooms among the wraps and top with tomatoes and cheese.
Per Serving
Calories: 273 | fat: 20g | protein: 18g | carbs: 5g | net carbs: 4g | fiber: 1g

Easy Skillet Pancakes

Prep time: 5 minutes | Cook time: 5 minutes | Makes 8 pancakes

8 ounces (227 g) cream cheese
8 eggs
2 tablespoons coconut flour
2 teaspoons baking powder
1 teaspoon ground cinnamon

½ teaspoon vanilla extract
1 teaspoon liquid stevia or sweetener of choice (optional)
2 tablespoons butter

1. In a blender, combine the cream cheese, eggs, coconut flour, baking powder, cinnamon, vanilla, and stevia (if using). Blend until smooth. 2. In a large skillet over medium heat, melt the butter. 3. Use half the mixture to pour four evenly sized pancakes and cook for about a minute, until you see bubbles on top. Flip the pancakes and cook for another minute. Remove from the pan and add more butter or oil to the skillet if needed. Repeat with the remaining batter. 4. Top with butter and eat right away, or freeze the pancakes in a freezer-safe resealable bag with sheets of parchment in between, for up to 1 month.
Per Serving 1 pancake
Calories: 179 | fat: 15g | protein: 8g | carbs: 3g | net carbs: 2g | fiber: 1g

Blackberry-Chia Pudding

Prep time: 10 minutes | Cook time: 0 minutes | Serves 2

1 cup unsweetened full-fat coconut milk
1 teaspoon liquid stevia 1 teaspoon vanilla extract

½ cup blackberries, fresh or frozen (no sugar added if frozen)
¼ cup chia seeds

1. In a food processor (or blender), process the coconut milk, stevia, and vanilla until the mixture starts to thicken. 2. Add the blackberries, and process until thoroughly mixed and purple. Fold in the chia seeds. 3. Divide the mixture between two small cups with lids, and refrigerate overnight or up to 3 days before serving.

Per Serving
Calories: 437 | fat: 38g | protein: 8g | carbs: 23g | net carbs: 8g | fiber: 15g

Mocha Pre-Workout Smoothie

Prep time: 5 minutes | Cook time: 0 minutes | Serves 2

1 cup full-fat coconut milk
1 cup almond milk
2 scoops (25-28 g) chocolate protein powder (use something with no or very few carbs—I use

Primal Fuel)
½ banana
½ cup brewed espresso
1 tablespoon cocoa powder
4 ice cubes

1. Blend the smoothie. Put the coconut milk, almond milk, protein powder, banana, espresso, cocoa powder, and ice in a blender and blend until smooth and creamy. 2. Serve. Pour into two tall glasses and serve.

Per Serving
Calories: 372 | fat: 27g | protein: 26g | carbs: 14g | net carbs: 9g | fiber: 5g

Chapter 3 Beef, Pork, and Lamb

Easy Smoked Ham Hocks with Smoky Whole-Grain Mustard

Prep time: 5 minutes | Cook time: 10 minutes | Serves 4

Smoky Whole-Grain Mustard:
¼ cup prepared yellow mustard
¼ cup brown mustard seeds
2 tablespoons Swerve confectioners'-style sweetener or equivalent amount of liquid or powdered sweetener
¼ cup coconut vinegar or apple cider vinegar

2 teaspoons chili powder
½ teaspoon freshly ground black pepper
2 tablespoons coconut oil, melted
½ teaspoon liquid smoke
4 (3 ounces/85 g) smoked ham hock steaks
2 cups sauerkraut, warmed, for serving
Cornichons or other pickles of choice, for serving

To Make the Mustard: 1. In a small bowl, stir together the prepared mustard, mustard seeds, sweetener, vinegar, chili powder, and pepper. Stir in the melted coconut oil and liquid smoke; mix well to combine. Refrigerate overnight to allow the flavors to blend before using. 2. Preheat the oven to 425ºF (220ºC). Place the smoked ham hocks on a rimmed baking sheet and bake for 10 minutes, or until the skin gets crispy. 3. Place each ham hock on a plate with ½ cup sauerkraut and 2 to 4 tablespoons of the smoky mustard. 4. Store extras in an airtight container in the fridge for up to 3 days. To reheat, place in a skillet over medium heat and sauté for 3 minutes per side, or until warmed to your liking.
Per Serving
Calories: 195 | fat: 15g | protein: 9g | carbs: 6g | net carbs: 4g | fiber: 2g

Beef Meatball Stroganoff

Prep time: 10 minutes | Cook time: 14 minutes | Serves 4

1 pound (454 g) ground beef
1 egg
4 tablespoons heavy cream, divided
3 cloves garlic, minced
1 tablespoon chopped fresh parsley, plus more for garnish

½ teaspoon salt
Pinch of black pepper
1 cup beef broth
8 ounces (227 g) sliced baby bella mushrooms
¼ cup sour cream
1 teaspoon xanthan gum

1. In a large bowl, combine the beef, egg, 2 tablespoons of the heavy cream, garlic, parsley, salt, and pepper. Use a spoon to work everything evenly into the beef. 2. Use a cookie scoop to divide out 24 meatballs, about 1 ounce (28 g) each. Roll them between your hands to round them out. 3. Add the broth and mushrooms to the pot. Place the meatballs on top of the mushrooms. 4. Close the lid and seal the vent. Cook on High Pressure for 12 minutes. Quick release the steam. Press Cancel. 5. Use a slotted spoon to transfer the meatballs from the pot to a bowl or platter. 6. Turn the pot to Sauté mode. Whisk in the sour cream and the remaining 2 tablespoons heavy cream. Once the broth begins to lightly boil, whisk in the xanthan gum. Continue whisking until a thin gravy consistency is reached, about 2 minutes. Pour the gravy on top of the meatballs. Garnish with fresh parsley.
Per Serving
Calories: 408 | fat: 27g | protein: 29g | carbs: 14g | net carbs: 6g | fiber: 8g

Spaghetti Squash and Ground Pork Stir-Fry with Kale

Prep time: 10 minutes | Cook time: 1 hour 25 minutes | Serves 3 to 4

1 medium spaghetti squash, halved lengthwise and seeded
2 tablespoons avocado or macadamia nut oil, divided
1 pound (454 g) ground free-range pork
Salt and freshly ground black pepper, to taste

1 bunch kale, stems removed, leaves chopped (2 to 3 cups)
1 teaspoon garlic powder
1 teaspoon onion powder
1 teaspoon dried parsley
½ teaspoon dry mustard powder
½ teaspoon dried rosemary
½ teaspoon dried oregano

1. Preheat the oven to 400ºF (205ºC). Line a baking sheet with aluminum foil. 2. Brush the cut side of the spaghetti squash with 1 tablespoon of the oil. Place it cut side down on the baking sheet and roast for 45 minutes to 1 hour, or until tender when pierced with a fork. Remove from the oven and let sit until cool enough to handle. 3. In a large skillet or a wok, heat the oil over medium-high heat. Add the ground pork and season with salt and pepper. Cook for about 5 minutes, stirring and breaking the meat up into pieces. 4. Scoop the squash flesh (the spaghetti strands) into the skillet or wok and stir to combine with the meat. Reserve the spaghetti squash shells for serving, if you'd like. 5. Add the kale, garlic and onion powders, parsley, dry mustard powder, rosemary, oregano, and salt and pepper to taste. Mix everything together until well combined and cook for 10 minutes, or until the meat is no longer pink and the kale is wilted. 6. To serve, scoop the pork mixture into the reserved spaghetti squash shells or simply serve up in bowls or on plates!
Per Serving
Calories: 355 | fat: 23g | protein: 23g | carbs: 14g | net carbs: 8g | fiber: 6g

Beef Tenderloin with Red Wine Sauce

Prep time: 30 minutes | Cook time: 10 minutes | Serves 5

2 pounds (907 g) beef tenderloin
Salt and black pepper, to taste
2 tablespoons avocado oil
½ cup beef broth
½ cup dry red wine

2 cloves garlic, minced
1 teaspoon Worcestershire sauce
1½ teaspoons dried rosemary
¼ teaspoon xanthan gum
Chopped fresh rosemary, for garnish (optional)

1. Thirty minutes prior to cooking, take the tenderloin out of the fridge and let it come to room temperature. Crust the outside of the tenderloin in salt and pepper. 2. Turn the pot to Sauté mode and add the avocado oil. Once hot, add the tenderloin and sear on all sides, about 5 minutes. Press Cancel. 3. Add the broth, wine, garlic, Worcestershire sauce, and rosemary to the pot around the beef. 4. Close the lid and seal the vent. Cook on High Pressure for 8 minutes. Quick release the steam. 5. Remove the tenderloin to a platter, tent with aluminum foil, and let it rest for 10 minutes. Press Cancel. 6. Turn the pot to Sauté mode. Once the broth has begun a low boil, add the xanthan gum and whisk until a thin sauce has formed, 2 to 3 minutes. 7. Slice the tenderloin against the grain into thin rounds. Top each slice with the red wine glaze. Garnish with rosemary, if desired.
Per Serving
Calories: 575 | fat: 44g | protein: 33g | carbs: 2g | net carbs: 1g | fiber: 1g

Feta-Stuffed Burgers ✗ ✗

Prep time: 10 minutes | Cook time: 10 minutes | Serves 2

2 tablespoons fresh mint leaves, finely chopped
1 scallion, white and green parts, thinly sliced
1 tablespoon Dijon mustard
Pink Himalayan salt
Freshly ground black pepper

12 ounces (6 ounces/170 g each) ground beef and ground lamb mixture
2 ounces (57 g) crumbled feta cheese
1 tablespoon ghee

1. In a large bowl, mix to combine the mint leaves with the scallion and mustard. Season with pink Himalayan salt and pepper. 2. Add the ground beef and lamb to the bowl. Mix together thoroughly, and form into 4 patties. 3. Press the feta crumbles into 2 of the patties, and put the other 2 patties on top so the cheese is in the middle. Pinch all the way around the edges of the burgers to seal in the feta cheese. 4. In a medium skillet over medium heat, heat the ghee. Add the burger patties to the hot oil. Cook each side for 4 to 5 minutes, until done to your preference, and serve.

Per Serving
Calories: 607 | fat: 48g | protein: 41g | carbs: 2g | net carbs: 2g | fiber: 1g

Cheesesteak Stuffed Peppers

Prep time: 10 minutes | Cook time: 8 minutes | Serves 4

1 tablespoon butter
1 pound (454 g) shaved beef
4 ounces (113 g) mushrooms, coarsely chopped
2½ ounces (71 g) sliced onion
1 tablespoon Worcestershire

sauce
1 teaspoon seasoned salt
¼ teaspoon salt
¼ teaspoon black pepper
4 large bell peppers (any color)
½ cup water
4 slices provolone cheese

1. Heat the broiler. 2. Turn the pot to Sauté mode and add the butter. Once melted, add the beef, mushrooms, and onion. Sauté until softened, 2 to 3 minutes. Add the Worcestershire sauce, seasoned salt, salt, and black pepper. Stir to evenly combine. Press Cancel. 3. Slice the tops off the bell peppers and remove the cores and seeds. Fill each pepper with 4¼ ounces (120 g) of the meat mixture. Rinse out the pot. 4. Place the pot back into the base. Add the water and the trivet. Place the peppers on top of the trivet. 5. Close the lid and seal the vent. Cook on High Pressure for 5 minutes. Quick release the steam. 6. Carefully remove the trivet from the pot. Transfer the peppers to a baking sheet. Place one slice of provolone cheese on top of each pepper and broil for about 1 minute to melt the cheese.
Per Serving
Calories: 294 | fat: 18g | protein: 26g | carbs: 5g | net carbs: 4g | fiber: 1g

BLTA Lettuce Wraps ✗ ✗

Prep time: 15 minutes | Cook time: 5 minutes | Serves 4

6 slices bacon
3 tablespoons mayonnaise
4 butter lettuce leaves

½ avocado
2 slices tomato, halved
Salt and pepper

1. In a large skillet over medium heat, fry the bacon until crispy, about 5 minutes. Set aside on a paper towel–lined plate to cool. When cool enough to handle, cut each strip in half crosswise. 2. Squeeze a line of mayonnaise onto each of the lettuce leaves. Top each leaf with a half-slice of tomato, 3. half-slices of bacon, and a slice of avocado. Season to taste with salt and pepper and enjoy!
Per Serving
Calories: 387 | fat: 34g | protein: 15g | carbs: 5g | net carbs: 2g | fiber: 3g

Chile Verde Pulled Pork with Tomatillos

Prep time: 15 minutes | Cook time: 1 hour 3 minutes | Serves 6

2 pounds (907 g) pork shoulder, cut into 6 equal-sized pieces
1 teaspoon sea salt
½ teaspoon ground black pepper
2 jalapeño peppers, deseeded and stemmed
1 pound (454 g) tomatillos, husks removed and quartered
3 garlic cloves
1 tablespoon lime juice
3 tablespoons fresh cilantro, chopped
1 medium white onion, chopped
1 teaspoon ground cumin
½ teaspoon dried oregano
1⅔ cups chicken broth
1½ tablespoons olive oil

1. Season the pork pieces with the salt and pepper. Gently rub the seasonings into the pork cuts. Set aside. 2. Combine the jalapeños, tomatillos, garlic cloves, lime juice, cilantro, onions, cumin, oregano, and chicken broth in the blender. Pulse until well combined. Set aside. 3. Select Sauté mode and add the olive oil to the pot. Once the oil is hot, add the pork cuts and sear for 4 minutes per side or until browned. 4. Pour the jalapeño sauce over the pork and lightly stir to coat well. 5. Lock the lid. Select Manual mode and set cooking time for 55 minutes on High Pressure. 6. When cooking is complete, allow the pressure to release naturally for 10 minutes and then release the remaining pressure. 7. Open the lid. Transfer the pork pieces to a cutting board and use two forks to shred the pork. 8. Transfer the shredded pork back to the pot and stir to combine the pork with the sauce. Transfer to a serving platter. Serve warm.
Per Serving
Calories: 381 | fat: 24.8g | protein: 29.3g | carbs: 11.1g | net carbs: 8.3g | fiber: 2.8g

Cajun Sausage and Rice

Prep time: 10 minutes | Cook time: 25 minutes | serves 4

2 tablespoons avocado oil
14 ounces (397 g) fully cooked andouille sausage, sliced
½ cup diced onions
½ cup diced green bell peppers
1 rib celery, diced
1 (12-ounce) bag frozen riced cauliflower
1 cup vegetable broth
1 teaspoon Creole seasoning
1 bay leaf

1. Heat the oil in a large, deep skillet over medium heat. Brown the sausage for 2 to 3 minutes. Add the onions, green peppers, and celery to the skillet and cook until the vegetables are tender and the onions are translucent. 2. Add the cauliflower, broth, Creole seasoning, and bay leaf to the skillet. Continue cooking, stirring occasionally, until the cauliflower is tender. 3. Reduce the heat to low and simmer for 10 more minutes, until the mixture is slightly thickened. Remove the bay leaf before serving.
Per Serving
Calories: 308 | fat: 25g | protein: 17g | carbs: 7g | net carbs: 4g | fiber: 3g

Beef Provençal

Prep time: 10 minutes | Cook time: 35 minutes | Serves 4

12 ounces (340 g) beef steak racks
2 fennel bulbs, sliced
Salt and black pepper, to taste
3 tablespoons olive oil
½ cup apple cider vinegar
1 teaspoon herbs de Provence
1 tablespoon swerve

1. In a bowl, mix the fennel with 2 tablespoons of oil, swerve, and vinegar, toss to coat well, and set to a baking dish. Season with herbs de Provence, pepper and salt, and cook in the oven at 400ºF for 15 minutes. 2. Sprinkle black pepper and salt to the beef, place into an oiled pan over medium heat, and cook for a couple of minutes. Place the beef to the baking dish with the fennel, and bake for 20 minutes. Split everything among plates and enjoy.
Per Serving
Calories: 251 | fat: 15g | protein: 19g | carbs: 8g | net carbs: 4g | fiber: 4g

Spicy Sausage and Cabbage Skillet

Prep time: 5 minutes | Cook time: 35 minutes | Serves 4

1 tablespoon olive oil
1 small white onion, diced
1 garlic clove, minced
1 pound (454 g) hot Italian sausage, casings removed
1 head cabbage, chopped
Salt, to taste
Freshly ground black pepper, to taste
1 cup shredded provolone cheese

1. Preheat the oven to 350ºF (180ºC). 2. In a large cast-iron skillet over medium heat, heat the olive oil. 3. Add the onion and garlic. Sauté for 5 to 7 minutes until the onion is softened and translucent. 4. Add the sausage and cook for 7 to 10 minutes or until browned. Remove from the heat, slice the sausage, and return it to the skillet. 5. Add the cabbage and season with salt and pepper. 6. Top with the provolone and transfer the skillet to the oven. Bake for 20 minutes or until the cheese melts. Refrigerate leftovers in an airtight container for up to 6 days.
Per Serving
Calories: 602 | fat: 48g | protein: 28g | carbs: 17g | net carbs: 11g | fiber: 6g

Beef Satay Skewers

Prep time: 30 minutes | Cook time: 15 minutes | Serves 6

Marinade:
½ cup full-fat coconut milk
3 tablespoons coconut aminos
2 to 3 dashes of fish sauce
½ small yellow onion, finely chopped
2 cloves garlic, grated or minced
1 teaspoon ground cumin
¼ teaspoon ground ginger
Pinch of red pepper flakes
Pinch of sea salt
Pinch of ground black pepper
2 pounds (907 g) sirloin steak, sliced
1 medium red onion, cut

into 1½-inch chunks
Satay Sauce:
½ cup coconut aminos
½ cup unsweetened peanut, almond, or sunflower seed butter
¼ cup rice vinegar
2 to 3 dashes of fish sauce
½ teaspoon toasted sesame seeds
¼ teaspoon ground black pepper
¼ teaspoon sea salt
¼ teaspoon red pepper flakes
For Garnish:
¼ cup chopped fresh cilantro leaves
1 lime, cut into wedges

1. Whisk together all the ingredients for the marinade in a large mixing bowl. 2. Place the steak in the bowl with the marinade and massage the marinade into it. Cover and place in the refrigerator to marinate overnight. 3. When you're ready to grill the steak, soak 12 to 16 (depending on how many slices of meat you have) bamboo or wooden skewers for 10 minutes and preheat a grill or grill pan to medium-high heat. Thread the marinated steak pieces on the skewers, alternating them with the onion pieces. 4. Grill the skewers for 4 to 6 minutes on each side, or to your desired level of doneness, so the steak is seared but not burned. Remove from the heat, cover with foil, and let rest for 5 minutes. 5. While the skewers are resting, **make the satay sauce:** Whisk together all the ingredients for the sauce in a small mixing bowl. 6. Garnish the skewers with cilantro, squeeze lime juice over the meat, and serve with the satay sauce on the side.
Per Serving
Calories: 605 | fat: 30g | protein: 57g | carbs: 19g | net carbs: 16g | fiber: 3g

Baked Crustless Pizza

Prep time: 5 minutes | Cook time: 20 minutes | Serves 2

8 ounces (227 g) chopped Italian sausage
15 slices pepperoni

10 large black olives, sliced
½ cup grated Mozzarella cheese

1. Preheat the oven to 350°F (180°C). 2. In a skillet over medium heat, cook the sausage. Drain the grease and spread the sausage on the bottom of an 8-by-8-inch baking dish or pie pan. 3. Layer the pepperoni slices, black olives,
and cheese over the sausage. 4. Bake, covered, for 10 to 15 minutes or until the cheese is melted and hot throughout.
Per Serving ½ skillet
Calories: 480 | fat: 40g | protein: 27g | carbs: 3g | net carbs: 2g | fiber: 1g

Lamb Shashlyk

Prep time: 5 minutes | Cook time: 10 minutes | Serves 4

1 pound ground lamb
¼ teaspoon cinnamon
1 egg

1 grated onion
Salt and ground black pepper, to taste

1. Place all ingredients in a bowl. Mix with your hands to combine well. Divide the meat into 4 pieces. Shape all meat portions around previously-soaked skewers. 2. Preheat grill to medium and grill the kebabs for about 5 minutes per side.
Per Serving
Calories: 246 | fat: 15g | protein: 25g | carbs: 3g | net carbs: 2g | fiber: 1g

Keto BLTs with Soft-Boiled Eggs

Prep time: 7 minutes | Cook time: 15 minutes | Makes 12 wraps

12 slices bacon
6 large eggs (omit for egg-free)
Coarse sea salt and freshly ground black pepper, to taste
12 thick slices tomato

(about 3 tomatoes)
12 large lettuce leaves, such as romaine, green leaf, or Boston
¾ cup mayonnaise and/or baconnaise, homemade or store-bought

1. If using standard-sliced bacon, preheat the oven to 400°F (205°C); if using thick-cut bacon, preheat the oven to 375°F (190°C). Place the bacon on a wire rack set inside a rimmed baking sheet. Bake until crispy, 10 to 15 minutes, depending on how thick the bacon is. 2. Meanwhile, **make the soft-boiled eggs:** Place the eggs in a pot of simmering (not boiling) water, cover, and simmer for 6 minutes. Immediately rinse the eggs under cold water. Peel the eggs, then cut them in half and place on a large serving platter. Sprinkle the eggs with flaky sea salt and pepper. 3. Place the tomato slices on the serving platter with the eggs and sprinkle them with flaky sea salt. Then add the cooked bacon to the platter. 4. Place the lettuce leaves in a bowl and have mayo out for serving. 5. Let everyone assemble their wraps!
Per Serving
Calories: 461 | fat: 42g | protein: 16g | carbs: 5g | net carbs: 4g | fiber: 1g

The Classic Juicy Lucy

Prep time: 10 minutes | Cook time: 10 minutes | Serves 4 ⚹⚹

1 pound (454 g) ground beef
8 ounces (227 g) Cheddar cheese, shredded or cubed
Salt, to taste
Freshly ground black pepper, to taste

1. Divide the ground beef into 4 equal portions. (This makes 4 quarter-pound burgers—if you want 2 larger ones, just divide the meat in half.) Form each portion into a patty, pressing down on the center to flatten it out a bit. 2. Add ¼ of the Cheddar to the center of each burger and roll the sides of the patty up to cover the cheese, like a big meatball. Smooth the burger out in your hands and gently press down with your palms to re-form it into a patty. Season both sides generously with salt and pepper. 3. In a large skillet, cast-iron pan, or on the grill over medium-high heat, cook the burgers for 7 to 10 minutes per side, depending on how you like them done. This timing will give you medium burgers; cook for a little less time if you prefer yours medium-rare. Remove the burgers from the heat and serve immediately with your favorite keto toppings (lettuce, pickles, sliced onion).

Per Serving
Calories: 602 | fat: 53g | protein: 30g | carbs: 1g | net carbs: 1g | fiber: 0g

Shepherd's Pie

Prep time: 15 minutes | Cook time: 70 minutes | Serves 6

4 tablespoons extra-virgin olive oil, divided
2 cups cauliflower florets (from about half a head of cauliflower)
2 tablespoons unsalted butter
½ cup heavy cream
1 cup shredded Cheddar cheese
2 teaspoons salt, divided
2 teaspoons dried thyme, divided
½ teaspoon freshly ground black pepper, divided
1 pound (454 g) ground beef, preferably grass-fed
½ small yellow onion, diced
1 cup chopped cabbage
1 carrot, peeled and diced
2 ribs celery, diced
4 ounces (113 g) mushrooms, sliced
4 cloves garlic, minced
1 (14½ ounces/411 g) can diced tomatoes, with juices
2 tablespoons tomato paste
½ cup beef stock
8 ounces (227 g) cream cheese, room temperature

1. Heat the oven to 375ºF (190ºC). 2. Heat 2 tablespoons of olive oil in a pan over medium-low heat. Add the cauliflower and sauté for 6-8 minutes. Add the butter and heavy cream, cover, reduce heat to low, and cook another 6-8 minutes. Remove from the heat and cool slightly. 3. Add the cheese, 1 teaspoon of salt, 1 teaspoon of thyme, and ¼ teaspoon of pepper to the cauliflower. Puree until very smooth. 4. Heat the remaining 2 tablespoons of olive oil. Add the ground beef and sauté for 5 minutes, breaking apart the meat. Add the onion, cabbage, carrot, celery, and mushrooms and sauté for another 5-6 minutes. Add the garlic, remaining salt, thyme, and pepper and stir-fry for another 30 seconds. 5. Stir in the tomatoes with their juices and the tomato paste. Bring to a simmer, reduce heat to low, cover, and simmer for 8-10 minutes. 6. In a small microwave-safe bowl, combine the stock and cream cheese and microwave on high for 1 minute or until cheese is melted. Whisk until creamy. 7. Add the cream cheese mixture to the meat and vegetables and stir to combine. Place the mixture in a dish. Spread the pureed cauliflower over the meat mixture and bake until golden, 25-30 minutes.

Per Serving
Calories: 868 | fat: 74g | protein: 37g | carbs: 18g | net carbs: 13g | fiber: 5g

Parsley Beef Burgers

Prep time: 5 minutes | Cook time: 18 minutes | Serves 6

2 pounds (907 g) ground beef
1 tablespoon onion flakes
¾ cup almond flour
¼ cup beef broth
1 tablespoon chopped parsley
1 tablespoon Worcestershire sauce

1. Combine all ingredients in a bowl. Mix well with your hands and make 6 patties out of the mixture. Arrange on a lined baking sheet. Bake at 370ºF, for about 18 minutes, until nice and crispy.

Per Serving
Calories: 300 | fat: 19g | protein: 30g | carbs: 2g | net carbs: 2g | fiber: 0g

Turmeric Pork Loin

Prep time: 10 minutes | Cook time: 22 minutes | Serves 4

1 pound (454 g) pork loin
1 teaspoon ground turmeric
1 teaspoon coconut oil
½ teaspoon salt
½ cup organic almond milk

1. Cut the pork loin into the strips and sprinkle with salt and ground turmeric. 2. Heat up the coconut oil on Sauté mode for 1 minute and add pork strips. 3. Sauté them for 6 minutes. Stir the meat from time to time. 4. After this, add almond milk and close the lid. 5. Sauté the pork for 15 minutes.

Per Serving
Calories: 226 | fat: 11g | protein: 30g | carbs: 2g | net carbs: 2g | fiber: 0g

Slow Cooker Short Rib Tacos

Prep time: 5 minutes | Cook time: 6 to 8 hours | Serves 12

Ribs:
¼ cup diced onions
4 pounds (1.8 kg) boneless beef short ribs
1 cup green or red salsa
1 cup beef or chicken bone broth, homemade or store-bought
2 cloves garlic, minced
2 teaspoons fine sea salt

1 teaspoon freshly ground black pepper
For Serving:
Purple cabbage, radicchio, or lettuce leaves, for "shells"
Guacamole
Salsa verde
Lime wedges
Chopped fresh cilantro

1. Place the onions in a 6-quart (or larger) slow cooker. Set the ribs on top of the onions. Add the rest of the ingredients and stir to combine the seasonings. Cover and cook on low until the meat is fork-tender and falls apart easily, 6 to 8 hours. 2. Remove the ribs from the slow cooker. Pull the meat off the bones, discard the bones, and use two forks to shred the meat. Place the meat in a serving bowl. 3. Serve with purple cabbage, radicchio, or lettuce wraps for taco "shells," along with guacamole, salsa verde, lime wedges, and cilantro. Store extras in an airtight container in the fridge for up to 4 days.
Per Serving
Calories: 296 | fat: 16g | protein: 32g | carbs: 6g | net carbs: 4g | fiber: 2g

Italian Beef Meatloaf

Prep time: 10 minutes | Cook time: 25 minutes | Serves 6

1 pound (454 g) ground beef
1 cup crushed pork rinds
1 egg
¼ cup grated Parmesan cheese
¼ cup Italian dressing
2 teaspoons Italian seasoning

½ cup water
½ cup sugar-free tomato sauce
1 tablespoon chopped fresh herbs (such as parsley or basil)
1 clove garlic, minced

1. In large bowl, combine the beef, pork rinds, egg, cheese, dressing, and Italian seasoning. Use a wooden spoon to incorporate everything into the meat, but do not overwork the meat or it will turn out tough. 2. Turn the meat mixture out onto a piece of aluminum foil. Use your hands to shape into a loaf. Wrap the foil up around the meat like a packet, but do not cover the top. Place the trivet in the pot and add the water. Place the meatloaf on top of the trivet. 3. Close the lid and seal the vent. Cook on High Pressure 20 minutes. Quick release the steam. 4. While the meat is cooking, whisk together the tomato sauce, herbs, and garlic in a small bowl. Heat the broiler. 5. Remove the meat and foil packet from the pot. Place on a baking sheet and spread the tomato sauce mixture on top. Broil until the glaze becomes sticky, about 5 minutes. Slice into six equal pieces.
Per Serving
Calories: 358 | fat: 25g | protein: 29g | carbs: 2g | net carbs: 2g | fiber: 0g

Bistecca Alla Fiorentina

Prep time: 10 minutes | Cook time: 15 minutes | Serves 4

2 (1-inch-thick) bone-in porterhouse steaks, about 2 pounds (907 g)
6 tablespoons good-quality olive oil, divided
Sea salt, for seasoning

Freshly ground black pepper, for seasoning
½ cup white wine
2 rosemary sprigs
Lemon wedges, for serving

1. Preheat the grill. Preheat the grill to high heat. 2. Prepare the steaks. Rub the steaks with 2 tablespoons of the olive oil and season them generously with salt and pepper. 3. Prepare the basting liquid. In a small bowl, stir together the white wine and the remaining 4 tablespoons of olive oil. 4. Grill the steaks. Using the rosemary sprigs as basters, baste the steaks on both sides with the wine mixture. Grill the steaks, flipping them once, until they're seared on both sides, 6 to 8 minutes in total (125°F internal temperature) for medium rare. 5. Serve. Let the steaks rest for 10 minutes, then divide them between four plates, and serve them with lemon wedges.
Per Serving
Calories: 569 | fat: 45g | protein: 35g | carbs: 0g | net carbs: 0g | fiber: 0g

Winter Veal and Sauerkraut

Prep time: 10 minutes | Cook time: 1 hour | Serves 4

1 pound veal, cut into cubes
18 ounces (504 g) sauerkraut, rinsed and drained
Salt and black pepper, to taste
½ cup ham, chopped

1 onion, chopped
2 garlic cloves, minced
1 tablespoon butter
½ cup Parmesan cheese, grated
½ cup sour cream

1. Heat a pot with the butter over medium heat, add in the onion, and cook for 3 minutes. Stir in garlic, and cook for 1 minute. Place in the veal and ham, and cook until slightly browned. Place in the sauerkraut, and cook until the meat becomes tender, about 30 minutes. Stir in sour cream, pepper, and salt. Top with Parmesan cheese and bake for 20 minutes at 350ºF.

Slow Cooker Herb-and-Garlic Short Rib Stew

Prep time: 10 minutes | Cook time: 4 to 6 hours | Serves 4

1 pound (454 g) boneless beef short ribs
1 teaspoon salt
½ teaspoon garlic powder
¼ teaspoon freshly ground black pepper
4 tablespoons extra-virgin olive oil, divided
½ small yellow onion, diced
1 carrot, peeled and diced
2 ribs celery, diced

4 ounces (113 g) sliced mushrooms
6 cloves garlic, minced
2 teaspoons dried thyme
2 teaspoons dried rosemary (or 2 tablespoons fresh)
1 teaspoon dried oregano
3 cups beef stock
1 (14½ ounces/411 g) can diced tomatoes, with juices
½ cup dry red wine

1. Season the short ribs with the salt, garlic powder, and pepper. 2. Heat 2 tablespoons of olive oil in a large skillet over high heat. Add the short ribs and brown until dark in color, 2 to 3 minutes per side. Transfer to the bowl of a slow cooker. 3. Add the remaining 2 tablespoons of olive oil to the skillet and reduce heat to medium. Add the onion, carrot, celery, and mushrooms and sauté until just tender but not fully cooked, 3 to 4 minutes. Add the garlic and sauté, stirring, for an additional 30 seconds. Transfer the contents of the skillet to the slow cooker with the ribs. 4. Add the thyme, rosemary, oregano, stock, tomatoes with their juices, and wine, and cook on low for 4 to 6 hours, or until meat is very tender. 5. Remove the ribs from the stew and shred using two forks. Return the shredded meat to the stew and stir to combine well. Serve warm.

Per Serving
Calories: 549 | fat: 43g | protein: 24g | carbs: 14g | net carbs: 9g | fiber: 5g

Cabbage Casserole

Prep time: 10 minutes | Cook time: 35 minutes | Serves 4

1 tablespoon olive oil
¼ white onion, diced
½ pound (227 g) ground beef
½ pound (227 g) ground pork
Salt, to taste
Freshly ground black pepper, to taste

2 eggs
½ cup heavy (whipping) cream
2 tablespoons tomato paste
1 cup shredded provolone cheese, divided
1 large head cabbage, shredded

1. Preheat the oven to 350°F (180°C). 2. In a large skillet over medium heat, heat the olive oil. 3. Add the onion.

Sauté for 5 to 7 minutes until softened and translucent. 4. Add the beef and pork. Cook for 5 to 7 minutes until browned. Season with salt and pepper. Drain off the grease and transfer the meat mixture to a 7-by-11-inch baking dish. 5. In a medium bowl, whisk together the eggs, cream, tomato paste, and ½ cup of provolone. Season with salt and pepper. 6. Top the meat mixture with the shredded cabbage and pour the egg mixture over it. Gently shake the dish and tap it on the counter to ensure the mixture makes it through to the bottom and sides of the dish. Top with the remaining ½ cup of provolone. Bake for 25 minutes until the cheese melts and the corners are set and bubbling slightly. Cover and refrigerate leftovers for up to 3 days.

Per Serving
Calories: 650 | fat: 48g | protein: 36g | carbs: 22g | net carbs: 14g | fiber: 8g

Low-Carb Chili

Prep time: 15 minutes | Cook time: 3 hours | Serves 6

2 tablespoons olive oil
1 large onion, diced
3 garlic cloves, minced
1 medium red bell pepper, chopped
1 medium yellow bell pepper, chopped
2 pounds (907 g) ground beef
1 (6 ounces/170 g) can tomato paste
4 cups water
1 tablespoon chili powder
1½ teaspoons red pepper flakes

1 teaspoon ground cumin
1 teaspoon paprika
¾ teaspoon dry mustard
¾ teaspoon ground coriander
½ teaspoon dried oregano
½ teaspoon ground allspice
2 cups beef broth
1½ teaspoons ground cayenne pepper (more or less depending on your heat preference)
½ cup apple cider vinegar
Sliced scallion, green parts only, for garnish

1. In a large saucepan over medium heat, heat the olive oil. 2. Add the onion, garlic, and red and yellow bell peppers. Sauté for about 5 minutes until the vegetables cook down. 3. Add the beef. Cook for 5 to 7 minutes, stirring with a wooden spoon and breaking up the beef until mostly browned. 4. Add the tomato paste and water. Give it a good stir. 5. Stir in the chili powder, red pepper flakes, cumin, paprika, mustard, coriander, oregano, and allspice. Bring the chili to a low boil, reduce the heat to simmer, cover the pan, and cook for at least 2 hours. Periodically check the chili and stir in some broth when it starts getting thick. 6. About 20 minutes before serving, stir in the cayenne and vinegar. Spoon into bowls and top with scallion.

Per Serving
Calories: 551 | fat: 43g | protein: 28g | carbs: 13g | net carbs: 10g | fiber: 3g

Drunken Pot Roast

Prep time: 5 minutes | Cook time: 8 hours | Serves 8

1 (4 pounds/1.8 kg) roast	½ cup unsalted butter, softened
1 (1 ounce/28 g) package ranch dressing mix	1 (12 ounces/340 g) can low-carb beer
1 cup chopped celery	

1. Place roast in slow cooker and cover with dressing mix, celery, butter, and beer. 2. Cover and cook on low heat for 8 hours. 3. After cooking is finished, let roast sit 15 minutes. Carve and serve warm.

Per Serving
Calories: 556 | fat: 34g | protein: 49g | carbs: 4g | net carbs: 4g | fiber: 0g

Per Serving
Calories: 410 | fat: 25g | protein: 32g | carbs: 10g | net carbs: 6g | fiber: 4g

Stuffed Pork Roll-Ups

Prep time: 15 minutes | Cook time: 1 hour | Serves 4

2 tablespoons butter	boneless pork chops
1 large onion, sliced	½ cup chicken broth
2 garlic cloves, minced	1 teaspoon dried thyme
10 ounces (283 g) mushrooms, sliced	½ cup freshly grated Parmesan cheese, divided, plus more for garnish
Salt, to taste	¼ cup heavy (whipping) cream
Freshly ground black pepper, to taste	
4 (4-6 ounces/113-170 g)	

1. Preheat the oven to 350ºF (180ºC). 2. In a large skillet over medium heat, melt the butter. 3. Add the onion and garlic. Sauté for 10 minutes. 4. Add the mushrooms and cook for 8 to 10 minutes. Season with salt and pepper. 5. While the mushrooms reduce, slice each pork chop in half widthwise. Open the chop like a book, cover with plastic wrap, and pound the meat thinly. Season with salt and pepper and set aside. 6. Once the mushrooms have reduced, stir in the chicken broth and thyme. Bring to a simmer and cook for about 10 minutes. Remove from the heat and add ¼ cup of Parmesan and the cream, stirring well to combine. 7. Spoon some mushroom mixture onto the edge of each piece of pork. Add another tablespoon of Parmesan to each and roll up the pork tightly, securing with toothpicks if desired. Transfer to a baking dish and cover with the remaining mushroom sauce. Bake for 25 to 30 minutes or until the pork is cooked through. 8. Remove the roll-ups from the oven and serve topped with the remaining ¼ cup of Parmesan. Refrigerate leftovers in an airtight container for up to 1 week.

Per Serving
Calories: 398 | fat: 26g | protein: 33g | carbs: 8g | net carbs: 6g | fiber: 2g

Beef Burger

Prep time: 20 minutes | Cook time: 12 minutes | Serves 4

1¼ pounds (567 g) lean ground beef	1 clove garlic, minced
1 tablespoon coconut aminos	½ teaspoon cumin powder
1 teaspoon Dijon mustard	¼ cup scallions, minced
A few dashes of liquid smoke	⅓ teaspoon sea salt flakes
1 teaspoon shallot powder	⅓ teaspoon freshly cracked mixed peppercorns
	1 teaspoon celery seeds
	1 teaspoon parsley flakes

1. Mix all of the above ingredients in a bowl; knead until everything is well incorporated. 2. Shape the mixture into four patties. Next, make a shallow dip in the center of each patty to prevent them puffing up during air frying. 3. Spritz the patties on all sides using nonstick cooking spray. Cook approximately 12 minutes at 360ºF (182ºC). 4. Check for doneness, an instant-read thermometer should read 160ºF (71ºC). Bon appétit!

Per Serving
Calories: 193 | fat: 7g | protein: 31g | carbs: 1g | fiber: 0g | sodium: 304mg

Cider-Herb Pork Tenderloin

Prep time: 15 minutes | Cook time: 18 minutes | Serves 4

¼ teaspoon ground cumin	1 pound (454 g) pork tenderloin
½ teaspoon ground nutmeg	2 tablespoons apple cider vinegar
½ teaspoon dried thyme	1 cup water
½ teaspoon ground coriander	
1 tablespoon sesame oil	

1. In the mixing bowl, mix up ground cumin, ground nutmeg, thyme, ground coriander, and apple cider vinegar. 2. Then rub the meat with the spice mixture. 3. Heat up sesame oil on Sauté mode for 2 minutes. 4. Put the pork tenderloin in the hot oil and cook it for 5 minutes from each side or until meat is light brown. 5. Add water. 6. Close and seal the lid. Cook the meat on Manual mode (High Pressure) for 5 minutes. 7. When the time is finished, allow the natural pressure release for 15 minutes.

Per Serving
Calories: 196 | fat: 7g | protein: 29g | carbs: 0g | net carbs: 0g | fiber: 0g

Beef Meatballs

Prep time: 5 minutes | Cook time: 32 minutes | Serves 5

½ cup pork rinds, crushed
1 egg
Salt and black pepper, to taste
1½ pounds (680 g) ground beef
10 ounces canned onion soup
1 tablespoon almond flour
¼ cup free-sugar ketchup
3 teaspoons Worcestershire sauce
½ teaspoon dry mustard
¼ cup water

1. In a bowl, combine ⅓ cup of the onion soup with the beef, pepper, pork rinds, egg, and salt. Heat a pan over medium heat, shape the mixture into 12 meatballs. Brown in the pan for 12 minutes on both sides. 2. In a separate bowl, combine the rest of the soup with the almond flour, dry mustard, ketchup, Worcestershire sauce, and water. Pour this over the beef meatballs, cover the pan, and cook for 20 minutes as you stir occasionally. Split among serving bowls and serve.

Per Serving
Calories: 417 | fat: 30g | protein: 31g | carbs: 6g | net carbs: 5g | fiber: 1g

Slow Cooker Swedish Meatballs

Prep time: 20 minutes | Cook time: 4 hours | Serves 8

1 pound (454 g) ground Italian pork sausage
1 pound (454 g) ground beef, preferably grass-fed
½ small yellow onion, minced
¼ cup almond flour
1 large egg, beaten
3 teaspoons Worcestershire sauce, divided
2 teaspoons salt, divided
1 teaspoon ground allspice
½ teaspoon ground nutmeg
½ teaspoon ground ginger
½ teaspoon freshly ground black pepper, divided
1½ cups beef stock or broth
1 cup heavy cream
1 tablespoon Dijon mustard
4 ounces (113 g) cream cheese, room temperature
1 cup sour cream, room temperature

1. In a large bowl, combine the pork, beef, onion, almond flour, egg, 1 teaspoon of Worcestershire, 1 teaspoon of salt, the allspice, nutmeg, ginger, and ¼ teaspoon of pepper and mix well with a fork. 2. Form the meat mixture into small 1-inch meatballs, and place on a baking sheet or cutting board. 3. In the bowl of a 5- or 6-quart slow cooker, whisk together the stock, heavy cream, mustard, remaining 2 teaspoons of Worcestershire sauce, remaining 1 teaspoon of salt, and remaining ¼ teaspoon of pepper until smooth and creamy. Place the meatballs in the sauce, trying to not overcrowd. Set the slow cooker to low and cook for 4 hours. 4. After 4 hours of cooking, whisk together the cream cheese and sour cream and add to the warm mixture, gently stirring to incorporate well. 5. Serve the meatballs in their sauce with toothpicks, or over spiralized zucchini

for a complete meal. Leftover meatballs and sauce can be frozen for up to 3 months.

Per Serving
Calories: 544 | fat: 49g | protein: 23g | carbs: 5g | net carbs: 4g | fiber: 1g

Lemon Pork Chops with Buttered Brussels Sprouts

Prep time: 10 minutes | Cook time: 22 minutes | Serves 6

3 tablespoons lemon juice
3 cloves garlic, pureed
1 tablespoon olive oil
6 pork loin chops
1 tablespoon butter
1 pound (454 g) brussels sprouts, trimmed and halved
2 tablespoons white wine
Salt and black pepper to taste

1. Preheat broiler to 400°F and mix the lemon juice, garlic, salt, black pepper, and oil in a bowl. 2. Brush the pork with the mixture, place in a baking sheet, and cook for 6 minutes on each side until browned. Share into 6 plates and make the side dish. 3. Melt butter in a small wok or pan and cook in brussels sprouts for 5 minutes until tender. Drizzle with white wine, sprinkle with salt and black pepper and cook for another 5 minutes. Ladle brussels sprouts to the side of the chops and serve with a hot sauce.

Per Serving
Calories: 300 | fat: 11g | protein: 42g | carbs: 7g | net carbs: 4g | fiber: 3g

Zucchini Rolls

Prep time: 10 minutes | Cook time: 0 minutes | Serves 4

Rolls:
1 medium zucchini (about 7 ounces/198 g)
1 cup cooked beef strips
5 medium radishes, sliced thin

Dipping Sauce:
¼ cup extra-virgin olive oil or refined avocado oil
2 tablespoons hot sauce
2 teaspoons fresh lime juice

1. Place the zucchini on a cutting board and, using a vegetable peeler, peel long strips from the zucchini until it is next to impossible to create a full, long strip. 2. Place a zucchini strip on a cutting board, with a short end facing you. Place a couple of pieces of beef and 3 or 4 radish slices at the short end closest to you. Roll it up, then stab with a toothpick to secure. Repeat with the remaining zucchini strips, placing the completed rolls on a serving plate. 3. In a small serving dish, whisk together the dipping sauce ingredients. Serve the dipping sauce alongside the rolls.

Per Serving
Calories: 370 | fat: 33g | protein: 14g | carbs: 4g | net carbs: 3g | fiber: 1g

Beef and Cauliflower Burgers

Prep time: 15 minutes | Cook time: 15 minutes | Serves 2

½ cup shredded cauliflower
5 ounces (142 g) ground beef
1 teaspoon garlic salt
¼ teaspoon ground cumin
1 tablespoon scallions, diced
1 egg, beaten
1 tablespoon coconut oil
¼ cup hot water

1. In the mixing bowl, mix up shredded cauliflower, ground beef, garlic salt, ground cumin, and diced scallions. 2. When the meat mixture is homogenous, add egg and stir it well. 3. Make the burgers from the cauliflower and meat mixture. 4. After this, heat up the coconut oil on Sauté mode. 5. Place the burgers in the hot oil in one layer and cook them for 5 minutes from each side. 6. Then add water and close the lid. Cook the meal on Sauté mode for 5 minutes more.
Per Serving
Calories: 235 | fat: 13g | protein: 25g | carbs: 3g | net carbs: 2g | fiber: 1g

Chili-Stuffed Avocados

Prep time: 10 minutes | Cook time: 30 minutes | Serves 8

2 tablespoons tallow or bacon grease
1 pound (455 g) ground beef (20% to 30% fat)
1 (14½ ounces/408 g) can whole tomatoes with juices
1½ tablespoons chili powder
2 small cloves garlic, minced
2 teaspoons paprika
¾ teaspoon finely ground gray sea salt
¼ teaspoon ground cinnamon
2 tablespoons finely chopped fresh parsley
4 large Hass avocados, sliced in half, pits removed (leave skin on), for serving

1. Place the tallow into a large saucepan. Melt on medium heat before adding the ground beef. Cook until beef is no longer pink, 7 to 8 minutes, stirring often to break the meat up into small clumps. 2. Add the tomatoes, chili powder, garlic, paprika, salt, and cinnamon. Cover and bring to a boil on high heat. Once boiling, reduce the heat to medium-low and simmer for 20 to 25 minutes, with the cover slightly askew to let steam out. 3. Once thickened, remove from the heat and stir in the chopped parsley. 4. Place an avocado half on a small serving plate or on a platter if you plan to serve them family style. Scoop ⅓ scant cup (180g) of chili into the hollow of
Per Serving
Calories: 385 | fat: 31g | protein: 17g | carbs: 10g | net carbs: 3g | fiber: 7g

Classic Italian Bolognese Sauce

Prep time: 10 minutes | Cook time: 22 minutes | Serves 5

1 pound (454 g) ground beef
2 garlic cloves
1 onion, chopped
1 teaspoon oregano
1 teaspoon sage
1 teaspoon rosemary
7 ounces (198 g) canned chopped tomatoes
1 tablespoon olive oil

1. Heat olive oil in a saucepan. Add onion and garlic and cook for 3 minutes. Add beef and cook until browned, about 4-5 minutes. Stir in the herbs and tomatoes. Cook for 15 minutes. Serve with zoodles.
Per Serving
Calories: 216 | fat: 14g | protein: 18g | carbs: 4g | net carbs: 3g | fiber: 1g

Pan-Seared Steak with Mushroom Sauce

Prep time: 10 minutes | Cook time: 20 minutes | Serves 4

4 top sirloin steaks (6 ounces/170 g each), at room temperature
½ teaspoon sea salt, or more to taste
¼ teaspoon black pepper, or more to taste
4 tablespoons (½ stick) butter, divided into 2 tablespoons and 2
tablespoons
2 cloves garlic, minced
8 ounces (227 g) baby portobello mushrooms, thinly sliced
¼ cup beef broth
1 teaspoon fresh thyme, chopped
¼ cup heavy cream

1. Season the steaks on both sides with the sea salt and black pepper. Let rest at room temperature for 30 minutes. 2. Heat a large sauté pan over medium-high heat. Add 2 tablespoons of the butter and melt. 3. Place the steaks in the pan in a single layer. Cook based on desired level of doneness on each side. **Rare:** 2 to 4 minutes per side. **Medium-rare:** 3 to 5 minutes per side. **Medium:** 4 to 6 minutes per side. **Medium-well:** 5 to 7 minutes per side. **Well-done:** 7 to 9 minutes per side. 4. When the steaks are ready, transfer to a plate, and cover with foil. 5. Return the sauté pan to medium heat. Melt the remaining 2 tablespoons butter. Add the garlic and sauté for about 1 minute, until fragrant. 6. Add the mushrooms, beef broth, and thyme. Scrape any browned bits from the bottom of the pan. Adjust the heat to bring to a simmer, cover, and stir occasionally, for 5-8 minutes. 7. Reduce the heat to medium, add the cream, and simmer for 1 to 3 minutes, until the sauce thickens. Adjust salt and pepper to taste, if needed. 8. Spoon the mushroom sauce over the steaks to serve.
Per Serving
Calories: 420 | fat: 27g | protein: 39g | carbs: 3g | net carbs: 3g | fiber: 0g

Beef Cotija Cheeseburger

Prep time: 10 minutes | Cook time: 14 minutes | Serves 4

1 pound (454 g) ground beef	Salt and black pepper to taste
1 teaspoon dried parsley	1 cup cotija cheese, shredded
½ teaspoon Worcestershire sauce	4 low carb buns, halved

1. Preheat a grill to 400°F and grease the grate with cooking spray. 2. Mix the beef, parsley, Worcestershire sauce, salt, and black pepper with your hands until evenly combined. Make medium sized patties out of the mixture, about 4 patties. Cook on the grill for 7 minutes one side to be cooked through and no longer pink. 3. Flip the patties and top with cheese. Cook for 7 minutes, until the cheese melts. Remove the patties and sandwich into two halves of a bun each. Serve with a tomato dipping sauce and zucchini fries.

Per Serving

Calories: 324 | fat: 23g | protein: 29g | carbs: 2g | net carbs: 2g | fiber: 0g

Crispy Baked Pork Chops with Mushroom Gravy

Prep time: 10 minutes | Cook time: 25 minutes | Serves 4

4 tablespoons extra-virgin olive oil, divided	4 (4 ounces/113 g) boneless pork chops
½ cup almond flour	1 tablespoon unsalted butter
2 teaspoons dried sage, divided	4 ounces (113 g) chopped mushrooms
1½ teaspoons salt, divided	2 cloves garlic, minced
½ teaspoon freshly ground black pepper, divided	1 teaspoon dried thyme
1 large egg	8 ounces (227 g) cream cheese, room temperature
¼ cup flax meal	½ cup heavy cream
¼ cup walnuts, very finely chopped	¼ cup chicken stock

1. Preheat the oven to 400°F (205°C). Line a baking sheet with aluminum foil and coat with 1 tablespoon of olive oil. 2. Combine the almond flour, 1 teaspoon of sage, ½ teaspoon of salt, and ¼ teaspoon of pepper in a first bowl. In a second bowl, whisk the egg. In a third bowl, stir together the flax meal and walnuts. 3. One at a time, dredge each pork chop first in the flour mixture, then in the egg, then in the flax-and-walnut mixture to fully coat all sides. Place on the prepared baking sheet and drizzle the pork chops evenly with 1 tablespoon of olive oil. 4. Bake until cooked through and golden brown, 18 to 25 minutes. 5. Prepare the gravy. Heat the remaining 2 tablespoons of olive oil and the butter in a medium saucepan over medium heat. Add the mushrooms and sauté until very tender, 4 to

6 minutes. Add the garlic, remaining 1 teaspoon of sage and 1 teaspoon of salt, thyme, and remaining ¼ teaspoon of pepper, and sauté for an additional 30 seconds. 6. Add the cream cheese to the mushrooms, reduce heat to low, and stir until melted, 2 to 3 minutes. Whisk in the cream and stock until smooth. Cook over low heat, whisking frequently, until the mixture is thick and creamy, another 3 to 4 minutes. 7. Serve each pork chop covered with a quarter of the mushroom gravy.

Per Serving

Calories: 799 | fat: 69g | protein: 36g | carbs: 11g | net carbs: 7g | fiber: 4g

Oregano Pork Chops with Spicy Tomato Sauce

Prep time: 10 minutes | Cook time: 45 minutes | Serves 4

4 pork chops	diced tomatoes
1 tablespoon fresh oregano, chopped	1 tablespoon tomato paste
2 garlic cloves, minced	Salt and black pepper, to taste
1 tablespoon canola oil	¼ cup tomato juice
15 ounces (425 g) canned	1 red chili, finely chopped

1. Set a pan over medium heat and warm oil, place in the pork, season with pepper and salt, cook for 6 minutes on both sides; remove to a bowl. Add in the garlic, and cook for 30 seconds. Stir in the tomato paste, tomatoes, tomato juice, and chili; bring to a boil, and reduce heat to medium-low. 2. Place in the pork chops, cover the pan and simmer everything for 30 minutes. Remove the pork to plates and sprinkle with fresh oregano to serve.

Per Serving

Calories: 382 | fat: 10g | protein: 40g | carbs: 5g | net carbs: 3g | fiber: 2g

Bacon Stew with Cauliflower

Prep time: 10 minutes | Cook time: 35 minutes | Serves 6

4 ounces (113 g) mozzarella cheese, grated	4 garlic cloves, minced
2 cups chicken broth	¼ cup heavy cream
½ teaspoon garlic powder	3 cups bacon, chopped
½ teaspoon onion powder	1 head cauliflower, cut into florets
Salt and black pepper, to taste	

1. In a pot, combine the bacon with broth, cauliflower, salt, heavy cream, black pepper, garlic powder, cheese, onion powder, and garlic, and cook for 35 minutes. Share into serving plates, and enjoy.

Per Serving

Per serving: Kcal 380, Fat 25g, Net Carbs 6g, Protein 33g

Beef Sausage Meat Loaf

Prep time: 10 minutes | Cook time: 1 hour 15 minutes | Serves 6

1½ pounds (680 g) Italian sausage meat
1 pound (454 g) grass-fed ground beef
½ cup almond flour
¼ cup heavy (whipping) cream
1 egg, lightly beaten

½ onion, finely chopped
½ red bell pepper, chopped
2 teaspoons minced garlic
1 teaspoon dried oregano
¼ teaspoon sea salt
⅛ teaspoon freshly ground black pepper

1. Preheat the oven. Set the oven temperature to 400°F.
2. Make the meat loaf. In a large bowl, mix together the sausage, ground beef, almond flour, cream, egg, onion, red bell pepper, garlic, oregano, salt, and pepper until everything is well combined. Press the mixture into a 9-inch loaf pan. 3. Bake. Bake for 1 hour to 1 hour and 15 minutes, or until the meat loaf is cooked through. Drain off and throw out any grease and let the meat loaf stand for 10 minutes. 4. Serve. Cut the meat loaf into six slices, divide them between six plates, and serve it immediately.

Per Serving

Calories: 394 | fat: 34g | protein: 19g | carbs: 1g | net carbs: 1g | fiber: 0g

Reverse Sear Garlic Rosemary Rib-Eye Steaks

Prep time: 5 minutes | Cook time: 27 minutes | serves 2

2 (6 ounces/170 g) bone-in rib-eye steaks (1½ inches thick)
Salt and ground black pepper

2 tablespoons salted butter
2 fresh rosemary sprigs
2 cloves garlic, minced

1. Take the steaks out of the refrigerator. Generously salt and pepper both sides of the steaks. Allow to sit at room temperature for 30 minutes. 2. Preheat the oven to 275°F. Line a sheet pan with foil and place a wire cooling rack on top. 3. Place the steaks on the rack on top of the foil-lined pan. Bake for 25 minutes or until the internal temperature of the meat reaches 125°F. Remove from the oven and let rest for 15 minutes. 4. Preheat a cast-iron skillet over medium-high heat. Put the butter in the hot pan; it will melt quickly. Place the steaks in the skillet and hard sear the first side for 1 minute (see Note), then flip the steaks. Add the rosemary and garlic to the pan and swirl it around. Hard sear the steaks for 1 more minute, tilting the pan to spoon the melted butter and herbs over them. Serve immediately.

Per Serving

Calories: 559 | fat: 46g | protein: 33g | carbs: 4g | net carbs: 2g | fiber: 2g

Sweet Chipotle Grilled Ribs

Prep time: 5 minutes | Cook time: 50 minutes | Serves 4

2 tablespoons erythritol
Pink salt and black pepper to taste
1 tablespoon olive oil
3 teaspoons chipotle powder
1 teaspoon garlic powder

1 pound (454 g) beef spare ribs
4 tablespoons sugar-free BBQ sauce + extra for serving

1. Mix the erythritol, salt, pepper, oil, chipotle, and garlic powder. Brush on the meaty sides of the ribs and wrap in foil. Sit for 30 minutes to marinate. 2. Preheat oven to 400ºF, place wrapped ribs on a baking sheet, and cook for 40 minutes to be cooked through. Remove ribs and aluminium foil, brush with BBQ sauce, and brown under the broiler for 10 minutes on both sides. Slice and serve with extra BBQ sauce and lettuce tomato salad.

Per Serving

Calories: 449 | fat: 37g | protein: 18g | carbs: 10g | net carbs: 9g | fiber: 1g

Pork Burgers with Sriracha Mayo

Prep time: 10 minutes | Cook time: 10 minutes | Serves 2

12 ounces (340 g) ground pork
2 scallions, white and green parts, thinly sliced
1 tablespoon toasted sesame oil

Pink Himalayan salt
Freshly ground black pepper
1 tablespoon ghee
1 tablespoon Sriracha sauce
2 tablespoons mayonnaise

1. In a large bowl, mix to combine the ground pork with the scallions and sesame oil, and season with pink Himalayan salt and pepper. Form the pork mixture into 2 patties. Create an imprint with your thumb in the middle of each burger so the pork will heat evenly. 2. In a large skillet over medium-high heat, heat the ghee. When the ghee has melted and is very hot, add the burger patties and cook for 4 minutes on each side. 3. Meanwhile, in a small bowl, mix the Sriracha sauce and mayonnaise. 4. Transfer the burgers to a plate and let rest for at least 5 minutes. 5. Top the burgers with the Sriracha mayonnaise and serve.

Per Serving

Calories: 575 | fat: 49g | protein: 31g | carbs: 2g | net carbs: 1g | fiber: 1g

Pepperoni Pizza Casserole

Prep time: 10 minutes | Cook time: 30 minutes | Serves 4

1 tablespoon olive oil
¼ white onion, diced
1 pound (454 g) pepperoni, roughly chopped
2 teaspoons dried oregano
1 teaspoon red pepper flakes
2 eggs
½ cup heavy (whipping) cream
2 tablespoons tomato paste
1 cup shredded Mozzarella cheese, divided
Salt, to taste
Freshly ground black pepper, to taste

1. Preheat the oven to 350ºF (180ºC). 2. In a large skillet over medium heat, heat the olive oil. 3. Add the onion and sauté for 5 to 7 minutes until softened and translucent. 4. Stir in the pepperoni, oregano, and red pepper flakes and remove from the heat. 5. In a medium bowl, whisk the eggs, cream, tomato paste, and ½ cup of Mozzarella. Season with salt and pepper and whisk again. 6. Spread the pepperoni and onions in a 7-by-11-inch baking dish. Pour the egg mixture over it. Gently shake the dish and tap it on the counter to ensure the mixture makes it through to the bottom and sides of the dish. Top with the remaining ½ cup of Mozzarella. Bake for 25 minutes. Refrigerate leftovers in an airtight container for up to 1 week.

Per Serving
Calories: 772 | fat: 68g | protein: 36g | carbs: 4g | net carbs: 3g | fiber: 1g

Shoulder Chops with Lemon-Thyme Gravy

Prep time: 30 minutes | Cook time: 40 minutes | Serves 6

¼ cup refined avocado oil or melted coconut oil, for frying
2½ pounds (1.2 kg) bone-in pork shoulder blade chops (aka shoulder chops, blade steaks, or pork shoulder steaks), about ½ inch (1.25 cm) thick
1½ teaspoons finely ground gray sea salt, divided
1 teaspoon ground black pepper
⅓ cup white wine, such as Pinot Grigio, Sauvignon Blanc, or unoaked Chardonnay
2 tablespoons unflavored gelatin
Grated zest of 1 lemon
Juice of 1 lemon
1 teaspoon dried thyme leaves
⅔ cup full-fat coconut milk

1. Place the oil in a large frying pan over high heat. While the oil is heating, sprinkle 1 teaspoon of the salt and the pepper on both sides of the chops. Place the chops in the hot oil and sear for 4 minutes per side. Transfer the seared chops to a clean plate. 2. Remove the pan from the heat. Leaving the fat in the pan, add the wine, gelatin, lemon zest, lemon juice, thyme, and remaining ½ teaspoon of salt. Whisk to combine. 3. Return the chops to the frying pan. Cover and cook over medium-low heat for 30 minutes, flipping them halfway through cooking. 4. Place an oven rack in the top position and turn on the broiler to low, if that is an option (if not, simply "broil" is fine). Place the chops in an oven-safe pan (I like to use cast iron) and set the pan on the top rack of the oven. Broil the chops for 3 minutes per side, or until just browned. Allow to rest for 5 minutes. 5. Meanwhile, add the coconut milk to the liquid in the frying pan. Cook over medium heat for 15 minutes, whisking occasionally, until slightly thickened. 6. If serving individually instead of family style, remove the bones from each chop and divide the steaks into 6 servings. Serve the chops drizzled with the gravy.

Per Serving
Calories: 511 | fat: 40g | protein: 33g | carbs: 2g | net carbs: 2g | fiber: 0g

Chorizo Sausage and Mushroom Casserole

Prep time: 10 minutes | Cook time: 10 minutes | Serves 4

¼ cup Paleo fat, such as coconut oil or lard
1 pound (454 g) Mexican-style fresh (raw) chorizo, removed from casings
1 pound (454 g) baby portobello or button mushrooms, quartered
¼ cup diced onions
1½ teaspoons fine sea salt
½ teaspoon freshly ground black pepper
Sausage Vinaigrette:
1 clove garlic
2 ounces (57 g) dry-cured Spanish-style chorizo, casing removed, chopped
½ cup coconut vinegar
2 teaspoons smoked paprika
1 teaspoon lemon juice
¼ teaspoon ground coriander
¼ cup MCT oil or extra-virgin olive oil
2 tablespoons beef bone broth, homemade or store-bought
1 teaspoon fine sea salt
Chopped fresh flat-leaf parsley or cilantro, for garnish (optional)

1. Heat the Paleo fat in a large skillet over medium heat. Add the fresh chorizo, mushrooms, and onions and sauté, breaking up the chorizo with a spoon as it cooks, until the sausage is cooked through and the mushrooms are tender and browned, about 10 minutes. Season with the salt and pepper. 2. Meanwhile, **make the vinaigrette:** In a blender, purée the garlic, cured chorizo, coconut vinegar, paprika, lemon juice, and coriander until smooth. With the blender running, drizzle in the oil and broth until well combined. Season the vinaigrette with the salt. 3. Pour the vinaigrette into the skillet with the chorizo mixture and toss to coat. Divide among four plates and garnish with parsley, if desired. 4. Store extras in an airtight container in the fridge for up to 4 days. To reheat, place in a skillet over medium heat until warmed.

Per Serving
Calories: 596 | fat: 56g | protein: 17g | carbs: 7g | net carbs: 6g | fiber: 1g

Italian Beef Ragout

Prep time: 15 minutes | Cook time: 1 hour 50 minutes | Serves 4

1 pound (454 g) chuck steak, trimmed and cubed
2 tablespoons olive oil
Salt and black pepper to taste
2 tablespoons almond flour
1 medium onion, diced
½ cup dry white wine
1 red bell pepper, seeded and diced
2 teaspoons Worcestershire sauce
4 ounces (113 g) tomato puree
3 teaspoons smoked paprika
1 cup beef broth
Thyme leaves to garnish

1. First, lightly dredge the meat in the almond flour and set aside. Place a large skillet over medium heat, add 1 tablespoon of oil to heat and then sauté the onion, and bell pepper for 3 minutes. Stir in the paprika, and add the remaining olive oil. 2. Add the beef and cook for 10 minutes in total while turning them halfway. Stir in white wine, let it reduce by half, about 3 minutes, and add Worcestershire sauce, tomato puree, and beef broth. 3. Let the mixture boil for 2 minutes, then reduce the heat to lowest and let simmer for 1½ hours; stirring now and then. Adjust the taste and dish the ragout. Serve garnished with thyme leaves.
Per Serving
Calories: 426 | fat: 26g | protein: 41g | carbs: 7g | net carbs: 4g | fiber: 3g

Cheeseburger "Mac" Helper

Prep time: 5 minutes | Cook time: 20 or 40 minutes | serves 4

1 pound (454 g) ground beef
½ cup chopped onions, or
2 tablespoons dried minced onions
2 teaspoons paprika
1 teaspoon chili powder
1 teaspoon garlic powder
1 teaspoon dried parsley
½ teaspoon salt
½ teaspoon ground black pepper
1 (8 ounces/227 g) can tomato sauce
1 (12 ounces/340 g) bag frozen cauliflower florets
2 cups shredded cheddar cheese
Fresh flat-leaf parsley, for garnish (optional)

1. In a large skillet over medium heat, cook the ground beef with the onions, crumbling the meat with a large spoon as it cooks, until the meat is browned and the onions are translucent, about 10 minutes. Drain the fat, if necessary. 2. Stir in the paprika, chili powder, garlic powder, parsley, salt, pepper, and tomato sauce and simmer for 5 minutes. 3. Stir in the cauliflower, cover, and continue cooking, stirring occasionally, until the cauliflower is tender. 4. Stir in the cheese and serve immediately, or reduce the heat to low and simmer for an additional 20 minutes for more depth of flavor, then stir in the cheese. Garnish with parsley, if desired. Leftovers can be stored in an airtight container in the refrigerator for up to 5 days.
Per Serving
Calories: 381 | fat: 28g | protein: 24g | carbs: 9g | net carbs: 6g | fiber: 3g

Broccoli & Ground Beef Casserole

Prep time: 10 minutes | Cook time: 4 hours | Serves 6

1 tablespoon olive oil
2 pounds (907 g) ground beef
1 head broccoli, cut into florets
Salt and black pepper, to taste
2 teaspoons mustard
2 teaspoons Worcestershire sauce
28 ounces (784 g) canned diced tomatoes
2 cups mozzarella cheese, grated
16 ounces (454 g) tomato sauce
2 tablespoons fresh parsley, chopped
1 teaspoon dried oregano

1. Apply black pepper and salt to the broccoli florets, set them into a bowl, drizzle over the olive oil, and toss well to coat completely. In a separate bowl, combine the beef with Worcestershire sauce, salt, mustard, and black pepper, and stir well. Press on the slow cooker's bottom. 2. Scatter in the broccoli, add the tomatoes, parsley, mozzarella, oregano, and tomato sauce. 3. Cook for 4 hours on low; covered. Split the casserole among bowls and enjoy while hot.
Per Serving
Calories: 440 | fat: 24g | protein: 48g | carbs: 8g | net carbs: 5g | fiber: 3g

Barbacoa Beef Roast

Prep time: 10 minutes | Cook time: 8 hours | Serves 2

1 pound (454 g) beef chuck roast
Pink Himalayan salt
Freshly ground black pepper
4 chipotle peppers in adobo sauce (I use La Costeña
12-ounce can)
1 (6 ounces/170 g) can green jalapeño chiles
2 tablespoons apple cider vinegar
½ cup beef broth

1. With the crock insert in place, preheat the slow cooker to low. 2. Season the beef chuck roast on both sides with pink Himalayan salt and pepper. Put the roast in the slow cooker. 3. In a food processor (or blender), combine the chipotle peppers and their adobo sauce, jalapeños, and apple cider vinegar, and pulse until smooth. Add the beef broth, and pulse a few more times. Pour the chile mixture over the top of the roast. 4. Cover and cook on low for 8 hours. 5. Transfer the beef to a cutting board, and use two forks to shred the meat. 6. Serve hot.
Per Serving
Calories: 723 | fat: 46g | protein: 66g | carbs: 7g | net carbs: 2g | fiber: 5g

White Wine Lamb Chops

Prep time: 10 minutes | Cook time: 1 hour 10 minutes | Serves 6

6 lamb chops
1 tablespoon sage
1 teaspoon thyme
1 onion, sliced
3 garlic cloves, minced
2 tablespoons olive oil
½ cup white wine
Salt and black pepper, to taste

1. Heat the olive oil in a pan. Add onion and garlic and cook for 3 minutes, until soft. Rub the sage and thyme over the lamb chops. Cook the lamb for about 3 minutes per side. Set aside. 2. Pour the white wine and 1 cup of water into the pan, bring the mixture to a boil. Cook until the liquid is reduced by half. Add the chops in the pan, reduce the heat, and let simmer for 1 hour.
Per Serving
Calories: 388 | fat: 35g | protein: 18g | carbs: 1g | net carbs: 1g | fiber: 0g

Beef Back Ribs with Barbecue Glaze

Prep time: 10 minutes | Cook time: 35 minutes | Serves 4

½ cup water
1 (3 pounds/1.4 kg) rack beef back ribs, prepared with rub of choice
¼ cup unsweetened tomato purée
¼ teaspoon Worcestershire sauce
¼ teaspoon garlic powder
2 teaspoons apple cider vinegar
¼ teaspoon liquid smoke
¼ teaspoon smoked paprika
3 tablespoons Swerve
Dash of cayenne pepper

1. Pour the water in the pot and place the trivet inside. 2. Arrange the ribs on top of the trivet. 3. Close the lid. Select Manual mode and set cooking time for 25 minutes on High Pressure. 4. Meanwhile, prepare the glaze by whisking together the tomato purée, Worcestershire sauce, garlic powder, vinegar, liquid smoke, paprika, Swerve, and cayenne in a medium bowl. Heat the broiler. 5. When timer beeps, quick release the pressure. Open the lid. Remove the ribs and place on a baking sheet. 6. Brush a layer of glaze on the ribs. Put under the broiler for 5 minutes. 7. Remove from the broiler and brush with glaze again. Put back under the broiler for 5 more minutes, or until the tops are sticky. 8. Serve immediately.
Per Serving
Calories: 758 | fat: 26.8g | protein: 33.7g | carbs: 0.9g | net carbs: 0.7g | fiber: 0.2g

Sirloin with Blue Cheese Compound Butter

Prep time: 10 minutes | Cook time: 12 minutes | Serves 4

6 tablespoons butter, at room temperature
4 ounces (113 g) blue cheese, such as Stilton or Roquefort
4 (5 ounces/142 g) beef sirloin steaks
1 tablespoon olive oil
Sea salt
Freshly ground black pepper

1. Place the butter in a blender and pulse until the butter is whipped, about 2 minutes. 2. Add the cheese and pulse until just incorporated. 3. Spoon the butter mixture onto a sheet of plastic wrap and roll it into a log about 1½ inches in diameter by twisting both ends of the plastic wrap in opposite directions. 4. Refrigerate the butter until completely set, about 1 hour. 5. Slice the butter into ½-inch disks and set them on a plate in the refrigerator until you are ready to serve the steaks. Store leftover butter in the refrigerator for up to 1 week. 6. Preheat a barbecue to medium-high heat. 7. Let the steaks come to room temperature. 8. Rub the steaks all over with the olive oil and season them with salt and pepper. 9. Grill the steaks until they reach your desired doneness, about 6 minutes per side for medium. 10. If you do not have a barbecue, broil the steaks in a preheated oven for 7 minutes per side for medium. 11. Let the steaks rest for 10 minutes. Serve each topped with a disk of the compound butter.
Per Serving
Calories: 544 | fat: 44g | protein: 35g | carbs: 0g | net carbs: 0g | fiber: 0g

Homemade Classic Beef Burgers

Prep time: 10 minutes | Cook time: 6 minutes | Serves 4

1 pound (454 g) ground beef
½ teaspoon onion powder
½ teaspoon garlic powder
2 tablespoons ghee
1 teaspoon Dijon mustard
4 low carb buns, halved
¼ cup mayonnaise
1 teaspoon sriracha sauce
4 tablespoons cabbage slaw
Salt and black pepper to taste

1. Mix together the beef, onion powder, garlic powder, mustard, salt, and black pepper; create 4 burgers. Melt the ghee in a skillet and cook the burgers for about 3 minutes per side. 2. Serve in buns topped with mayo, sriracha, and cabbage slaw.
Per Serving
Calories: 679 | fat: 55g | protein: 39g | carbs: 7g | net carbs: 6g | fiber: 1g

Italian Sausage Soup

Prep time: 5 minutes | Cook time: 25 minutes | Serves 4

1 tablespoon olive oil
½ onion, diced
3 garlic cloves, minced
8 ounces (227 g) hot Italian sausage, removed from their casings
2 cups chicken broth
1 (14½ ounces/411 g) can diced tomatoes
1 to 2 teaspoons red pepper flakes
1 teaspoon dried oregano
1 teaspoon dried basil
Salt, to taste
Freshly ground black pepper, to taste
¼ cup freshly grated Parmesan cheese, divided
2 cups chopped fresh spinach

1. In a large saucepan over medium heat, heat the olive oil. 2. Add the onion and garlic. Sauté for 5 to 7 minutes until the onion is softened and translucent. 3. Add the sausage to the pan. Cook for about 5 minutes as you crumble it, allowing the meat to brown. 4. Stir in the chicken broth and tomatoes. Bring to a boil and reduce the heat to low. 5. Add the red pepper flakes, oregano, and basil. Season with salt and pepper, and stir in 2 tablespoons of Parmesan. Simmer for 10 minutes and remove from the heat. 6. Stir in the spinach until wilted. Serve sprinkled with the remaining 2 tablespoons of Parmesan.
Per Serving
Calories: 365 | fat: 20g | protein: 33g | carbs: 11g | net carbs: 9g | fiber: 2g

Rib Eye with Chimichurri Sauce

Prep time: 15 minutes | Cook time: 15 minutes | Serves 4

For the Chimichurri:
½ cup good-quality olive oil
½ cup finely chopped fresh parsley
2 tablespoons red wine vinegar
2 tablespoons finely chopped fresh cilantro
1½ tablespoons minced garlic
1 tablespoon finely chopped chile pepper
½ teaspoon sea salt
¼ teaspoon freshly ground black pepper
For the Steak:
4 (5 ounces/142 g) rib eye steaks
1 tablespoon good-quality olive oil
Sea salt, for seasoning
Freshly ground black pepper, for seasoning

To Make the Chimichurri: Make the chimichurri. In a medium bowl, stir together the olive oil, parsley, vinegar, cilantro, garlic, chile, salt, and pepper. Let it stand for 15 minutes to mellow the flavors. **To Make the Steak:** 1. Prepare the steaks. Let the steaks come to room temperature and lightly oil them with the olive oil and season them with salt and pepper. 2. Grill the steaks. Preheat the grill to high heat. Grill the steaks for 6 to 7 minutes per side for medium (140°F internal temperature) or until they're done the way you like them. 3. Rest and serve. Let the steaks rest for 10 minutes and then serve them topped with generous spoonfuls of the chimichurri sauce.
Per Serving
Calories: 503 | fat: 42g | protein: 29g | carbs: 1g | net carbs: 1g | fiber: 0g

Spicy Spinach Pinwheel Steaks

Prep time: 5 minutes | Cook time: 30 minutes | Serves 6

1½ pounds (680 g) beef flank steak
Salt and black pepper to taste
1 cup crumbled feta cheese
½ loose cup baby spinach
1 jalapeño pepper, chopped
¼ cup chopped basil leaves

1. Preheat oven to 400ºF and grease a baking sheet with cooking spray. 2. Wrap the steak in plastic wrap, place on a flat surface, and gently run a rolling pin over to flatten. Take off the wraps. Sprinkle with half of the feta cheese, top with spinach, jalapeno, basil leaves, and the remaining cheese. Roll the steak over on the stuffing and secure with toothpicks. 3. Place in the baking sheet and cook for 30 minutes, flipping once until nicely browned on the outside and the cheese melted within. Cool for 3 minutes, slice into pinwheels and serve with sautéed veggies.
Per Serving
Calories: 228 | fat: 11g | protein: 28g | carbs: 3g | net carbs: 2g | fiber: 1g

Crispy Pork Lettuce Wraps

Prep time: 10 minutes | Cook time: 10 minutes | Serves 4

2 tablespoons olive oil
2 garlic cloves, minced
¼ cup sesame oil, divided
1 pound (454 g) pork, sliced thinly
2 to 3 tablespoons gluten-free soy sauce
1 teaspoon chili garlic sauce
2 to 3 tablespoons rice wine vinegar
1 large carrot, julienned
½ large cucumber, julienned
2 tablespoons chopped fresh cilantro
1 small head butter lettuce, or romaine lettuce

1. In a large skillet over medium heat, heat the olive oil. 2. Add the garlic and sauté for 1 to 2 minutes until fragrant. 3. Add 2 tablespoons of sesame oil and the pork. Cook for 5 to 6 minutes or until the pork is cooked through and starts to get crispy. Remove from the heat. 4. In a small bowl, whisk the remaining 2 tablespoons of sesame oil, the soy sauce, chili garlic sauce, and vinegar. 5. Add the carrot and cucumber to the dressing and toss to combine. 6. **Assemble the lettuce wraps:** Layer pork and veggies in lettuce cups and serve with a sprinkle of fresh cilantro.
Per Serving
Calories: 340 | fat: 24g | protein: 23g | carbs: 8g | net carbs: 7g | fiber: 1g

Saucy Beef Fingers

Prep time: 30 minutes | Cook time: 14 minutes | Serves 4

1½ pounds (680 g) sirloin
steak
¼ cup red wine
¼ cup fresh lime juice
1 teaspoon garlic powder
1 teaspoon shallot powder
1 teaspoon celery seeds

1 teaspoon mustard seeds
Coarse sea salt and ground
black pepper, to taste
1 teaspoon red pepper flakes
2 eggs, lightly whisked
1 cup Parmesan cheese
1 teaspoon paprika

1. Place the steak, red wine, lime juice, garlic powder, shallot powder, celery seeds, mustard seeds, salt, black pepper, and red pepper in a large ceramic bowl; let it marinate for 3 hours. 2. Tenderize the cube steak by pounding with a mallet; cut into 1-inch strips. 3. In a shallow bowl, whisk the eggs. In another bowl, mix the Parmesan cheese and paprika. 4. Dip the beef pieces into the whisked eggs and coat on all sides. Now, dredge the beef pieces in the Parmesan mixture. 5. Cook at 400ºF (204ºC) for 14 minutes, flipping halfway through the cooking time. 6. Meanwhile, make the sauce by heating the reserved marinade in a saucepan over medium heat; let it simmer until thoroughly warmed. Serve the steak fingers with the sauce on the side. Enjoy!

Per Serving
Calories: 483 | fat: 29g | protein: 49g | carbs: 4g | fiber: 1g | sodium: 141mg

Flaky Beef Empanadas

Prep time: 30 minutes | Cook time: 25 minutes | Serves 6

For the Dough:
1 cup mozzarella cheese,
shredded
5 tablespoons cream cheese
¾ cup almond flour
2 tablespoons coconut milk
1 tablespoon coconut flour
1 egg, lightly beaten
1 teaspoon garlic powder
½ teaspoon sea salt
For the Filling:
¼ cup grass-fed butter

1 pound (454 g) grass-fed
ground beef
1 onion, chopped
1 tablespoon minced garlic
2 tablespoons sugar-free
tomato paste
2 teaspoons ground cumin
2 teaspoons dried oregano
1 teaspoon chili powder
Sea salt, for seasoning
Freshly ground black pepper,
for seasoning

To Make the Dough: 1. In a small saucepan over low heat, melt the mozzarella and cream cheese together, stirring often. Remove the pan from the heat. 2. Transfer the cheese mixture to a medium bowl and stir in the almond flour, coconut milk, coconut flour, egg, garlic powder, and salt until well blended and the mixture holds together in a ball. Cover the bowl with plastic wrap, pressing it down onto the surface of the dough, and place the bowl in the refrigerator for 30 minutes. **To Make the Filling:** 1. In a large skillet over medium-high heat, melt the butter. Add the beef and

cook it until it's browned, about 7 minutes. 2. Add the onion and garlic and sauté until they've softened, about 4 minutes. Stir in the tomato paste, cumin, oregano, and chili powder. Season the filling with salt and pepper and set it aside to cool. **To Make the Empanadas:** 1. Set the oven temperature to 425°F. Line a baking sheet with parchment paper. 2. Spread some parchment paper on your work surface. Press the dough out into a thin layer on the paper, then cut the dough into 12 (3-inch) circles. 3. Spoon the filling equally onto the middle of each dough circle. Fold the dough over and press the edges together using a fork to seal them. 4. Transfer the empanadas to the baking sheet and bake them for 10 to 12 minutes until they're golden brown. 5. Divide the empanadas between six plates and serve them immediately.
Per Serving
Calories: 436 | fat: 38g | protein: 19g | carbs: 4g | net carbs: 3g | fiber: 1g

Kung Pao Beef

Prep time: 15 minutes | Cook time: 20 minutes | Serves 4

Sauce/Marinade:
¼ cup coconut aminos
1½ tablespoons white wine
vinegar
1½ tablespoons sherry wine
1 tablespoon avocado oil
1 teaspoon chili paste
Stir-Fry:
1 pound (454 g) flank steak,
thinly sliced against the
grain and cut into bite-size

pieces
2 tablespoons avocado oil,
divided into 1 tablespoon and
1 tablespoon
2 medium bell peppers (6
ounces/170 g each), red and
green, chopped into bite-size
pieces
2 cloves garlic, minced
¼ cup roasted peanuts

Make the Sauce/Marinade: 1. In a small bowl, whisk together the coconut aminos, white wine vinegar, sherry wine, avocado oil, and chili paste. **Make the Stir-fry:** 1. Place the sliced steak into a medium bowl. Pour half of the sauce/marinade (about ¼ cup) over it and stir to coat. Cover and chill for at least 30 minutes, up to 2 hours. 2. About 10 minutes before marinating time is up or when you are ready to cook, in a large wok or sauté pan, heat 1 tablespoon of the oil over medium-high heat. Add the bell peppers and sauté for 7 to 8 minutes, until soft and browned. 3. Add the garlic and sauté for about 1 minute, until fragrant. 4. Remove the peppers and garlic, and cover to keep warm. 5. Add the remaining 1 tablespoon oil to the pan and heat over very high heat. Add the steak, arrange in a single layer, and cook undisturbed for 2 to 4 minutes per side, until browned on each side. If it's not cooked through yet, you can stir-fry for longer. Remove the meat from the pan and cover to keep warm. 6. Add the reserved marinade to the pan. Bring to a vigorous simmer and continue to simmer for a few minutes, until thickened. 7. Add the cooked meat, cooked peppers, and roasted peanuts to the pan and toss in the sauce.
Per Serving
Calories: 341 | fat: 20g | protein: 27g | carbs: 9g | net carbs: 7g | fiber: 2g

Deconstructed Egg Rolls

Prep time: 10 minutes | Cook time: 15 minutes | Serves 6

1 pound (454 g) ground pork
1 tablespoon untoasted, cold-pressed sesame oil
6 cups finely shredded cabbage
2 teaspoons minced garlic
1 tablespoon minced fresh ginger
1 tablespoon coconut aminos or wheat-free tamari
1 teaspoon fish sauce (optional)
¼ cup chopped green onions, for garnish

1. Place the pork and oil in a large cast-iron skillet over medium-high heat and cook, crumbling the meat with a wooden spoon, until cooked through, about 10 minutes. (Do not drain the drippings from the pan.) 2. Add the cabbage, garlic, ginger, coconut aminos, and fish sauce, if using, to the skillet. Sauté until the cabbage is soft, 3 to 5 minutes. 3. Divide among six plates or bowls and serve garnished with the green onions.

Per Serving
Calories: 250 | fat: 19g | protein: 14g | carbs: 6g | net carbs: 3g | fiber: 3g

Bacon Mac 'n' Cheese

Prep time: 10 minutes | Cook time: 50 minutes | Serves 4

1 large head cauliflower (about 1⅔ pounds/750 g), cored and broken into ½-inch (1.25-cm) pieces
⅓ cup finely chopped fresh parsley
6 strips bacon (about 6 ounces/170 g), cooked until crisp, then crumbled (reserve the grease)
2 cups unsweetened nondairy milk
2 tablespoons unflavored gelatin
1 tablespoon fresh lemon juice
1 teaspoon onion powder
1 teaspoon finely ground gray sea salt
¼ teaspoon garlic powder
⅓ cup nutritional yeast
2 large eggs, beaten
2 teaspoons prepared yellow mustard
2 ounces (57 g) pork dust or ground pork rinds

1. Preheat the oven to 350°F (177°C) and grease a shallow 1½-quart (1.4-L) casserole dish with coconut oil. Set aside. 2. Place the cauliflower, parsley, and bacon in a large bowl and toss to combine. 3. Place the reserved bacon grease, milk, gelatin, lemon juice, onion powder, salt, and garlic powder in a medium-sized saucepan. Bring to a boil over medium heat, whisking occasionally. Once boiling, continue to boil for 5 minutes. 4. Whisk in the nutritional yeast, eggs, and mustard and gently cook for 3 minutes, whisking constantly. 5. Remove the saucepan from the heat and pour the "cheese" sauce over the cauliflower mixture. (If you've overcooked the sauce or didn't whisk it well enough, you may end up with small pieces of cooked egg; for an ultra-smooth sauce, pour the sauce through a fine-mesh strainer.) Toss with a spatula until all the cauliflower pieces are coated in the cheese sauce. 6. Transfer the coated cauliflower to the prepared casserole dish and smooth it out with the back of a spatula. Sprinkle the pork dust evenly over the top. Bake for 40 to 45 minutes, until the cauliflower is fork-tender, checking with a sharp knife on the edge of the casserole. 7. Allow to sit for 15 minutes before serving.

Per Serving
Calories: 440 | fat: 27g | protein: 35g | carbs: 15g | net carbs: 8g | fiber: 7g

Cheesy Southwestern Meat Loaf

Prep time: 30 minutes | Cook time: 1 hour | Serves 8

½ cup avocado or extra-virgin olive oil, divided
2 cups shredded (not spiralized) zucchini, from 2 small or 1 large zucchini
1½ teaspoons salt, divided
1 pound (454 g) ground beef, preferably grass-fed
1 pound (454 g) ground pork chorizo
½ cup chopped cilantro
¼ cup chopped scallions, green and white parts
1 large egg, beaten
1 tablespoon chopped chipotle pepper with adobo sauce
1 teaspoon garlic powder
¼ cup almond flour
2 cups shredded Mexican cheese blend or Cheddar cheese, divided
1 tablespoon tomato paste (no sugar added)

1. Preheat the oven to 375°F (190°C). Coat a loaf pan with 2 tablespoons of avocado oil. 2. Line a colander with a layer of paper towels and add the shredded zucchini. Sprinkle with ½ teaspoon of salt, tossing to coat. Let sit for 10 minutes, then press down with another layer of paper towels to release some of the excess moisture. 3. While the zucchini drains, in a large bowl, combine the ground beef, chorizo, cilantro, scallions, ¼ cup of oil, egg, chipotle with adobo, garlic powder, and remaining 1 teaspoon of salt. Mix well with a fork. 4. Add the almond flour to the drained zucchini and toss to coat. Add the zucchini to the meat mixture and mix until well combined. Add half of the mixture to the prepared pan and spread evenly. Top with 1 cup of shredded cheese, spreading evenly. Top with the remaining half of the mixture and spread evenly. In a small bowl, whisk together the tomato paste and remaining 2 tablespoons of oil and spread evenly on top of the meat mixture. Sprinkle with the remaining 1 cup of cheese. Bake for 50 to 55 minutes, or until cooked through. Let sit for 10 minutes before cutting.

Per Serving
Calories: 623 | fat: 53g | protein: 33g | carbs: 4g | net carbs: 3g | fiber: 1g

Braised Short Ribs with Red Wine

Prep time: 10 minutes | Cook time: 1 hour 30 minutes to 2 hours | Serves 4

1½ pounds (680 g) boneless beef short ribs (if using bone-in, use 3½ pounds)
1 teaspoon salt
½ teaspoon freshly ground black pepper
½ teaspoon garlic powder

¼ cup extra-virgin olive oil
1 cup dry red wine (such as cabernet sauvignon or merlot)
2 to 3 cups beef broth, divided
4 sprigs rosemary

1. Preheat the oven to 350°F(180°C). 2. Season the short ribs with salt, pepper, and garlic powder. Let sit for 10 minutes. 3. In a Dutch oven or oven-safe deep skillet, heat the olive oil over medium-high heat. 4. When the oil is very hot, add the short ribs and brown until dark in color, 2 to 3 minutes per side. Remove the meat from the oil and keep warm. 5. Add the red wine and 2 cups beef broth to the Dutch oven, whisk together, and bring to a boil. Reduce the heat to low and simmer until the liquid is reduced to about 2 cups, about 10 minutes. 6. Return the short ribs to the liquid, which should come about halfway up the meat, adding up to 1 cup of remaining broth if needed. Cover and braise until the meat is very tender, about 1½ to 2 hours. 7. Remove from the oven and let sit, covered, for 10 minutes before serving. Serve warm, drizzled with cooking liquid.
Per Serving
Calories: 525 | fat: 37g | protein: 34g | carbs: 5g | fiber: 1g | sodium: 720mg

Grilled Herbed Pork Kebabs

Prep time: 10 minutes | Cook time: 15 minutes | Serves 4

¼ cup good-quality olive oil
1 tablespoon minced garlic
2 teaspoons dried oregano
1 teaspoon dried basil
1 teaspoon dried parsley
½ teaspoon sea salt

¼ teaspoon freshly ground black pepper
1 (1 pound/454 g) pork tenderloin, cut into 1½-inch pieces

1. Marinate the pork. In a medium bowl, stir together the olive oil, garlic, oregano, basil, parsley, salt, and pepper. Add the pork pieces and toss to coat them in the marinade. Cover the bowl and place it in the refrigerator for 2 to 4 hours. 2. Make the kebabs. Divide the pork pieces between four skewers, making sure to not crowd the meat. 3. Grill the kebabs. Preheat your grill to medium-high heat. Grill the skewers for about 12 minutes, turning to cook all sides of the pork, until the pork is cooked through. 4. Serve. Rest the skewers for 5 minutes. Divide the skewers between four plates and serve them immediately.
Per Serving
Calories: 261 | fat: 18g | protein: 24g | carbs: 1g | net carbs: 1g | fiber: 0g

Crack Slaw

Prep time: 5 minutes | Cook time: 35 minutes | Serves 4

2 tablespoons butter, ghee, or coconut oil
1 pound (454 g) ground pork or sausage
1 small head green cabbage, shredded
2 tablespoons liquid or coconut aminos
1 tablespoon fish sauce
1 tablespoon coconut vinegar

or apple cider vinegar
1 teaspoon garlic powder
1 teaspoon onion powder
¼ teaspoon ground ginger
Pinch red pepper flakes
Pinch sea salt
Pinch freshly ground black pepper
1 scallion, chopped

1. In a large skillet over medium heat, melt the butter or heat the oil and add the ground pork or sausage. Cook, stirring, until browned, 5 to 7 minutes. Add the shredded cabbage and mix to combine. Add the aminos, fish sauce, vinegar, garlic powder, onion powder, ginger, and red pepper flakes and mix well. 2. Simmer on low for 20 to 30 minutes, stirring occasionally, until the cabbage is cooked down and tender. 3. Season with salt and pepper and top with the chopped scallion. 4. Serve immediately or store in refrigerator for up to 1 week.
Per Serving
Calories: 356 | fat: 24g | protein: 24g | carbs: 11g | net carbs: 7g | fiber: 4g

BLTA Cups

Prep time: 5 minutes | Cook time: 20 minutes | Serves 2

12 bacon slices
¼ head romaine lettuce, chopped

½ avocado, diced
½ cup halved grape tomatoes
2 tablespoons sour cream

1. Preheat the oven to 400°F. You will need a muffin tin. (I use a jumbo muffin tin, but you can use a standard muffin tin if that's what you have.) 2. Turn a muffin tin upside down, and lay it on a baking sheet. Make a cross with 2 bacon strip halves over the upside-down muffin tin. Take 2 more bacon strip halves and put them around the perimeter of the crossed halves. Take 1 full bacon strip and circle it around the base of the upside down tin and then use a toothpick to hold that piece together tightly. Repeat to make 4 cups total. 3. Bake for 20 minutes, or until the bacon is crispy. Transfer to a cooling rack and let rest for at least 10 minutes. 4. Once the bacon cups have become firm, carefully remove them from the muffin cups and place two cups on each of two plates. Fill the cups evenly with the romaine, add the avocado, tomatoes, and a dollop of sour cream, and serve.
Per Serving 2 bowls
Calories: 354 | fat: 28g | protein: 20g | carbs: 7g | net carbs: 3g | fiber: 4g

Pecorino Veal Cutlets

Prep time: 10 minutes | Cook time: 45 minutes | Serves 6

6 veal cutlets
½ cup Pecorino cheese, grated
6 provolone cheese slices
Salt and black pepper, to taste

4 cups tomato sauce
A pinch of garlic salt
2 tablespoons butter
2 tablespoons coconut oil, melted
1 teaspoon Italian seasoning

1. Season the veal cutlets with garlic salt, black pepper, and salt. Set a pan over medium heat and warm oil and butter, place in the veal, and cook until browned on all sides. Spread half of the tomato sauce on the bottom of a baking dish that is coated with some cooking spray. 2. Place in the veal cutlets then spread with Italian seasoning and sprinkle over the remaining sauce. Set in the oven at 360° F, and bake for 40 minutes. Scatter with the provolone cheese, then sprinkle with Pecorino cheese, and bake for another 5 minutes until the cheese is golden and melted. Serve.

Per Serving
Calories: 362 | fat: 21g | protein: 26g | carbs: 8g | net carbs: 6g | fiber: 2g

Parmesan Pork Chops and Roasted Asparagus

Prep time: 10 minutes | Cook time: 25 minutes | Serves 2

¼ cup grated Parmesan cheese
¼ cup crushed pork rinds
1 teaspoon garlic powder
2 boneless pork chops
Pink Himalayan salt

Freshly ground black pepper
Olive oil, for drizzling
½ pound (227 g) asparagus spears, tough ends snapped off

1. Preheat the oven to 350°F. Line a baking sheet with aluminum foil or a silicone baking mat. 2. In a medium bowl, mix to combine the Parmesan cheese, pork rinds, and garlic powder. 3. Pat the pork chops dry with a paper towel, and season with pink Himalayan salt and pepper. 4. Place a pork chop in the bowl with the Parmesan–pork rind mixture, and press the "breading" to the pork chop so it sticks. Place the coated pork chop on the prepared baking sheet. Repeat for the second pork chop. 5. Drizzle a small amount of olive oil over each pork chop. 6. Place the asparagus on the baking sheet around the pork chops. Drizzle with olive oil, and season with pink Himalayan salt and pepper. Sprinkle any leftover Parmesan cheese–pork rind mixture over the asparagus. 7. Bake for 20 to 25 minutes. Thinner pork chops will cook faster than thicker ones. 8. Serve hot.

Per Serving
Calories: 370 | fat: 21g | protein: 40g | carbs: 6g | net carbs: 4g | fiber: 3g

Beef Sausage Casserole

Prep time: 10 minutes | Cook time: 25 minutes | Serves 8

⅓ cup almond flour
2 eggs
2 pounds (907 g) beef sausage, chopped
Salt and black pepper, to taste
1 tablespoon dried parsley
¼ teaspoon red pepper flakes
¼ cup Parmesan cheese,

grated
¼ teaspoon onion powder
½ teaspoon garlic powder
¼ teaspoon dried oregano
1 cup ricotta cheese
1 cup sugar-free marinara sauce
1½cups cheddar cheese, shredded

1. In a bowl, combine the sausage, black pepper, pepper flakes, oregano, eggs, Parmesan cheese, onion powder, almond flour, salt, parsley, and garlic powder. Form balls, lay them on a greased baking sheet, place in the oven at 370°F, and bake for 15 minutes. 2. Remove the balls from the oven and cover with half of the marinara sauce. Pour ricotta cheese all over followed by the rest of the marinara sauce. Scatter the cheddar cheese and bake in the oven for 10 minutes. Allow the meatballs casserole to cool before serving.

Per Serving
Calories: 519 | fat: 39g | protein: 36g | carbs: 6g | net carbs: 4g | fiber: 2g

Carnitas

Prep time: 10 minutes | Cook time: 8 hours | Serves 2

½ tablespoon chili powder
1 tablespoon olive oil
1 pound (454 g) boneless pork butt roast
2 garlic cloves, minced

½ small onion, diced
Pinch pink Himalayan salt
Pinch freshly ground black pepper
Juice of 1 lime

1. With the crock insert in place, preheat the slow cooker to low. 2. In a small bowl, mix to combine the chili powder and olive oil, and rub it all over the pork. 3. Place the pork in the slow cooker, fat-side up. 4. Top the pork with the garlic, onion, pink Himalayan salt, pepper, and lime juice. 5. Cover and cook on low for 8 hours. 6. Transfer the pork to a cutting board, shred the meat with two forks, and serve.

Per Serving
Calories: 446 | fat: 26g | protein: 45g | carbs: 6g | net carbs: 4g | fiber: 2g

Pork Fried Cauliflower Rice

Prep time: 10 minutes | Cook time: 20 minutes | Serves 4

1 pound (454 g) ground pork
Sea salt and freshly ground black pepper, to taste
3 tablespoons toasted sesame oil
3 cups thinly sliced cabbage
1 cup chopped broccoli
1 red bell pepper, cored and

chopped
1 garlic clove, minced
1½ cups riced cauliflower
1 tablespoon sriracha
2 tablespoons liquid aminos or tamari
1 teaspoon rice wine vinegar
1 teaspoon sesame seeds, for garnish

1. Heat a medium skillet over medium-high heat. Add the pork and sprinkle generously with salt and pepper. Cook, stirring frequently, until browned, about 10 minutes. Remove the meat from the skillet. 2. Reduce the heat to medium and add the sesame oil to the skillet along with the cabbage, broccoli, bell pepper, riced cauliflower, and garlic. Cook for about 5 minutes until slightly softened, then add the sriracha, liquid aminos, and vinegar and mix well. 3. Return the browned pork to the skillet. Simmer together for about 5 minutes more until the cabbage is crisp-tender. Season with salt and pepper, then garnish with the sesame seeds and serve right away.

Per Serving
Calories: 460 | fat: 36g | protein: 23g | carbs: 11g | net carbs: 5g | fiber: 6g

Beef with Grilled Vegetables

Prep time: 15 minutes | Cook time: 15 minutes | Serves 4

4 sirloin steaks
Salt and black pepper to taste
4 tablespoons olive oil
3 tablespoons balsamic vinegar
Vegetables
½ pound (227 g) asparagus, trimmed

1 cup green beans
1 cup snow peas
1 red bell peppers, seeded, cut into strips
1 orange bell peppers, seeded, cut into strips
1 medium red onion, quartered

1. Set the grill pan over high heat. 2. Grab 2 separate bowls; put the beef in one and the vegetables in another. Mix salt, pepper, olive oil, and balsamic vinegar in a small bowl, and pour half of the mixture over the beef and the other half over the vegetables. Coat the ingredients in both bowls with the sauce and cook the beef first. 3. Place the steaks in the grill pan and sear both sides for 2 minutes each, then continue cooking for 6 minutes on each side.

When done, remove the beef onto a plate; set aside. 4. Pour the vegetables and marinade in the pan; and cook for 5 minutes, turning once. Share the vegetables into plates. Top with each piece of beef, the sauce from the pan, and serve with a rutabaga mash.

Per Serving
Calories: 515 | fat: 32g | protein: 66g | carbs: 11g | net carbs: 5g | fiber: 6g

Kung Pao Pork

Prep time: 15 minutes | Cook time: 10 minutes | Serves 4

Stir-Fried Pork:
2 tablespoons refined avocado oil or hazelnut oil
1 pound (454 g) pork stir-fry pieces
4 small cloves garlic, minced
1 (1-inch/2.5-cm) piece fresh ginger root
2 to 4 dried chilis
2 tablespoons coconut aminos
2 teaspoons apple cider vinegar
2 drops liquid stevia
¼ cup roasted cashews,

roughly chopped
Salad Dressing:
2 tablespoons unsweetened smooth almond butter
2 tablespoons refined avocado oil or hazelnut oil
1 tablespoon plus 1 teaspoon apple cider vinegar
1 tablespoon toasted sesame oil
1 tablespoon coconut aminos
For Serving:
1 cucumber, spiral sliced
½ bunch fresh cilantro (about 1 ounce/28 g), chopped

1. If you want to marinate the pork before cooking, place all the ingredients for the stir-fry, except the cashews, in a large casserole dish. Toss to coat, then refrigerate for at least 1 hour and up to 12 hours. 2. **To Prepare the Stir-fry:** Place a medium-sized frying pan over medium heat. If you didn't marinate the pork, pour the oil into the hot pan and wait until the oil is hot, about 1 minute, then add the remaining stir-fry ingredients. If you did marinate the pork, add the marinated stir-fry ingredients, including the marinating juices, to the hot pan. Cook for 10 minutes, stirring frequently, or until the pork is cooked through. Remove from the heat and stir in the chopped cashews. 3. Meanwhile, **make the salad dressing:** Place the ingredients for the dressing in a small bowl and whisk to combine. 4. Place the spiral-sliced cucumber and cilantro on a serving platter and toss quickly. Place the stir-fried pork on the platter, next to the salad, and drizzle the salad and pork with the dressing.

Per Serving
Calories: 453 | fat: 32g | protein: 28g | carbs: 12g | net carbs: 10g | fiber: 2g

Lamb Stew with Veggies

Prep time: 20 minutes | Cook time: 1 hour 50 minutes | Serves 2

1 garlic clove, minced
1 parsnip, chopped
1 onion, chopped
1 tablespoon olive oil
1 celery stalk, chopped
10 ounces lamb fillet, cut into pieces
Salt and black pepper, to taste
1¼ cups vegetable stock
1 carrot, chopped
½ tablespoon fresh rosemary, chopped
1 leek, chopped
1 tablespoon mint sauce
1 teaspoon stevia
1 tablespoon tomato puree
½ head cauliflower, cut into florets
½ head celeriac, chopped
2 tablespoons butter

1. Set a pot over medium heat and warm the oil, stir in the celery, onion, and garlic, and cook for 5 minutes. Stir in the lamb pieces, and cook for 3 minutes. 2. Add in the stevia, carrot, parsnip, rosemary, mint sauce, stock, leek, tomato puree, boil the mixture, and cook for 1 hour and 30 minutes. 3. Meanwhile, heat a pot with water over medium heat, place in the celeriac, cover, and simmer for 10 minutes. Place in the cauliflower florets, cook for 15 minutes, drain everything, and combine with butter, black pepper, and salt. 4. Mash using a potato masher, and split the mash between 2 plates. Top with vegetable mixture and lamb and enjoy.

Per Serving

Calories: 479 | fat: 32g | protein: 33g | carbs: 15g | net carbs: 8g | fiber: 7g

Chipotle-Spiced Meatball Subs

Prep time: 15 minutes | Cook time: 35 minutes | Serves 15

Meatballs:
1⅔ pounds (750 g) ground pork
1 pound (454 g) ground chicken
½ cup grated white onions
1½ teaspoons dried oregano leaves
1¼ teaspoons ground cumin
1 teaspoon finely ground gray sea salt
Sauce:
2½ cups crushed tomatoes
½ cup refined avocado oil or melted chicken fat
⅔ cup chicken bone broth
1 tablespoon dried oregano leaves
1¼ teaspoons chipotle powder
1 teaspoon garlic powder
½ teaspoon onion powder
½ teaspoon smoked paprika
½ teaspoon finely ground gray sea salt
¼ teaspoon ground black pepper
For Serving:
1 large head green cabbage
Finely chopped fresh cilantro (optional)

1. Preheat the oven to 350°F (177°C) and line a rimmed baking sheet with parchment paper or a silicone baking mat. 2. Place the ingredients for the meatballs in a large bowl. Mix with your hands until combined. 3. Wet your hands and pinch a 1½-tablespoon piece from the bowl, then roll it between your palms to form a ball. Place on the prepared baking sheet and repeat with the remaining meat mixture, making a total of 30 meatballs. Keeping your palms wet will help you shape the meatballs quicker. 4. Bake the meatballs for 25 to 30 minutes, until the internal temperature reaches 165°F (74°C). 5. Meanwhile, place the ingredients for the sauce in a large saucepan. Stir to combine, then cover, placing the lid slightly askew to allow steam to escape. Bring to a boil over medium-high heat, then reduce the heat to low and simmer for 20 minutes. 6. While the meatballs and sauce are cooking, remove 30 medium-sized leaves from the head of cabbage and lightly steam for 1 to 2 minutes. 7. Remove the meatballs from the oven and transfer to the saucepan with the sauce. Turn them to coat, cover, and cook on low for 5 minutes. 8. To serve, stack 2 cabbage leaves on top of one another, top with 2 meatballs, a dollop of extra sauce, and a sprinkle of cilantro, if using.

Per Serving

Calories: 253 | fat: 17g | protein: 18g | carbs: 8g | net carbs: 5g | fiber: 3g

Spicy Barbecued Pork Wings

Prep time: 10 minutes | Cook time: 10 minutes to 3 hours | Serves 2

4 pork wings or trimmed pork shanks
¼ cup water
1 teaspoon extra-virgin olive oil
¼ cup sugar-free barbecue
sauce
2 tablespoons butter
1 teaspoon hot sauce of choice
Cayenne pepper

1. If the wings did not come already cooked, preheat the oven to 300°F (150°C). (If they did, skip to step 3.) 2. Place the wings in an 8-inch square baking pan and add the water. Seal the pan with aluminum foil. Bake for 2 to 3 hours, until the meat is tender. 3. In a medium sauté pan or skillet, heat the olive oil over medium-high heat. Add the wings and crisp for 2 to 3 minutes on each side. 4. Transfer the pork to a platter. Lower the heat to medium and add the barbecue sauce, butter, and hot sauce to the skillet. Season to taste with cayenne. 5. Stir the sauce until it starts to simmer, then put the wings back in the skillet and coat with the sauce. 6. Simmer until the sauce has thickened and sticks to the wings, about 2 minutes. Serve.

Per Serving

Calories: 458 | fat: 35g | protein: 34g | carbs: 2g | net carbs: 1g | fiber: 1g

Steak Diane

Prep time: 10 minutes | Cook time: 15 minutes | Serves 4

4 tablespoons Paleo fat, such as lard, coconut oil, or avocado oil, divided
4 (4 ounces/113 g) beef or venison tenderloins
1¼ teaspoons fine sea salt, plus more for the sauce
½ teaspoon freshly ground black pepper, plus more for the sauce
¼ cup minced shallots or onions
1 teaspoon minced garlic
½ pound (227 g) button mushrooms, sliced ¼ inch thick (small mushrooms can be left whole)
¼ cup beef bone broth, homemade or store-bought
¼ cup full-fat coconut milk
2 teaspoons Dijon mustard

1. Heat a cast-iron skillet over medium-high heat; once hot, place 1 tablespoon of the fat in the pan. While the pan is heating, **prepare the tenderloins:** Pat the tenderloins dry and season them well with the salt and pepper. 2. When the fat is hot, place the tenderloins in the skillet and sear for 3 minutes, then flip them over and sear for another 3 minutes. Remove from the skillet for rare meat, or continue to cook until done to your liking. Allow to rest for 10 minutes before slicing or serving. 3. While the meat is resting, **make the pan sauce:** Add the remaining 3 tablespoons of fat to the pan, then add the shallots, garlic, and mushrooms, season with a couple pinches each of salt and pepper, and sauté until the mushrooms are golden brown on both sides, about 6 minutes. (Add the mushrooms to the pan in batches if necessary to avoid overcrowding.) Pour in the broth and, using a whisk, scrape up the brown bits from the bottom of the pan to incorporate them into the sauce. Add the coconut milk and mustard, stir to combine, and heat until simmering. Simmer over low heat until thickened, about 3 minutes. Season to taste with salt and pepper. 4. Serve the steaks with the sauce.

Per Serving
Calories: 332 | fat: 20g | protein: 36g | carbs: 2g | net carbs: 1g | fiber: 1g

Keto Chili

Prep time: 20 minutes | Cook time: 5 TO 8 hours | Serves 6

1 pound (454 g) ground beef
1 pound (454 g) bulk sausage, mild or hot
1 green bell pepper, diced
½ medium yellow onion, chopped
3 to 4 cloves garlic, minced, or 1 tablespoon garlic powder
1 (14½-ounce) can diced tomatoes (with juices)
1 (6 ounces/170 g) can tomato paste
1 tablespoon chili powder
1½ teaspoons ground cumin
⅓ cup water
Topping Suggestions:
Shredded cheddar cheese
Sliced green onions
Sour cream
Sliced jalapeños

1. In a large pot, brown the ground beef and sausage, using a wooden spoon to break up the clumps. Drain the meat, reserving half of the drippings. 2. Transfer the drained meat to a slow cooker. Add the reserved drippings, bell pepper, onion, garlic, tomatoes with juices, tomato paste, chili powder, cumin, and water and mix well. 3. Place the lid on the slow cooker and cook on low for 6 to 8 hours or on high for 5 hours, until the veggies are soft. 4. Serve topped with shredded cheese, green onions, sour cream, and/or sliced jalapeños, if desired.

Per Serving
Calories: 387 | fat: 25g | protein: 34g | carbs: 11g | net carbs: 8g | fiber: 3g

Steak and Egg Bibimbap

Prep time: 10 minutes | Cook time: 15 minutes | Serves 2

For the Steak:
1 tablespoon ghee or butter
8 ounces (227 g) skirt steak
Pink Himalayan salt
Freshly ground black pepper
1 tablespoon soy sauce (or coconut aminos)
For the Egg and Cauliflower Rice:
2 tablespoons ghee or butter,
divided
2 large eggs
1 large cucumber, peeled and cut into matchsticks
1 tablespoon soy sauce
1 cup cauliflower rice
Pink Himalayan salt
Freshly ground black pepper

To Make the Steak: 1. Over high heat, heat a large skillet. 2. Using a paper towel, pat the steak dry. Season both sides with pink Himalayan salt and pepper. 3. Add the ghee or butter to the skillet. When it melts, put the steak in the skillet. 4. Sear the steak for about 3 minutes on each side for medium-rare. 5. Transfer the steak to a cutting board and let it rest for at least 5 minutes. 6. Slice the skirt steak across the grain and divide it between two bowls. **To Make the Egg and Cauliflower Rice:** 1. In a second large skillet over medium-high heat, heat 1 tablespoon of ghee. When the ghee is very hot, crack the eggs into it. When the whites have cooked through, after 2 to 3 minutes, carefully transfer the eggs to a plate. 2. In a small bowl, marinate the cucumber matchsticks in the soy sauce. 3. Clean out the skillet from the eggs, and add the remaining 1 tablespoon of ghee or butter to the pan over medium-high heat. Add the cauliflower rice, season with pink Himalayan salt and pepper, and stir, cooking for 5 minutes. Turn the heat up to high at the end of the cooking to get a nice crisp on the "rice." 4. Divide the rice between two bowls. 5. Top the rice in each bowl with an egg, the steak, and the marinated cucumber matchsticks and serve.

Per Serving
Calories: 590 | fat: 45g | protein: 39g | carbs: 8g | net carbs: 5g | fiber: g

Southern Pulled Pork "Spaghetti"

Prep time: 5 minutes | Cook time: 0 minutes | Serves 6

Pork "Spaghetti":
2 pounds (907 g) boneless pork shoulder
1 cup chicken bone broth
1 teaspoon finely ground sea salt
Barbecue Pork Sauce:
2 tablespoons avocado oil

1 red bell pepper, diced
1 small white onion, diced
8 cremini mushrooms, diced
1 pound (454 g) ground pork
¾ cup sugar-free barbecue sauce
½ cup reserved pork shoulder cooking liquid (from above)

1. **Make the "Spaghetti":** Place all the ingredients for the spaghetti in a pressure cooker or slow cooker. 2. If using a pressure cooker, seal the lid and cook on high pressure for 45 minutes. Allow the pressure to release naturally before removing the lid. Remove ½ cup (120 ml) of the cooking liquid and set aside for the sauce. Drain the meat almost completely, leaving ¼ cup (60 ml) of the cooking liquid in the cooker. If using a slow cooker, cook on high for 4 hours or low for 6 hours. When the meat is done, remove ½ cup (120 ml) of the cooking liquid and set aside for the sauce. Drain the meat almost completely, leaving ⅓ cup (80 ml) of the cooking liquid in the cooker. 3. Meanwhile, **make the sauce:** Heat the oil in a large frying pan over medium heat. Add the bell pepper, onion, and mushrooms and sauté for 5 minutes, until softened. Add the ground pork and cook until no longer pink, 5 to 7 minutes, stirring to break up the meat as it cooks. Add the barbecue sauce and the reserved cooking liquid. Stir to combine, then cover and cook for another 3 minutes, just to heat through. 4. Shred the meat with two forks. Divide the shredded pork among 6 dinner plates, top with the barbecue pork sauce, and dig in!
Per Serving
Calories: 683 | fat: 46g | protein: 58g | carbs: 7g | net carbs: 5g | fiber: 2g

Mississippi Pot Roast

Prep time: 5 minutes | Cook time: 8 minutes | Serves 4

1 pound (454 g) beef chuck roast
Pink Himalayan salt
Freshly ground black pepper
1 (1 ounce/28 g) packet dry Au Jus Gravy Mix

1 (1 ounce/28 g) packet dry ranch dressing
8 tablespoons butter (1 stick)
1 cup whole pepperoncini (I use Mezzetta)

1. With the crock insert in place, preheat the slow cooker to low. 2. Season both sides of the beef chuck roast with pink Himalayan salt and pepper. Put in the slow cooker. 3. Sprinkle the gravy mix and ranch dressing packets on top of the roast. 4. Place the butter on top of the roast, and sprinkle the pepperoncini around it. 5. Cover and cook on low for 8 hours. 6. Shred the beef using two forks, and serve hot.
Per Serving
Calories: 504 | fat: 34g | protein: 36g | carbs: 6g | net carbs: 6g | fiber: 0g

Adobo Beef Fajitas

Prep time: 10 minutes | Cook time: 20 minutes | Serves 4

2 pounds (907 g) skirt steak
2 tablespoons adobo seasoning
Salt to taste
2 tablespoons olive oil

2 large white onion, chopped
1 cup mixed bell peppers, chopped
12 low carb tortillas

1. Season the steak with adobo seasoning and marinate in the fridge for one hour. 2. Preheat grill to 425ºF and cook steak for 6 minutes on each side, flipping once until lightly browned. Remove from heat and wrap in foil and let sit for 10 minutes. This allows the meat to cook in its heat for a few more minutes before slicing. 3. Heat olive oil in a skillet over medium heat and sauté onion and bell peppers for 5 minutes, until soft. Cut steak against the grain into strips and share on the tortillas. Top with the veggies and serve.
Per Serving
Calories: 350 | fat: 26g | protein: 23g | carbs: 6g | net carbs: 5g | fiber: 1g

Italian Beef Burgers

Prep time: 10 minutes | Cook time: 12 minutes | Serves 4

1 pound (454 g) 75% lean ground beef
¼ cup ground almonds
2 tablespoons chopped fresh basil
1 teaspoon minced garlic

¼ teaspoon sea salt
1 tablespoon olive oil
1 tomato, cut into 4 thick slices
¼ sweet onion, sliced thinly

1. In a medium bowl, mix together the ground beef, ground almonds, basil, garlic, and salt until well mixed. 2. Form the beef mixture into four equal patties and flatten them to about ½ inch thick. 3. Place a large skillet on medium-high heat and add the olive oil. 4. Panfry the burgers until cooked through, flipping them once, about 12 minutes in total. 5. Pat away any excess grease with paper towels and serve the burgers with a slice of tomato and onion.
Per Serving
Calories: 441 | fat: 37g | protein: 22g | carbs: 4g | net carbs: 3g | fiber: 1g

Chili Cheese Pot Pie

Prep time: 15 minutes | Cook time: 45 minutes | serves 6

Filling:

2 pounds (907 g) ground beef

½ cup diced onions, or 2 tablespoons dried minced onions

2 cloves garlic, minced

1 (14½ ounces/411 g) can petite diced tomatoes

1½ tablespoons chili powder

2 teaspoons ground cumin

1 teaspoon smoked paprika

Biscuit Topping:

1½ cups finely ground blanched almond flour

2 teaspoons baking powder

½ teaspoon garlic powder

¼ teaspoon salt

½ cup shredded cheddar cheese

¼ cup sour cream

2 large eggs

2 tablespoons salted butter, melted but not hot

1. **Make the Filling:** In a 12-inch cast-iron skillet or other ovenproof skillet, cook the ground beef with the onions and garlic over medium heat, crumbling the meat with a large spoon as it cooks, until the meat is browned and the onions and garlic are translucent, about 10 minutes. Drain the fat, if necessary. 2. Stir in the tomatoes and seasonings. Simmer over low heat for 15 minutes, then remove from the heat. 3. Preheat the oven to 375°F. 4. **Make the Biscuit Topping:** In a bowl, whisk together the almond flour, baking powder, garlic powder, and salt until well combined. In a separate bowl, stir together the cheese, sour cream, eggs, and melted butter. Add the wet ingredients to the dry ingredients and gently stir until well combined. 5. Drop the biscuit topping mixture by the large spoonful onto the chili beef mixture in the skillet. 6. Bake for 20 minutes or until the biscuits are cooked through and browned on top. Leftovers can be stored in an airtight container in the refrigerator for up to 5 days.

Per Serving

Calories: 477 | fat: 37g | protein: 24g | carbs: 10g | net carbs: 7g | fiber: 4g

Grilled Skirt Steak with Jalapeño Compound Butter

Prep time: 10 minutes | Cook time: 10 minutes | Serves 4

¼ cup unsalted grass-fed butter, at room temperature

½ jalapeño pepper, seeded and minced very finely

Zest and juice of ½ lime

½ teaspoon sea salt

4 (4 ounces/113 g) skirt steaks

1 tablespoon olive oil

Sea salt, for seasoning

Freshly ground black pepper, for seasoning

1. Make the compound butter. In a medium bowl, stir together the butter, jalapeño pepper, lime zest, lime juice,

and salt until everything is well combined. Lay a piece of plastic wrap on a clean work surface and spoon the butter mixture into the middle. Form the butter into a log about 1 inch thick by folding the plastic wrap over the butter and twisting the two ends in opposite directions. Roll the butter log on the counter to smooth the edges and put it in the freezer until it's very firm, about 4 hours. 2. Grill the steak. Preheat the grill to high heat. Lightly oil the steaks with the olive oil and season them lightly with salt and pepper. Grill the steaks for about 5 minutes per side for medium (140°F internal temperature) or until they're done the way you like them. 3. Rest and serve. Let the steaks rest for 10 minutes and serve them sliced across the grain, topped with a thick slice of the compound butter.

Per Serving

Calories: 404 | fat: 32g | protein: 29g | carbs: 0g | net carbs: 0g | fiber: 0g

Stuffed Pork Loin with Sun-Dried Tomato and Goat Cheese

Prep time: 15 minutes | Cook time: 30 to 40 minutes | Serves 6

1 to 1½ pounds (454 to 680 g) pork tenderloin

1 cup crumbled goat cheese

4 ounces (113 g) frozen spinach, thawed and well drained

2 tablespoons chopped sun-dried tomatoes

2 tablespoons extra-virgin

olive oil (or seasoned oil marinade from sun-dried tomatoes), plus ¼ cup, divided

½ teaspoon salt

½ teaspoon freshly ground black pepper

Zucchini noodles or sautéed greens, for serving

1. Preheat the oven to 350°F(180ºC). Cut cooking twine into eight (6-inch) pieces. 2. Cut the pork tenderloin in half lengthwise, leaving about an inch border. Open the tenderloin to form a large rectangle. Place it between two pieces of parchment paper and pound to about ¼-inch thickness. 3. In a small bowl, mix the goat cheese, spinach, sun-dried tomatoes, 2 tablespoons olive oil, salt, and pepper. 4. Spread the filling over the surface of the pork, leaving a 1-inch border from one long edge and both short edges. Roll the pork. Tie cooking twine around the pork to secure it closed, evenly spacing each of the eight pieces of twine along the length of the roll. 5. In a Dutch oven or large oven-safe skillet, heat ¼ cup olive oil over medium-high heat. Add the pork and brown on all sides. Remove from the heat, cover, and bake until the pork is cooked through, 45 to 75 minutes. Remove from the oven and let rest for 10 minutes at room temperature. 6. To serve, remove the twine. Slice the pork into medallions and serve over zucchini noodles or sautéed greens, spooning the cooking oil and any bits of filling that fell out during cooking over top.

Per Serving

Calories: 270 | fat: 20g | protein: 20g | carbs: 2g | fiber: 1g | sodium: 392mg

Bacon Cheeseburger Mini Meatloaves

Prep time: 15 minutes | Cook time: 30 minutes | Makes 8 mini meatloaves

8 slices bacon, partially cooked
1 pound (454 g) ground beef
1 cup shredded cheddar cheese
1 large egg
½ cup sugar-free ketchup, plus extra for the tops
¼ cup chopped dill pickles
2 tablespoons dried minced onions
1 tablespoon Worcestershire sauce
¼ teaspoon salt
½ teaspoon ground black pepper

1. Preheat the oven to 375°F. Grease 8 wells of a standard-size 12-well muffin pan or line with parchment paper. 2. Wrap a slice of partially cooked bacon around the side of each prepared muffin well. 3. Place the rest of the ingredients in a large bowl. Use your hands to combine the ingredients until just blended, being careful not to overmix. 4. Divide the meat mixture evenly among the bacon-lined wells of the muffin pan, filling each well to the top of the bacon. Brush the tops of the meatloaves with ketchup. 5. Bake for 30 minutes or until a meat thermometer registers 160°F when inserted in the middle of a meatloaf. Leftovers can be stored in an airtight container in the refrigerator for up to 5 days.

Per Serving
Calories: 548 | fat: 42g | protein: 35g | carbs: 5g | net carbs: 5g | fiber: 0g

Soy-Glazed Meatloaf

Prep time: 15 minutes | Cook time: 50 minutes | Serves 6

1 cup white mushrooms, chopped
2 pounds (907 g) ground beef
2 tablespoons fresh parsley, chopped
2 garlic cloves, minced
1 onion, chopped
1 red bell pepper, seeded and chopped
½ cup almond flour
⅓ cup Parmesan cheese, grated
2 eggs
Salt and black pepper, to taste
1 teaspoon balsamic vinegar
1 tablespoon swerve
1 tablespoon soy sauce
2 tablespoons sugar-free ketchup
2 cups balsamic vinegar

1. In a bowl, combine the beef with salt, mushrooms, bell pepper, Parmesan cheese, 1 teaspoon vinegar, parsley, garlic, black pepper, onion, almond flour, salt, and eggs. Set this into a loaf pan, and bake for 30 minutes in the oven at 370°F. 2. Meanwhile, heat a small pan over medium heat, add in the 2 cups vinegar, swerve, soy sauce, and ketchup, and cook for 20 minutes. Remove the meatloaf from the oven, spread the glaze over the meatloaf, and bake in the oven for 20 more minutes. Allow the meatloaf to cool, slice, and enjoy.

Per Serving
Calories: 429 | fat: 25g | protein: 43g | carbs: 8g | net carbs: 5g | fiber: 3g

Italian Beef and Pork Rind Meatloaf

Prep time: 6 minutes | Cook time: 25 minutes | Serves 6

1 pound (454 g) ground beef
1 cup crushed pork rinds
1 egg
¼ cup grated Parmesan cheese
¼ cup Italian dressing
2 teaspoons Italian seasoning
½ cup water
½ cup unsweetened tomato purée
1 tablespoon chopped fresh parsley
1 clove garlic, minced

1. In large bowl, combine the beef, pork rinds, egg, cheese, dressing, and Italian seasoning. Stir to mix well. 2. Pour the mixture in a baking pan and level with a spatula. 3. Place the trivet in the pot and add the water. Place the pan on top of the trivet. 4. Close the lid. Select Manual mode and set cooking time for 20 minutes on High Pressure. 5. When timer beeps, use a quick pressure release. Open the lid. 6. Meanwhile, whisk together the tomato purée, parsley, and garlic in a small bowl. Heat the broiler. 7. Remove the pan from the pot. Spread the tomato purée mixture on top. 8. Broil for 5 minutes or until sticky. Slice and serve.

Per Serving
Calories: 358 | fat: 25.2g | protein: 29.2g | carbs: 2.3g | net carbs: 2.3g | fiber: 0g

Rolled Lamb Shoulder with Basil & Pine Nuts

Prep time: 10 minutes | Cook time: 50 minutes | Serves 4

1 pound (454 g) rolled lamb shoulder, boneless
1½ cups basil leaves, chopped
5 tablespoons pine nuts,
chopped
½ cup green olives, pitted and chopped
3 cloves garlic, minced
Salt and black pepper to taste

1. Preheat the oven to 450°F. 2. In a bowl, combine the basil, pine nuts, olives, and garlic. Season with salt and pepper. Untie the lamb flat onto a chopping board, spread the basil mixture all over, and rub the spices onto the meat. 3. Roll the lamb over the spice mixture and tie it together using 3 to 4 strings of butcher's twine. Place the lamb onto a baking dish and cook in the oven for 10 minutes. Reduce the heat to 350°F and continue cooking for 40 minutes. When ready, transfer the meat to a cleaned chopping board; let it rest for 10 minutes before slicing. Serve with roasted root vegetables.

Per Serving
Calories: 291 | fat: 20g | protein: 25g | carbs: 5g | net carbs: 3g | fiber: 2g

Creamy Pork Marsala

Prep time: 5 minutes | Cook time: 30 minutes | Serves 4

4 (4 ounces/113 g) boneless pork cutlets
Salt and freshly ground black pepper, to taste
4 tablespoons butter, divided
8 ounces (227 g) sliced mushrooms (cremini, portabella, button, or other)
4 ounces (113 g) prosciutto, chopped
1 garlic clove, minced
½ cup Marsala cooking wine
½ cup bone broth
1 teaspoon chopped fresh thyme
½ teaspoon xanthan or guar gum, to thicken (optional)
Chopped fresh parsley, for garnish

1. Sprinkle the cutlets with salt and pepper. 2. Heat a large skillet over medium-high heat and melt 2 tablespoons of butter. Add the cutlets and cook for at least 5 minutes on each side until cooked through. Remove the cutlets from the skillet. 3. Reduce the heat to medium-low and add the remaining 2 tablespoons of butter. Add the mushrooms, prosciutto, and garlic, and cook, stirring frequently, until the mushrooms brown, about 5 minutes. 4. Add the wine, bone broth, and thyme. Simmer for about 15 minutes until the sauce thickens. Add the xanthan gum (if using), to thicken the sauce even more. Return the pork to the skillet and raise the heat to medium-high. Cook until the cutlets are heated through. 5. Serve garnished with parsley.

Per Serving
Calories: 339 | fat: 19g | protein: 36g | carbs: 6g | net carbs: 5g | fiber: 1g

Mustard-Lemon Beef

Prep time: 15 minutes | Cook time: 17 minutes | Serves 4

2 tablespoons olive oil
1 tablespoon fresh rosemary, chopped
2 garlic cloves, minced
1½ pounds (680 g) beef rump steak, thinly sliced
Salt and black pepper, to taste
1 shallot, chopped
½ cup heavy cream
½ cup beef stock
1 tablespoon mustard
2 teaspoons Worcestershire sauce
2 teaspoons lemon juice
1 teaspoon erythritol
2 tablespoons butter
A sprig of rosemary
A sprig of thyme

1. In a bowl, combine 1 tablespoon of oil with black pepper, garlic, rosemary, and salt. Toss in the beef to coat, and set aside for some minutes. Heat a pan with the rest of the oil over medium heat, place in the beef steak, cook for 6 minutes, flipping halfway through; set aside and keep warm. 2. Set the pan to medium heat, stir in the shallot, and cook for 3 minutes; stir in the stock, Worcestershire sauce, erythritol, thyme, cream, mustard, and rosemary, and cook for 8 minutes. 3. Stir in the butter, lemon juice, black pepper, and salt. Get rid of the rosemary and thyme, and remove from heat. Arrange the beef slices on serving plates, sprinkle over the sauce, and enjoy.

Per Serving
Calories: 477 | fat: 33g | protein: 37g | carbs: 8g | net carbs: 6g | fiber: 2g

Kalua Pork with Cabbage

Prep time: 10 minutes | Cook time: 8 hours | Serves 2

1 pound (454 g) boneless pork butt roast
Pink Himalayan salt
Freshly ground black pepper
1 tablespoon smoked paprika or Liquid Smoke
½ cup water
½ head cabbage, chopped

1. With the crock insert in place, preheat the slow cooker to low. 2. Generously season the pork roast with pink Himalayan salt, pepper, and smoked paprika. 3. Place the pork roast in the slow-cooker insert, and add the water. 4. Cover and cook on low for 7 hours. 5. Transfer the cooked pork roast to a plate. Put the chopped cabbage in the bottom of the slow cooker, and put the pork roast back in on top of the cabbage. 6. Cover and cook the cabbage and pork roast for 1 hour. 7. Remove the pork roast from the slow cooker and place it on a baking sheet. Use two forks to shred the pork. 8. Serve the shredded pork hot with the cooked cabbage. 9. Reserve the liquid from the slow cooker to remoisten the pork and cabbage when reheating leftovers.

Per Serving
Calories: 550 | fat: 41g | protein: 39g | carbs: 10g | net carbs: 5g | fiber: 5g

Breaded Pork Chops

Prep time: 5 minutes | Cook time: 20 minutes | Serves 2

2 (8 ounces/227 g) boneless pork loin chops
¼ cup pork panko crumbs
1 teaspoon extra-virgin olive oil
1 teaspoon grated Parmesan cheese
¼ teaspoon pink Himalayan sea salt
¼ teaspoon onion powder
¼ teaspoon paprika
¼ teaspoon garlic powder
⅛ teaspoon freshly ground black pepper
⅛ teaspoon dried parsley
⅛ teaspoon dried basil
⅛ teaspoon dried oregano
Pinch of cayenne pepper

1. Preheat the oven to 425ºF (220ºC). Place a baking rack on a small baking sheet. 2. Pat the chops dry with a paper towel. 3. In a food processor, combine the pork crumbs, olive oil, Parmesan, salt, onion powder, paprika, garlic powder, pepper, parsley, basil, oregano, and cayenne and run on high until the mixture forms a uniform, fine powder. Transfer the mixture to a resealable 1-gallon plastic bag. 4. Add the chops to the bag, one at a time, shaking to coat them in the breading. 5. Transfer the chops to the rack and bake for 20 minutes, until an instant-read thermometer registers 160ºF (71ºC) or the juices run clear when the meat is pierced.

Per Serving
Calories: 435 | fat: 23g | protein: 57g | carbs: 0g | net carbs: 0g | fiber: 0g

Lamb and Beef Kebabs

Prep time: 15 minutes | Cook time: 25 minutes | Serves 2

Coconut oil cooking spray
¼ medium onion, chopped
8 ounces (227 g) ground beef (80/20)
8 ounces (227 g) ground lamb
1 large egg
1 garlic clove, minced
½ teaspoon pink Himalayan sea salt
½ teaspoon freshly ground black pepper
½ teaspoon ground sumac
¼ teaspoon ground turmeric
2 tablespoons butter, melted

1. Preheat the oven to 450ºF (235ºC). Line a large baking sheet with aluminum foil and spray with the cooking spray. 2. In a food processor, purée the onion on high speed until a smooth paste forms. You may need to scrape down the sides of the bowl. 3. Transfer the onion paste to a fine-mesh strainer over the sink and toss it around a few times to drain off any liquid. 4. In a large bowl, combine the onion paste with the beef, lamb, egg, garlic, salt, pepper, sumac, and turmeric. Using your hands, mix the meat with the seasonings until well combined. 5. Divide the mixture into 4 equal portions, then roll each into a cylinder. Slide metal skewers through the cylinders, if desired, or you can bake them as is. 6. Transfer the kebabs to the baking sheet and bake for 15 minutes. 7. Brush the tops of the kebabs with the melted butter, then return them to the oven for an additional 5 to 10 minutes of baking. An instant-read thermometer should reach 155ºF (68ºC) when inserted in the center, and no pink should remain in the meat. 8. Let the kebabs cool for 5 minutes, then serve.
Per Serving
Calories: 724 | fat: 60g | protein: 46g | carbs: 2g | net carbs: 2g | fiber: 0g

Baked Pork Meatballs in Pasta Sauce

Prep time: 10 minutes | Cook time: 35 minutes | Serves 6

2 pounds (907 g) ground pork
1 tablespoon olive oil
1 cup pork rinds, crushed
3 cloves garlic, minced
½ cup coconut milk
2 eggs, beaten
½ cup grated Parmesan cheese
½ cup grated asiago cheese
Salt and black pepper to taste
¼ cup chopped parsley
2 jars sugar-free marinara sauce
½ teaspoon Italian seasoning
1 cup Italian blend kinds of cheeses
Chopped basil to garnish

1. Preheat the oven to 400ºF, line a cast iron pan with foil and oil it with cooking spray. Set aside. 2. Combine the coconut milk and pork rinds in a bowl. Mix in the ground pork, garlic, Asiago cheese, Parmesan cheese, eggs, salt, and pepper, just until combined. Form balls of the mixture and place them in the prepared pan. Bake in the oven for 20 minutes at a reduced temperature of 370ºF. 3. Transfer the meatballs to a plate. Pour half of the marinara sauce in the baking pan. Place the meatballs back in the pan and pour the remaining marinara sauce all over them. Sprinkle with the Italian blend cheeses, drizzle with the olive oil, and then sprinkle with Italian seasoning. 4. Cover the pan with foil and put it back in the oven to bake for 10 minutes. After, remove the foil, and cook for 5 minutes. Once ready, take out the pan and garnish with basil. Serve on a bed of squash spaghetti.
Per Serving
Calories: 575 | fat: 43g | protein: 39g | carbs: 8g | net carbs: 5g | fiber: 3g

Slow Cooker Pastrami-Style Pork Ribs

Prep time: 5 minutes | Cook time: 7 to 8 hours | Serves 8

Pastrami Seasoning:
1 tablespoon freshly ground pepper
1 tablespoon ground coriander
1 tablespoon dry mustard
1 tablespoon smoked paprika
2 teaspoons fine sea salt
½ teaspoon cayenne pepper
4 pounds (1.8 kg) boneless country-style pork ribs
½ cup water or beef bone broth, homemade or store-bought
Sauce:
¾ cup Dijon mustard
¼ cup coconut vinegar or apple cider vinegar
¼ cup Swerve confectioners'-style sweetener or equivalent amount of liquid or powdered sweetener
2 tablespoons coconut aminos or wheat-free tamari
For Serving (optional):
Sauerkraut, warmed
Cornichons

1. Combine the pastrami seasoning ingredients and rub over the surface of the ribs. 2. Place the ribs in a 4-quart (or larger) slow cooker, standing them on their edge with the meaty side out. 3. Add the water or broth to the slow cooker. Cover and cook on low until the meat is falling apart and very tender, 7 to 8 hours. 4. Meanwhile, **make the sauce:** Place all the ingredients in a small bowl and stir to combine. 5. When the meat is done, preheat the oven to broil. Place the ribs on a rimmed baking sheet and spoon the sauce all over the top of the ribs. Broil for 3 to 5 minutes, until charred to your liking. 6. Serve with sauerkraut and cornichons, if desired. Store extras in an airtight container in the fridge for up to 4 days.
Per Serving
Calories: 353 | fat: 18g | protein: 47g | carbs: 1g | net carbs: 0g | fiber: 1g

Crispy Fish Nuggets

Prep time: 15 minutes | Cook time: 9 minutes | Serves 4

1 pound (454 g) tilapia fillet
½ cup almond flour
3 eggs, beaten
¼ cup avocado oil
1 teaspoon salt

1. Cut the fish into the small pieces (nuggets) and sprinkle withs alt. 2. Then dip the fish nuggets in the eggs and coat in the almond flour. 3. Heat up avocado oil for 3 minutes on Sauté mode. 4. Put the prepared fish nuggets in the hot oil and cook them on Sauté mode for 3 minutes from each side or until they are golden brown.
Per Serving
Calories: 179 | fat: 8g | protein: 26g | carbs: 2g | net carbs: 1g | fiber: 1g

Sushi

Prep time: 15 minutes | Cook time: 3 to 5 minutes | Serves 2 to 4

4 cups cauliflower rice
2 tablespoons grass-fed gelatin
1 tablespoon apple cider vinegar
1 teaspoon salt
2 to 4 nori sheets
½ pound (227 g) sushi-grade fish, thinly sliced
1 small avocado, halved, pitted, peeled, and thinly sliced
1 small cucumber (or any other vegetable you'd like), thinly sliced
Sesame seeds, for topping (optional)
Coconut aminos or tamari, wasabi, sugar-free pickled ginger, sliced avocado, and/ or avocado oil mayonnaise mixed with sugar-free hot sauce, for serving (optional)

1. In a shallow pot with a lid, combine the cauliflower with 3 tablespoons of water. Turn the heat to medium, cover the pot, and steam for 3 to 5 minutes. 2. Drain the cauliflower and transfer to a mixing bowl. Stir in the gelatin, vinegar, and salt. Stir together until the mixture is smooth and sticky. Set aside. 3. Fold a dish towel in half lengthwise and place it on your counter. Cover the towel in plastic wrap. 4. Place a nori sheet on top of the plastic wrap, then spread with a layer of the cauliflower rice. 5. Layer slices of fish, avocado, and cucumber over the cauliflower on the end of the nori sheet closest to you. 6. Starting at the end closest to you, gently roll the nori sheet over all the ingredients, using the towel as your rolling aid. (Emphasis on the word "gently" because you don't want to tear the nori sheet.) When you're done rolling, remove the towel and plastic wrap as you slide the roll onto a plate or cutting board. Using a sharp knife, cut the roll into equal pieces. Repeat steps 4 through 7 with the remaining nori and filling ingredients. 7. Sprinkle sesame seeds on top of your sushi, if desired, and serve with any of the other optional ingredients you'd like.
Per Serving
Calories: 295 | fat: 15g | protein: 30g | carbs: 10g | net carbs: 2g | fiber: 8g

Gambas al Ajillo

Prep time: 10 minutes | Cook time: 10 minutes | Serves 4

½ cup extra-virgin olive oil
10 to 12 garlic cloves, thinly sliced
1 pound (454 g) jumbo
shrimp, tails removed
Salt, to taste
Freshly ground black pepper, to taste

1. In a large skillet over medium heat, heat the olive oil. 2. Add the garlic. Cook for 2 to 3 minutes until fragrant. 3. Add the shrimp and cook for 2 to 3 minutes per side until pink. Season with salt and pepper and serve right away. Refrigerate leftovers in an airtight container for up to 3 days.
Per Serving
Calories: 370 | fat: 29g | protein: 24g | carbs: 4g | net carbs: 4g | fiber: 0g

Blackened Fish Tacos with Slaw

Prep time: 10 minutes | Cook time: 6 minutes | Serves 4

1 tablespoon olive oil
1 teaspoon chili powder
2 tilapia fillets
1 teaspoon paprika
4 low carb tortillas slaw
½ cup red cabbage, shredded
1 tablespoon lemon juice
1 teaspoon apple cider vinegar
1 tablespoon olive oil
Salt and black pepper to taste

1. Season the tilapia with chili powder and paprika. Heat the olive oil in a skillet over medium heat. 2. Add tilapia and cook until blackened, about 3 minutes per side. Cut into strips. Divide the tilapia between the tortillas. Combine all slaw ingredients in a bowl and top the fish to serve.
Per Serving
Calories: 236 | fat: 10g | protein: 15g | carbs: 10g | net carbs: 8g | fiber: 2g

Clam Chowder

Prep time: 5 minutes | Cook time: 15 minutes | Serves 4

4 slices bacon, chopped into ½-inch squares
2 tablespoons unsalted butter
½ small yellow onion, chopped
4 ribs celery, cut into ¼-inch-thick half-moons
1 cup chopped cauliflower florets, cut to about ½ inch thick
4 ounces (113 g) chopped mushrooms
4 cloves garlic, minced
1 teaspoon dried tarragon
1 teaspoon salt
¼ teaspoon freshly ground black pepper
8 ounces (227 g) bottled clam juice
1 cup vegetable stock or broth
½ cup heavy cream
8 ounces (227 g) cream cheese, room temperature
3 (6½ ounces/184 g) cans chopped clams, with juice
¼ cup freshly chopped Italian parsley

1. Place the bacon in a medium saucepan over medium heat. Fry until just browned and most of the fat has been rendered, 3 to 4 minutes. Remove the bacon with a slotted spoon, reserving the rendered fat. 2. Add the butter to the pan with the fat and melt over medium heat. Add the onion, celery, cauliflower, and mushrooms and sauté until vegetables are just tender, 4 to 5 minutes. Add the garlic, tarragon, salt, and pepper and sauté for another 30 seconds or until fragrant. 3. Add the clam juice, stock, cream, and cream cheese and whisk until the cheese is melted and creamy, 2 to 3 minutes. Add the clams and their juice, bring to a simmer, and cook for 1 to 2 minutes so the flavors meld. Stir in the parsley and serve warm.
Per Serving
Calories: 671 | fat: 54g | protein: 34g | carbs: 15g | net carbs: 13g | fiber: 2g

Pan-Seared Lemon-Garlic Salmon

Prep time: 5 minutes | Cook time: 10 minutes | Serves 2

1 tablespoon extra-virgin olive oil
2 (8 ounces/227 g) salmon fillets
1 lemon, halved
Pink Himalayan sea salt
Freshly ground black pepper
2 tablespoons butter
1 tablespoon chopped fresh parsley
2 garlic cloves, minced

1. In a medium sauté pan or skillet, heat the olive oil over medium-high heat. 2. Squeeze the juice from a lemon half over the fillets. Season the salmon with salt and pepper. 3. Place the salmon skin-side up in the skillet. Cook for 4 to 5 minutes, then flip the fish and cook for an additional 2 to 3 minutes on the other side. 4. Add the butter, the juice from the other lemon half, the parsley, and garlic to the pan. Toss

to combine. Allow the fish to cook for 2 to 3 more minutes, until the flesh flakes easily with a fork. 5. Transfer the fish to a serving plate, then top with the butter sauce and serve.
Per Serving
Calories: 489 | fat: 33g | protein: 45g | carbs: 0g | net carbs: 0g | fiber: 0g

Cream Cheese and Salmon Cucumber Bites

Prep time: 15 minutes | Cook time: 0 minutes | Serves 6

6 ounces (170 g) full-fat cream cheese, at room temperature
1 large cucumber, washed, peeled or unpeeled, cut into coins about ½ inch thick
(about 12)
6 ounces (170 g) smoked salmon
Salt, to taste
Freshly ground black pepper, to taste

1. Spread about ½ ounce (14 g) of cream cheese onto each cucumber slice. Top each cucumber slice with ½ ounce (14 g) of smoked salmon. Season with salt and pepper. Serve immediately or refrigerate in an airtight container for up to 2 days.
Per Serving
Calories: 126 | fat: 11g | protein: 7g | carbs: 3g | net carbs: 3g | fiber: 0g

Simple Lemon-Herb Whitefish

Prep time: 5 minutes | Cook time: 14 minutes | Serves 6

6 white fish fillets (5 ounces/142 g each), preferably lake whitefish, grouper, or halibut
1 teaspoon sea salt
½ teaspoon black pepper
3 tablespoons olive oil
2 teaspoons lemon zest
2 teaspoons lemon juice
2 cloves garlic, minced
1 teaspoon minced capers (optional)
3 tablespoons minced fresh parsley
3 tablespoons minced fresh dill

1. Preheat the oven to 400ºF (205ºC). Line a sheet pan with foil or parchment paper and grease lightly. 2. Place the fish fillets in a single layer on the pan. Season the fish on both sides with the sea salt and black pepper. 3. In a small bowl, whisk together the oil, lemon zest, lemon juice, garlic, capers (if using), parsley, and dill. Spoon about 1 tablespoon of the lemon-herb oil over each piece of fish, then use a brush to spread it. 4. Bake for 10 to 14 minutes, depending on the thickness of the fish, until the fish flakes easily with a fork.
Per Serving
Calories: 325 | fat: 17g | protein: 37g | carbs: 0g | net carbs: 0g | fiber: 0g

Basil Halibut Red Pepper Packets

Prep time: 10 minutes | Cook time: 20 minutes | Serves 4

2 cups cauliflower florets
1 cup roasted red pepper strips
½ cup sliced sun-dried tomatoes
4 (4 ounces/113 g) halibut fillets
¼ cup chopped fresh basil
Juice of 1 lemon
¼ cup good-quality olive oil
Sea salt, for seasoning
Freshly ground black pepper, for seasoning

1. Preheat the oven. Set the oven temperature to 400°F. Cut four (12-inch) square pieces of aluminum foil. Have a baking sheet ready. 2. Make the packets. Divide the cauliflower, red pepper strips, and sun-dried tomato between the four pieces of foil, placing the vegetables in the middle of each piece. Top each pile with 1 halibut fillet, and top each fillet with equal amounts of the basil, lemon juice, and olive oil. Fold and crimp the foil to form sealed packets of fish and vegetables and place them on the baking sheet. 3. Bake. Bake the packets for about 20 minutes, until the fish flakes with a fork. Be careful of the steam when you open the packet! 4. Serve. Transfer the vegetables and halibut to four plates, season with salt and pepper, and serve immediately.

Per Serving
Calories: 294 | fat: 18g | protein: 25g | carbs: 8g | net carbs: 5g | fiber: 3g

Salmon Cakes

Prep time: 10 minutes | Cook time: 15 minutes | Serves 4

1 (16 ounces/454 g) can pink salmon, drained and bones removed
¼ cup almond flour
¼ cup crushed pork rinds
2 scallions, diced
1 large egg
3 tablespoons mayonnaise
1 teaspoon garlic salt
1 teaspoon freshly ground black pepper
2 tablespoons extra-virgin olive oil

1. Line a plate with paper towels and set aside. 2. In a bowl, combine the salmon, almond flour, pork rinds, scallions, egg, mayonnaise, garlic salt, and pepper, and mix together well, using your hands or a spatula. 3. Form 8 small patties or 4 large patties. If the patties seem too dry, add a little more mayonnaise. If they seem too wet, add a little more almond flour or pork rinds. 4. In a skillet over medium heat, heat the oil. Cook the patties for 4 to 5 minutes on each side, until crispy. Larger patties may need to cook a little longer. 5. Transfer the patties to the lined plate to drain.

Per Serving 2 small patties
Calories: 313 | fat: 21g | protein: 26g | carbs: 5g | net carbs: 5g | fiber: 0g

Shrimp Ceviche Salad

Prep time: 15 minutes | Cook time: 0 minutes | Serves 4

1 pound (454 g) fresh shrimp, peeled and deveined
1 small red or yellow bell pepper, cut into ½-inch chunks
½ English cucumber, peeled and cut into ½-inch chunks
½ small red onion, cut into thin slivers
¼ cup chopped fresh cilantro or flat-leaf Italian parsley
⅓ cup freshly squeezed lime juice
2 tablespoons freshly squeezed lemon juice
2 tablespoons freshly squeezed clementine juice or orange juice
½ cup extra-virgin olive oil
1 teaspoon salt
½ teaspoon freshly ground black pepper
2 ripe avocados, peeled, pitted, and cut into ½-inch chunks

1. Cut the shrimp in half lengthwise. In a large glass bowl, combine the shrimp, bell pepper, cucumber, onion, and cilantro. 2. In a small bowl, whisk together the lime, lemon, and clementine juices, olive oil, salt, and pepper. Pour the mixture over the shrimp and veggies and toss to coat. Cover and refrigerate for at least 2 hours, or up to 8 hours. Give the mixture a toss every 30 minutes for the first 2 hours to make sure all the shrimp "cook" in the juices. 3. Add the cut avocado just before serving and toss to combine.

Per Serving
Calories: 520 | fat: 42g | protein: 26g | carbs: 14g | fiber: 8g | sodium: 593mg

Dilled Salmon in Creamy Sauce

Prep time: 5 minutes | Cook time: 8 minutes | Serves 2

2 salmon fillets
¾ teaspoon dried tarragon
2 tablespoons olive oil
¾ teaspoon dried dill
Sauce:
2 tablespoons butter
½ teaspoon dill
½ teaspoon tarragon
¼ cup heavy cream
Salt and black pepper to taste

1. Season the salmon with dill and tarragon. Warm the olive oil in a pan over medium heat. Add salmon and cook for about 4 minutes on both sides. Set aside. 2. **To Make the Sauce:** melt the butter and add the dill and tarragon. Cook for 30 seconds to infuse the flavors. Whisk in the heavy cream, season with salt and black pepper, and cook for 2-3 minutes. Serve the salmon topped with the sauce.

Per Serving
Calories: 391 | fat: 31g | protein: 26g | carbs: 2g | net carbs: 2g | fiber: 0g

Scallops & Mozza Broccoli Mash

Prep time: 5 minutes | Cook time: 35 minutes | Serves 4

Mozza Broccoli Mash:
¼ cup coconut oil or ghee, or ¼ cup avocado oil
6 cups broccoli florets
4 cloves garlic, minced
1 (2-in/5-cm) piece fresh ginger root, grated
⅔ cup chicken bone broth
½ cup shredded mozzarella cheese (dairy-free or

regular)
Scallops:
1 pound (455 g) sea scallops
¼ teaspoon finely ground sea salt
¼ teaspoon ground black pepper
2 tablespoons coconut oil, avocado oil, or ghee
Lemon wedges, for serving

1. **Prepare the Mash:** Heat the oil in a large frying pan over low heat. Add the broccoli, garlic, and ginger and cook, uncovered, for 5 minutes, or until the garlic is fragrant. 2. Pour in the broth, then cover and cook on low for 25 minutes, or until the broccoli is easily mashed. 3. About 5 minutes before the broccoli is ready, **prepare the scallops:** Pat the scallops dry and season them on both sides with the salt and pepper. Heat the oil in a medium-sized frying pan over medium heat. When the oil is hot, add the scallops. Cook for 2 minutes per side, or until lightly golden. 4. When the broccoli is done, add the cheese and mash with a fork. Divide the mash among 4 dinner plates and top with the scallops. Serve with lemon wedges and enjoy!

Per Serving
Calories: 353 | fat: 25g | protein: 19g | carbs: 12g | net carbs: 5g | fiber: 7g

Seared Scallops with Chorizo and Asiago Cheese

Prep time: 10 minutes | Cook time: 15 minutes | Serves 4

2 tablespoons ghee
16 fresh scallops
8 ounces (227 g) chorizo, chopped
1 red bell pepper, seeds

removed, sliced
1 cup red onions, finely chopped
1 cup asiago cheese, grated
Salt and black pepper to taste

1. Melt half of the ghee in a skillet over medium heat, and cook the onion and bell pepper for 5 minutes until tender. Add the chorizo and stir-fry for another 3 minutes. Remove and set aside. 2. Pat dry the scallops with paper towels, and season with salt and pepper. Add the remaining ghee to the skillet and sear the scallops for 2 minutes on each side to have a golden brown color. Add the chorizo mixture back and warm through. Transfer to serving platter and top with asiago cheese.

Per Serving
Calories: 496 | fat: 38g | protein: 30g | carbs: 8g | net carbs: 7g | fiber: 1g

Herb Butter Scallops

Prep time: 10 minutes | Cook time: 10 minutes | Serves 4

1 pound (454 g) sea scallops, cleaned
Freshly ground black pepper
8 tablespoons butter, divided
2 teaspoons minced garlic

Juice of 1 lemon
2 teaspoons chopped fresh basil
1 teaspoon chopped fresh thyme

1. Pat the scallops dry with paper towels and season them lightly with pepper. 2. Place a large skillet over medium heat and add 2 tablespoons of butter. 3. Arrange the scallops in the skillet, evenly spaced but not too close together, and sear each side until they are golden brown, about 2½ minutes per side. 4. Remove the scallops to a plate and set aside. 5. Add the remaining 6 tablespoons of butter to the skillet and sauté the garlic until translucent, about 3 minutes. 6. Stir in the lemon juice, basil, and thyme and return the scallops to the skillet, turning to coat them in the sauce. 7. Serve immediately.

Per Serving
Calories: 306 | fat: 24g | protein: 19g | carbs: 4g | net carbs: 4g | fiber: 0g

Coconut Curry Mussels

Prep time: 15 minutes | Cook time: 12 minutes | Serves 6

3 pounds (1.2 kg) mussels, cleaned, de-bearded
1 cup minced shallots
3 tablespoons minced garlic
1½ cups coconut milk

2 cups dry white wine
2 teaspoons red curry powder
⅓ cup coconut oil
⅓ cup chopped green onions
⅓ cup chopped parsley

1. Pour the wine into a large saucepan and cook the shallots and garlic over low heat. Stir in the coconut milk and red curry powder and cook for 3 minutes. 2. Add the mussels and steam for 7 minutes or until their shells are opened. Then, use a slotted spoon to remove to a bowl leaving the sauce in the pan. Discard any closed mussels at this point. 3. Stir the coconut oil into the sauce, turn the heat off, and stir in the parsley and green onions. Serve the sauce immediately with a butternut squash mash.

Per Serving
Calories: 275 | fat: 19g | protein: 23g | carbs: 3g | net carbs: 2g | fiber: 1g

Tuna Slow-Cooked in Olive Oil

Prep time: 5 minutes | Cook time: 45 minutes | Serves 4

1 cup extra-virgin olive oil, plus more if needed	sliced
4 (3- to 4-inch) sprigs fresh rosemary	2 (2-inch) strips lemon zest
8 (3- to 4-inch) sprigs fresh thyme	1 teaspoon salt
2 large garlic cloves, thinly	½ teaspoon freshly ground black pepper
	1 pound (454 g) fresh tuna steaks (about 1 inch thick)

1. Select a thick pot just large enough to fit the tuna in a single layer on the bottom. The larger the pot, the more olive oil you will need to use. Combine the olive oil, rosemary, thyme, garlic, lemon zest, salt, and pepper over medium-low heat and cook until warm and fragrant, 20 to 25 minutes, lowering the heat if it begins to smoke. 2. Remove from the heat and allow to cool for 25 to 30 minutes, until warm but not hot. 3. Add the tuna to the bottom of the pan, adding additional oil if needed so that tuna is fully submerged, and return to medium-low heat. Cook for 5 to 10 minutes, or until the oil heats back up and is warm and fragrant but not smoking. Lower the heat if it gets too hot. 4. Remove the pot from the heat and let the tuna cook in warm oil 4 to 5 minutes, to your desired level of doneness. For a tuna that is rare in the center, cook for 2 to 3 minutes. 5. Remove from the oil and serve warm, drizzling 2 to 3 tablespoons seasoned oil over the tuna. 6. To store for later use, remove the tuna from the oil and place in a container with a lid. Allow tuna and oil to cool separately. When both have cooled, remove the herb stems with a slotted spoon and pour the cooking oil over the tuna. Cover and store in the refrigerator for up to 1 week. Bring to room temperature to allow the oil to liquify before serving.

Per Serving
Calories: 606 | fat: 55g | protein: 28g | carbs: 1g | fiber: 0g | sodium: 631mg

Sole Meunière

Prep time: 5 minutes | Cook time: 10 minutes | Serves 2

½ cup almond flour	divided
4 (6 ounces/170 g) sole fillets	Juice of ½ lemon
Salt, to taste	2 tablespoons minced fresh parsley leaves
Freshly ground black pepper, to taste	4 lemon wedges (from the other half of the lemon), for serving
6 tablespoons butter,	

1. Put the almond flour into a shallow dish. 2. Pat the fish dry with a paper towel and coat each side with almond flour. Season with salt and pepper. 3. In a large skillet over medium heat, melt 3 tablespoons of butter. 4. Add the fish to the skillet and cook for 2 to 3 minutes per side or until the fish is completely opaque. Transfer the fish to a serving platter. 5. Return the skillet to the heat and add the remaining 3 tablespoons of butter and the lemon juice. When melted, pour it over the fish, garnish with the parsley, and serve with the lemon wedges. Refrigerate leftovers in an airtight container for up to 4 days.

Per Serving
Calories: 624 | fat: 40g | protein: 65g | carbs: 2g | net carbs: 2g | fiber: 0g

Cod Cakes

Prep time: 5 minutes | Cook time: 20 minutes | Serves 2

2 tablespoons plus 1 teaspoon extra-virgin olive oil, divided	2 tablespoons ground flaxseed
¼ medium onion, chopped	1 tablespoon freshly squeezed lemon juice
1 garlic clove, minced	1 teaspoon dried dill
1 cup cauliflower rice, fresh or thawed frozen	½ teaspoon ground cumin
1 pound (454 g) cod fillets	½ teaspoon pink Himalayan sea salt
½ cup almond flour	¼ teaspoon freshly ground black pepper
1 large egg	Tartar sauce
2 tablespoons chopped fresh parsley	

1. In a medium sauté pan or skillet, heat 1 tablespoon of olive oil over medium heat. Add the onion and garlic and cook for about 7 minutes, until tender. 2. Add the cauliflower rice and continue to stir for 5 to 7 minutes, until warmed through and tender. Transfer to a large bowl. 3. In the same skillet, heat 1 teaspoon of olive oil over medium-high heat. Cook the cod for 4 to 5 minutes on each side, until cooked through. Let the cod cool for a couple of minutes. 4. Add the almond flour, egg, parsley, flaxseed, lemon juice, dill, cumin, salt, and pepper to the bowl with the cauliflower rice. Using your hands, mix until the ingredients are well combined. 5. Add the fish to the bowl and mix well. I like to use a fluffing motion to keep the fish in chunks, rather than smashing it all. 6. In the skillet, heat the remaining 1 tablespoon of olive oil over medium heat. 7. Using a ½ cup measuring cup, form the fish cakes by packing the mixture into the cup, then slipping the cake out of the cup onto a plate. You should be able to shape 4 cakes. 8. Place the fish cakes in the hot oil and cook for about 5 minutes per side, flipping once, until golden brown on both sides. 9. Place the cod cakes on serving plates, and serve with tartar sauce.

Per Serving
Calories: 531 | fat: 34g | protein: 45g | carbs: 12g | net carbs: 6g | fiber: 6g

Tuna Salad Wrap

Prep time: 5 minutes | Cook time: 0 minutes | Serves 2

2 (5 ounces/142 g) cans tuna packed in olive oil, drained
3 tablespoons mayonnaise
1 tablespoon chopped red onion
2 teaspoons dill relish
¼ teaspoon pink Himalayan sea salt
¼ teaspoon freshly ground black pepper
Pinch of dried or fresh dill
2 low-carb tortillas
2 romaine lettuce leaves
¼ cup grated Cheddar cheese

1. In a medium bowl, combine the tuna, mayonnaise, onion, relish, salt, pepper, and dill. 2. Place a lettuce leaf on each tortilla, then split the tuna mixture evenly between the wraps, spreading it evenly over the lettuce. 3. Sprinkle the Cheddar on top of each, then fold the tortillas and serve.

Per Serving
Calories: 549 | fat: 33g | protein: 42g | carbs: 21g | net carbs: 5g | fiber: 16g

Souvlaki Spiced Salmon Bowls

Prep time: 10 minutes | Cook time: 20 minutes | Serves 4

For the Salmon:
¼ cup good-quality olive oil
Juice of 1 lemon
2 tablespoons chopped fresh oregano
1 tablespoon minced garlic
1 tablespoon balsamic vinegar
1 tablespoon smoked sweet paprika
½ teaspoon sea salt
¼ teaspoon freshly ground black pepper
4 (4 ounces/113 g) salmon fillets

For the Bowls:
2 tablespoons good-quality olive oil
1 red bell pepper, cut into strips
1 yellow bell pepper, cut into strips
1 zucchini, cut into ½-inch strips lengthwise
1 cucumber, diced
1 large tomato, chopped
½ cup sliced Kalamata olives
6 ounces (170 g) feta cheese, crumbled
½ cup sour cream

To Make the Salmon: 1. Marinate the fish. In a medium bowl, stir together the olive oil, lemon juice, oregano, garlic, vinegar, paprika, salt, and pepper. Add the salmon and turn to coat it well with the marinade. Cover the bowl and let the salmon sit marinating for 15 to 20 minutes. 2. Grill the fish. Preheat the grill to medium-high heat and grill the fish until just cooked through, 4 to 5 minutes per side. Set the fish aside on a plate. **To Make the Bowls:** 1. Grill the vegetables. In a medium bowl, toss together the oil, red and yellow bell peppers, and zucchini. Grill the vegetables, turning once, until they're lightly charred and soft, about 3 minutes per side. 2. Assemble and serve. Divide the grilled vegetables between four bowls. Top each bowl with cucumber, tomato, olives, feta cheese, and the sour cream. Place one salmon fillet on top of each bowl and serve immediately.

Per Serving
Calories: 553 | fat: 44g | protein: 30g | carbs: 10g | net carbs: 7g | fiber: 3g

Nut-Crusted Baked Fish

Prep time: 10 minutes | Cook time: 20 minutes | Serves 4

½ cup extra-virgin olive oil, divided
1 pound (454 g) flaky white fish (such as cod, haddock, or halibut), skin removed
½ cup shelled finely chopped pistachios
½ cup ground flaxseed
Zest and juice of 1 lemon, divided
1 teaspoon ground cumin
1 teaspoon ground allspice
½ teaspoon salt (use 1 teaspoon if pistachios are unsalted)
¼ teaspoon freshly ground black pepper

1. Preheat the oven to 400°F(205°C). 2. Line a baking sheet with parchment paper or aluminum foil and drizzle 2 tablespoons olive oil over the sheet, spreading to evenly coat the bottom. 3. Cut the fish into 4 equal pieces and place on the prepared baking sheet. 4. In a small bowl, combine the pistachios, flaxseed, lemon zest, cumin, allspice, salt, and pepper. Drizzle in ¼ cup olive oil and stir well. 5. Divide the nut mixture evenly atop the fish pieces. Drizzle the lemon juice and remaining 2 tablespoons oil over the fish and bake until cooked through, 15 to 20 minutes, depending on the thickness of the fish.

Per Serving
Calories: 499 | fat: 41g | protein: 26g | carbs: 41g | fiber: 6g | sodium: 358mg

Oven-Baked Dijon Salmon

Prep time: 5 minutes | Cook time: 10 minutes | Serves 4

4 (6 ounces/170 g) salmon fillets
2 tablespoons olive oil
Salt, to taste
Freshly ground black pepper, to taste
¼ cup grainy Dijon mustard

1. Preheat the oven to 450°F (235°C). 2. Drizzle the fillets with the olive oil and season with salt and pepper. Brush the mustard over each piece of fish and place on a baking sheet. Bake for 10 to 12 minutes or until the salmon is opaque and flakes easily with a fork. (Cook a few minutes longer if you prefer it cooked more than medium.)

Per Serving
Calories: 370 | fat: 25g | protein: 34g | carbs: 1g | net carbs: 0g | fiber: 1g

Shrimp in Curry Sauce

Prep time: 10 minutes | Cook time: 5 minutes | Serves 2

½ ounce (14 g) grated
Parmesan cheese
1 egg, beaten
¼ teaspoon curry powder
2 teaspoons almond flour
12 shrimp, shelled
3 tablespoons coconut oil

Sauce:
2 tablespoons curry leaves
2 tablespoons butter
½ onion, diced
½ cup heavy cream
½ ounce (14 g) cheddar
cheese, shredded

1. Combine all dry ingredients for the batter. Melt the coconut oil in a skillet over medium heat. Dip the shrimp in the egg first, and then coat with the dry mixture. Fry until golden and crispy. 2. In another skillet, melt butter. Add onion and cook for 3 minutes. Add curry leaves and cook for 30 seconds. Stir in heavy cream and cheddar and cook until thickened. Add shrimp and coat well. Serve.

Per Serving
Calories: 570 | fat: 52g | protein: 20g | carbs: 10g | net carbs: 5g | fiber: 5g

One-Pot Shrimp Alfredo and Zoodles

Prep time: 10 minutes | Cook time: 25 minutes | Serves 5

Zoodles:
3 medium zucchini (about
21 ounces/595 g)
1 teaspoon sea salt
Shrimp and Sauce:
2 tablespoons butter or ghee
3 garlic cloves, minced
1 pound (454 g) shrimp,
peeled and deveined
4 ounces (113 g) cream

cheese, at room temperature
½ cup heavy (whipping)
cream
½ teaspoon sea salt
¼ teaspoon freshly ground
black pepper
1 cup freshly grated
Parmesan cheese
¼ teaspoon cayenne pepper
(optional)

Make the Zoodles: 1. Trim off the ends of the zucchini. Using a vegetable spiral slicer, swirl the zucchini into noodle shapes (zoodles). 2. Lay the zoodles on a kitchen towel and sprinkle with the salt. Let sit while you prepare the Alfredo sauce. 3. While the sauce is simmering, fold the zoodles up in the towel and squeeze out as much water as you can. **Make the Shrimp and Sauce:** 4. In a large pot, melt the butter over medium heat. Add the garlic and cook for 3 minutes until fragrant. Add the shrimp and cook for 4 to 6 minutes, just until the shrimp start to turn pink. Remove the shrimp to a plate. 5. Add the cream cheese to the pot and whisk until melted. Pour in the cream slowly, whisking constantly. Add the salt and pepper. Let the sauce simmer for 5 to 10 minutes, whisking often, until thickened. 6. Remove the pot from the heat and stir in the

Parmesan and cayenne (if using). Taste and adjust the salt and pepper to your liking. 7. Add the zoodles, cover, and cook for 5 minutes. The zoodles will release a bit of water, which will thin out the thick sauce a bit. 8. Add the shrimp and toss before serving.

Per Serving
Calories: 329 | fat: 25g | protein: 20g | carbs: 6g | net carbs: 5g | fiber: 1g

Halibut Curry

Prep time: 5 minutes | Cook time: 35 minutes | Serves 4

1 tablespoon avocado oil
½ cup finely chopped celery
½ cup frozen butternut
squash cubes
1 cup full-fat coconut milk
½ cup seafood stock
1½ tablespoons curry
powder
1 tablespoon dried cilantro

½ tablespoon garlic powder
½ tablespoon ground
turmeric
1 teaspoon ground ginger
1 pound (454 g) skinless
halibut fillet, cut into chunks
Cooked cauliflower rice, for
serving (optional)

1. In a large pot with a lid, heat the avocado oil over medium-high heat. Add the celery and cook for about 3 minutes. Add the squash and cook for 5 minutes more. 2. Pour in the coconut milk and seafood stock and cook, stirring, for another 3 minutes. Stir in the curry powder, cilantro, garlic, turmeric, and ginger. 3. Add the halibut to the pot and stir into the rest of the mixture. Reduce the heat to medium, cover the pot, and cook for 15 to 20 minutes, or until the fish is completely white and flakes easily with a fork. 4. Serve the halibut curry over cauliflower rice if you'd like, or just eat it by itself!

Per Serving
Calories: 362 | fat: 22g | protein: 33g | carbs: 8g | net carbs: 5g | fiber: 3g

Coconut Crab Patties

Prep time: 5 minutes | Cook time: 6 minutes | Serves 8

2 tablespoons coconut oil
1 tablespoon lemon juice
1 cup lump crab meat

2 teaspoons Dijon mustard
1 egg, beaten
1½ tablespoons coconut flour

1. In a bowl to the crabmeat, add all the ingredients, except for the oil; mix well to combine. Make patties out of the mixture. Melt the coconut oil in a skillet over medium heat. Add the crab patties and cook for about 2-3 minutes per side.

Per Serving
Calories: 209 | fat: 13g | protein: 17g | carbs: 6g | net carbs: 4g | fiber: 2g

Salmon Panzanella

Prep time: 15 minutes | Cook time: 8 minutes | Serves 4

1 pound (454 g) skinned salmon, cut into 4 steaks each
1 cucumber, peeled, seeded, cubed
Salt and black pepper to taste
8 black olives, pitted and chopped
1 tablespoon capers, rinsed

2 large tomatoes, diced
3 tablespoons red wine vinegar
¼ cup thinly sliced red onion
3 tablespoons olive oil
2 slices zero carb bread, cubed
¼ cup thinly sliced basil leaves

1. Preheat a grill to 350ºF and prepare the salad. In a bowl, mix the cucumbers, olives, pepper, capers, tomatoes, wine vinegar, onion, olive oil, bread, and basil leaves. Let sit for the flavors to incorporate. 2. Season the salmon steaks with salt and pepper; grill them on both sides for 8 minutes in total. Serve the salmon steaks warm on a bed of the veggies' salad.
Per Serving
Calories: 335 | fat: 20g | protein: 26g | carbs: 13g | net carbs: 11g | fiber: 2g

Pork Rind Salmon Cakes

Prep time: 10 minutes | Cook time: 10 minutes | Serves 2

6 ounces (170 g) canned Alaska wild salmon, drained
2 tablespoons crushed pork rinds
1 egg, lightly beaten
3 tablespoons mayonnaise,

divided
Pink Himalayan salt
Freshly ground black pepper
1 tablespoon ghee
½ tablespoon Dijon mustard

1. In a medium bowl, mix to combine the salmon, pork rinds, egg, and 1½ tablespoons of mayonnaise, and season with pink Himalayan salt and pepper. 2. With the salmon mixture, form patties the size of hockey pucks or smaller. Keep patting the patties until they keep together. 3. In a medium skillet over medium-high heat, melt the ghee. When the ghee sizzles, place the salmon patties in the pan. Cook for about 3 minutes per side, until browned. Transfer the patties to a paper towel–lined plate. 4. In a small bowl, mix together the remaining 1½ tablespoons of mayonnaise and the mustard. 5. Serve the salmon cakes with the mayo-mustard dipping sauce.
Per Serving
Calories: 362 | fat: 31g | protein: 24g | carbs: 1g | net carbs: 1g | fiber: 0g

Baked Lemon-Butter Fish

Prep time: 10 minutes | Cook time: 20 minutes | Serves 2

4 tablespoons butter, plus more for coating
2 (5 ounces/142 g) tilapia fillets
Pink Himalayan salt

Freshly ground black pepper
2 garlic cloves, minced
1 lemon, zested and juiced
2 tablespoons capers, rinsed and chopped

1. Preheat the oven to 400°F. Coat an 8-inch baking dish with butter. 2. Pat dry the tilapia with paper towels, and season on both sides with pink Himalayan salt and pepper. Place in the prepared baking dish. 3. In a medium skillet over medium heat, melt the butter. Add the garlic and cook for 3 to 5 minutes, until slightly browned but not burned. 4. Remove the garlic butter from the heat, and mix in the lemon zest and 2 tablespoons of lemon juice. 5. Pour the lemon-butter sauce over the fish, and sprinkle the capers around the baking pan. 6. Bake for 12 to 15 minutes, until the fish is just cooked through, and serve.
Per Serving
Calories: 299 | fat: 26g | protein: 16g | carbs: 5g | net carbs: 3g | fiber: 1g

Crispy Fried Cod

Prep time: 15 minutes | Cook time: 15 minutes | Serves 4

1 cup crushed pork rinds
¼ cup grated Parmesan cheese
½ cup heavy cream
1 large egg
4 (4 ounces/113 g) cod fillets, patted dry

Extra-virgin olive oil, for frying
1 (10 ounces/283 g) can original Ro-Tel (drained)
2 tablespoons lemon juice (optional)

1. In a small bowl, combine the pork rinds and grated Parmesan. 2. In another bowl, whisk together the heavy cream and egg. 3. Dip each cod fillet completely in the egg mixture, then dip on both sides into the pork rind mixture, making sure the entire fillet is covered. Place the fillets on a plate and refrigerate while the oil heats. 4. In a heavy skillet over medium heat, heat 2 to 3 inches of oil. 5. Heat the oil to 365°F (185°C). (Dip a wooden spoon into the oil. If the oil steadily bubbles around the wooden spoon, it's ready.) 6. Working in batches if necessary, fry each fillet for about 2 minutes on each side or until the outside is golden brown. 7. Drain on a paper towel if needed, then plate and serve, topping each fillet with one-quarter of the can of Ro-Tel.
Per Serving 1 fillet
Calories: 375 | fat: 28g | protein: 36g | carbs: 6g | net carbs: 6g | fiber: 0g

Low-Carb Lowcountry Seafood Boil

Prep time: 30 minutes | Cook time: 1 hour | Serves 8

4 gallons water
6 bay leaves
2 onions, quartered
2 lemons, halved
3 tablespoons salt
2½ tablespoons paprika
1½ tablespoons ground coriander
1 tablespoon ground allspice
1 tablespoon red pepper flakes
1 tablespoon chili powder
1 tablespoon dried marjoram
1 tablespoon onion powder
1 tablespoon garlic powder
1 tablespoon dry mustard

1 tablespoon dried tarragon
1 tablespoon dried thyme
1 tablespoon dried rosemary
2½ teaspoons peppercorns
1 teaspoon ground cumin
½ teaspoon ground cayenne pepper
2 pounds (907 g) Italian sausage, each link cut into thirds
1½ pounds (680 g) mussels
2½ pounds (1.1 kg) cod fillets
3½ pounds (1.6 kg) snow crab legs
1½ pounds (680 g) large raw shrimp, shells on

1. Fill a large stockpot over high heat about three-fourths full with the water. Bring to a boil. Add the bay leaves, onions, lemons, salt, paprika, coriander, allspice, red pepper flakes, chili powder, marjoram, onion powder, garlic powder, mustard, tarragon, thyme, rosemary, peppercorns, cumin, and cayenne. 2. In a large skillet over medium heat, cook the sausage for about 3 minutes per side, turning to brown all sides. They don't have to be fully cooked because they'll finish cooking in the stockpot. Remove from the heat and set aside. 3. Remove any excess fat from the skillet and place it back over medium heat. Add the mussels and 1 cup of seasoned water from the stockpot. Cover the skillet and steam the mussels for 5 to 7 minutes. Discard any that don't open. 4. Add the sausage to the stockpot, followed by the cod. Keep the water at a low boil and cook for 5 minutes. 5. Add the mussels and crab legs. Cook for 5 minutes more. 6. About 5 minutes before you're ready to serve, add the shrimp. Cook for 4 to 5 minutes until completely pink and opaque. 7. Carefully drain the contents of the stockpot and transfer everything to a large serving bowl. Serve immediately. Go traditional and pour the contents of the bowl onto a newspaper-lined table and dig in with your hands!
Per Serving
Calories: 805 | fat: 40g | protein: 96g | carbs: 7g | net carbs: 7g | fiber: 0g

Spicy Sea Bass with Hazelnuts

Prep time: 5 minutes | Cook time: 15 minutes | Serves 2

2 sea bass fillets
2 tablespoons butter

⅓ cup roasted hazelnuts
A pinch of cayenne pepper

1. Preheat your oven to 425ºF. Line a baking dish with waxed paper. Melt the butter and brush it over the fish. Process the cayenne pepper and hazelnuts in a food processor to achieve a smooth consistency. Coat the sea bass with the hazelnut mixture. Place in the oven and bake for about 15 minutes.
Per Serving
Calories: 403 | fat: 27g | protein: 37g | carbs: 3g | net carbs: 3g | fiber: 0g

Grilled Calamari

Prep time: 10 minutes | Cook time: 5 minutes | Serves 4

2 pounds (907 g) calamari tubes and tentacles, cleaned
½ cup good-quality olive oil
Zest and juice of 2 lemons
2 tablespoons chopped fresh

oregano
1 tablespoon minced garlic
¼ teaspoon sea salt
⅛ teaspoon freshly ground black pepper

1. Prepare the calamari. Score the top layer of the calamari tubes about 2 inches apart. 2. Marinate the calamari. In a large bowl, stir together the olive oil, lemon zest, lemon juice, oregano, garlic, salt, and pepper. Add the calamari and toss to coat it well, then place it in the refrigerator to marinate for at least 30 minutes and up to 1 hour. 3. Grill the calamari. Preheat a grill to high heat. Grill the calamari, turning once, for about 3 minutes total, until it's tender and lightly charred. 4. Serve. Divide the calamari between four plates and serve it hot.
Per Serving
Calories: 455 | fat: 30g | protein: 35g | carbs: 8g | net carbs: 7g | fiber: 1g

Cheesy Garlic Salmon ✗✗

Prep time: 10 minutes | Cook time: 12 minutes | Serves 4

½ cup Asiago cheese
2 tablespoons freshly squeezed lemon juice
2 tablespoons butter, at room temperature
2 teaspoons minced garlic
1 teaspoon chopped fresh

basil
1 teaspoon chopped fresh oregano
4 (5 ounces/142 g) salmon fillets
1 tablespoon olive oil

1. Preheat the oven to 350ºF. Line a baking sheet with parchment paper and set aside. 2. In a small bowl, stir together the Asiago cheese, lemon juice, butter, garlic, basil, and oregano. 3. Pat the salmon dry with paper towels and place the fillets on the baking sheet skin-side down. Divide the topping evenly between the fillets and spread it across the fish using a knife or the back of a spoon. 4. Drizzle the fish with the olive oil and bake until the topping is golden and the fish is just cooked through, about 12 minutes. 5. Serve.
Per Serving
Calories: 357 | fat: 28g | protein: 24g | carbs: 2g | net carbs: 2g | fiber: 0g

Pan-Seared Scallops with Lemon Butter

Prep time: 10 minutes | Cook time: 20 minutes | Serves 4

1 pound (454 g) scallops, rinsed under cold water and patted dry with a paper towel
Salt, to taste
Freshly ground black pepper, to taste
4 tablespoons butter, divided
1 lemon, halved
Zest of ½ lemon

1. Season the scallops on both sides with salt and pepper. 2. In a large nonstick skillet over medium-high heat, melt 2 tablespoons of butter. 3. Add the scallops. Cook for 5 to 7 minutes per side or until the scallops begin to get crispy. 4. Squeeze 1 lemon half over the scallops. Transfer the scallops to a serving platter. 5. Return the skillet to low heat. Add the remaining 2 tablespoons of butter. 6. Stir in the lemon zest and squeeze the remaining lemon half into the skillet. Stir continuously until the butter reduces slightly, 4 to 5 minutes. Pour the sauce over the scallops and serve immediately. Refrigerate leftovers in an airtight container for up to 2 days.
Per Serving
Calories: 200 | fat: 12g | protein: 19g | carbs: 3g | net carbs: 3g | fiber: 0g

Escabeche

Prep time: 10 minutes | Cook time: 20 minutes | Serves 4

1 pound (454 g) wild-caught Spanish mackerel fillets, cut into four pieces
1 teaspoon salt
½ teaspoon freshly ground black pepper
8 tablespoons extra-virgin olive oil, divided
1 bunch asparagus, trimmed
and cut into 2-inch pieces
1 (13¾ ounces/390 g) can artichoke hearts, drained and quartered
4 large garlic cloves, peeled and crushed
2 bay leaves
¼ cup red wine vinegar
½ teaspoon smoked paprika

1. Sprinkle the fillets with salt and pepper and let sit at room temperature for 5 minutes. 2. In a large skillet, heat 2 tablespoons olive oil over medium-high heat. Add the fish, skin-side up, and cook 5 minutes. Flip and cook 5 minutes on the other side, until browned and cooked through. Transfer to a serving dish, pour the cooking oil over the fish, and cover to keep warm. 3. Heat the remaining 6 tablespoons olive oil in the same skillet over medium heat. Add the asparagus, artichokes, garlic, and bay leaves and sauté until the vegetables are tender, 6 to 8 minutes. 4. Using a slotted spoon, top the fish with the cooked vegetables, reserving the oil in the skillet. Add the vinegar and paprika to the oil and whisk to combine well. Pour the vinaigrette over the fish and vegetables and let sit at room temperature for at least 15 minutes, or

marinate in the refrigerator up to 24 hours for a deeper flavor. Remove the bay leaf before serving.
Per Serving
Calories: 459 | fat: 34g | protein: 26g | carbs: 13g | fiber: 6g | sodium: 597mg

Creamy Dill Salmon

Prep time: 10 minutes | Cook time: 10 minutes | Serves 2

2 tablespoons ghee, melted
2 (6 ounces/170 g) salmon fillets, skin on
Pink Himalayan salt
Freshly ground black pepper
¼ cup mayonnaise
1 tablespoon Dijon mustard
2 tablespoons minced fresh dill
Pinch garlic powder

1. Preheat the oven to 450°F. Coat a 9-by-13-inch baking dish with the ghee. 2. Pat dry the salmon with paper towels, season on both sides with pink Himalayan salt and pepper, and place in the prepared baking dish. 3. In a small bowl, mix to combine the mayonnaise, mustard, dill, and garlic powder. 4. Slather the mayonnaise sauce on top of both salmon fillets so that it fully covers the tops. 5. Bake for 7 to 9 minutes, depending on how you like your salmon—7 minutes for medium-rare and 9 minutes for well-done—and serve.
Per Serving
Calories: 510 | fat: 41g | protein: 33g | carbs: 3g | net carbs: 2g | fiber: 1g

Herbed Coconut Milk Steamed Mussels

Prep time: 10 minutes | Cook time: 15 minutes | Serves 4

2 tablespoons coconut oil
½ sweet onion, chopped
2 teaspoons minced garlic
1 teaspoon grated fresh ginger
½ teaspoon turmeric
1 cup coconut milk
Juice of 1 lime
1½ pounds (680 g) fresh mussels, scrubbed and debearded
1 scallion, finely chopped
2 tablespoons chopped fresh cilantro
1 tablespoon chopped fresh thyme

1. Sauté the aromatics. In a large skillet, warm the coconut oil. Add the onion, garlic, ginger, and turmeric and sauté until they've softened, about 3 minutes. 2. Add the liquid. Stir in the coconut milk and lime juice and bring the mixture to a boil. 3. Steam the mussels. Add the mussels to the skillet, cover, and steam until the shells are open, about 10 minutes. Take the skillet off the heat and throw out any unopened mussels. 4. Add the herbs. Stir in the scallion, cilantro, and thyme. 5. Serve. Divide the mussels and the sauce between four bowls and serve them immediately.
Per Serving
Calories: 319 | fat: 23g | protein: 23g | carbs: 8g | net carbs: 6g | fiber: 2g

Shrimp Fry

Prep time: 5 minutes | Cook time: 20 minutes | Serves 4

¼ cup coconut oil
1 pound (455 g) medium shrimp, peeled, deveined, and tails removed
12 ounces (340 g) smoked sausage (chicken, pork, beef—anything goes), cubed
5 asparagus spears, woody ends snapped off, thinly sliced
4 ounces (113 g) cremini mushrooms, sliced
1 medium zucchini, cubed

1 tablespoon paprika
2 teaspoons garlic powder
1 teaspoon onion powder
1 teaspoon dried thyme leaves
½ teaspoon finely ground sea salt
¼ teaspoon ground black pepper
Pinch of cayenne pepper (optional)
Handful of fresh parsley leaves, chopped, for serving

1. Melt the oil in a large frying pan over medium heat.
2. Add the remaining ingredients, except the parsley. Toss to coat in the oil, then cover and cook for 15 to 20 minutes, until the asparagus is tender and the shrimp has turned pink. 3. Divide the mixture among 4 serving plates, sprinkle with parsley, and serve.

Per Serving
Calories: 574 | fat: 40g | protein: 45g | carbs: 8g | net carbs: 6g | fiber: 2g

Creamy Shrimp and Bacon Skillet

Prep time: 5 minutes | Cook time: 20 minutes | Serves 4

10 ounces (283 g) thick-cut bacon, diced
½ onion, diced
2 garlic cloves, minced
1 pound (454 g) shrimp, peeled, deveined, tails removed
Salt, to taste

Freshly ground black pepper, to taste
4 ounces (113 g) cream cheese
Dash chicken broth (optional)
¼ cup grated Parmesan cheese

1. Preheat the broiler. 2. In a large ovenproof skillet over medium-high heat, cook the bacon in its own fat for about 5 minutes until it starts to get crispy. 3. Add the onion and garlic. Sauté for 5 to 7 minutes until the onion is softened and translucent. 4. Add the shrimp. Season with salt and pepper. Cook for 2 to 3 minutes, stirring, or until the shrimp start to turn pink. 5. Add the cream cheese and stir well to combine as it melts. If necessary, add a splash of chicken broth to thin it out. 6. Top with the Parmesan and transfer the skillet to the oven. Broil for 4 to 5 minutes until the Parmesan is lightly browned. Refrigerate leftovers in an airtight container for up to 5 days.

Per Serving
Calories: 574 | fat: 45g | protein: 36g | carbs: 5g | net carbs: 5g | fiber: 0g

Muffin Top Tuna Pops

Prep time: 10 minutes | Cook time: 25 minutes | Serves 6

1 (5 ounces/142 g) can tuna in water, drained
2 large eggs
¾ cup shredded Cheddar cheese
¾ cup shredded pepper jack cheese
¼ cup full-fat sour cream

¼ cup full-fat mayonnaise
¼ cup chopped yellow onion
1 tablespoon dried parsley
¼ teaspoon salt
18 pieces sliced jalapeño from jar
2 tablespoons unsalted butter

1. Preheat oven to 350°F. Grease six cups of a muffin tin. 2. Combine all ingredients except the jalapeño slices and butter in a medium mixing bowl. 3. Evenly fill six muffin cups with the mixture, topping each with three jalapeño slices. 4. Bake 25 minutes. Serve warm with butter.

Per Serving
Calories: 275 | fat: 22g | protein: 14g | carbs: 1g | net carbs: 1g | fiber: 0g

Shrimp Alfredo

Prep time: 10 minutes | Cook time: 10 minutes | Serves 2

2 tablespoons butter
2 tablespoons olive oil, divided
1 garlic clove, minced
1 cup heavy (whipping) cream
¾ cup grated Parmesan

cheese
Salt, to taste
Freshly ground black pepper, to taste
1 pound (454 g) shrimp, shells and tails removed, deveined

1. In a small saucepan over medium-low heat, melt together the butter and 1 tablespoon of olive oil. 2. Stir in the garlic and cream. Bring to a low simmer and cook for 5 to 7 minutes until thickened. 3. Slowly add the Parmesan, stirring well to mix as it melts. Continue to stir until smooth. Season with salt and pepper. Set aside. 4. In a skillet over medium heat, heat the remaining 1 tablespoon of olive oil. 5. Add the shrimp and sauté for about 3 minutes per side or until they turn pink. Remove from the heat and toss with the Alfredo sauce. Serve immediately. Refrigerate leftovers in an airtight container for up to 5 days.

Per Serving
Calories: 1034 | fat: 84g | protein: 63g | carbs: 7g | net carbs: 7g | fiber: 0g

Shrimp Scampi with Zucchini Noodles

Prep time: 5 minutes | Cook time: 10 minutes | Serves 4

½ cup extra-virgin olive oil, divided
1 pound (454 g) shrimp, peeled and deveined
1 teaspoon salt
¼ teaspoon freshly ground black pepper
2 tablespoons unsalted butter
6 garlic cloves, minced
2 tablespoons dry white wine or chicken broth
½ teaspoon red pepper flakes
Zest and juice of 1 lemon
¼ cup chopped fresh Italian parsley
4 cups spiralized zucchini noodles (about 2 medium zucchini)

1. In a large skillet, heat ¼ cup of olive oil over medium-high heat. Add the shrimp, sprinkle with salt and pepper, and sauté for 2 to 3 minutes, or until the shrimp is just pink. Using a slotted spoon, transfer the shrimp to a bowl and cover to keep warm. 2. Reduce heat to low and add the remaining ¼ cup of olive oil, butter, and garlic. Cook the garlic, stirring frequently, until very fragrant, 3 to 4 minutes. 3. Whisk in the wine, red pepper flakes, and lemon zest and juice. Increase the heat to medium-high and bring to a simmer. Remove the skillet from the heat as soon as the liquid simmers. Return the shrimp to the skillet, add the parsley, and toss. 4. To serve, place the raw zucchini noodles in a large bowl. Add the shrimp and sauce and toss to coat.
Per Serving
Calories: 414 | fat: 34g | protein: 25g | carbs: 5g | net carbs: 3g | fiber: 2g

Salmon Poke

Prep time: 5 minutes | Cook time: 0 minutes | Serves 2

½ pound (227 g) sushi-grade salmon, chopped into ½-inch cubes
¼ small red onion, finely chopped
1 tablespoon dried chives
½ tablespoon capers
1 tablespoon dried basil
1 teaspoon Dijon mustard
½ teaspoon olive oil
Juice of ½ small lemon
Salt and freshly ground black pepper, to taste
1 cucumber, sliced into rounds, for serving (optional)

1. Put the salmon, red onion, and chives in a mixing bowl. Add the capers, basil, mustard, olive oil, and lemon juice and season with salt and pepper. Mix the contents of the bowl together until everything is evenly coated. 2. If desired, spoon the poke onto cucumber rounds (enough to cover the cucumber slice, but not so much that it's falling off). You can certainly eat this poke by itself, too, though.

Per Serving
Calories: 177 | fat: 9g | protein: 23g | carbs: 1g | net carbs: 1g | fiber: 0g

Sour Cream Salmon with Parmesan

Prep time: 10 minutes | Cook time: 17 minutes | Serves 4

1 cup sour cream
½ tablespoon minced dill
½ lemon, zested and juiced
Pink salt and black pepper to
season
4 salmon steaks
½ cup grated Parmesan cheese

1. Preheat oven to 400°F and line a baking sheet with parchment paper; set aside. In a bowl, mix the sour cream, dill, lemon zest, juice, salt and black pepper, and set aside. 2. Season the fish with salt and black pepper, drizzle lemon juice on both sides of the fish and arrange them in the baking sheet. Spread the sour cream mixture on each fish and sprinkle with Parmesan. 3. Bake the fish for 15 minutes and after broil the top for 2 minutes with a close watch for a nice a brown color. Plate the fish and serve with buttery green beans.
Per Serving
Calories: 289 | fat: 14g | protein: 31g | carbs: 8g | net carbs: 7g | fiber: 1g

Swordfish in Tarragon-Citrus Butter

Prep time: 5 minutes | Cook time: 20 minutes | Serves 4

1 pound (454 g) swordfish steaks, cut into 2-inch pieces
1 teaspoon salt
¼ teaspoon freshly ground black pepper
¼ cup extra-virgin olive oil, plus 2 tablespoons, divided
2 tablespoons unsalted
butter
Zest and juice of 2 clementines
Zest and juice of 1 lemon
2 tablespoons chopped fresh tarragon
Sautéed greens, riced cauliflower, or zucchini noodles, for serving

1. In a bowl, toss the swordfish with salt and pepper. 2. In a large skillet, heat ¼ cup olive oil over medium-high heat. Add the swordfish chunks to the hot oil and sear on all sides, 2 to 3 minutes per side, until they are lightly golden brown. Using a slotted spoon, remove the fish from the pan and keep warm. 3. Add the remaining 2 tablespoons olive oil and butter to the oil already in the pan and return the heat to medium-low. Once the butter has melted, whisk in the clementine and lemon zests and juices, along with the tarragon. Season with salt. Return the fish pieces to the pan and toss to coat in the butter sauce. Serve the fish drizzled with sauce over sautéed greens, riced cauliflower, or zucchini noodles.
Per Serving
Calories: 330 | fat: 26g | protein: 23g | carbs: 1g | fiber: 0g | sodium: 585mg

Cod in Garlic Butter Sauce

Prep time: 5 minutes | Cook time: 12 minutes | Serves 6

2 teaspoons olive oil
6 Alaska cod fillets
Salt and black pepper to taste
4 tablespoons salted butter
4 cloves garlic, minced
⅓ cup lemon juice
3 tablespoons white wine
2 tablespoons chopped chives

1. Heat the oil in a skillet over medium heat and season the cod with salt and black pepper. Fry the fillets in the oil for 4 minutes on one side, flip and cook for 1 minute. Take out, plate, and set aside. 2. In another skillet over low heat, melt the butter and sauté the garlic for 3 minutes. Add the lemon juice, wine, and chives. Season with salt, black pepper, and cook for 3 minutes until the wine slightly reduces. Put the fish in the skillet, spoon sauce over, cook for 30 seconds and turn the heat off. 3. Divide fish into 6 plates, top with sauce, and serve with buttered green beans.

Per Serving
Calories: 145 | fat: 7g | protein: 18g | carbs: 2g | net carbs: 2g | fiber: 1g

Parmesan Wings with Yogurt Sauce

Prep time: 5 minutes | Cook time: 20 minutes | Serves 6

For the Dipping Sauce:	wings
1 cup plain yogurt	Salt and black pepper to taste
1 teaspoon fresh lemon juice	Cooking spray
Salt and black pepper to taste	½ cup melted butter
	½ cup Hot sauce
For the Wings:	¼ cup grated Parmesan cheese
2 pounds (907 g) chicken	

1. Mix the yogurt, lemon juice, salt, and black pepper in a bowl. Chill while making the chicken. 2. Preheat oven to 400°F and season wings with salt and black pepper. Line them on a baking sheet and grease lightly with cooking spray. Bake for 20 minutes until golden brown. Mix butter, hot sauce, and Parmesan cheese in a bowl. Toss chicken in the sauce to evenly coat and plate. Serve with yogurt dipping sauce and celery strips.

Per Serving
Calories: 435 | fat: 31g | protein: 33g | carbs: 6g | net carbs: 4g | fiber: 2g

Cream of Mushroom–Stuffed Chicken

Prep time: 10 minutes | Cook time: 45 minutes | Serves 4

3 tablespoons coconut oil, avocado oil, or ghee	¼ teaspoon ground black pepper
7 ounces (198 g) cremini mushrooms, chopped	1 pound (454 g) boneless, skin-on chicken breasts
4 cloves garlic, minced	1 teaspoon onion powder
3 teaspoons dried parsley, divided	1 teaspoon garlic powder
¾ teaspoon finely ground sea salt, divided	½ cup milk (nondairy or regular)
	4 cups spinach, for serving

1. Preheat the oven to 400°F (205°C). Line a rimmed baking sheet with parchment paper or a silicone baking mat. 2. Heat the oil in a large frying pan over medium heat. Add the mushrooms, garlic, 2 teaspoons of the parsley, ¼ teaspoon of the salt, and the pepper. Toss to coat and sauté for 10 minutes. 3. Meanwhile, slice each chicken breast horizontally, stopping the knife about ½ inch (1.25 cm) from the opposite side, so that it opens like a book; be careful not to slice the breasts all the way through. The best way to do this is to use a sharp knife and place your palm on the top of the breast to hold it steady. 4. Place the chicken breasts on the lined baking sheet and open them up. Place one-quarter of the mushroom mixture in the middle of each opened breast. If there is leftover mushroom mixture, simply drop it into the pan, around the chicken. 5. Fold over the chicken breasts to cover the filling. Dust the stuffed breasts with the garlic powder, onion powder, remaining 1 teaspoon of parsley, and remaining ½ teaspoon of salt. 6. Pour the milk between the chicken breasts, directly into the pan. 7. Bake for 30 to 35 minutes, until the internal temperature of the chicken reaches 165°F (74°C). 8. Divide the spinach among 4 dinner plates. Divide the stuffed chicken breasts among the plates, drizzle the spinach with the creamy pan juices, and enjoy! (**Note:** If you did not end up with one breast half per person in the package, cut the stuffed breasts into portions and divide them equally among the plates.)

Per Serving
Calories: 388 | fat: 24g | protein: 38g | carbs: 7g | net carbs: 4g | fiber: 2g

Thanksgiving Turkey

Prep time: 5 minutes | Cook time: 60 minutes | Serves 8

1 turkey breast (7 pounds/3.2 kg), giblets removed	2 teaspoons black pepper
	½ onion, quartered
4 tablespoons butter, softened	1 rib celery, cut into 3 or 4 pieces
2 teaspoons ground sage	1 cup chicken broth
2 teaspoons garlic powder	2 or 3 bay leaves
2 teaspoons salt	1 teaspoon xanthan gum

1. Pat the turkey dry with a paper towel. 2. In a small bowl, combine the butter with the sage, garlic powder, salt, and pepper. Rub the butter mixture all over the top of the bird. Place the onion and celery inside the cavity. 3. Place the trivet in the pot. Add the broth and bay leaves to the pot. 4. Place the turkey on the trivet. If you need to remove the trivet to make the turkey fit, you can. The turkey will be near the top of the pot, which is fine. 5. Close the lid and seal the vent. Cook on High Pressure for 35 minutes. It is normal if it takes your pot a longer time to come to pressure. 6. Let the steam naturally release for 20 minutes before Manually releasing. Press Cancel. 7. Heat the broiler. 8. Carefully remove the turkey to a sheet pan. Place under the broiler for 5 to 10 minutes to crisp up the skin. 9. While the skin is crisping, use the juices to make a gravy. Pour the juices through a mesh sieve, reserving 2 cups of broth. Return the reserved broth to the pot. Turn the pot to Sauté mode. When the broth starts to boil, add the xanthan gum and whisk until the desired consistency is reached. Add more xanthan gum if you like a thicker gravy. 10. Remove the turkey from the broiler and place on a platter. Carve as desired and serve with the gravy.

Per Serving
Calories: 380 | fat: 18g | protein: 47g | carbs: 3g | net carbs: 1g | fiber: 2g

Lemon & Rosemary Chicken in a Skillet

Prep time: 5 minutes | Cook time: 14 minutes | Serves 4

8 chicken thighs
1 teaspoon salt
2 tablespoons lemon juice
1 teaspoon lemon zest
2 tablespoons olive oil

1 tablespoon chopped rosemary
¼ teaspoon black pepper
1 garlic clove, minced

1. Combine all ingredients in a bowl. Place in the fridge for one hour. Heat a skillet over medium heat. Add the chicken along with the juices and cook until crispy, about 7 minutes per side.

Per Serving
Calories: 457 | fat: 33g | protein: 37g | carbs: 3g | net carbs: 2g | fiber: 1g

Crispy Thighs & Mash

Prep time: 15 minutes | Cook time: 30 minutes | Serves 6

Crispy Chicken:
6 small or 3 large boneless, skinless chicken thighs (about 1 pound/454 g)
¼ cup melted coconut oil or avocado oil
1 teaspoon garlic powder
½ teaspoon onion powder
¼ teaspoon finely ground sea salt
¼ teaspoon ground black pepper

Butternut Mash:
1 medium butternut squash (about 1¼ pounds/570 g)
2 tablespoons coconut oil or ghee
½ teaspoon finely ground sea salt
⅛ teaspoon ground black pepper
⅓ cup milk (nondairy or regular)
1½ tablespoons chicken bone broth

1. **Cook the Chicken:** Preheat the oven to 400°F (205°C). If using large chicken thighs, cut them in half to make 6 pieces. Place the chicken on a rimmed baking sheet. Pour the oil over the thighs and dust them with the spices. Turn the thighs until they're fully coated in the oil and spices. Bake for 25 to 30 minutes, until the internal temperature of the chicken reaches 165°F (74°C). Cut the chicken into ½-inch (1.25-cm) slices. 2. Meanwhile, **Make the Mash:** Peel and seed the squash, then cut the flesh into cubes. Measure 3 cups (455 g) of the cubes for the mash; store any remaining squash in the fridge for another use. 3. Heat the oil in a large frying pan over medium heat. Add the squash, salt, and pepper. Cover and cook for 10 to 15 minutes, until the squash is lightly browned. Add the milk and broth, cover, and continue to cook for 15 minutes, or until the squash is soft enough to mash easily. When the squash is done, mash it with the back of a fork right there

in the pan. 4. To serve, divide the mash among 6 dinner plates. Top each portion with an equal amount of the sliced chicken thighs and enjoy!

Per Serving
Calories: 331 | fat: 26g | protein: 16g | carbs: 10g | net carbs: 8g | fiber: 2g

Chicken Pot Pie Crumble

Prep time: 25 minutes | Cook time: 45 minutes | Serves 4

Filling:
¼ cup coconut oil or duck fat
1 pound (454 g) boneless, skinless chicken thighs, cubed
⅓ cup diced celery
¼ cup diced white onions
¼ cup diced carrots
2 small cloves garlic, minced
1 small head cauliflower
2 cups chicken bone broth

¾ teaspoon finely ground gray sea salt
½ teaspoon onion powder
Crumble:
1 tablespoon hot cauliflower cooking liquid (from above)
¼ cup plus 2 tablespoons coconut flour
¼ cup coconut oil
1 large egg
½ teaspoon garlic powder
½ teaspoon onion powder

1. Preheat the oven to 350°F (177°C) and grease a shallow 1½-quart (1.4-L) casserole dish with coconut oil. 2. **Make the Filling:** Melt the coconut oil in a frying pan over medium heat. Add the chicken and sauté for 10 minutes, or until cooked through. Add the celery, onions, carrots, and garlic and continue to cook for 5 minutes. Remove from the heat. 3. Meanwhile, break up the cauliflower into large florets (you should have about 14 ounces/397 g of florets) and place them in a saucepan with the broth. Cover and bring to a boil over high heat. Reduce the heat to medium-low and simmer for 15 minutes, until the cauliflower is fork-tender. Transfer the cauliflower and ½ cup (120 ml) of the cooking liquid (reserve the rest for later) to a blender. Add the salt and onion powder and blend on high until smooth, about 1 minute. 4. Pour the cauliflower cream into the frying pan with the chicken pieces. Stir to combine, then transfer to the prepared casserole dish. 5. **Make the Crumble:** Place 1 tablespoon of the hot cauliflower cooking liquid, the coconut flour, coconut oil, egg, garlic powder, and onion powder in a medium-sized bowl. Combine with your hands until the mixture forms a ball. 6. Crumble the dough over the top of the filling, distributing it evenly. Bake for 25 to 30 minutes, until the top is golden. Serve immediately.

Per Serving
Calories: 474 | fat: 35g | protein: 30g | carbs: 10g | net carbs: 6g | fiber: 4g

Tuscan Chicken Sauté

Prep time: 10 minutes | Cook time: 35 minutes | Serves 4

1 pound (454 g) boneless chicken breasts, each cut into three pieces
Sea salt, for seasoning
Freshly ground black pepper, for seasoning
3 tablespoons olive oil
1 tablespoon minced garlic
¾ cup chicken stock

1 teaspoon dried oregano
½ teaspoon dried basil
½ cup heavy (whipping) cream
½ cup shredded Asiago cheese
1 cup fresh spinach
¼ cup sliced Kalamata olives

1. Prepare the chicken. Pat the chicken breasts dry and lightly season them with salt and pepper. 2. Sauté the chicken. In a large skillet over medium-high heat, warm the olive oil. Add the chicken and sauté until it is golden brown and just cooked through, about 15 minutes in total. Transfer the chicken to a plate and set it aside. 3. Make the sauce. Add the garlic to the skillet and sauté until it's softened, about 2 minutes. Stir in the chicken stock, oregano, and basil, scraping up any browned bits in the skillet. Bring to a boil, then reduce the heat to low and simmer until the sauce is reduced by about one-quarter, about 10 minutes. 4. Finish the dish. Stir in the cream and Asiago and simmer, stirring the sauce frequently, until it has thickened, about 5 minutes. Return the chicken to the skillet along with any accumulated juices. Stir in the spinach and olives and simmer until the spinach is wilted, about 2 minutes. 5. Serve. Divide the chicken and sauce between four plates and serve it immediately.
Per Serving
Calories: 483 | fat: 38g | protein: 31g | carbs: 5g | net carbs: 3g | fiber: 1g

Lemon Threaded Chicken Skewers

Prep time: 10 minutes | Cook time: 12 minutes | Serves 4

3 chicken breasts, cut into cubes
2 tablespoons olive oil, divided
2/3 jar preserved lemon, flesh removed, drained
2 cloves garlic, minced

½ cup lemon juice
Salt and black pepper to taste
1 teaspoon rosemary leaves to garnish
2 to 4 lemon wedges to garnish

1. First, thread the chicken onto skewers and set aside. 2. In a wide bowl, mix half of the oil, garlic, salt, pepper, and lemon juice, and add the chicken skewers, and lemon rind. Cover the bowl and let the chicken marinate for at least 2 hours in the refrigerator. 3. When the marinating time is almost over, preheat a grill to 350ºF, and remove the chicken onto the grill. Cook for 6 minutes on each side. 4.

Remove and serve warm garnished with rosemary leaves and lemons wedges.
Per Serving
Calories: 350 | fat: 11g | protein: 34g | carbs: 5g | net carbs: 4g | fiber: 1g

Crunchy Chicken Milanese

Prep time: 10 minutes | Cook time: 10 minutes | Serves 2

2 boneless skinless chicken breasts
½ cup coconut flour
1 teaspoon ground cayenne pepper

Pink Himalayan salt
Freshly ground black pepper
1 egg, lightly beaten
½ cup crushed pork rinds
2 tablespoons olive oil

1. Pound the chicken breasts with a heavy mallet until they are about ½ inch thick. (If you don't have a kitchen mallet, you can use the thick rim of a heavy plate.) 2. Prepare two separate prep plates and one small, shallow bowl. On plate 1, put the coconut flour, cayenne pepper, pink Himalayan salt, and pepper. Mix together. Crack the egg into the small bowl, and lightly beat it with a fork or whisk. On plate 2, put the crushed pork rinds. 3. In a large skillet over medium-high heat, heat the olive oil. 4. Dredge 1 chicken breast on both sides in the coconut-flour mixture. Dip the chicken into the egg, and coat both sides. Dredge the chicken in the pork-rind mixture, pressing the pork rinds into the chicken so they stick. Place the coated chicken in the hot skillet and repeat with the other chicken breast. 5. Cook the chicken for 3 to 5 minutes on each side, until brown, crispy, and cooked through, and serve.
Per Serving
Calories: 604 | fat: 29g | protein: 65g | carbs: 17g | net carbs: 7g | fiber: 10g

Chicken Breasts with Walnut Crust

Prep time: 5 minutes | Cook time: 15 minutes | Serves 4

1 egg, whisked
Salt and black pepper, to taste
3 tablespoons coconut oil

1½ cups walnuts, ground
4 chicken breast halves, boneless and skinless

1. In a bowl, add in walnuts and the whisked egg in another. Season the chicken, dip in the egg and then in pecans. Warm oil in a pan over medium heat and brown the chicken. Remove the chicken pieces to a baking sheet, set in the oven, and bake for 10 minutes at 350º F. Serve topped with lemon slices.
Per Serving
Calories: 322 | fat: 18g | protein: 35g | carbs: 5g | net carbs: 2g | fiber: 3g

Jamaican Jerk Chicken

Prep time: 10 minutes | Cook time: 45 minutes | Serves 4

¼ medium white onion
¼ cup extra-virgin olive oil
1 to 3 habanero chiles
2 tablespoons granulated erythritol
2 tablespoons jerk seasoning
1 tablespoon coconut

aminos or soy sauce
Juice of 1 lime
1 tablespoon minced garlic
4 chicken leg quarters (thighs and drumsticks)
2 scallions, white and green parts, sliced

1. In a food processor, combine the onion, olive oil, chiles, erythritol, jerk seasoning, coconut aminos, lime juice, and garlic. Purée on high until the mixture is smooth. Transfer this marinade to a resealable 1-gallon plastic bag. 2. Add the chicken to the bag, then seal and shake the bag until the chicken is well coated with the seasoning. Allow to marinate in the refrigerator for 12 to 24 hours, preferably 24. 3. Set a grill to high or preheat the oven to 425°F (220°C). 4. Remove the chicken from the marinade bag and place it on the grill or on a rack set on a baking sheet. Reserve the marinade. Cook the chicken for 30 to 35 minutes, flipping the pieces every 15 minutes. An instant-read thermometer inserted between the thigh and drumstick should read 165°F (74°C), and the juices should run clear when the chicken is pierced. 5. Transfer the marinade to a small saucepan and set it over high heat. Cook for about 10 minutes, or until it reaches just over 165°F (74°C). 6. Place the chicken on a serving platter. Top with the scallions and serve with the jerk sauce on the side.
Per Serving
Calories: 884 | fat: 68g | protein: 58g | carbs: 7g | net carbs: 6g | fiber: 1g

Roasted Stuffed Chicken with Tomato Basil Sauce

Prep time: 5 minutes | Cook time: 30 minutes | Serves 6

4 ounces (113 g) cream cheese
3 ounces mozzarella slices
10 ounces spinach
⅓ cup shredded mozzarella

cheese
1 tablespoon olive oil
1 cup tomato basil sauce
3 whole chicken breasts

1. Preheat your oven to 400°F. Combine the cream cheese, shredded mozzarella cheese, and spinach in the microwave. Cut the chicken a couple of times horizontally and stuff with the spinach mixture. Brush with olive oil. place on a lined baking dish and bake in the oven for 25 minutes. 2. Pour the tomato basil sauce over and top with mozzarella slices. Return to the oven and cook for an additional 5 minutes.

Per Serving
Calories: 338 | fat: 28g | protein: 37g | carbs: 5g | net carbs: 3g | fiber: 2g

Verde Chicken Enchiladas

Prep time: 20 minutes | Cook time: 20 minutes | Serves 8

2 (4.2 ounces/118 g) boneless, skinless chicken breasts, cooked
½ cup cooked, diced mushrooms
½ cup cooked, diced zucchini
8 small low-carb flour tortillas

1 cup green enchilada sauce
1 cup shredded Cheddar cheese
1 medium green onion, finely chopped
¼ cup freshly minced cilantro, divided
¼ cup sliced black olives
⅓ cup full-fat sour cream

1. Preheat oven to 350°F. Grease a 9" × 9" baking dish. 2. In a medium bowl, finely shred cooked chicken breasts. Add mushrooms and zucchini and stir to combine. 3. On a large baking sheet or clean cutting board, lay out tortillas one at a time and evenly distribute chicken and vegetable mixture in center of each tortilla. Roll each tortilla over chicken and vegetables to make tight rolls. 4. Put rolls in baking dish. Cover with green enchilada sauce and evenly top with cheese, green onion, half of the cilantro, and olives. 5. Bake 15–20 minutes until cheese melts. 6. Let cool 10 minutes. Top with sour cream and remaining cilantro and serve.
Per Serving
Calories: 200 | fat: 10g | protein: 15g | carbs: 18g | net carbs: 9g | fiber: 9g

Duck & Vegetable Casserole

Prep time: 15 minutes | Cook time: 20 minutes | Serves 2

2 duck breasts, skin on and sliced
2 zucchinis, sliced
1 tablespoon coconut oil
1 green onion bunch, chopped

1 carrot, chopped
2 green bell peppers, seeded and chopped
Salt and ground black pepper, to taste

1. Set a pan over medium heat and warm oil, stir in the green onions, and cook for 2 minutes. Place in the zucchini, bell peppers, black pepper, salt, and carrot, and cook for 10 minutes. 2. Set another pan over medium heat, add in duck slices and cook each side for 3 minutes. 3. Pour the mixture into the vegetable pan. Cook for 3 minutes. Set in bowls and enjoy.
Per Serving
Calories: 433 | fat: 21g | protein: 53g | carbs: 13g | net carbs: 8g | fiber: 5g

Easy Chicken Meatloaf

Prep time: 15 minutes | Cook time: 35 minutes | Serves 8

1 cup sugar-free marinara sauce
2 pounds (907 g) ground chicken
2 tablespoons fresh parsley, chopped
3 garlic cloves, minced
2 teaspoons onion powder
2 teaspoons Italian seasoning
Salt and ground black

pepper, to taste
For the Filling:
½ cup ricotta cheese
1 cup Grana Padano cheese, grated
1 cup Colby cheese, shredded
2 teaspoons fresh chives, chopped
2 tablespoons fresh parsley, chopped
1 garlic clove, minced

1. In a bowl, combine the chicken with half of the marinara sauce, pepper, onion powder, Italian seasoning, salt, and 2 garlic cloves. In a separate bowl, combine the ricotta cheese with half of the Grana Padano cheese, chives, pepper, 1 garlic clove, half of the Colby cheese, salt, and 2 tablespoons parsley. 2. Place half of the chicken mixture into a loaf pan, and spread evenly. Top with cheese filling. Cover with the rest of the meat mixture and spread again. Set the meatloaf in the oven at 380ºF and bake for 25 minutes. 3. Remove meatloaf from the oven, spread the rest of the marinara sauce, Grana Padano cheese and Colby cheese, and bake for 18 minutes. Allow meatloaf cooling and serve in slices sprinkled with 2 tablespoons of chopped parsley.
Per Serving
Calories: 399 | fat: 28g | protein: 31g | carbs: 5g | net carbs: 4g | fiber: 1g

Slow Cooker Chicken Cacciatore

Prep time: 15 minutes | Cook time: 10 minutes | Serves 4

¼ cup good-quality olive oil
4 (4 ounces/113 g) boneless chicken breasts, each cut into three pieces
1 onion, chopped
2 celery stalks, chopped
1 cup sliced mushrooms
2 tablespoons minced garlic

1 (28 ounces/784 g) can sodium-free diced tomatoes
½ cup red wine
½ cup tomato paste
1 tablespoon dried basil
1 teaspoon dried oregano
⅛ teaspoon red pepper flakes

1. Brown the chicken. In a skillet over medium-high heat, warm the olive oil. Add the chicken breasts and brown them, turning them once, about 10 minutes in total. 2. Cook in the slow cooker. Place the chicken in the slow cooker and stir in the onion, celery, mushrooms, garlic, tomatoes, red wine, tomato paste, basil, oregano, and red pepper flakes. Cook it on high for 3 to 4 hours or on low for 6 to 8 hours, until the chicken is fully cooked and tender. 3.

Serve. Divide the chicken and sauce between four bowls and serve it immediately.
Per Serving
Calories: 383 | fat: 26g | protein: 26g | carbs: 11g | net carbs: 7g | fiber: 4g

One Pot Chicken with Mushrooms

Prep time: 10 minutes | Cook time: 20 minutes | Serves 6

2 cups sliced mushrooms
½ teaspoon onion powder
½ teaspoon garlic powder
¼ cup butter
1 teaspoon Dijon mustard

1 tablespoon tarragon, chopped
2 pounds (907 g) chicken thighs
Salt and black pepper, to taste

1. Season the thighs with salt, pepper, garlic, and onion powder. Melt the butter in a skillet, and cook the chicken until browned; set aside. Add mushrooms to the same fat and cook for about 5 minutes. 2. Stir in Dijon mustard and ½ cup of water. Return the chicken to the skillet. Season to taste with salt and pepper, reduce the heat and cover, and let simmer for 15 minutes. Stir in tarragon. Serve warm.
Per Serving
Calories: 404 | fat: 32g | protein: 27g | carbs: 2g | net carbs: 1g | fiber: 1g

Chicken Quesadilla

Prep time: 5 minutes | Cook time: 5 minutes | Serves 2

1 tablespoon olive oil
2 low-carbohydrate tortillas
½ cup shredded Mexican blend cheese
2 ounces (57 g) shredded

chicken (I usually use a store-bought rotisserie chicken)
1 teaspoon Tajín seasoning salt
2 tablespoons sour cream

1. In a large skillet over medium-high heat, heat the olive oil. Add a tortilla, then layer on top ¼ cup of cheese, the chicken, the Tajín seasoning, and the remaining ¼ cup of cheese. Top with the second tortilla. 2. Peek under the edge of the bottom tortilla to monitor how it is browning. Once the bottom tortilla gets golden and the cheese begins to melt, after about 2 minutes, flip the quesadilla over. The second side will cook faster, about 1 minute. 3. Once the second tortilla is crispy and golden, transfer the quesadilla to a cutting board and let sit for 2 minutes. Cut the quesadilla into 4 wedges using a pizza cutter or chef's knife. 4. Transfer half the quesadilla to each of two plates. Add 1 tablespoon of sour cream to each plate, and serve hot.
Per Serving
Calories: 414 | fat: 28g | protein: 26g | carbs: 24g | net carbs: 7g | fiber: 17g

Chicken Cauliflower Bake

Prep time: 10 minutes | Cook time: 45 minutes | Serves 6

3 cups cubed leftover chicken
3 cups spinach
2 cauliflower heads, cut into florets
3 cups water
3 eggs, lightly beaten
2 cups grated sharp cheddar

cheese
1 cup pork rinds, crushed
½ cup unsweetened almond milk
3 tablespoons olive oil
3 cloves garlic, minced
Salt and black pepper to taste
Cooking spray

1. Preheat the oven to 350ºF and grease a baking dish with cooking spray. Set aside. 2. Pour the cauli florets and water in a pot; bring to boil over medium heat. Cover and steam the cauli florets for 8 minutes. Drain them through a colander and set aside. 3. Also, combine the cheddar cheese and pork rinds in a large bowl and mix in the chicken. Set aside. 4. Heat the olive oil in a skillet and cook the garlic and spinach until the spinach has wilted, about 5 minutes. Season with salt and black pepper, and add the spinach mixture and cauli florets to the chicken bowl. 5. Top with the eggs and almond milk, mix and transfer everything to the baking dish. Layer the top of the ingredients and place the dish in the oven to bake for 30 minutes. 6. By this time the edges and top must have browned nicely, then remove the chicken from the oven, let rest for 5 minutes, and serve. Garnish with steamed and seasoned green beans.
Per Serving
Calories: 395 | fat: 31g | protein: 24g | carbs: 5g | net carbs: 3g | fiber: 2g

Eggplant & Tomato Braised Chicken Thighs

Prep time: 10 minutes | Cook time: 25 minutes | Serves 4

2 tablespoons ghee
1 pound (454 g) chicken thighs
Salt and black pepper to taste
2 cloves garlic, minced

1 (14 ounces/397 g) can whole tomatoes
1 eggplant, diced
10 fresh basil leaves, chopped + extra to garnish

1. Melt ghee in a saucepan over medium heat, season the chicken with salt and black pepper and fry for 4 minutes on each side until golden brown. Remove to a plate. 2. Sauté the garlic in the ghee for 2 minutes, pour in the tomatoes, and cook covered for 8 minutes. Add in the eggplant and basil. Cook for 4 minutes. Season the sauce with salt and black pepper, stir and add the chicken. Coat with sauce and simmer for 3 minutes. 3. Serve chicken with sauce on a bed of squash pasta. Garnish with extra basil.
Per Serving
Calories: 468 | fat: 40g | protein: 26g | carbs: 7g | net carbs: 2g | fiber: 5g

Chicken and Zucchini Bake

Prep time: 10 minutes | Cook time: 30 minutes | Serves 4

1 zucchini, chopped
Salt and black pepper, to taste
1 teaspoon garlic powder
1 tablespoon avocado oil
2 chicken breasts, skinless,

boneless, sliced
1 tomato, cored and chopped
½ teaspoon dried oregano
½ teaspoon dried basil
½ cup mozzarella cheese, shredded

1. Apply pepper, garlic powder and salt to the chicken. Set a pan over medium heat and warm avocado oil, add in the chicken slices, cook until golden; remove to a baking dish. To the same pan add the zucchini, tomato, pepper, basil, oregano, and salt, cook for 2 minutes, and spread over chicken. 2. Bake in the oven at 330ºF for 20 minutes. Sprinkle the mozzarella over the chicken, return to the oven, and bake for 5 minutes until the cheese is melted and bubbling. Serve with green salad.
Per Serving
Calories: 279 | fat: 15g | protein: 33g | carbs: 3g | net carbs: 2g | fiber: 1g

Chicken with Parmesan Topping

Prep time: 15 minutes | Cook time: 40 minutes | Serves 4

4 chicken breast halves, skinless and boneless
Salt and black pepper, to taste
¼ cup green chilies, chopped
5 bacon slices, chopped
6 ounces (170 g) cream cheese
¼ cup onion, chopped

½ cup mayonnaise
½ cup Grana Padano cheese, grated
1 cup cheddar cheese, grated
2 ounces (57 g) pork rinds, crushed
2 tablespoons olive oil
½ cup Parmesan cheese, shredded

1. Season the chicken with salt and pepper. Heat the olive oil in a pan over medium heat and fry the chicken for approximately 4-6 minutes until cooked through with no pink showing. Remove to a baking dish. 2. In the same pan, fry bacon until crispy and remove to a plate. Sauté the onion for 3 minutes, until soft. Remove from heat, add in the fried bacon, cream cheese, 1 cup of water, Grana Padano cheese, mayonnaise, chilies, and cheddar cheese, and spread over the chicken. 3. Bake in the oven for 10-15 minutes at 370ºF. Remove and sprinkle with mixed Parmesan cheese and pork rinds and return to the oven. Bake for another 10-15 minutes until the cheese melts. Serve immediately.
Per Serving
Calories: 361 | fat: 15g | protein: 25g | carbs: 6g | net carbs: 5g | fiber: 1g

Roasted Chicken Breasts with Capers

Prep time: 10 minutes | Cook time: 55 minutes | Serves 6

3 medium lemons, sliced
½ teaspoon salt
1 teaspoon olive oil
3 chicken breasts, halved
Salt and black pepper to season
¼ cup almond flour

2 teaspoons olive oil
2 tablespoons capers, rinsed
1¼ cup chicken broth
2 teaspoons butter
1½ tablespoons chopped fresh parsley
Parsley for garnish

1. Preheat the oven to 350ºF and lay a piece of parchment paper on a baking sheet. 2. Lay the lemon slices on the baking sheet, drizzle with olive oil and sprinkle with salt. Roast in the oven for 25 minutes to brown the lemon rinds. 3. Cover the chicken with plastic wrap, place them on a flat surface, and gently pound with the rolling pin to flatten to about ½ -inch thickness. Remove the plastic wraps and season with salt and pepper. 4. Next, dredge the chicken in the almond flour on each side, and shake off any excess flour. Set aside. 5. Heat the olive oil in a skillet over medium heat and fry the chicken on both sides to a golden brown, for about 8 minutes in total. Pour the chicken broth in, shake the skillet, and let the broth boil and reduce to a thick consistency, about 12 minutes. 6. Lightly stir in the capers, roasted lemon, pepper, butter, and parsley, and simmer on low heat for 10 minutes. Turn the heat off and serve the chicken with the sauce hot, an extra garnish of parsley with a creamy squash mash.
Per Serving
Calories: 366 | fat: 26g | protein: 27g | carbs: 6g | net carbs: 4g | fiber: 2g

Keto Greek Avgolemono

Prep time: 10 minutes | Cook time: 30 minutes | Serves 4

4 bone-in, skin-on chicken thighs
¼ cup diced onions
1 sprig fresh thyme
4 cups chicken bone broth, homemade or store-bought, plus more if needed
Fine sea salt and freshly ground black pepper, to taste
2 large eggs

2 tablespoons lemon juice
4 tablespoons extra-virgin olive oil or MCT oil, for drizzling (optional)
Cracklings:
Chicken skin (from above)
½ teaspoon fine sea salt
½ teaspoon freshly ground black pepper
1½ teaspoons Paleo fat, such as lard, tallow, or avocado oil

1. Remove the skin from the chicken thighs. Place the skinless chicken, diced onions, and thyme in a large pot and fill with broth so that the broth covers the thighs by 1 inch. Add a couple pinches each of salt and pepper. Bring to a boil and cook for 20 minutes. 2. While the chicken is cooking, **make the cracklings:** Cut the chicken skin into ¼-inch pieces and season with the ½ teaspoon each of salt and pepper. Heat the Paleo fat in a skillet over medium-high heat, then add the chicken skin and fry until golden brown and crispy, about 8 minutes. Set the cracklings aside on a paper towel to drain. 3. Place them in individual serving bowls. 4. In a medium bowl, whisk the eggs and lemon juice. While whisking, very slowly pour in ½ cup of the hot broth. Slowly whisk another cup of hot soup into the egg mixture. 5. Pour the hot egg mixture into the pot while stirring to create a creamy soup without the cream. Reduce the heat and simmer for 10 minutes, stirring constantly. 6. Pour one-quarter (about 1 cup) of the creamy soup over each chicken thigh. Top with the cracklings. Drizzle each bowl with 1 tablespoon of olive oil, if desired.
Per Serving
Calories: 275 | fat: 20g | protein: 22g | carbs: 2g | net carbs: 1g | fiber: 1g

Merry Christmas Chicken

Prep time: 10 minutes | Cook time: 23 minutes | Serves 4

4 (4.2 ounces/118 g) boneless, skinless chicken breasts
1 medium red bell pepper, seeded and chopped
1 medium green bell pepper, seeded and chopped

4 ounces (113 g) full-fat cream cheese, softened
¼ teaspoon salt
¼ teaspoon black pepper
¼ teaspoon paprika
¼ teaspoon dried parsley

1. Preheat oven to 375°F. 2. Place wax paper on both sides of chicken breasts. Use a rolling pin, kitchen mallet, or cast iron skillet to pound chicken until thin (less than ¼"). 3. In a medium microwave-safe bowl, microwave bell peppers 3 minutes. 4. In a separate medium bowl, mix cream cheese and softened bell peppers. Add salt and pepper. 5. Cover a large baking sheet with foil. Coat evenly with cooking spray. Lay flattened breasts on baking sheet. 6. Place one-quarter of the cream cheese mixture into the center of each pounded chicken and roll. Secure with a wet toothpick. 7. Garnish chicken with paprika and parsley to continue Christmas theme. 8. Bake 20 minutes. Serve warm.
Per Serving
Calories: 240 | fat: 11g | protein: 28g | carbs: 5g | net carbs: 4g | fiber: 1g

White Wine Seared Chicken Breasts

Prep time: 10 minutes | Cook time: 30 minutes | Serves 4

4 medium boneless, skinless chicken breasts (8 ounces/227 g each)
1 teaspoon sea salt
¼ teaspoon black pepper
4 tablespoons (½ stick) butter, cut into 1-tablespoon pats
2 cloves garlic, minced
1 medium shallot, finely chopped
½ cup white cooking wine
½ cup chicken broth
½ tablespoon chopped fresh parsley
½ tablespoon fresh thyme, chopped

1. Season the chicken on both sides with sea salt and black pepper. 2. In a large skillet or sauté pan, melt 1 tablespoon of the butter over medium-high heat. Add the chicken and sauté for 5 to 8 minutes per side, until cooked through and browned. 3. Remove the chicken from the pan and cover with foil. 4. Add another 1 tablespoon butter to the pan. Add the garlic and shallot, and sauté for about 1 minute, until fragrant. 5. Add the wine and broth to the pan and use a wooden spoon to scrape any browned bits from the bottom. Bring to a gentle boil, then lower the heat and simmer for about 7 to 8 minutes, until the liquid volume is reduced by half. 6. Reduce the heat to low. Stir in the remaining 2 tablespoons butter, parsley, and thyme, just until the butter melts. 7. Serve the sauce over the chicken.

Per Serving
Calories: 288 | fat: 14g | protein: 29g | carbs: 2g | net carbs: 2g | fiber: 0g

Chicken with Anchovy Tapenade

Prep time: 10 minutes | Cook time: 10 minutes | Serves 2

1 chicken breast, cut into 4 pieces
2 tablespoons coconut oil
3 garlic cloves, crushed
For the Tapenade:
1 cup black olives, pitted
1 ounce anchovy fillets, rinsed
1 garlic clove, crushed
Salt and ground black pepper, to taste
2 tablespoons olive oil
¼ cup fresh basil, chopped
1 tablespoon lemon juice

1. Using a food processor, combine the olives, salt, olive oil, basil, lemon juice, anchovy, and black pepper, blend well. Set a pan over medium heat and warm coconut oil, stir in the garlic, and sauté for 2 minutes. 2. Place in the chicken pieces and cook each side for 4 minutes. Split the chicken among plates and apply a topping of the anchovy tapenade.

Per Serving
Calories: 155 | fat: 13g | protein: 25g | carbs: 5g | net carbs: 3g | fiber: 2g

Turkey Burgers with Fried Brussels Sprouts

Prep time: 10 minutes | Cook time: 10 minutes | Serves 4

For the Burgers:
1 pound (454 g) ground turkey
1 free-range egg
½ onion, chopped
1 teaspoon salt
½ teaspoon ground black pepper
1 teaspoon dried thyme
2 ounces (57 g) butter
For the Fried Brussels Sprouts:
1½ pounds (680 g) Brussels sprouts, halved
3 ounces butter
1 teaspoon salt
½ teaspoon ground black pepper

1. Combine the burger ingredients in a mixing bowl. Create patties from the mixture. Set a large pan over medium heat, warm butter, and fry the patties until cooked completely. 2. Place on a plate and cover with aluminium foil to keep warm. Fry brussels sprouts in butter, season to your preference, then set to a bowl. Plate the burgers and brussels sprouts and serve.

Per Serving
Calories: 432 | fat: 25g | protein: 31g | carbs: 21g | net carbs: 6g | fiber: 15g

Chipotle Chicken Fajita Bowl

Prep time: 10 minutes | Cook time: 30 minutes | Serves 4

3 tablespoons unsalted butter
1½ pounds (680 g) boneless, skinless chicken thighs, cut into thin strips
¼ teaspoon salt
1 small yellow onion, peeled and diced
1 large green bell pepper, seeded and diced
2 tablespoons taco seasoning
6 cups chopped romaine lettuce
1 cup shredded Mexican cheese
½ cup full-fat sour cream
2 large avocados, peeled, pitted, and diced
1 small tomato, chopped
4 tablespoons finely chopped cilantro

1. In a large skillet over medium heat, add butter and fry chicken for 5 minutes while stirring just to brown. Season chicken with salt. Sauté 10–15 minutes, stirring regularly. 2. Add onion, bell pepper, and taco seasoning. Reduce heat to low and cook 7–10 minutes. Stir often until vegetables have softened. 3. Distribute lettuce evenly to serving bowls, then add cooked chicken and vegetables. Top with cheese, sour cream, diced avocados, tomato, and cilantro.

Per Serving
Calories: 610 | fat: 40g | protein: 39g | carbs: 16g | net carbs: 8g | fiber: 8g

Bruschetta and Cheese Stuffed Chicken

Prep time: 10 minutes | Cook time: 10 minutes | Serves 4

6 ounces (170 g) diced Roma tomatoes
2 tablespoons avocado oil
1 tablespoon thinly sliced fresh basil, plus more for garnish
1½ teaspoons balsamic vinegar
Pinch of salt

Pinch of black pepper
4 boneless, skinless chicken breasts (about 2 pounds/907 g)
12 ounces (340 g) goat cheese, divided
2 teaspoons Italian seasoning, divided
1 cup water

1. Prepare the bruschetta by mixing the tomatoes, avocado oil, basil, vinegar, salt, and pepper in a small bowl. Let it marinate until the chicken is done. 2. Pat the chicken dry with a paper towel. Butterfly the breast open but do not cut all the way through. Stuff each breast with 3 ounces (85 g) of the goat cheese. Use toothpicks to close the edges. 3. Sprinkle ½ teaspoon of the Italian seasoning on top of each breast. 4. Pour the water into the pot. Place the trivet inside. Lay a piece of aluminum foil on top of the trivet and place the chicken breasts on top. It is okay if they overlap. 5. Close the lid and seal the vent. Cook on High Pressure for 10 minutes. Quick release the steam. 6. Remove the toothpicks and top each breast with one-fourth of the bruschetta.

Per Serving
Calories: 581 | fat: 34g | protein: 64g | carbs: 5g | net carbs: 4g | fiber: 1g

Cacio e Pepe Spaghetti Squash with Grilled Chicken Thighs

Prep time: 5 minutes | Cook time: 50 minutes | Serves 6

1 medium spaghetti squash (about 3 pounds/1.4 kg)
¼ cup (½ stick) butter
1 cup finely grated hard cheese, such as Parmigiano-Reggiano or Pecorino Romano, plus extra for

garnish
½ teaspoon ground black pepper
Sea salt, to taste
2 pounds (907 g) bone-in, skin-on chicken thighs, grilled or baked, then sliced

1. Preheat the oven to 375ºF (190ºC). 2. **Make the Spaghetti Squash Noodles:** Slice the spaghetti squash in half crosswise. Scoop out the seeds, then sprinkle the cut sides with salt and pepper. Place both halves face down on a rimmed baking sheet and roast for 35 to 45 minutes, until the flesh of the squash is translucent and the skin begins to soften and easily separates from the "noodles" inside. 3.

Allow the squash to cool enough that you can handle it (or carefully use tongs to hold it while still hot), then scoop out the "noodles" into a large serving bowl. Set aside. 4. Melt the butter in a large skillet and add the spaghetti squash noodles, cheese, and pepper, tossing everything together until the cheese begins to melt and coats the noodles. 5. Garnish with a pinch or two of sea salt and more black pepper and grated cheese, and serve with the chicken thighs.

Per Serving
Calories: 561 | fat: 41g | protein: 40g | carbs: 8g | net carbs: 8g | fiber: 0g

Butter Chicken

Prep time: 10 minutes | Cook time: 45 minutes | Serves 4

⅓ cup coconut oil
1⅓ pounds (600 g) boneless, skinless chicken thighs, cubed
½ cup sliced yellow onions
2 small cloves garlic, minced
1 (1-in/2.5-cm) piece fresh ginger root, grated
1 (14½ ounces/400 g) can diced tomatoes
1 cup chicken bone broth
1 bay leaf
1 tablespoon garam masala or curry powder
1 teaspoon ground cumin
1 teaspoon finely ground

gray sea salt
½ teaspoon ground coriander
¼ teaspoon ground cloves
⅛ teaspoon ground black pepper
⅛ teaspoon ground cardamom
⅓ cup full-fat coconut milk
3 tablespoons blanched almond flour
1 tablespoon fresh lemon juice
Handful of fresh cilantro, roughly chopped, for garnish
Sliced green onions, for garnish

1. Melt the coconut oil in a large saucepan or deep sauté pan over medium-high heat. Add the cubed chicken to the pan and cook for 10 minutes, or until the chicken is no longer pink. 2. Add the onions, garlic, and ginger and continue to cook for 5 minutes, until fragrant. 3. Add the tomatoes, bone broth, bay leaf, garam masala, cumin, salt, coriander, cloves, pepper, and cardamom and give everything a stir. Cover and bring to a boil, then reduce the heat to low and lightly simmer for 20 minutes. 4. Stir in the coconut milk, almond flour, and lemon juice. Increase the heat to medium-high and cook for 5 minutes, until slightly thickened. 5. Remove the bay leaf. Divide the chicken and sauce among 4 serving bowls. Top with cilantro and green onions and enjoy.

Per Serving
Calories: 450 | fat: 31g | protein: 34g | carbs: 8g | net carbs: 5g | fiber: 2g

Spinach Chicken Cheesy Bake

Prep time: 10 minutes | Cook time: 35 minutes | Serves 6

6 chicken breasts, skinless and boneless
1 teaspoon mixed spice seasoning
Pink salt and black pepper to season

2 loose cups baby spinach
3 teaspoons olive oil
4 ounces (113 g) cream cheese, cubed
1¼ cups shredded mozzarella cheese

1. Preheat oven to 370ºF. 2. Season chicken with spice mix, salt, and black pepper. Pat with your hands to have the seasoning stick on the chicken. Put in the casserole dish and layer spinach over the chicken. Mix the oil with cream cheese, mozzarella, salt, and black pepper and stir in water a tablespoon at a time. Pour the mixture over the chicken and cover the pot with aluminium foil. 3. Bake for 20 minutes, remove foil and continue cooking for 15 minutes until a nice golden brown color is formed on top. Take out and allow sitting for 5 minutes. Serve warm with braised asparagus.

Per Serving
Calories: 340 | fat: 30g | protein: 15g | carbs: 3g | net carbs: 3g | fiber: 0g

Caprese Chicken Thighs

Prep time: 10 minutes | Cook time: 28 minutes | Serves 4

⅓ cup olive oil
3 tablespoons balsamic vinegar, divided into 2 tablespoons and 1 tablespoon
1 teaspoon Italian seasoning
½ teaspoon garlic powder
½ teaspoon sea salt
¼ teaspoon black pepper

8 boneless, skinless chicken thighs (2½ ounces/71 g each)
4 ounces (113 g) fresh Mozzarella cheese, cut into 8 slices
2 medium Roma (plum) tomatoes, thinly sliced
2 tablespoons fresh basil, cut into ribbons

1. In a large bowl, whisk together the oil, 2 tablespoons of balsamic vinegar, the Italian seasoning, garlic powder, sea salt, and black pepper. 2. Add the chicken thighs and push down into the marinade. Set aside for 20 minutes, or refrigerate until ready to use. 3. Meanwhile, preheat the oven to 375ºF (190ºC). Line a sheet pan with foil or parchment paper. 4. Shake off any excess marinade from each piece of chicken and arrange on the baking sheet in a single layer without touching. 5. Top each chicken thigh with a slice of Mozzarella, covering most of it. You may need to cut a piece in half to cover the chicken better. Place 2 slices of tomato on top of the Mozzarella. 6. Roast for 23 to 28 minutes, until the chicken is cooked through. You may need to pour off extra liquid from the pan at the end. 7. Drizzle the chicken with the remaining 1 tablespoon balsamic vinegar (or with a reduction by simmering more balsamic vinegar in a small saucepan). Garnish with basil ribbons.

Per Serving
Calories: 564 | fat: 46g | protein: 31g | carbs: 4g | net carbs: 4g | fiber: 0g

Chili Turkey Patties with Cucumber Salsa

Prep time: 10 minutes | Cook time: 6 minutes | Serves 4

2 spring onions, thinly sliced
1 pound (454 g) ground turkey
1 egg
2 garlic cloves, minced
1 tablespoon chopped herbs
1 small chili pepper, deseeded and diced
2 tablespoons ghee

Cucumber Salsa:
1 tablespoon apple cider vinegar
1 tablespoon chopped dill
1 garlic clove, minced
2 cucumbers, grated
1 cup sour cream
1 jalapeño pepper, minced
2 tablespoons olive oil

Place all turkey ingredients, except the ghee, in a bowl. Mix to combine. Make patties out of the mixture. 2. Melt the ghee in a skillet over medium heat. Cook the patties for 3 minutes per side. Place all salsa ingredients in a bowl and mix to combine. Serve the patties topped with salsa.
Calories: 484 | fat: 36g | protein: 35g | carbs: 10g | net carbs: 9g | fiber: 1g

Paprika Chicken

Prep time: 10 minutes | Cook time: 25 minutes | Serves 4

4 (4 ounces/113 g) chicken breasts, skin-on
Sea salt
Freshly ground black pepper
1 tablespoon olive oil
½ cup chopped sweet onion

½ cup heavy (whipping) cream
2 teaspoons smoked paprika
½ cup sour cream
2 tablespoons chopped fresh parsley

1. Lightly season the chicken with salt and pepper. 2. Place a large skillet over medium-high heat and add the olive oil. 3. Sear the chicken on both sides until almost cooked through, about 15 minutes in total. Remove the chicken to a plate. 4. Add the onion to the skillet and sauté until tender, about 4 minutes. 5. Stir in the cream and paprika and bring the liquid to a simmer. 6. Return the chicken and any accumulated juices to the skillet and simmer the chicken for 5 minutes until completely cooked. 7. Stir in the sour cream and remove the skillet from the heat. 8. Serve topped with the parsley.

Per Serving
Calories: 389 | fat: 30g | protein: 25g | carbs: 4g | net carbs: 4g | fiber: 0g

Chicken with Green Sauce

Prep time: 10 minutes | Cook time: 25 minutes | Serves 4

2 tablespoons butter
4 scallions, chopped
4 chicken breasts, skinless and boneless

Salt and black pepper, to taste
6 ounces (170 g) sour cream
2 tablespoons fresh dill, chopped

1. Heat a pan with the butter over medium heat, add in the chicken, season with pepper and salt, and fry for 2-3 per side until golden. Transfer to a baking dish and cook in the oven for 15 minutes at 390ºF, until no longer pink. 2. To the pan add scallions, and cook for 2 minutes. Pour in the sour cream, warm through without boil. Slice the chicken and serve on a platter with green sauce spooned over and fresh dill.

Per Serving
Calories: 209 | fat: 13g | protein: 21g | carbs: 2g | net carbs: 2g | fiber: 0g

Grilled Paprika Chicken with Steamed Broccoli

Prep time: 10 minutes | Cook time: 22 minutes | Serves 6

3 tablespoons smoked paprika
Salt and black pepper to taste
2 teaspoons garlic powder

1 tablespoon olive oil
6 chicken breasts
1 head broccoli, cut into florets

1. Place broccoli florets onto the steamer basket over the boiling water; steam approximately 8 minutes or until crisp-tender. Set aside. Grease grill grate with cooking spray and preheat to 400ºF. 2. Combine paprika, salt, black pepper, and garlic powder in a bowl. Brush chicken with olive oil and sprinkle spice mixture over and massage with hands. 3. Grill chicken for 7 minutes per side until well-cooked, and plate. Serve warm with steamed broccoli.

Per Serving
Calories: 388 | fat: 32g | protein: 22g | carbs: 3g | net carbs: 2g | fiber: 1g

Pancetta & Chicken Casserole

Prep time: 10 minutes | Cook time: 25 minutes | Serves 3

8 pancetta strips, chopped
⅓ cup Dijon mustard
Salt and black pepper, to taste
1 onion, chopped

1 tablespoon olive oil
1½ cups chicken stock
3 chicken breasts, skinless and boneless
¼ teaspoon sweet paprika

1. In a bowl, combine paprika, black pepper, salt, and mustard. Sprinkle this on chicken breasts and massage. Set

a pan over medium heat, stir in the pancetta, cook until it browns, and remove to a plate. 2Place oil in the same pan and heat over medium heat, add in the chicken breasts, cook for each side for 2 minutes and set aside. Put in the stock, and bring to a simmer. Stir in black pepper, pancetta, salt, and onion. Return the chicken to the pan as well, stir gently, and simmer for 20 minutes over medium heat, turning the meat halfway through. Split the chicken on serving plates, sprinkle the sauce over it to serve.

Per Serving
Calories: 313 | fat: 18g | protein: 26g | carbs: 11g | net carbs: 3g | fiber: 8g

Buffalo Chicken Crust Pizza

Prep time: 10 minutes | Cook time: 30 minutes | Serves 2

Buffalo Sauce:
¼ cup Frank's RedHot sauce
¼ cup (½ stick) unsalted butter
2¼ teaspoons apple cider vinegar
Crust:
2 (5 ounces/142 g) cans chunk chicken breast in

water, drained
¼ cup grated Parmesan cheese
1 large egg
Toppings:
4 ounces (113 g) fresh mozzarella cheese, sliced
1 tablespoon sliced scallions (optional)

1. Preheat the oven to 350°F and line a pizza stone or metal pizza pan with parchment paper. 2. **Make the Sauce:** Put the hot sauce, butter, and vinegar in a small saucepan over medium heat. Once the butter melts, stir to combine and remove from the heat. Set aside. 3. **Prepare the Crust:** Spread the drained chicken on the lined pizza stone/pan and bake for 10 minutes to remove all the moisture. Remove from the oven and transfer the chicken to a medium-sized bowl. Increase the oven temperature to 500°F. 4. To the bowl with the chicken, add the Parmesan cheese and egg. Mix thoroughly with a fork. 5. Place a clean sheet of parchment paper on the counter and pour the chicken mixture onto it. Spread the chicken into a thin layer with a rubber spatula. Place another piece of parchment paper on top of the chicken mixture and flatten it into a ¼-inch-thick circle using a rolling pin. Remove the top piece of parchment, transfer the bottom piece of parchment with the crust on it to the pizza stone/pan, and bake the crust for 8 minutes, until slightly browned and hardened. 6. Remove the crust from the oven and top with the Buffalo sauce and mozzarella cheese. Bake for 6 to 8 more minutes, until the cheese is melted and starting to brown. Remove from the oven, top with the sliced scallions, if using, and cut into 6 slices. 7. Store leftovers in a sealed container in the refrigerator for up to 3 days. Reheat in a 250°F oven.

Per Serving
Calories: 600 | fat: 45g | protein: 48g | carbs: 2g | net carbs: 2g | fiber: 0g

Spanish Chicken

Prep time: 20 minutes | Cook time: 50 minutes | Serves 4

½ cup mushrooms, chopped
1 pound (454 g) chorizo
sausages, chopped
2 tablespoons avocado oil
4 cherry peppers, chopped
1 red bell pepper, seeded,
chopped
1 onion, peeled and sliced
2 tablespoons garlic, minced

2 cups tomatoes, chopped
4 chicken thighs
Salt and black pepper, to taste
½ cup chicken stock
1 teaspoon turmeric
1 tablespoon vinegar
2 teaspoons dried oregano
Fresh parsley, chopped, for
serving

1. Set a pan over medium heat and warm half of the avocado oil, stir in the chorizo sausages, and cook for 5-6 minutes until browned; remove to a bowl. Heat the rest of the oil, place in the chicken thighs, and apply pepper and salt for seasoning. Cook each side for 3 minutes and set aside on a bowl. 2. In the same pan, add the onion, bell pepper, cherry peppers, and mushrooms, and cook for 4 minutes. Stir in the garlic and cook for 2 minutes. Pour in the stock, turmeric, salt, tomatoes, pepper, vinegar, and oregano. Stir in the chorizo sausages and chicken, place everything to the oven at 400°F, and bake for 30 minutes. Ladle into serving bowls and garnish with chopped parsley to serve.

Per Serving
Calories: 507 | fat: 39g | protein: 29g | carbs: 10g | net carbs: 6g | fiber: 4g

"K.F.C." Keto Fried Chicken

Prep time: 15 minutes | Cook time: 10 minutes | Serves 4

1 cup vegetable oil, for
frying
2 large eggs
2 tablespoons heavy
whipping cream
⅔ cup blanched almond
flour
⅔ cup grated Parmesan

cheese
¼ teaspoon salt
½ teaspoon black pepper
½ teaspoon paprika
½ teaspoon ground cayenne
1 pound (454 g)
(approximately 4) boneless,
skinless chicken thighs

1. In a medium pot over medium heat add vegetable oil. Make sure it is about 1" deep. Heat oil to 350°F, frequently monitoring to maintain the temperature by adjusting heat during frying. 2. In a medium bowl, add eggs and heavy whipping cream. Beat until well mixed. 3. In a separate medium bowl, add almond flour, Parmesan cheese, salt, pepper, paprika, and cayenne and mix. 4. Cut each thigh into two even pieces. If wet, pat dry. 5. Coat each piece first in the dry breading, then in the egg wash, and then the breading again. 6. Shake off any excess breading and lower the chicken into the hot oil. Fry until deep brown and cooked through, about 3–5 minutes on each side, and then drain on paper towels. 7. Repeat until all chicken is cooked. Serve right away while hot and crispy.

Per Serving
Calories: 470 | fat: 34g | protein: 31g | carbs: 5g | net carbs: 3g | fiber: 2g

Biscuit-Topped Chicken Pot Pie

Prep time: 25 minutes | Cook time: 30 minutes | Serves 4

Biscuits:
1 cup almond flour
1½ teaspoons baking
powder
½ teaspoon salt
2 tablespoons cold butter,
diced into small chunks
2 tablespoons heavy cream
1 large egg
2 ounces (57 g) shredded
Mozzarella or Cheddar
cheese
Filling:
2 tablespoons extra-virgin
olive oil
½ small yellow onion, finely
chopped
4 ribs celery, diced small
(about 1 cup diced celery)

4 ounces (113 g) chopped
mushrooms
¼ cup diced carrot (about 1
small carrot)
1½ teaspoons dried thyme
1 teaspoon salt
¼ teaspoon freshly ground
black pepper
4 cloves garlic, minced
¼ cup dry white wine or
chicken stock
1 cup heavy cream, divided
4 ounces (113 g) cream
cheese, room temperature
1 teaspoon Worcestershire
sauce
2 cups (4 or 5 thighs) cooked
chicken thigh meat, diced

1. Preheat the oven to 375°F (190°C). 2. **To make the biscuits:** In a large bowl, combine the almond flour, baking powder, and salt in a large bowl and mix well. Add the cubed butter and use a fork or your hands to crumble it into the flour mixture until it resembles coarse pebbles. 3. Whisk in the heavy cream, 1 tablespoon at a time. Whisk in the egg and cheese until the mixture forms a smooth dough. Set aside. 4. **To make the filling:** Heat the olive oil in a large skillet over medium-high heat. Add the onion, celery, mushrooms, carrot, thyme, salt, and pepper and sauté until vegetables are just tender, 5 to 6 minutes. Add the garlic and sauté for an additional 30 seconds. 5. Add the wine or stock, stirring until most of the liquid has evaporated. Whisk in ¾ cup of heavy cream, and bring to just below a simmer. Reduce heat to low and cook, stirring occasionally, for 4 to 5 minutes. 6. In a microwave-safe bowl, combine the remaining ¼ cup of heavy cream, cream cheese, and Worcestershire sauce and microwave on high for 45 to 60 seconds, or until the cream cheese is melted. Whisk until smooth. Add the cream mixture to the vegetable mixture, stirring until smooth. 7. Add the diced chicken and stir to combine. Pour the chicken-and-vegetable mixture into an 8-inch square glass baking dish or pie pan. 8. Form the biscuit dough into 8 balls (the mixture will be sticky), flatten into 8 flat biscuits, and place atop the chicken and vegetables. Bake until bubbly and biscuits are golden brown, 16 to 18 minutes.

Per Serving
Calories: 776 | fat: 68g | protein: 32g | carbs: 13g | net carbs: 9g | fiber: 4g

Stuffed Chicken Breasts with Cucumber Noodle Salad ✗

Prep time: 10 minutes | Cook time: 45 minutes | Serves 4

For the Chicken:
4 chicken breasts
⅓ cup baby spinach
¼ cup goat cheese
¼ cup shredded cheddar cheese
4 tablespoons butter
Salt and black pepper, to taste
For the Tomato Sauce:
1 tablespoon butter
1 shallot, chopped
2 garlic cloves, chopped

½ teaspoon red wine vinegar
2 tablespoons tomato paste
14 ounces (397 g) canned crushed tomatoes
½ teaspoon salt
1 teaspoon dried basil
1 teaspoon dried oregano
Black pepper, to taste
For the Salad:
2 cucumbers, spiralized
2 tablespoons olive oil
1 tablespoon rice vinegar

1. Set oven to 400ºF and grease a baking dish. Set aside. 2. Place a pan over medium heat. Melt 2 tablespoons of butter and sauté spinach until it shrinks; season with salt and pepper. Transfer to a bowl containing goat cheese, stir and set aside. Cut the chicken breasts lengthwise and stuff with the cheese mixture and set into the baking dish. On top, spread the grated cheddar cheese, add 2 tablespoons of butter then set into the oven. Bake until cooked through for 20-30 minutes. 3. Set a pan over medium-high heat and warm 1 tablespoon of butter. Add in garlic and shallot and cook until soft. Place in herbs, tomato paste, vinegar, tomatoes, salt, and pepper. Bring the mixture to a boil. Set heat to low and simmer for 15 minutes. Arrange the cucumbers on a serving platter, season with salt, pepper, olive oil, and vinegar, Top with the chicken and pour over the sauce.
Per Serving
Calories: 484 | fat: 36g | protein: 40g | carbs: 10g | net carbs: 5g | fiber: 5g

Chicken Skewers with Celery Fries

Prep time: 5 minutes | Cook time: 40 minutes | Serves 4

2 chicken breasts
½ teaspoon salt
¼ teaspoon ground black pepper
2 tablespoons olive oil
¼ cup chicken broth

For the Fries:
1 pound (454 g) celery root
2 tablespoons olive oil
½ teaspoon salt
¼ teaspoon ground black pepper

1. Set oven to 400ºF. Grease and line a baking sheet. In a bowl, mix oil, spices and the chicken; set in the fridge for 10 minutes while covered. Peel and chop celery root to form fry shapes and place into a separate bowl. Apply oil to coat and add pepper and salt for seasoning. Arrange to the baking tray in an even layer and bake for 10 minutes. 2. Take the chicken from the refrigerator and thread onto the skewers. Place over the celery, pour in the chicken broth, then set in the oven for 30 minutes. Serve with lemon wedges.
Per Serving
Calories: 579 | fat: 43g | protein: 39g | carbs: 9g | net carbs: 6g | fiber: 3g

Greek Chicken with Gravy and Asparagus

Prep time: 15 minutes | Cook time: 1½ hours | Serves 6

1 (3½ pounds/1.6 kg) whole chicken, giblets removed and reserved
3 tablespoons refined avocado oil or melted coconut oil
1½ tablespoons Greek seasoning
1 apple, roughly chopped

Handful of fresh parsley
6 sprigs fresh oregano
6 sprigs fresh thyme
4 small cloves garlic
Gravy:
Giblets (from above)
3 tablespoons melted duck fat
1 teaspoon tapioca starch

1. pound (455 g) asparagus, tough ends removed, for serving 1. Preheat the oven to 350°F (177°C). Set the chicken in a roasting pan or large cast-iron frying pan. Coat all sides of the bird with the oil, then top with the Greek seasoning. Stuff the bird with the apple, parsley, oregano, thyme, and garlic. Roast for 1 hour 15 minutes, or until the internal temperature in the thigh reaches 165°F (74°C) and the juices run clear. 2. While the bird is cooking, **cook the giblets:** Place the giblets in a small saucepan and cover with about 1½ cups (350 ml) of water, then cover the pan with a lid and bring to a boil. Reduce the heat to low and simmer for 30 minutes. Strain the giblet pieces, reserving the flavorful cooking liquid. Discard the giblets. 3. About 10 minutes before the bird is done, steam the asparagus. 4. When the chicken is done, remove it from the oven and transfer the bird to a serving platter. Remove the stuffing and surround the chicken with the steamed asparagus. 5. Place the roasting pan on the stovetop over medium heat. Add ½ cup (120 ml) of the giblet cooking liquid and the melted duck fat to the pan and whisk to combine. Add the tapioca starch and continue to whisk until the gravy has thickened. 6. Drizzle the gravy over the bird or serve on the side.
Per Serving
Calories: 580 | fat: 41g | protein: 50g | carbs: 4g | net carbs: 2g | fiber: 2g

Chicken Piccata with Mushrooms

Prep time: 25 minutes | Cook time: 25 minutes | Serves 4

1 pound (454 g) thinly sliced chicken breasts
1½ teaspoons salt, divided
½ teaspoon freshly ground black pepper
¼ cup ground flaxseed
2 tablespoons almond flour
8 tablespoons extra-virgin olive oil, divided
4 tablespoons butter, divided

2 cups sliced mushrooms
½ cup dry white wine or chicken stock
¼ cup freshly squeezed lemon juice
¼ cup roughly chopped capers
Zucchini noodles, for serving
¼ cup chopped fresh flat-leaf Italian parsley, for garnish

1. Season the chicken with 1 teaspoon salt and the pepper. On a plate, combine the ground flaxseed and almond flour and dredge each chicken breast in the mixture. Set aside. 2. In a large skillet, heat 4 tablespoons olive oil and 1 tablespoon butter over medium-high heat. Working in batches if necessary, brown the chicken, 3 to 4 minutes per side. Remove from the skillet and keep warm. 3. Add the remaining 4 tablespoons olive oil and 1 tablespoon butter to the skillet along with mushrooms and sauté over medium heat until just tender, 6 to 8 minutes. 4. Add the white wine, lemon juice, capers, and remaining ½ teaspoon salt to the skillet and bring to a boil, whisking to incorporate any little browned bits that have stuck to the bottom of the skillet. Reduce the heat to low and whisk in the final 2 tablespoons butter. 5. Return the browned chicken to skillet, cover, and simmer over low heat until the chicken is cooked through and the sauce has thickened, 5 to 6 more minutes. 6. Serve chicken and mushrooms warm over zucchini noodles, spooning the mushroom sauce over top and garnishing with chopped parsley.

Per Serving

Calories: 596 | fat: 48g | protein: 30g | carbs: 8g | fiber: 4g | sodium: 862mg

Cheesy Chicken Sun-Dried Tomato Packets

Prep time: 15 minutes | Cook time: 40 minutes | Serves 4

1 cup goat cheese
½ cup chopped oil-packed sun-dried tomatoes
1 teaspoon minced garlic
½ teaspoon dried basil
½ teaspoon dried oregano

4 (4 ounces/113 g) boneless chicken breasts
Sea salt, for seasoning
Freshly ground black pepper, for seasoning
3 tablespoons olive oil

1. Preheat the oven. Set the oven temperature to 375°F.
2. Prepare the filling. In a medium bowl, stir together the goat cheese, sun-dried tomatoes, garlic, basil, and oregano until everything is well blended. 3. Stuff the chicken. Make a horizontal slice in the middle of each chicken breast to make a pocket, making sure not to cut through the sides or ends. Spoon one-quarter of the filling into each breast, folding the skin and chicken meat over the slit to form packets. Secure the packets with a toothpick. Lightly season the breasts with salt and pepper. 4. Brown the chicken. In a large oven-safe skillet over medium heat, warm the olive oil. Add the breasts and sear them, turning them once, until they are golden, about 8 minutes in total. 5. Bake the chicken. Place the skillet in the oven and bake the chicken for 30 minutes or until it's cooked through. 6. Serve. Remove the toothpicks. Divide the chicken between four plates and serve them immediately.

Per Serving

Calories: 388 | fat: 29g | protein: 28g | carbs: 4g | net carbs: 3g | fiber: 1g

My Favorite Creamy Pesto Chicken

Prep time: 10 minutes | Cook time: 20 minutes | Serves 4

Chicken:
¼ cup avocado oil
1 pound (454 g) boneless, skinless chicken breasts, thinly sliced
1 small white onion, thinly sliced
½ cup sun-dried tomatoes, drained and chopped
¾ teaspoon dried oregano leaves
½ teaspoon dried thyme leaves
⅛ teaspoon red pepper flakes

Pesto Cream Sauce:
2 cloves garlic
¼ cup pine nuts
¼ cup nutritional yeast
½ cup chicken bone broth
½ cup full-fat coconut milk
½ teaspoon finely ground sea salt
½ teaspoon ground black pepper
½ ounce (14 g) fresh basil leaves and stems
2 medium zucchinis, spiral sliced, raw or cooked, for serving

1. Heat the oil in a large frying pan over medium heat. When hot, add the chicken, onion, sun-dried tomatoes, oregano, thyme, and red pepper flakes. Sauté for 5 minutes, or until fragrant. 2. Meanwhile, place all the ingredients for the pesto cream sauce, except the basil, in a food processor or blender. Blend on high until smooth, about 30 seconds. Add the basil and pulse to break it up slightly, but before the sauce turns a bright green color—don't pulverize the basil! 3. Pour the sauce into the pan and toss the chicken to coat. Reduce the heat to low, cover, and cook for 15 minutes, stirring every couple of minutes, until the chicken is cooked through. 4. Divide the spiral-sliced zucchini among 4 dinner plates and top with equal portions of the chicken and sauce. Dig in!

Per Serving

Calories: 455 | fat: 29g | protein: 32g | carbs: 16g | net carbs: 11g | fiber: 4g

Spicy Creamy Chicken Soup

Prep time: 10 minutes | Cook time: 30 minutes | Serves 15

2 (32 ounces/907 g) cartons chicken broth or bone broth
1 (8 ounces/227 g) brick cream cheese, cubed
4 (12½ ounces/354 g) cans chicken or 1¾ pounds (794 g) chopped cooked boneless skinless chicken breasts or rotisserie chicken
2 (10 ounces/283 g) cans

diced tomatoes and green chilies, undrained
½ cup ranch dressing
½ cup heavy cream
1 teaspoon garlic powder
1 teaspoon sea salt
1 teaspoon freshly ground black pepper
15 ounces (425 g) grated Cheddar cheese

1. In a stockpot over medium heat, combine the broth, cream cheese, chicken, tomatoes and green chilies, ranch dressing, heavy cream, garlic powder, salt, and pepper. 2. Simmer for 30 minutes, stirring occasionally. 3. Portion into individual bowls and sprinkle each with ¼ cup of Cheddar cheese. Enjoy!

Per Serving 8 ounces
Calories: 383 | fat: 27g | protein: 27g | carbs: 7g | net carbs: 7g | fiber: 0g

Chicken Alfredo

Prep time: 5 minutes | Cook time: 20 minutes | Serves 2

2 teaspoons extra-virgin olive oil, divided
8 ounces (227 g) boneless, skinless chicken thighs, cubed
2 tablespoons butter
½ teaspoon minced garlic
½ cup heavy (whipping) cream
⅔ cup grated Parmesan

cheese
¼ cup shredded low-moisture mozzarella cheese
Pinch of red pepper flakes
Pink Himalayan sea salt
Freshly ground black pepper
1 (7 ounces/198 g) package shirataki noodles, drained, or 7 ounces (198 g) zoodles (spiralized zucchini)

1. In a small sauté pan or skillet, heat 1 teaspoon of olive oil over medium heat and cook the chicken for 10 to 12 minutes, until cooked through. 2. In a medium saucepan, melt the butter over medium heat. Add the garlic and cook for 1 to 2 minutes, until slightly browned. Add the cream and bring to a simmer. 3. Slowly add the Parmesan and mozzarella while stirring. The cheese should melt into the sauce. 4. Reduce the heat, add the chicken, and heat through, without allowing the sauce to boil. Season with the salt and pepper. 5. In the same skillet as you cooked the chicken, add the remaining 1 teaspoon of olive oil and drop in the shirataki noodles. Cook the noodles over medium heat for 2 to 3 minutes, until heated through. 6. Spoon the noodles onto 2 serving plates and top with the sauce.

Per Serving
Calories: 810 | fat: 70g | protein: 36g | carbs: 11g | net carbs: 9g | fiber: 2g

Zucchini Spaghetti with Turkey Bolognese Sauce

Prep time: 10 minutes | Cook time: 35 minutes | Serves 6

3 cups sliced mushrooms
2 teaspoons olive oil
1 pound (454 g) ground turkey

3 tablespoons pesto sauce
1 cup diced onion
2 cups broccoli florets
6 cups zucchini, spiralized

1. Heat the oil in a skillet. Add zucchini and cook for 2-3 minutes, stirring continuously; set aside. 2. Add turkey to the skillet and cook until browned, about 7-8 minutes. Transfer to a plate. Add onion and cook until translucent, about 3 minutes. Add broccoli and mushrooms, and cook for 7 more minutes. Return the turkey to the skillet. Stir in the pesto sauce. Cover the pan, lower the heat, and simmer for 15 minutes. Stir in zucchini pasta and serve immediately.

Per Serving
Calories: 279 | fat: 19g | protein: 22g | carbs: 5g | net carbs: 3g | fiber: 2g

Indoor BBQ Chicken

Prep time: 10 minutes | Cook time: 45 minutes | Serves 4

1 tablespoon sriracha sauce
2 teaspoons chili powder
2 teaspoons garlic powder
2 teaspoons onion powder
1 teaspoon salt
1 teaspoon black pepper
1 tablespoon apple cider vinegar

1 tablespoon paprika
1 (1 g) packet 0g net carb sweetener
½ teaspoon xanthan gum
1 cup crushed tomatoes
4 medium chicken thighs with skin

1. Preheat oven to 375°F. Line a baking sheet with parchment paper or greased foil. 2. In a small saucepan over medium-high heat, make the barbecue sauce by mixing all the ingredients except the chicken and bring to boil. Let simmer 5 minutes, stirring regularly. 3. Using a basting brush, apply about half the barbecue sauce to both sides of thighs. Place chicken on baking sheet. 4. Cook 20 minutes. Flip chicken and reapply remaining sauce. Cook another 20 minutes until chicken is thoroughly cooked. 5. Serve warm or cold.

Per Serving
Calories: 362 | fat: 19g | protein: 34g | carbs: 10g | net carbs: 7g | fiber: 3g

Habanero Chicken Wings

Prep time: 10 minutes | Cook time: 50 minutes | Serves 4

2 pounds (907 g) chicken wings
Salt and black pepper, to taste
3 tablespoons coconut aminos

3 tablespoons rice vinegar
3 tablespoons stevia
¼ cup chives, chopped
½ teaspoon xanthan gum
5 dried habanero peppers, chopped

1. Spread the chicken wings on a lined baking sheet and sprinkle with 2 tablespoons of water, black pepper and salt. Bake in the oven at 370ºF for 35 minutes. Put a small pan over medium heat and add in the remaining ingredients. Bring the mixture to a boil and cook for 2 minutes. 2Pour the sauce over the chicken and bake for 10 more minutes. Serve warm.

Per Serving
Calories: 410 | fat: 25g | protein: 26g | carbs: 20g | net carbs: 2g | fiber: 18g

Mezze Cake

Prep time: 10 minutes | Cook time: 35 minutes | Serves 2 to 4

Nonstick cooking spray
2 coconut wraps (one of them is optional)
1 small eggplant, thinly sliced lengthwise
Salt, to taste
1 zucchini, thinly sliced lengthwise
1 (8 ounces/227 g) jar sun-dried tomatoes packed in olive oil (do not discard oil), chopped or whole
½ (14 ounces/397 g) can

quartered artichoke hearts
½ cup cauliflower rice
¼ cup black olives, pitted and coarsely chopped
2 precooked sugar-free chicken sausages, cut into bite-size pieces
1 tablespoon dried oregano or marjoram
½ tablespoon garlic powder
Freshly ground black pepper, to taste

1. Preheat the oven to 350ºF (180ºC). Coat a shallow baking dish with nonstick spray and place a coconut wrap in the bottom. 2. Sprinkle the eggplant with ½ teaspoon of salt and let sit for 5 minutes to let the moisture come to the surface. Get a damp towel and wipe off the salt and excess water from the eggplant. 3. Lay the eggplant slices on top of the coconut wrap, then lay the zucchini slices on top of the eggplant. Next add the sun-dried tomatoes and drizzle in the olive oil they're packed in. Sprinkle in the artichoke hearts, then add the cauliflower rice. Scatter the olives on top, then shower the chicken sausage over all the vegetables. Season everything with the oregano, garlic powder, salt, and pepper. 4. Place another coconut wrap over the top of everything, if desired, and bake this vegetable layer "cake" in the oven for about 25 minutes, or until the vegetables are a bit wilted.

5. Turn the oven to broil and cook for another 5 minutes, or until the top is crisp. 6. Remove from the oven and let cool before slicing and serving.

Per Serving
Calories: 510 | fat: 38g | protein: 17g | carbs: 25g | net carbs: 13g | fiber: 12g

Greek Chicken with Capers

Prep time: 10 minutes | Cook time: 15 minutes | Serves 4

¼ cup olive oil
1 onion, chopped
4 chicken breasts, skinless and boneless
4 garlic cloves, minced
Salt and ground black pepper, to taste

½ cup kalamata olives, pitted and chopped
1 tablespoon capers
1 pound (454 g) tomatoes, chopped
½ teaspoon red chili flakes

1. Sprinkle black pepper and salt on the chicken, and rub with half of the oil. Add the chicken to a pan set over high heat, cook for 2 minutes, flip to the other side, and cook for 2 more minutes. Set the chicken breasts in the oven at 450ºF and bake for 8 minutes. Split the chicken into serving plates. 2. Set the same pan over medium heat and warm the remaining oil, place in the onion, olives, capers, garlic, and chili flakes, and cook for 1 minute. Stir in the tomatoes, black pepper, and salt, and cook for 2 minutes. Sprinkle over the chicken breasts and enjoy.

Per Serving
Calories: 329 | fat: 21g | protein: 25g | carbs: 10g | net carbs: 2g | fiber: 3g

Chicken Tenders

Prep time: 10 minutes | Cook time: 25 to 30 minutes | Serves 4

2 cups crushed pork rinds
¼ cup grated Parmesan cheese
1 teaspoon garlic powder
1 teaspoon freshly ground black pepper

1 large egg
½ cup heavy cream
1 pound (454 g) boneless skinless chicken tenderloins (10 to 12 tenderloins), patted dry

1. Preheat the oven to 425ºF (220ºC). Line a baking sheet with parchment paper and set aside. 2. In a shallow bowl, mix the pork rinds, Parmesan cheese, garlic powder, and pepper. 3. In a separate bowl, whisk together the egg and heavy cream. 4. Dip a tenderloin entirely in the egg mixture, then lay the tenderloin in the pork rind mixture, turning to coat both sides. 5. Lay the coated tenderloin on the prepared baking sheet and repeat with the remaining tenderloins. 6. Bake for 25 to 30 minutes.

Per Serving3 tenderloins: Calories: 460 | fat: 32g | protein: 41g | carbs: 2g | net carbs: 2g | fiber: 0g

Easy Marinated Chicken Thighs

Prep time: 10 minutes | Cook time: 15 minutes | Serves 3

½ cup olive oil
¼ cup balsamic vinegar
1 teaspoon minced garlic
(1 or 2 cloves)
Juice of ½ lemon
½ teaspoon red pepper flakes

1 pound (454 g) boneless
skinless chicken thighs
Salt, to taste
Freshly ground black pepper,
to taste

1. In a large container (or in a plastic freezer bag), whisk together the olive oil, vinegar, garlic, lemon juice, and red pepper flakes. Add the chicken and toss well to combine. Season with salt and black pepper. Refrigerate to marinate for at least 30 minutes, and preferably a couple of hours.
2. Cook the chicken on a grill, in a grill pan, large pan, or cast-iron skillet over medium-high heat, for 5 to 7 minutes per side or until browned and cooked through. Serve hot. Refrigerate leftovers in an airtight container for up to 1 week.
Per Serving
Calories: 496 | fat: 40g | protein: 30g | carbs: 4g | net carbs: 4g | fiber: 0g

Stuffed Chicken for Suppah

Prep time: 10 minutes | Cook time: 24 minutes | Serves 4

6 ounces (170 g) chopped
fresh spinach
2 cloves garlic, peeled and
minced
1½ cups crumbled feta
cheese, divided
2 ounces (57 g) full-fat

cream cheese, softened
4 (4.8 ounces/134 g)
boneless, skinless chicken
breasts
¼ teaspoon black pepper
2 medium Roma tomatoes,
each sliced into 8 rounds

1. Preheat oven to 450°F. Line a baking sheet with parchment paper or greased foil. 2. Steam spinach in microwave 2–3 minutes (or cook in a medium skillet 3–5 minutes over medium heat). Let cooked spinach cool, then squeeze out excess moisture. 3. To a medium bowl, add spinach, garlic, and ¾ cup feta cheese. 4. Microwave cream cheese to soften for 15–30 seconds. Add to spinach mixture, stirring thoroughly. 5. Place chicken on baking sheet. Cut horizontal slit in each breast, creating a pocket. (Center your cut midway, between top and bottom of the breast.) 6. Stuff each breast with one-quarter of the total spinach mixture. Sprinkle lightly with pepper. 7. Top each breast with four tomato slices and remaining feta. 8. Bake 16–20 minutes until chicken is thoroughly cooked. Tent pan with foil if cheese starts to brown before chicken is done.
Per Serving
Calories: 364 | fat: 19g | protein: 40g | carbs: 7g | net carbs: 5g | fiber: 2g

Red Wine Chicken

Prep time: 10 minutes | Cook time: 15 minutes | Serves 4

3 tablespoons coconut oil
2 pounds (907 g) chicken
breast halves, skinless and
boneless
3 garlic cloves, minced
Salt and black pepper, to
taste

1 cup chicken stock
3 tablespoons stevia
½ cup red wine
2 tomatoes, sliced
6 mozzarella slices
Fresh basil, chopped, for
serving

1. Set a pan over medium heat and warm oil, add the chicken, season with pepper and salt, cook until brown. Stir in the stevia, garlic, stock, and red wine, and cook for 10 minutes. 2. Remove to a lined baking sheet and arrange mozzarella cheese slices on top. Broil in the oven over medium heat until cheese melts and lay tomato slices over chicken pieces. 3Sprinkle with chopped basil to serve.
Per Serving
Calories: 381 | fat: 38g | protein: 26g | carbs: 4g | net carbs: 4g | fiber: 0g
Per Serving
Calories: 297 | fat: 21g | protein: 22g | carbs: 5g | net carbs: 3g | fiber: 2g

Steph's Stuffed Peppers

Prep time: 10 minutes | Cook time: 40 minutes | Serves 6

4 medium green bell
peppers, seeded
1 medium red bell pepper,
seeded
1 medium yellow bell
pepper, seeded
1 pound (454 g) lean ground
turkey
1 cup cooked riced

cauliflower
¾ cup no-sugar-added salsa
1 teaspoon chili powder
1 teaspoon ground cumin
½ teaspoon black pepper
¼ teaspoon salt
1 cup shredded Cheddar
cheese

1. Preheat oven to 375°F. Grease a 9" × 13" baking dish. 2. Remove stems from peppers by cutting tight circle around stem. Cut peppers in half vertically from stem to bottom. Remove the seeds and membranes from insides. Wash gently and pat dry. 3. In a medium skillet over medium-high heat, cook ground turkey, stirring regularly, about 10 minutes. 4. Add riced cauliflower. Stir in salsa and spices. 5. Arrange bell pepper halves open-side up in baking dish. Fill each pepper half with one-twelfth of meat mixture and top with cheese. 6. Bake 30 minutes, or until peppers are softened and cheese is fully melted. Remove from oven and let cool. Serve warm.
Per Serving
Calories: 159 | fat: 6g | protein: 6g | carbs: 10g | net carbs: 7g | fiber: 3g

Chipotle Dry-Rub Wings

Prep time: 10 minutes | Cook time: 45 minutes | Serves 4

Chipotle Rub:

1 tablespoon ground chipotle pepper	1 teaspoon onion powder
1 teaspoon paprika	1 teaspoon pink Himalayan salt
1 teaspoon ground cumin	2 pounds (907 g) chicken wings
1 teaspoon ground mustard	
1 teaspoon garlic powder	1 teaspoon baking powder

1. Preheat the oven to 250°F and place a wire baking rack inside a rimmed baking sheet. 2. Put the seasonings for the rub in a small bowl and stir with a fork. Divide the spice rub into 2 equal portions. 3. Cut the wings in half, if whole (see Tip), and place in a large zip-top plastic bag. Add the baking powder and half of the spice rub to the bag and shake thoroughly to coat the wings. 4. Lay the wings on the baking rack in a single layer. Bake for 25 minutes. 5. Turn the heat up to 450°F and bake the wings for an additional 20 minutes, until golden brown and crispy. 6. Once the wings are done, place them in a large plastic container with the remaining half of the spice rub and shake to coat. Serve immediately.

Per Serving
Calories: 507 | fat: 36g | protein: 42g | carbs: 3g | net carbs: 3g | fiber: 0g

Stewed Chicken and Sausage

Prep time: 10 minutes | Cook time: 1 hour 10 minutes | Serves 8

2 pounds (907 g) Mexican-style fresh (raw) chorizo	3 tablespoons minced garlic
1 tablespoon coconut oil	2 tablespoons smoked paprika
2 boneless, skinless chicken thighs, cut into ½-inch pieces	1 tablespoon ground cumin
	1 tablespoon dried oregano leaves
1 cup chopped onions	2 teaspoons fine sea salt
1½ (18 ounces/510 g) jars whole peeled tomatoes with juices	1 teaspoon cayenne pepper
	2 cups chicken bone broth, homemade or store-bought
3 chipotle chiles in adobo sauce	¼ cup lime juice
	¼ cup chopped fresh cilantro

1. Slice 1 pound (454 g) of the chorizo into rounds; crumble the remaining pound. 2. Heat the oil in large soup pot over medium-high heat. Add the sliced and crumbled chorizo, chicken, and onions and cook until the onions are soft and the chicken is cooked through, about 5 minutes, stirring to break up the crumbled chorizo. 3. Meanwhile, place the tomatoes and their juices and the chiles in a food processor. Purée until smooth; set aside. 4. Add the garlic, paprika, cumin, oregano, salt, and cayenne pepper to the soup pot and sauté for another minute while stirring. 5. Add the puréed tomato mixture and broth to the soup pot. Bring to a gentle boil, then reduce the heat to low and simmer for 1 hour to allow the flavors to open up. Just before serving, stir in the lime juice and cilantro. 6. Store extras in an airtight container in the fridge for up to 2 days. Reheat in a saucepan over medium heat until warmed.

Per Serving
Calories: 415 | fat: 33g | protein: 20g | carbs: 10g | net carbs: 8g | fiber: 2g

Roasted Chicken with Tarragon

Prep time: 10 minutes | Cook time: 40 minutes | Serves 4

2 pounds (907 g) chicken thighs	4 ¼ ounces (120 g) butter
	1 tablespoon tarragon
2 pounds (907 g) radishes, sliced	Salt and black pepper, to taste
	1 cup mayonnaise

1. Set oven to 400°F and grease a baking dish. 2. Add in the chicken, radishes, tarragon, pepper, and salt. 3. Place in butter then set into the oven and cook for 40 minutes at 360°F. 4. Remove to a serving plate and serve with mayonnaise.

Per Serving
Calories: 957 | fat: 81g | protein: 43g | carbs: 13g | net carbs: 8g | fiber: 5g

Bacon Wrapped Chicken with Grilled Asparagus

Prep time: 5 minutes | Cook time: 40 minutes | Serves 4

6 chicken breasts	spears
Pink salt and black pepper to taste	3 tablespoons olive oil
8 bacon slices	2 tablespoons fresh lemon juice
3 tablespoons olive oil	Manchego cheese for topping
1 pound (454 g) asparagus	

1. Preheat the oven to 400°F. 2. Season chicken breasts with salt and black pepper, and wrap 2 bacon slices around each chicken breast. Arrange on a baking sheet that is lined with parchment paper, drizzle with oil and bake for 25-30 minutes until bacon is brown and crispy. 3. Preheat your grill to high heat. 4. Brush the asparagus spears with olive oil and season with salt. Grill for 8-10 minutes, frequently turning until slightly charred. Remove to a plate and drizzle with lemon juice. Grate over Manchego cheese so that it melts a little on contact with the hot asparagus and forms a cheesy dressing.

Per Serving
Calories: 464 | fat: 36g | protein: 32g | carbs: 3g | net carbs: 3g | fiber: 0g

Crunchy Chicken Tacos

Prep time: 5 minutes | Cook time: 30 minutes to 8 hours | Serves 4

1 pound (454 g) frozen boneless, skinless chicken thighs
1 cup chicken broth
1 cup low-carb green salsa
½ medium onion, chopped
2 teaspoons minced garlic
8 slices provolone cheese
1 cup shredded lettuce
¼ cup chopped ripe tomato
½ cup sour cream

1. In a slow cooker or electric pressure cooker, combine the chicken thighs, broth, salsa, onion, and garlic. 2. Place the lid on the pot. If using a slow cooker, cook on the low setting for 7 to 8 hours or on high for 3 to 4 hours. If using a pressure cooker, cook for 20 minutes on high pressure, then quick-release the pressure. 3. Place a slice of the provolone on a piece of parchment paper (not wax paper). Microwave on high power for 45 seconds; the cheese should just begin to turn a brownish orange in a few spots. 4. Quickly and carefully remove the parchment paper from the microwave. Holding opposite edges of the paper, form the melted cheese into a U shape. Hold it in this position for about 10 seconds, until it cools enough to hold its shape. (You can also hang the microwaved cheese slice over a wooden spoon handle to form the shape.) Remove the taco from the parchment paper. Repeat with the remaining 7 cheese slices. 5. Using a slotted spoon, remove the chicken from the cooker. Using 2 forks, shred the chicken, then return it to the cooker. 6. Use tongs or a slotted spoon to fill the tacos with equal portions of the chicken, being careful to drain off some of the liquid so the tacos don't get soggy. 7. Top the chicken filling with shredded lettuce, tomato, and sour cream, then serve.

Per Serving
Calories: 528 | fat: 40g | protein: 35g | carbs: 8g | net carbs: 6g | fiber: 2g

Chicken Fajitas with Bell Peppers

Prep time: 10 minutes | Cook time: 5 minutes | Serves 4

1½ pounds (680 g) boneless, skinless chicken breasts
¼ cup avocado oil
2 tablespoons water
1 tablespoon Mexican hot sauce
2 cloves garlic, minced
1 teaspoon lime juice
1 teaspoon ground cumin
1 teaspoon salt
1 teaspoon erythritol
¼ teaspoon chili powder
¼ teaspoon smoked paprika
5 ounces (142 g) sliced yellow bell pepper strips
5 ounces (142 g) sliced red bell pepper strips
5 ounces (142 g) sliced green bell pepper strips

1. Slice the chicken into very thin strips lengthwise. Cut each strip in half again. Imagine the thickness of restaurant fajitas when cutting. 2. In a measuring cup, whisk together the avocado oil, water, hot sauce, garlic, lime juice, cumin, salt, erythritol, chili powder, and paprika to form a marinade. Add to the pot, along with the chicken and peppers. 3. Close the lid and seal the vent. Cook on High Pressure for 5 minutes. Quick release the steam.

Per Serving
Calories: 319 | fat: 18g | protein: 34g | carbs: 6g | net carbs: 4g | fiber: 2g

Chicken Broccoli Alfredo

Prep time: 15 minutes | Cook time: 15 minutes | Serves 4

1 tablespoon butter
1 garlic clove, minced
1 pound (454 g) boneless skinless chicken breasts, diced
Salt, to taste
Freshly ground black pepper, to taste
1 large head broccoli, cut into florets
1½ cups Alfredo sauce
¼ cup grated Parmesan cheese

1. Preheat the oven to 350ºF (180ºC). 2. In a large ovenproof skillet over medium heat, melt the butter. 3. Add the garlic. Sauté for about 2 minutes until fragrant. 4. Add the chicken and stir. Season with salt and pepper. Cook for 5 to 7 minutes, stirring, until the chicken begins to brown. 5. Add the broccoli and continue to stir. Cook for 3 to 4 minutes more. 6. Pour the Alfredo sauce over everything, stirring to combine. 7. Top with the Parmesan and transfer to the oven for 5 to 7 minutes or until the cheese browns slightly. Refrigerate leftovers in an airtight container for up to 5 days.

Per Serving
Calories: 597 | fat: 43g | protein: 42g | carbs: 13g | net carbs: 9g | fiber: 4g

Baked Chicken with Acorn Squash and Goat's Cheese

Prep time: 15 minutes | Cook time: 45 minutes | Serves 6

6 chicken breasts, butterflied
1 pound (454 g) acorn squash, cubed
Salt and black pepper, to taste
1 cup goat's cheese, shredded
1 tablespoon dried parsley
3 tablespoons olive oil

1. Arrange the chicken breasts and squash in a baking dish. Season with salt, black pepper, and parsley. Drizzle with olive oil and pour a cup of water. Cover with aluminium foil and bake in the oven for 30 minutes at 420ºF. Discard the foil, scatter goat's cheese, and bake for 15-20 minutes. Remove to a serving plate and enjoy.

Per Serving
Calories: 266 | fat: 18g | protein: 21g | carbs: 5g | net carbs: 5g | fiber: 0g

Garlic & Ginger Chicken with Peanut Sauce

Prep time: 10 minutes | Cook time: 14 minutes | Serves 6

1 tablespoon wheat-free soy sauce
1 tablespoon sugar-free fish sauce
1 tablespoon lime juice
1 teaspoon cilantro
1 teaspoon minced garlic
1 teaspoon minced ginger
1 tablespoon olive oil
1 tablespoon rice wine vinegar
1 teaspoon cayenne pepper
1 teaspoon erythritol

6 chicken thighs

Peanut Sauce:
½ cup peanut butter
1 teaspoon minced garlic
1 tablespoon lime juice
2 tablespoons water
1 teaspoon minced ginger
1 tablespoon chopped jalapeño
2 tablespoons rice wine vinegar
2 tablespoons erythritol
1 tablespoon fish sauce

1. Combine all chicken ingredients in a large Ziploc bag. Seal the bag and shake to combine. Refrigerate for 1 hour. Remove from fridge about 15 minutes before cooking. 2. Preheat the grill to medium heat and cook the chicken for 7 minutes per side. Whisk together all sauce ingredients in a mixing bowl. Serve the chicken drizzled with peanut sauce.

Per Serving
Calories: 536 | fat: 38g | protein: 34g | carbs: 12g | net carbs: 11g | fiber: 1g

Sticky Sesame Chicken

Prep time: 10 minutes | Cook time: 30 minutes | Serves 2

Chicken:
½ cup coconut oil, for the pan
½ pound (227 g) boneless, skinless chicken thighs
½ teaspoon pink Himalayan salt
¼ teaspoon ground black pepper
⅓ cup coconut flour

Sauce:
1½ teaspoons toasted sesame oil
1 clove garlic, minced
1 (½-inch) piece fresh ginger, grated

¼ cup soy sauce
2½ tablespoons unseasoned rice wine vinegar
2½ tablespoons powdered erythritol
2 tablespoons water
½ teaspoon red pepper flakes
¼ teaspoon xanthan gum
2 cups riced cauliflower (see Tip, opposite)

For Garnish (Optional):
White and/or black sesame seeds
Sliced scallions

1. Heat the coconut oil in a saucepan over medium-high heat until it reaches 330°F to 350°F. 2. Meanwhile, **prepare the chicken:** Pat the thighs dry, cut them into bite-sized pieces, and season with the salt and pepper. Toss them in the coconut flour until fully coated. 3. Working in batches of 3 or 4 pieces, fry the coated chicken in the hot oil, turning them until light brown on the outside and cooked through in the center, 3 to 5 minutes. Remove with a slotted spoon and set on a paper towel–lined plate to drain while you fry the remaining pieces. 4. Once all the chicken is cooked, **make the sauce:** Heat the sesame oil in a small saucepan over medium heat. Add the garlic and ginger and cook for 30 seconds, or until fragrant. Add the remaining sauce ingredients, except for the xanthan gum, and whisk to combine. Simmer for about 3 minutes, then add the xanthan gum and whisk to combine. Turn the heat up to medium-high and allow the sauce to reduce and thicken, 5 to 7 minutes. 5. While the sauce reduces, **steam the rice:** Put the riced cauliflower in a microwave-safe bowl and cover with 2 or 3 damp paper towels. Microwave for 4 to 5 minutes, until tender but not mushy. Divide the steamed cauliflower rice between 2 bowls. 6. Add the chicken pieces to the saucepan with the thickened sauce and toss to coat them thoroughly; leave on the stovetop for 2 minutes to reheat. Divide the chicken and sauce between the bowls with the cauliflower rice and garnish with sesame seeds and sliced scallions, if desired.

Per Serving
Calories: 332 | fat: 16g | protein: 35g | carbs: 13g | net carbs: 6g | fiber: 7g

Duck Shish Kebab

Prep time: 10 minutes | Cook time: 20 minutes | Serves 2

2 boneless, skin-on duck breasts, cut into 1-inch cubes
1 teaspoon Chinese five-spice powder
¼ teaspoon pink Himalayan sea salt
¼ teaspoon freshly ground

black pepper
1 red bell pepper, cored, seeded, and cut into 1-inch chunks
½ small red onion, cut into 1-inch slices and then quartered 1 teaspoon extra-virgin olive oil

1. If using bamboo skewers, soak them in water for 30 minutes. Preheat the oven to 350°F (180°C). Line a baking sheet with parchment paper. 2. In a large bowl, sprinkle the duck cubes with the five-spice powder, salt, and pepper. Toss the duck to evenly distribute the seasonings. 3. Using metal or bamboo skewers, alternate pieces of bell pepper, duck, and onion, then repeat. Keep the fat side of the duck cubes facing outward in the same direction. 4. In a large sauté pan or skillet, heat the olive oil over medium-high heat. 5. Place the skewers in the skillet and cook for about 1 minute on each side, except the fat side. Cook the fat side for 2 to 3 minutes. The skewers should be browned on all sides. 6. Transfer the skewers to the baking sheet and bake for 15 to 20 minutes, until the duck is cooked through and the vegetables are tender. Serve.

Braised Chicken Legs with Olives and Artichokes

Prep time: 15 minutes | Cook time: 45 minutes | Serves 4

4 chicken legs
Sea salt, for seasoning
Freshly ground black pepper, for seasoning
¼ cup olive oil, divided
1 onion, chopped
1 red bell pepper, chopped
1 zucchini, chopped
2 tablespoons minced garlic
2 cups tomato sauce
1 cup chicken broth
1 cup chopped artichoke hearts
1 teaspoon smoked paprika
½ cup sliced Kalamata olives
2 tablespoons chopped fresh basil

1. Brown the chicken. Pat the chicken legs dry with a paper towel and season them lightly with salt and pepper. In a large skillet over medium-high heat, warm 2 tablespoons of the olive oil. Add the chicken legs and brown them, turning them once, about 10 minutes in total. Transfer them to a plate and set it aside. 2. Sauté the vegetables. Warm the remaining 2 tablespoons of olive oil in the skillet. Add the onion, red bell pepper, zucchini, and garlic and sauté until they've softened, about 5 minutes. 3. Make the sauce. Stir in the tomato sauce, chicken broth, artichoke hearts, and smoked paprika and bring it to a boil. 4. Braise the chicken. Reduce the heat to low and return the chicken and any accumulated juices on the plate to the skillet. Cover the skillet and simmer until the chicken is cooked through, 28 to 30 minutes. Remove the skillet from the heat and stir in the olives. 5. Serve. Divide the chicken between four plates and top with the chopped basil.
Per Serving
Calories: 456 | fat: 33g | protein: 29g | carbs: 11g | net carbs: 7g | fiber: 4g

Four Horsemen Butter Chicken

Prep time: 10 minutes | Cook time: 27 minutes | Serves 8

1 tablespoon unsalted butter
1 tablespoon olive oil
1 medium onion, peeled and diced
3 cloves garlic, peeled and minced
2 teaspoons peeled and grated fresh ginger
2 pounds (907 g) boneless, skinless chicken breasts, cooked and cut into ¾" chunks
3 ounces tomato paste
3 ounces red curry paste
1 tablespoon garam masala
1 teaspoon chili powder
1 teaspoon mustard seeds
1 teaspoon ground coriander
1 teaspoon curry
1 teaspoon salt
⅛ teaspoon black pepper
1 (14 ounces/397 g) can unsweetened coconut milk
1 teaspoon chopped cilantro

1. In a large skillet over medium-high heat, heat butter and olive oil. Add onion and fry until soft, about 3–5 minutes. Mix in garlic and ginger. Cook 1–2 minutes more. 2. Add cooked chicken to skillet. Add tomato paste, red curry paste, garam masala, chili powder, mustard seeds, coriander, and curry. Add salt and pepper. Stir until well mixed and chicken cubes are well coated. 3. Stir in coconut milk and bring to boil. Reduce heat. Cover and simmer 20 minutes. 4. Remove from heat. Let cool 10 minutes and serve warm with cilantro sprinkled on top.
Per Serving
Calories: 298 | fat: 16g | protein: 30g | carbs: 8g | net carbs: 7g | fiber: 1g

Chicken Fajitas

Prep time: 10 minutes | Cook time: 15 to 20 minutes | Serves 4

1 pound (454 g) boneless, skinless chicken breasts and/or thighs, sliced into thin strips
1 teaspoon salt
1 teaspoon dried oregano
1 teaspoon garlic powder
½ teaspoon freshly ground black pepper
1 teaspoon ground cumin
½ teaspoon red pepper flakes
½ teaspoon paprika
¼ teaspoon ground cinnamon
2 tablespoons avocado oil or
butter, divided
½ white onion, sliced
½ red bell pepper, sliced into strips
½ green bell pepper, sliced into strips
2 tablespoons chicken broth (optional)
2 to 4 coconut or almond flour wraps, or grain-free chips
1 cup shredded romaine lettuce
Sugar-free salsa, guacamole, sour cream, and shredded cheese, for serving (optional)

1. In a large bowl, combine the chicken with the salt, oregano, garlic powder, pepper, cumin, red pepper flakes, paprika, cinnamon, and 1 tablespoon of oil or butter. 2. Heat the remaining tablespoon of oil or butter in a large, shallow skillet over medium-high heat. Add the onion and cook for 3 to 5 minutes, stirring occasionally, until translucent. 3. Add the bell peppers and continue to cook, stirring, for another 5 minutes, until tender. 4. Add the chicken mixture and continue to cook and stir for another 2 to 3 minutes, then reduce the heat to medium, cover, and cook for about 5 minutes, or until the chicken is cooked through and no longer pink. If the chicken starts to burn, add the chicken broth. 5. Remove the chicken mixture from the heat and let cool a bit. 6. Divide the wraps or chips among plates, sprinkle the shredded romaine on top, and spoon the chicken fajita mixture on top of the lettuce. Serve the fajitas with salsa, guacamole, sour cream, and cheese, if you'd like.
Per Serving
Calories: 235 | fat: 13g | protein: 25g | carbs: 5g | net carbs: 3g | fiber: 2g

Buttered Duck Breast

Prep time: 10 minutes | Cook time: 12 minutes | Serves 1

1 medium duck breast, skin scored
1 tablespoon heavy cream
2 tablespoons butter
Salt and black pepper, to taste
1 cup kale
¼ teaspoon fresh sage

1. Set the pan over medium heat and warm half of the butter. Place in sage and heavy cream, and cook for 2 minutes. Set another pan over medium heat. Place in the remaining butter and duck breast as the skin side faces down, cook for 4 minutes, flip, and cook for 3 more minutes. 2. Place the kale to the pan containing the sauce, cook for 1 minute. Set the duck breast on a flat surface and slice. Arrange the duck slices on a platter and drizzle over the sauce.
Per Serving
Calories: 485 | fat: 37g | protein: 35g | carbs: 3g | net carbs: 2g | fiber: 1g

Thyme Chicken Thighs

Prep time: 5 minutes | Cook time: 15 minutes | Serves 4

½ cup chicken stock
1 tablespoon olive oil
½ cup chopped onion
4 chicken thighs
¼ cup heavy cream
2 tablespoons Dijon mustard
1 teaspoon thyme
1 teaspoon garlic powder

1. Heat the olive oil in a pan. Cook the chicken for about 4 minutes per side. Set aside. Sauté the onion in the same pan for 3 minutes, add the stock, and simmer for 5 minutes. Stir in mustard and heavy cream, along with thyme and garlic powder. Pour the sauce over the chicken and serve.
Per Serving
Calories: 528 | fat: 42g | protein: 33g | carbs: 5g | net carbs: 4g | fiber: 1g

Stuffed Mushrooms with Chicken

Prep time: 10 minutes | Cook time: 38 minutes | Serves 5

3 cups cauliflower florets
Salt and black pepper, to taste
1 onion, chopped
1½ pounds (680 g) ground chicken
3 teaspoons fajita seasoning
2 tablespoons butter
10 portobello mushrooms, stems removed
½ cup vegetable broth

1. In a food processor, add the cauliflower florets, pepper and salt, blend for a few times, and transfer to a plate. Set a pan over medium heat and warm butter, stir in onion and cook for 3 minutes. Add in the cauliflower rice, and cook for 3 minutes. 2Stir in the seasoning, pepper, chicken, broth, and salt and cook for a further 2 minutes. Arrange the mushrooms on a lined baking sheet, stuff each one with chicken mixture, put in the oven at 350°F, and bake for 30 minutes. Serve in serving plates and enjoy.
Per Serving
Calories: 269 | fat: 16g | protein: 26g | carbs: 7g | net carbs: 5g | fiber: 2g

Chicken and Bacon Rolls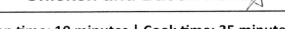

Prep time: 10 minutes | Cook time: 35 minutes | Serves 4

1 tablespoon fresh chives, chopped
8 ounces (227 g) blue cheese
2 pounds (907 g) chicken breasts, skinless, boneless,
halved
12 bacon slices
2 tomatoes, chopped
Salt and ground black pepper, to taste

1. Set a pan over medium heat, place in the bacon, cook until halfway done, remove to a plate. In a bowl, stir together blue cheese, chives, tomatoes, pepper and salt. Use a meat tenderizer to flatten the chicken breasts, season and lay blue cheese mixture on top. Roll them up, and wrap each in a bacon slice. Place the wrapped chicken breasts in a greased baking dish, and roast in the oven at 370°F for 30 minutes. Serve on top of wilted kale.
Per Serving
Calories: 623 | fat: 48g | protein: 38g | carbs: 6g | net carbs: 5g | fiber: 1g

Turkey & Mushroom Bake

Prep time: 15 minutes | Cook time: 40 minutes | Serves 8

4 cups mushrooms, sliced
1 egg, whisked
3 cups green cabbage, shredded
3 cups turkey meat, cooked and chopped
½ cup chicken stock
½ cup cream cheese
1 teaspoon poultry seasoning
2 cups cheddar cheese, grated
½ cup Parmesan cheese, grated
Salt and ground black pepper, to taste
¼ teaspoon garlic powder

1. Set a pan over medium-low heat. Stir in chicken broth, egg, Parmesan cheese, black pepper, garlic powder, poultry seasoning, cheddar cheese, cream cheese, and salt, and simmer. Place in the cabbage and turkey meat, and set away from the heat. 2Add the mushrooms, pepper, turkey mixture and salt in a baking dish and spread. Place aluminum foil to cover, set in an oven at 390°F, and bake for 35 minutes. Allow cooling and enjoy.
Per Serving
Calories: 245 | fat: 15g | protein: 25g | carbs: 4g | net carbs: 3g | fiber: 1g

Artichoke Dip

Prep time: 15 minutes | Cook time: 0 minutes | Serves 3

1 (14 ounces/397 g) can artichoke hearts, drained
1 pound (454 g) goat cheese
2 tablespoons extra-virgin olive oil
2 teaspoons lemon juice
1 garlic clove, minced
1 tablespoon chopped parsley

1 tablespoon chopped chives
½ tablespoon chopped basil
½ teaspoon sea salt
½ teaspoon freshly ground black pepper
Dash of cayenne pepper (optional)
½ cup freshly grated Pecorino Romano

1. In a food processor, combine all the ingredients, except the Pecorino Romano, and process until well incorporated and creamy. 2. Top with the freshly grated Pecorino Romano. Store in an airtight container in the refrigerator for up to 3 days.

Per Serving

Calories: 588 | fat: 44g | protein: 36g | carbs: 15g | fiber: 7g | sodium: 513mg

Clarified Butter and Ghee

Prep time: 5 minutes | Cook time: 30 minutes | Makes 4 cups

2 pounds (907 g) unsalted butter

Special Equipment: Cheesecloth

Make Clarified Butter 1. Slowly melt the butter in a medium-sized heavy-bottomed saucepan over low heat. As the butter comes to a simmer, the milk solids will float to the top and become foamy while the separated oil will become very clear. Skim off the milk solids and remove the butter from the heat. Pour it through cheesecloth to strain out any remaining milk solids. Store the strained liquid in a glass jar. Make Ghee 1. Follow the instructions for making clarified butter, but allow the milk solids to continue to cook slowly until they become browned and begin to sink to the bottom of the pan. When there are no longer any solids floating at the top, the ghee is finished. Pour it through cheesecloth to strain out the browned milk solids. Store the strained liquid in a glass jar. 2. Clarified butter and ghee are shelf-stable and will last indefinitely in the pantry. However, if some milk solids remain and the temperature in your home becomes very warm, they may go off. To prevent this, store them in the refrigerator—just be aware that they'll become solid when chilled.

Per Serving

Calories: 257 | fat: 29g | protein: 0g | carbs: 0g | net carbs: 0g | fiber: 0g

Green Goddess Dressing

Prep time: 5 minutes | Cook time: 0 minutes | Serves 4

2 tablespoon buttermilk
¼ cup Greek yogurt
1 teaspoon apple cider vinegar

1 garlic clove, minced
1 tablespoon olive oil
1 tablespoon fresh parsley leaves

1. In a food processor (or blender), combine the buttermilk, yogurt, apple cider vinegar, garlic, olive oil, and parsley. Blend until fully combined. 2. Pour into a sealed glass container and chill in the refrigerator for at least 30 minutes before serving. This dressing will keep in the fridge for up to 1 week.

Per Serving

Calories: 62 | fat: 6g | protein: 1g | carbs: 1g | net carbs: 1g | fiber: 0g

Traditional Caesar Dressing

Prep time: 10 minutes | Cook time: 5 minutes | Makes 1½ cups

2 teaspoons minced garlic
4 large egg yolks
¼ cup wine vinegar
½ teaspoon dry mustard
Dash Worcestershire sauce

1 cup extra-virgin olive oil
¼ cup freshly squeezed lemon juice
Sea salt and freshly ground black pepper, to taste

1. To a small saucepan, add the garlic, egg yolks, vinegar, mustard, and Worcestershire sauce and place over low heat. 2. Whisking constantly, cook the mixture until it thickens and is a little bubbly, about 5 minutes. 3. Remove from saucepan from the heat and let it stand for about 10 minutes to cool. 4. Transfer the egg mixture to a large stainless steel bowl. Whisking constantly, add the olive oil in a thin stream. 5. Whisk in the lemon juice and season the dressing with salt and pepper. 6. Transfer the dressing to an airtight container and keep in the refrigerator for up to 3 days.

Per Serving

Calories: 202 | fat: 21g | protein: 2g | carbs: 2g | fiber: 0g | sodium: 14mg

Classic Aioli

Prep time: 10 minutes | Cook time: 0 minutes | Serves 8

1 large egg
2 teaspoons Dijon mustard
1½ teaspoons minced garlic
1 cup olive oil

1 tablespoon freshly
squeezed lemon juice
Sea salt, for seasoning

1. Combine the base. In a medium bowl, whisk together the egg, mustard, and garlic until they're well blended, about 2 minutes. 2. Add the oil. Slowly add the olive oil in a thin, continuous stream, whisking constantly until the aioli is thick. Whisk in the lemon juice and season the aioli with salt. 3. Store. Store the aioli in an airtight container in the refrigerator for up to four days.

Per Serving
Calories: 124 | fat: 14g | protein: 0g | carbs: 0g | net carbs: 0g | fiber: 0g

Worcestershire Sauce

Prep time: 8 minutes | Cook time: 5 minutes | Makes 2½ cups

½ cup coconut vinegar
½ cup apple cider vinegar
½ cup Swerve
confectioners'-style
sweetener or equivalent
amount of liquid or
powdered sweetener
¼ cup fish sauce
2 tablespoons tamarind
paste
1 tablespoon coconut
aminos or wheat-free tamari
1 teaspoon onion powder

1 teaspoon freshly ground
black pepper
½ teaspoon ground cinnamon
½ teaspoon ground cloves
¼ teaspoon cayenne pepper
2 tablespoons MCT oil or
coconut oil
2 shallots, finely minced
4 cloves garlic, minced
1 teaspoon freshly grated
ginger
8 anchovies, minced
Juice of 1 lime

1. In a small bowl, combine the vinegars, sweetener, fish sauce, tamarind paste, coconut aminos, and onion powder. Set aside. 2. Heat a dry saucepan over medium heat. Add the black pepper, cinnamon, cloves, and cayenne pepper and toast until fragrant, about 1 minute. Pour the spices into a small bowl and set aside. 3. Heat the oil over medium heat in the same saucepan you used to toast the spices. Add the shallots and sauté for 3 minutes, or until transparent and beginning to brown. Add the garlic, ginger, anchovies, and toasted spices and continue to sauté just until fragrant, about 30 seconds. 4. Pour the vinegar mixture into the saucepan and scrape up any bits on the bottom of the pan. Bring to a boil, then remove from the heat and let cool completely. 5. Strain through a fine-mesh strainer into a bowl and stir in the lime juice. Store in an airtight container in the refrigerator for up to 2 weeks, or freeze for up to 2 months.

Per Serving
Calories: 48 | fat: 3g | protein: 2g | carbs: 3g | net carbs: 2g | fiber: 1g

Homemade Hazelnut Butter

Prep time: 5 minutes | Cook time: 20 minutes | Makes about 1⅓ cups

2 cups raw hazelnuts
1½ teaspoons sea salt
½ teaspoon ground

cinnamon (optional)
2 tablespoons MCT oil or
coconut oil

1. Preheat the oven to 275°F (135°C). 2. Pour the hazelnuts onto a baking sheet and roast in the oven for 15 to 20 minutes until golden brown. 3. Combine the hazelnuts, salt, and cinnamon (if using) in a food processor or blender. Pulse a few times and then drizzle in the oil and pulse until smooth. 4. Transfer to a glass jar with an airtight lid and store in the refrigerator.

Per Serving 1 tablespoon
Calories: 97 | fat: 9g | protein: 2g | carbs: 2g | net carbs: 1g | fiber: 1g

Cajun Seasoning

Prep time: 5 minutes | Cook time: 0 minutes | Makes about ¼ cup

2½ teaspoons smoked
paprika
2 teaspoons fine sea salt
2 teaspoons garlic powder
1¼ teaspoons onion powder
1¼ teaspoons dried oregano
leaves

1¼ teaspoons dried thyme
leaves
1 teaspoon freshly ground
black pepper
1 teaspoon cayenne pepper
½ teaspoon red pepper flakes

1. Place all the ingredients in a jar with a lid. Cover and shake until well combined. Store in the pantry for up to 2 months.

Per Serving
Calories: 4 | fat: 0g | protein: 0g | carbs: 1g | net carbs: 1g | fiber: 0g

Microwave Keto Bread

Prep time: 5 minutes | Cook time: 1 minute | Makes 1 roll or 2 thin slices

1 large egg
3 tablespoons almond flour
1 tablespoon extra-virgin

olive oil
¼ teaspoon baking powder
⅛ teaspoon salt

1. In a microwave-safe ramekin, small bowl, or mug, beat the egg. Add the almond flour, olive oil, baking powder, and salt and mix well with a fork. 2. Microwave on high for 90 seconds. 3. Slide a knife around the edges of the ramekin and flip to remove the bread. 4. Slice the bread in half with a serrated knife if you want to use it to make a sandwich.

Per Serving
Calories: 264 | fat: 24g | protein: 9g | carbs: 4g | net carbs: 2g | fiber: 2g

Blue Cheese Dressing

Prep time: 5 minutes | Cook time: 0 minutes | Serves 12

¾ cup sugar-free mayonnaise
¼ cup sour cream
½ cup heavy (whipping) cream
1 teaspoon minced garlic
1 tablespoon freshly

squeezed lemon juice
1 tablespoon apple cider vinegar
1 teaspoon hot sauce
½ teaspoon sea salt
4 ounces (113 g) blue cheese, crumbled (about ¾ cup)

1. In a medium bowl, whisk together the mayonnaise, sour cream, and heavy cream. 2. Stir in the garlic, lemon juice, apple cider vinegar, hot sauce, and sea salt. 3. Add the blue cheese crumbles, and stir until well combined. 4. Transfer to an airtight container, and refrigerate for up to 1 week.
Per Serving
Calories: 90| fat: 8g | protein: 2g | carbs: 3g | net carbs: 3g | fiber: 0g

 ## Greek Dressing

Prep time: 2 minutes | Cook time: 0 minutes | Makes ½ cup

¼ cup extra-virgin olive oil
2 tablespoons red wine vinegar
1 garlic clove, minced
1 teaspoon freshly squeezed lemon juice

1 teaspoon dried oregano
1 teaspoon dried parsley
½ teaspoon pink Himalayan sea salt
¼ teaspoon freshly ground black pepper

1. In a small glass canning jar, combine the olive oil, vinegar, garlic, lemon juice, oregano, parsley, salt, and pepper. Shake well, then use as desired.
Per Serving 2 tablespoons: Calories: 123 | fat: 14g | protein: 0g | carbs: 1g | net carbs: 1g | fiber: 0g

Tartar Sauce

Prep time: 10 minutes | Cook time: 0 minutes | Makes about 1 cup

1 cup mayonnaise
¼ cup dill relish
1 tablespoon freshly squeezed lemon juice
½ teaspoon Worcestershire sauce

1 tablespoon dried parsley leaves
1 teaspoon dried minced onions
Salt and ground black pepper, to taste

1. Put all the ingredients in a small bowl and stir until well blended. Refrigerate for 1 hour before serving. Store in an airtight container in the refrigerator for up to 5 days.

Per Serving
Calories: 204 | fat: 22g | protein: 0g | carbs: 0g | net carbs: 0g | fiber: 0g

Herb-Kale Pesto

Prep time: 15 minutes | Cook time: 0 minutes | Makes 1½ cups

1 cup chopped kale
1 cup fresh basil leaves
3 garlic cloves

2 teaspoons nutritional yeast
¼ cup extra-virgin olive oil

1. Place the kale, basil, garlic, and yeast in a food processor and pulse until the mixture is finely chopped, about 3 minutes. 2. With the food processor running, drizzle the olive oil into the pesto until a thick paste forms, scraping down the sides of the bowl at least once. 3. Add a little water if the pesto is too thick. 4. Store the pesto in an airtight container in the refrigerator for up to 1 week.
Per Serving
Calories: 44 | fat: 4g | protein: 1g | carbs: 1g | net carbs: 1g | fiber: 0g

"Nacho Cheese" Sauce

Prep time: 10 minutes | Cook time: 35 minutes | serves 6

½ head cauliflower, broken into florets
1 cup peeled and coarsely chopped butternut squash
2 cups vegetable broth, divided
1 cup almonds, soaked overnight

⅓ cup nutritional yeast
1 teaspoon sea salt
1 teaspoon freshly ground black pepper
2 teaspoons paprika
½ jalapeño pepper (optional)
1 tablespoon apple cider vinegar

1. Bring a large pot of water to a boil over medium-high heat. Add the cauliflower and butternut squash to the pot, reduce the heat to medium, and cook until completely tender, about 25 minutes. 2. Strain the vegetables and set them aside. 3. In a high-powered blender, combine 1 cup of broth, the almonds, nutritional yeast, salt, pepper, paprika, jalapeño (if using), and apple cider vinegar. Blend until smooth. 4. Slowly add the cauliflower and squash, blending as you go. Once the vegetables have been added, pulse until a smooth, thick, cheese-like consistency is reached. 5. Store in the refrigerator until ready to serve.
Per Serving
Calories: 181 | fat: 12g | protein: 9g | carbs: 14g | net carbs: 8g | fiber: 6g

Garlic-Rosemary Infused Olive Oil

Prep time: 5 minutes | Cook time: 45 minutes | Makes 1 cup

1 cup extra-virgin olive oil
4 large garlic cloves, smashed

4 (4- to 5-inch) sprigs rosemary

1. In a medium skillet, heat the olive oil, garlic, and rosemary sprigs over low heat. Cook until fragrant and garlic is very tender, 30 to 45 minutes, stirring occasionally. Don't let the oil get too hot or the garlic will burn and become bitter. 2. Remove from the heat and allow to cool slightly. Remove the garlic and rosemary with a slotted spoon and pour the oil into a glass container. Allow to cool completely before covering. Store covered at room temperature for up to 3 months.
Per Serving⅛ cup: Calories: 241 | fat: 27g | protein: 0g | carbs: 1g | fiber: 0g | sodium: 1mg

Thai Dressing

Prep time: 5 minutes | Cook time: 0 minutes | Makes 1 cup

¼ cup smooth unsweetened almond butter
¼ cup full-fat coconut milk
2 tablespoons apple cider vinegar
2 tablespoons coconut aminos

2 tablespoons toasted sesame oil
1 tablespoon lime juice
1 teaspoon garlic powder
½ teaspoon cayenne pepper
½ teaspoon finely ground sea salt

1. Place all the ingredients in a 12-ounce (350-ml) or larger airtight container. Cover and shake until incorporated. 2. When ready to serve, give the container a little shake and enjoy.
Per Serving
Calories: 22 | fat: 2g | protein: 0g | carbs: 1g | net carbs: 1g | fiber: 0g

Ginger-Lime Dressing

Prep time: 5 minutes | Cook time: 0 minutes | serves 8

1 cup cold-pressed olive oil
Juice of 3 limes
2 inches fresh ginger, peeled
1 teaspoon ground cumin

⅓ teaspoon ground cardamom
1 drop liquid stevia
Sea salt

1. Combine all the ingredients in a high-powered blender and blend on high until thoroughly amalgamated and smooth. 2. Store the dressing in a covered container in the refrigerator for up to 1 week.
Per Serving
Calories: 245 | fat: 27g | protein: 0g | carbs: 1g | net carbs: 1g | fiber: 0g

Versatile Sandwich Round

Prep time: 5 minutes | Cook time: 2 minutes | Serves 1

3 tablespoons almond flour
1 tablespoon extra-virgin olive oil
1 large egg
½ teaspoon dried rosemary,

oregano, basil, thyme, or garlic powder (optional)
¼ teaspoon baking powder
⅛ teaspoon salt

1. In a microwave-safe ramekin, combine the almond flour, olive oil, egg, rosemary (if using), baking powder, and salt. Mix well with a fork. 2. Microwave for 90 seconds on high. 3. Slide a knife around the edges of ramekin and flip to remove the bread. 4. Slice in half with a serrated knife if you want to use it to make a sandwich.
Per Serving
Calories: 354 | fat: 33g | protein: 12g | carbs: 6g | fiber: 3g | sodium: 388mg

Riced Cauliflower

Prep time: 5 minutes | Cook time: 10 minutes | Serves 6 to 8

1 small head cauliflower, broken into florets
¼ cup extra-virgin olive oil
2 garlic cloves, finely minced

1½ teaspoons salt
½ teaspoon freshly ground black pepper

1. Place the florets in a food processor and pulse several times, until the cauliflower is the consistency of rice or couscous. 2. In a large skillet, heat the olive oil over medium-high heat. Add the cauliflower, garlic, salt, and pepper and sauté for 5 minutes, just to take the crunch out but not enough to let the cauliflower become soggy. 3. Remove the cauliflower from the skillet and place in a bowl until ready to use. Toss with chopped herbs and additional olive oil for a simple side, top with sautéed veggies and protein, or use in your favorite recipe.
Per Serving
Calories: 69 | fat: 7g | protein: 1g | carbs: 2g | fiber: 1g | sodium: 446mg

Hot Sauce

Prep time: 5 minutes | Cook time: 5 minutes | Makes 4 cups

2 tablespoons MCT oil or coconut oil
15 medium serrano chiles, stemmed and cut crosswise into small pieces
½ cup diced onions
1 tablespoon minced garlic (about 3 cloves)

2 cups chicken bone broth, homemade or store-bought, or water (add ¼ teaspoon salt if using water)
1 cup coconut vinegar or apple cider vinegar
Fine sea salt, as needed

1. Heat the oil in a large cast-iron skillet over low heat. Add the chiles, onions, and garlic and cook for 5 minutes, or until the onions are translucent and the chiles are soft. Add the broth. 2. Transfer the sautéed veggies and broth to a high-speed blender or food processor and purée until smooth. With the machine running on low speed, add the vinegar in a slow, steady stream. Add salt to taste. 3. Strain the hot sauce and place in a jar. Cover and store in the fridge for up to 6 months. I recommend that you let the sauce sit for 2 weeks before using to allow the flavors to open up.

Per Serving
Calories: 146 | fat: 8g | protein: 13g | carbs: 5g | net carbs: 5g | fiber: 0g

Cheesy Garlic Biscuits

Prep time: 5 minutes | Cook time: 12 minutes | Makes 2 biscuits

Biscuits:
¼ cup almond flour
¼ cup grated Cheddar cheese
1 teaspoon baking powder
¼ teaspoon pink Himalayan sea salt
¼ teaspoon garlic powder

1 large egg
2 tablespoons butter, melted
1 tablespoon heavy (whipping) cream
Topping:
1 tablespoon butter, melted
¼ teaspoon dried parsley
Pinch of garlic powder

1. Preheat the oven to 425°F (220°C). Line a baking sheet with parchment paper. 2. **To Make the Biscuits:** In a medium bowl, combine the almond flour, cheese, baking powder, salt, and garlic powder. 3. In a small bowl, combine the egg, butter, and cream. Whisk the mixture until the egg is beaten. 4. Pour the wet ingredients into the dry, then mix just enough to combine the ingredients to form a dough. 5. Divide the dough in half and place both pieces on the baking sheet with a little space between. 6. Bake for 10 to 12 minutes, until the biscuits are golden brown tipped with a darker brown. 7. **To Make the Topping:** In a small bowl, combine the butter, parsley, and garlic powder. Brush the biscuits with the butter mixture, then serve immediately.

Per Serving 1 biscuit
Calories: 344 | fat: 33g | protein: 9g | carbs: 5g | net carbs: 3g | fiber: 2g

Seedy Crackers

Prep time: 25 minutes | Cook time: 15 minutes | Makes 24 crackers

1 cup almond flour
1 tablespoon sesame seeds
1 tablespoon flaxseed
1 tablespoon chia seeds
¼ teaspoon baking soda

¼ teaspoon salt
Freshly ground black pepper
1 large egg, at room temperature

1. Preheat the oven to 350°F (180°C). 2. In a large bowl, combine the almond flour, sesame seeds, flaxseed, chia seeds, baking soda, salt, and pepper and stir well. 3. In a small bowl, whisk the egg until well beaten. Add to the dry ingredients and stir well to combine and form the dough into a ball. 4. Place one layer of parchment paper on your counter-top and place the dough on top. Cover with a second layer of parchment and, using a rolling pin, roll the dough to ⅛-inch thickness, aiming for a rectangular shape. 5. Cut the dough into 1- to 2-inch crackers and bake on parchment until crispy and slightly golden, 10 to 15 minutes, depending on thickness. Alternatively, you can bake the large rolled dough prior to cutting and break into free-form crackers once baked and crispy. 6. Store in an airtight container in the fridge for up to 1 week.

Per Serving 2 crackers: Calories: 65 | fat: 5g | protein: 3g | carbs: 2g | fiber: 2g | sodium: 83mg

Strawberry Chia Seed Jam

Prep time: 15 minutes | Cook time: 20 minutes | Makes roughly 1½ cups

1 pound (454 g) fresh strawberries, hulled and halved
½ cup water

½ teaspoon plus 10 drops of liquid stevia
¼ cup chia seeds

1. Bring the strawberries and water to a boil in a heavy-bottomed saucepan over medium-high heat. 2. Once boiling, use a spoon to smash the strawberries in the saucepan. Add the stevia, reduce the heat to a simmer, and cook for an additional 10 to 15 minutes, until the mixture has a thick, jamlike consistency. 3. Turn off the heat, add the chia seeds, and stir for 1 to 2 minutes. 4. Store in a sealed container in the refrigerator for up to 3 months.

Per Serving
Calories: 24 | fat: 1g | protein: 1g | carbs: 3g | net carbs: 1g | fiber: 2g

Eggplant Dip

Prep time: 10 minutes | Cook time: 25 minutes | Serves 6

2 large eggplants, halved lengthwise
½ teaspoon salt
2 tablespoons tahini
1 tablespoon Greek yogurt (optional; if using, reduce the tahini sauce by 1 tablespoon)
¼ cup olive oil

1½ garlic cloves, minced
Juice of ½ lemon
Freshly ground black pepper, to taste
Chopped fresh parsley, for garnish
4 pitted Kalamata olives, for garnish (optional)

1. Preheat the oven to 400ºF (205ºC). 2. Season the eggplant with the salt and let sit for about 30 minutes to let the bitterness "sweat" out. 3. Wipe the eggplant off with a wet paper towel, then place cut-side up on a baking sheet. Bake in the oven for about 25 minutes, or until the eggplant flesh is fork-tender. Remove from the oven and let cool. 4. When the eggplant is cool enough to handle, scoop out the flesh and put in a blender or food processor. Add the tahini, yogurt (if using), olive oil, garlic, lemon juice, and black pepper to taste and blend to your desired consistency. I personally like my dip a bit chunkier. 5. Serve the dip sprinkled with chopped parsley and the Kalamata olives (if using).

Per Serving ¼ cup
Calories: 121 | fat: 9g | protein: 2g | carbs: 8g | net carbs: 4g | fiber: 4g

Egg-Free Mayonnaise

Prep time: 5 minutes | Cook time: 0 minutes | Makes 1¾ cups

¼ cup plus 2 tablespoons chickpea liquid (from a can of chickpeas)
2 tablespoons lemon juice
1 tablespoon plus 1 teaspoon Dijon mustard
1 tablespoon apple cider vinegar

½ teaspoon finely ground sea salt
½ teaspoon ground black pepper
1½ cups light-tasting oil, such as avocado oil or light olive oil

1. If using a countertop blender, put all the ingredients, except the oil, in the blender. Pulse just enough to combine. Then, with the blender running on medium speed, slowly drizzle in the oil, taking at least 2 minutes to add all the oil. After the oil has been added, continue to blend until the mixture has the consistency of mayonnaise. 2. If using an immersion blender, put all the ingredients, including the oil, in the blending jar or beaker. (If your immersion blender didn't come with a jar, use a wide-mouthed 1-quart/950-ml

jar or similar-sized container.) Insert the blender into the jar, turn it to high speed, and keep it at the base of the jar for 25 seconds. Then move the blender up and down in the jar until the ingredients are well incorporated.
Per Serving
Calories: 199 | fat: 22g | protein: 0g | carbs: 0g | net carbs: 0g | fiber: 0g

Ready-in-Seconds Hollandaise Sauce

Prep time: 2 minutes | Cook time: 0 minutes | Makes 1¾ cups

1¼ cups butter-flavored coconut oil or ghee, chilled in the fridge until hardened
6 large egg yolks
2 tablespoons lemon juice

1 teaspoon finely ground sea salt
Pinch of cayenne pepper (optional)

1. Place all the ingredients in a food processor or blender. Blend on medium speed for 15 to 25 seconds, until creamy. 2. Use immediately or transfer to an 18-ounce (530-ml) or larger airtight container for later use. When ready to serve, set the chilled sauce on the counter to come to room temperature, then transfer to the food processor or blender and blend again before using.
Per Serving
Calories: 100 | fat: 11g | protein: 1g | carbs: 0g | net carbs: 0g | fiber: 0g

Any-Herb Pesto

Prep time: 5 minutes | Cook time: 0 minutes | Makes about 1 cup

4 cups packed baby arugula leaves
1 cup packed basil leaves
1 cup walnuts, chopped
½ cup shredded Parmesan cheese

2 small garlic cloves, peeled and smashed
½ teaspoon salt
¾ cup extra-virgin olive oil

1. In a food processor, pulse the arugula, basil, walnuts, cheese, and garlic until very finely chopped. Add the salt. With the processor running, stream in the olive oil until well blended and smooth. 2. Transfer the mixture to a glass container and store, tightly covered in the refrigerator, for up to 2 weeks.
Per Serving
Calories: 305 | fat: 32g | protein: 4g | carbs: 4g | net carbs: 3g | fiber: 1g

Avocado Mayo

Prep time: 5 minutes | Cook time: 0 minutes | Serves 4

1 medium avocado, cut into chunks
½ teaspoon ground cayenne pepper
Juice of ½ lime

2 tablespoons fresh cilantro leaves (optional)
Pinch pink Himalayan salt
¼ cup olive oil

1. In a food processor (or blender), blend the avocado, cayenne pepper, lime juice, cilantro, and pink Himalayan salt until all the ingredients are well combined and smooth. 2. Slowly incorporate the olive oil, adding 1 tablespoon at a time, pulsing the food processor in between. 3. Keep in a sealed glass container in the refrigerator for up to 1 week.
Per Serving
Calories: 58 | fat: 5g | protein: 1g | carbs: 4g | net carbs: 1g | fiber: 3g

Coconut-Curry Simmer Sauce

Prep time: 5 minutes | Cook time: 5 minutes | Makes 2 cups

1 (14½ ounces/411 g) can full-fat coconut milk
Zest and juice of 1 lime
2 tablespoons curry powder
1 tablespoon soy sauce

1 teaspoon ground ginger
1 teaspoon garlic powder
½ to 1 teaspoon cayenne pepper

1. Whisk all the ingredients in a small saucepan over medium-high heat and bring just below a boil. Remove from heat and allow to cool to room temperature. The sauce will keep, tightly covered in the refrigerator, for up to 1 week.
Per Serving
Calories: 221 | fat: 22g | protein: 3g | carbs: 7g | net carbs: 5g | fiber: 2g

Keto Tortillas

Prep time: 10 minutes | Cook time: 10 minutes | Makes 4 tortillas

⅔ cup water
½ cup coconut flour
⅓ cup golden flax meal
3 tablespoons extra-virgin olive oil

1½ teaspoons xanthan gum
¼ teaspoon pink Himalayan sea salt

1. In a medium bowl, combine the water, coconut flour, flax meal, olive oil, xanthan gum, and salt. 2. Divide the dough into 4 equal portions. 3. Place each dough ball between 2 sheets of parchment paper, then roll the dough into a 1/16- to ⅛-inch-thick round. 4. Heat a griddle pan over medium heat. Place each tortilla on the griddle pan and cook for 60 seconds on each side, then transfer the tortilla to a plate. Cover the tortillas with a towel to retain the moisture. 5. Serve immediately or let cool for use later.
Per Serving 1 tortilla
Calories: 212 | fat: 16g | protein: 5g | carbs: 12g | net carbs: 5g | fiber: 7g

Zesty Parmesan Italian Dressing

Prep time: 10 minutes | Cook time: 0 minutes | Makes 2 cups

1 cup extra-virgin olive oil
½ cup white vinegar
1 tablespoon red wine vinegar
2 tablespoons water
2 tablespoons freshly grated Parmesan cheese
1 tablespoon minced garlic

1 tablespoon minced shallots
1 teaspoon dried basil
½ teaspoon dried oregano
¼ teaspoon sea salt
¼ teaspoon freshly ground black pepper
⅛ teaspoon dried marjoram
Pinch red pepper flakes

1. In an airtight container, combine the oil and vinegars and shake. Add the rest of the ingredients and shake again. 2. Let sit on the counter for at least 1 hour before serving, for the flavors to mix. 3. Refrigerate for up to 1 week, allowing 20 minutes before serving to bring to room temperature, and shake again.
Per Serving 2 tablespoons
Calories: 119 | fat: 13g | protein: 0g | carbs: 0g | net carbs: 0g | fiber: 0g

Cheese Sauce

Prep time: 5 minutes | Cook time: 5 minutes | Makes about ½ cup

2 tablespoons sour cream
2 tablespoons heavy (whipping) cream
¼ teaspoon pink Himalayan sea salt

⅛ teaspoon freshly ground black pepper
Pinch of garlic powder
Pinch of cayenne pepper
¼ cup grated Cheddar cheese

1. In a medium saucepan, heat the sour cream, cream, salt, pepper, garlic powder, and cayenne over medium heat.
2. Continue to stir until the sauce just begins to simmer.
3. Reduce the heat and slowly stir in the Cheddar cheese.
4. When the cheese is blended into the sauce, serve immediately.
Per Serving 2 tablespoons
Calories: 66 | fat: 6g | protein: 2g | carbs: 0g | net carbs: 0g | fiber: 0g

Chive & Onion Cream Cheese

Prep time: 5 minutes | Cook time: 0 minutes | Makes 1 cup

1 cup raw cashews
¼ cup unsweetened plain dairy-free yogurt
2 tablespoons apple cider vinegar
2 teaspoons nutritional yeast
¾ teaspoon onion powder
½ teaspoon finely ground sea salt
¼ teaspoon garlic powder
2 tablespoons sliced fresh chives

1. Place the cashews in a 12-ounce (350-ml) or larger sealable container. Cover with water. Seal and place in the fridge to soak for 12 hours. 2. Once the cashews are ready, drain and rinse them, then place in a food processor or blender along with the remaining ingredients, except the chives. Blend on high until smooth. 3. Transfer to a 12-ounce (350-ml) or larger airtight container. Stir in the sliced chives. Set on the counter for an hour before serving to allow the flavors to meld.

Per Serving
Calories: 55 | fat: 4g | protein: 2g | carbs: 3g | net carbs: 2g | fiber: 1g

Traditional Meat Sauce

Prep time: 15 minutes | Cook time: 40 minutes | Serves 4

2 tablespoons good-quality olive oil
1 pound (454 g) grass-fed ground beef
1 onion, chopped
2 celery stalks, chopped
2 tablespoons minced garlic
1 (28 ounces/784 g) can
sodium-free diced tomatoes
¼ cup red wine
¼ cup tomato paste
2 teaspoons dried oregano
2 teaspoons dried basil
1 teaspoon dried parsley
½ teaspoon sea salt
¼ teaspoon red pepper flakes

1. Brown the beef. In a large pot over medium-high heat, warm the olive oil. Brown the ground beef, stirring it occasionally, until it's cooked through, about 6 minutes. 2. Sauté the vegetables. Stir in the onion, celery, and garlic and sauté them until they've softened, about 3 minutes. 3. Add the rest of the ingredients. Stir in the tomatoes, red wine, tomato paste, oregano, basil, parsley, salt, and red pepper flakes. 4. Cook the sauce. Bring the sauce to a boil, then reduce the heat to low and simmer it for 25 to 30 minutes, stirring occasionally. 5. Store. Cool the sauce completely and store in a sealed container in the refrigerator for up to four days or freeze for up to one month.

Per Serving
Calories: 457 | fat: 35g | protein: 21g | carbs: 13g | net carbs: 8g | fiber: 5g

Bagna Cauda

Prep time: 5 minutes | Cook time: 20 minutes | Serves 8 to 10

½ cup extra-virgin olive oil
4 tablespoons (½ stick) butter
8 anchovy fillets, very finely chopped
4 large garlic cloves, finely minced
½ teaspoon salt
½ teaspoon freshly ground black pepper

1. In a small saucepan, heat the olive oil and butter over medium-low heat until the butter is melted. 2. Add the anchovies and garlic and stir to combine. Add the salt and pepper and reduce the heat to low. Cook, stirring occasionally, until the anchovies are very soft and the mixture is very fragrant, about 20 minutes. 3. Serve warm, drizzled over steamed vegetables, as a dipping sauce for raw veggies or cooked artichokes, or use as a salad dressing. Store leftovers in an airtight container in the refrigerator for up to 2 weeks.

Per Serving
Calories: 145 | fat: 16g | protein: 1g | carbs: 0g | fiber: 0g | sodium: 235mg

Honey Mustard Dressing & Marinade

Prep time: 5 minutes | Cook time: 0 minutes | Makes 1¾ cups

1 cup light-tasting oil, such as avocado oil or light olive oil
¼ cup apple cider vinegar
¼ cup Dijon mustard
2 tablespoons lemon juice
1 tablespoon plus 1 teaspoon honey
½ teaspoon finely ground sea salt

1. Place all the ingredients in an 18-ounce (530-ml) or larger airtight container. Cover and shake until incorporated. 2. When ready to serve, give the container a little shake and enjoy.

Per Serving
Calories: 74 | fat: 8g | protein: 0g | carbs: 1g | net carbs: 1g | fiber: 0g

Pepper Sauce

Prep time: 10 minutes | Cook time: 20 minutes | Makes 4 cups

2 red hot fresh chiles, seeded
2 dried chiles
½ small yellow onion,
roughly chopped
2 garlic cloves, peeled
2 cups water
2 cups white vinegar

1. In a medium saucepan, combine the fresh and dried chiles, onion, garlic, and water. Bring to a simmer and cook for 20 minutes, or until tender. Transfer to a food processor or blender. 2. Add the vinegar and blend until smooth.

Per Serving 1 cup
Calories: 41 | fat: 0g | protein: 1g | carbs: 5g | fiber: 1g | sodium: 11mg

Raw Keto Ranch

Prep time: 5 minutes | Cook time: 0 minutes | serves 12

1 cup raw cashews, soaked overnight
½ cup water
2 teaspoons apple cider vinegar
1½ teaspoons freshly squeezed lemon juice
2 tablespoons finely

chopped fresh dill
2 tablespoons finely chopped fresh chives
1 tablespoon finely chopped fresh Italian parsley
¼ teaspoon sea salt
¼ teaspoon onion powder
¼ teaspoon garlic powder

1. In a food processor or bullet blender, combine all the ingredients and blend on high until a creamy consistency is reached.

Per Serving
Calories: 61 | fat: 5g | protein: 2g | carbs: 3g | net carbs: 2g | fiber: 1g

Pea-NOT Sauce

Prep time: 10 minutes | Cook time: 0 minutes | Makes about 1 cup

½ cup raw almond butter
½ cup full-fat coconut milk
2 large garlic cloves, finely minced
Juice of 1 small lime
2 tablespoons tamari (gluten-free soy sauce)

1 tablespoon grated fresh ginger
½ tablespoon toasted sesame oil
½ tablespoon avocado oil
¼ teaspoon red pepper flakes (optional)

1. Mix all the ingredients in a medium bowl, or use a small food processor or an immersion blender. Store in an airtight container in the refrigerator. Finish within 2 to 3 weeks.

Per Serving
Calories: 153 | fat: 13g | protein: 4g | carbs: 5g | net carbs: 3g | fiber: 2g

Marinated Artichokes

Prep time: 10 minutes | Cook time: 0 minutes | Makes 2 cups

2 (13¾ ounces/390 g) cans artichoke hearts, drained and quartered
¾ cup extra-virgin olive oil
4 small garlic cloves, crushed with the back of a knife
1 tablespoon fresh rosemary

leaves
2 teaspoons chopped fresh oregano or 1 teaspoon dried oregano
1 teaspoon red pepper flakes (optional)
1 teaspoon salt

1. In a medium bowl, combine the artichoke hearts, olive oil, garlic, rosemary, oregano, red pepper flakes (if using), and salt. Toss to combine well. 2. Store in an airtight glass container in the refrigerator and marinate for at least 24 hours before using. Store in the refrigerator for up to 2 weeks.

Per Serving ¼ cup
Calories: 228 | fat: 20g | protein: 3g | carbs: 11g | fiber: 5g | sodium: 381mg

Miso-Ginger Dressing

Prep time: 10 minutes | Cook time: 0 minutes | Serves 4

1 tablespoon unseasoned rice vinegar
1 tablespoon red or white miso
1 teaspoon grated fresh

ginger
1 garlic clove, minced
3 tablespoons extra-virgin olive oil

1. In a small bowl, combine the vinegar and miso into a paste. Add the ginger and garlic, and mix well. While whisking, drizzle in the olive oil. 2. Store in the refrigerator in an airtight container for up to 1 week.

Per Serving
Calories: 100 | fat: 10g | protein: 1g | carbs: 2g | fiber: 0g | sodium: 159mg

Mole Sauce

Prep time: 5 minutes | Cook time: 15 minutes | Makes 1½ cups

2 tablespoons MCT oil
¼ cup finely chopped onions
1 clove garlic, minced
1 cup tomato sauce
1 (4 ounces/113 g) can diced

green chiles
1 tablespoon chopped fresh cilantro
1 tablespoon unsweetened cocoa powder
1 teaspoon ground cumin

1. Heat the oil in a sauté pan over medium heat. Add the onions and fry for 3 minutes, or until translucent. Add the garlic and cook until fragrant, about 1 minute. 2. Add the rest of the ingredients, stir to combine, and simmer for 10 minutes. Remove from heat and purée until smooth, if desired. Store in an airtight container in the fridge for up to 1 week.

Per Serving
Calories: 14 | fat: 1g | protein: 0g | carbs: 1g | net carbs: 1g | fiber: 0g

Berbere Spice Mix

Prep time: 5 minutes | Cook time: 0 minutes | Makes about ¾ cup

6 tablespoons paprika
3 tablespoons cayenne pepper
1 tablespoon fine sea salt
1 teaspoon garlic powder
1 teaspoon onion powder
1 teaspoon ground coriander

½ teaspoon ginger powder
½ teaspoon ground cardamom
½ teaspoon ground fenugreek
½ teaspoon freshly ground nutmeg
¼ teaspoon ground cloves

1. Place all the ingredients in a jar with a lid. Cover and shake until well combined. Store in the pantry for up to 2 months.

Per Serving
Calories: 201 | fat: 9g | protein: 9g | carbs: 38g | net carbs: 18g | fiber: 20g

Zucchini Noodles

Prep time: 5 minutes | Cook time: 0 minutes | Serves 4

2 medium to large zucchini

1. Cut off and discard the ends of each zucchini and, using a spiralizer set to the smallest setting, spiralize the zucchini to create zoodles. 2. To serve, simply place a ½ cup or so of spiralized zucchini into the bottom of each bowl and spoon a hot sauce over top to "cook" the zoodles to al dente consistency. Use with any of your favorite sauces, or just toss with warmed pesto for a simple and quick meal.

Per Serving
Calories: 27 | fat: 1g | protein: 2g | carbs: 5g | fiber: 2g | sodium: 13mg

Spicy and Sweet Hamburger Seasoning

Prep time: 5 minutes | Cook time: 0 minutes | Makes ½ cup plus 3 tablespoons

¼ cup paprika
1 tablespoon plus 2 teaspoons fine sea salt
1 tablespoon plus 1 teaspoon freshly ground black pepper
1 tablespoon plus 1 teaspoon Swerve confectioners'-style

sweetener or equivalent amount of powdered erythritol or monk fruit
1 tablespoon plus 1 teaspoon garlic powder
1 tablespoon plus 1 teaspoon onion powder
1 teaspoon cayenne pepper

1. Place all the ingredients in a large airtight container and shake until well combined. Store in the pantry for up to 2 months.

Per Serving
Calories: 8 | fat: 0g | protein: 0g | carbs: 2g | net carbs: 1g | fiber: 1g

Butternut Squash "Cheese" Sauce

Prep time: 10 minutes | Cook time: 10 minutes | Serves 6

2 cups frozen cubed butternut squash
1 tablespoon butter-flavored coconut oil
1 tablespoon tahini
2 tablespoons nutritional

yeast
1 teaspoon garlic powder
½ teaspoon onion powder
½ teaspoon paprika
Salt and freshly ground black pepper, to taste

1. In a shallow sauté pan over medium-high heat, cook the frozen butternut squash in the coconut oil until the squash is no longer frozen and the liquid in the pan has evaporated, 5 to 8 minutes. 2. Transfer the cooked squash to a blender, add the tahini, nutritional yeast, garlic and onion powders, paprika, and salt and pepper to taste. Blend until completely smooth.

Per Serving
Calories: 101 | fat: 5g | protein: 4g | carbs: 10g | net carbs: 6g | fiber: 4g

Tahini Goddess

Prep time: 5 minutes | Cook time: 0 minutes | serves 8

Juice of 1 large or 2 small lemons
3 tablespoons raw tahini
¼ cup water
½ teaspoon smoked paprika

⅛ teaspoon cayenne pepper (optional)
Freshly ground black pepper
Sea salt

1. In a medium bowl, whisk the lemon juice, tahini, and water until well blended. 2. Add the paprika and cayenne (if using), and season with salt and pepper. Mix until well combined. 3. Keep the dressing in a covered container in the pantry for up to 6 months. In the refrigerator, it will last for up to 1 year.

Per Serving
Calories: 40 | fat: 3g | protein: 1g | carbs: 2g | net carbs: 1g | fiber: 1g

Tennessee Dry Rub

Prep time: 5 minutes | Cook time: 0 minutes | Makes about ¼ cup

2 tablespoons brown sugar substitute
1 tablespoon smoked paprika
2 teaspoons ground black pepper

1 teaspoon ground cumin
1 teaspoon dried ground oregano
1 teaspoon salt
½ teaspoon onion powder
¼ teaspoon cayenne pepper

1. In a small bowl, stir the ingredients together until well combined. Store in a jar with a lid. Shake before use.
Per Serving
Calories: 65 | fat: 2g | protein: 3g | carbs: 13g | net carbs: 6g | fiber: 7g

Vegan "Sour Cream"

Prep time: 5 minutes | Cook time: 0 minutes | serves 12

1 cup raw almonds, soaked overnight
Juice of ½ lemon
1 teaspoon nutritional yeast

⅓ teaspoon sea salt
¼ cup water, plus more if needed

1. Put the soaked almonds in a high-powered blender with the lemon juice, nutritional yeast, salt, and water, and blend until creamy and smooth. Add more water if necessary. 2. Spoon the mixture into an airtight container and place in a cool, dark cabinet to allow the cream to ferment overnight. This fermentation is what gives the cream that tart "sour cream" flavor. 3. In the morning, place the mixture in the refrigerator to store until needed. It will last for up to 1 week.
Per Serving
Calories: 66 | fat: 6g | protein: 3g | carbs: 3g | net carbs: 2g | fiber: 1g

Homemade Chipotle Mayo

Prep time: 5 minutes | Cook time: 0 minutes | Makes 1¾ cups plus

2 large egg yolks
2 tablespoons Dijon mustard
1 tablespoon apple cider vinegar
1 teaspoon ground chipotle

pepper
½ teaspoon pink Himalayan salt
1½ cups avocado oil

1. Put the egg yolks, mustard, vinegar, chipotle pepper, and salt in a food processor and pulse to combine. 2. With the processor running, very slowly pour in the oil until you use it all and the mayo becomes thick. 3. Store in a sealed container in the refrigerator for up to 2 weeks.
Per Serving
Calories: 101 | fat: 12g | protein: 0g | carbs: 0g | net carbs: 0g | fiber: 0g

Mini Fat Bombs

Prep time: 5 minutes | Cook time: 0 minutes | Makes 60 fat bombs

½ cup coconut or MCT oil
½ cup butter or ghee
2 tablespoons unsweetened

cacao or cocoa powder
Dash sweetener
Pinch sea salt

1. In a microwave-safe cup or bowl (preferably with a spout) combine the oil, butter, and cacao powder. Microwave for 20 seconds, stir, and then microwave in 10-second increments until melted. 2. Add sweetener and season with salt. 3. Pour the mixture into mini chocolate molds or ice cube trays, about ½ tablespoon per mold. 4. Freeze for at least 1 hour and then pop out of the molds and store in a freezer-safe resealable plastic bag in the freezer.
Per Serving2 fat bombs: Calories: 63 | fat: 7g | protein: 0g | carbs: 0g | net carbs: 0g | fiber: 0g

Raspberry Sauce

Prep time: 5 minutes | Cook time: 10 minutes | Makes 1 cup

12 ounces (340 g) raspberries
2 tablespoons lemon juice

⅓ cup powdered erythritol, or to taste

1. In a small saucepan, combine the raspberries, lemon juice, and powdered erythritol. Cook over medium-low heat for 2 to 3 minutes, until the raspberries start to soften. 2. Adjust the heat to a gentle simmer, mash the berries with the back of a spoon, and continue cooking for 5 to 8 minutes, until thickened. Adjust the sweetener to taste. The sauce will thicken more as it cools.
Per Serving
Calories: 22 | fat: 0g | protein: 0g | carbs: 11g | net carbs: 4g | fiber: 7g

Crustless Cheesecake Bites

Prep time: 10 minutes | Cook time: 30 minutes | Serves 4

4 ounces (113 g) cream cheese, at room temperature
¼ cup sour cream
2 large eggs
⅓ cup Swerve natural sweetener
¼ teaspoon vanilla extract

1. Preheat the oven to 350°F. 2. In a medium mixing bowl, use a hand mixer to beat the cream cheese, sour cream, eggs, sweetener, and vanilla until well mixed. 3. Place silicone liners (or cupcake paper liners) in the cups of a muffin tin. 4. Pour the cheesecake batter into the liners, and bake for 30 minutes. 5. Refrigerate until completely cooled before serving, about 3 hours. Store extra cheesecake bites in a zip-top bag in the freezer for up to 3 months.

Per Serving
Calories: 169 | fat: 15g | protein: 5g | carbs: 18g | net carbs: 2g | fiber: 0g

Key Lime Pie Cupcakes

Prep time: 5 minutes | Cook time: 50 minutes | Makes 12 cupcakes

Crust:
¾ cup (3 ounces/85 g) coconut flour
2 tablespoons erythritol
4 tablespoons (½ stick) butter, melted
2 large eggs
Filling:
6 tablespoons (¾ stick) butter
3 cups heavy cream
¾ cup powdered erythritol
½ cup sour cream
1 tablespoon lime zest, plus more for garnish (optional)
½ cup lime juice
1 teaspoon vanilla extract
Sugar-free whipped cream, for garnish (optional)

1. Preheat the oven to 350ºF (180ºC). Line 12 cups of a muffin tin with paper liners. 2. **Make the Crust:** In a large bowl, stir together the coconut flour and erythritol. Stir in the melted butter and egg, until evenly combined. The dough will be crumbly, but you should be able to pinch it together. 3. Press a thin layer of the dough into the bottoms of the lined muffin cups. Bake for 10 to 12 minutes, until firm and slightly golden on the edges. Set aside to cool. 4. Meanwhile, **make the filling:** In a large sauté pan (not a saucepan), melt the butter over medium heat. Whisk in the heavy cream and powdered erythritol to combine. Bring to a boil, then reduce to a simmer for 30 to 45 minutes, stirring occasionally, until the mixture is thick, coats the back of a spoon. Remove from the heat and cool for about 10 minutes. Meanwhile, preheat the oven to 350ºF (180ºC) again. 5. Stir the sour cream, lime zest, lime juice, and vanilla into the condensed milk. 6. Pour the filling into the muffin cups over the cooled crust. 7. Return the pan to the oven for 5 to 10 minutes, until bubbles form on top and the cupcakes start to set on the edges but not in the center. Do not let the filling fully set or brown. 8. Remove the pan and cool completely, then chill for at least 1 to 2 hours, until set. 9. If desired, top with sugar-free whipped cream and/or additional lime zest.

Per Serving
Calories: 337 | fat: 33g | protein: 3g | carbs: 6g | net carbs: 4g | fiber: 2g

Sweetened Condensed Coconut Milk

Prep time: 10 minutes | Cook time: 35 minutes | Serves 12

1 (13½ ounces/400 ml) can full-fat coconut milk
2 tablespoons confectioners'-style erythritol

1. Place all the ingredients in a small saucepan and bring to a rapid boil over medium-high heat. Reduce the heat and simmer lightly for 32 to 35 minutes, until the milk has thickened and reduced by about half. Use immediately in a recipe that calls for it, or let it cool and store in the fridge for later use.

Per Serving
Calories: 68 | fat: 7g | protein: 1g | carbs: 1g | net carbs: 1g | fiber: 0g

Lavender Ice Cream

Prep time: 5 minutes | Cook time: 0 minutes | serves 4

2 (14 ounces/397 g) cans full-fat coconut cream
¾ cup monk fruit sweetener
½ cup raw cashews, soaked in water overnight
¼ cup coconut oil, melted
3 tablespoons dried lavender
1 teaspoon vanilla extract
1 teaspoon almond extract
Sea salt

1. Combine all the ingredients in a high-powered blender and blend on high for 5 minutes until the mixture grows in volume by about one-third and becomes fluffy. 2. Pour the mixture into a freezer-safe pan and freeze for 2 hours. 3. Remove the mixture from the freezer and break it into chunks. 4. Transfer the mixture to a food processor and blend until a soft-serve consistency is achieved. 5. Spoon the ice cream into a freezer-safe pan and place back in the freezer to set for 3 hours before serving.

Per Serving
Calories: 571 | fat: 60g | protein: 3g | carbs: 10g | net carbs: 9g | fiber: 1g

Glazed Coconut Bundt Cake

Prep time: 30 minutes | Cook time: 55 minutes | serves 10

Cake:
2 cups finely ground blanched almond flour
¼ cup coconut flour
¾ cup granular erythritol
2 teaspoons baking powder
½ teaspoon salt
5 large eggs
½ cup (1 stick) salted butter, softened
¼ cup coconut oil, softened
2 teaspoons vanilla extract
1 cup unsweetened coconut flakes

Garnish:
½ cup unsweetened coconut flakes

Glaze:
½ cup confectioners'-style erythritol
¼ cup heavy whipping cream
¼ teaspoon vanilla extract

1. Preheat the oven to 350°F. Grease a 12-cup Bundt pan with butter. 2. Whisk the almond flour, coconut flour, granular erythritol, baking powder, and salt. Blend the eggs, butter, coconut oil, and vanilla extract on low speed. Slowly blend in the flour mixture. Use a spoon to stir in the coconut flakes. 3. Spoon the batter into the prepared pan, then smooth the top. Bake for 45 minutes. Place the pan on a wire rack to cool completely. Lower the oven temperature to 325°F for toasting the coconut. 4. **Make the Toasted Coconut Garnish:** Line a sheet pan with parchment paper. Spread the coconut in a thin layer on the prepared pan. Bake for 5 minutes, stir the coconut, then return to the oven and bake until golden brown. Remove the coconut from the pan and allow to cool. 5. **Make the Glaze:** Put the confectioners'-style erythritol, cream, and vanilla extract in a small bowl and stir until smooth. 6. To serve, gently loosen the sides of the cooled cake from the pan with a knife and turn it onto a cake plate. Pour the glaze evenly over the cake. Garnish the cake with the toasted coconut.
Per Serving
Calories: 361 | fat: 31g | protein: 10g | carbs: 7g | net carbs: 3g | fiber: 4g

Fluffy Coconut Mousse

Prep time: 15 minutes | Cook time: 5 minutes | Serves 4

¼ cup cold water
2 teaspoons granulated gelatin
1 cup coconut milk
3 egg yolks
½ cup monk fruit sweetener, granulated form
1 cup heavy (whipping) cream

1. Prepare the gelatin. Pour the cold water into a small bowl, sprinkle the gelatin on top, and set it aside for 10 minutes. 2. Heat the coconut milk. Place a small saucepan over medium heat and pour in the coconut milk. Bring the coconut milk to a boil then remove the pan from the heat. 3. Thicken the base. Whisk the eggs and sweetener in a medium bowl. Pour the coconut milk into the yolks and whisk it to blend. Pour the yolk mixture back into the saucepan and place it over medium heat. Whisk until the base thickens, about 5 minutes. Remove the pan from the heat and whisk in the gelatin mixture. 4. Cool. Transfer the mixture to a medium bowl and cool it completely in the refrigerator, about 1 hour. 5. Make the mousse. When the coconut milk mixture is cool, whisk the cream in a large bowl until it's thick and fluffy, about 3 minutes. Fold the whipped cream into the coconut mixture until the mousse is well combined and fluffy. 6. Serve. Divide the mousse between four bowls and serve it immediately.
Per Serving
Calories: 261 | fat: 27g | protein: 5g | carbs: 3g | net carbs: 3g | fiber: 0g

Chocolate Chip Brownies

Prep time: 10 minutes | Cook time: 33 minutes | Serves 8

1½ cups almond flour
⅓ cup unsweetened cocoa powder
¾ cup granulated erythritol
1 teaspoon baking powder
2 eggs
1 tablespoon vanilla extract
5 tablespoons butter, melted
¼ cup sugar-free chocolate chips
½ cup water

1. In a large bowl, add the almond flour, cocoa powder, erythritol, and baking powder. Use a hand mixer on low speed to combine and smooth out any lumps. 2. Add the eggs and vanilla and mix until well combined. 3. Add the butter and mix on low speed until well combined. Scrape the bottom and sides of the bowl and mix again if needed. Fold in the chocolate chips. 4. Grease a baking dish with cooking spray. Pour the batter into the dish and smooth with a spatula. Cover tightly with aluminum foil. 5. Pour the water into the pot. Place the trivet in the pot and carefully lower the baking dish onto the trivet. 6. Close the lid. Select Manual mode and set cooking time for 33 minutes on High Pressure. 7. When timer beeps, use a quick pressure release and open the lid. 8. Use the handles to carefully remove the trivet from the pot. Remove the foil from the dish. 9. Let the brownies cool for 10 minutes before turning out onto a plate.
Per Serving
Calories: 235 | fat: 20.2g | protein: 7.0g | carbs: 6.7g | net carbs: 2.7g | fiber: 4.0g

Lemon Bars with Cashew Crust

Prep time: 5 minutes | Cook time: 35 minutes | Makes 12 bars

2 tablespoons butter, melted, plus 2 tablespoons, at room temperature, plus more for the baking dish
1 cup finely crushed cashews
1 cup almond flour
½ cup Swerve
Zest of 2 lemons
½ cup freshly squeezed lemon juice
6 egg yolks
2 tablespoons gelatin

1. Preheat the oven to 375°F (190°C). 2. Grease an 8- or 9-inch square baking dish with butter. 3. In a large bowl, stir together the cashews and almond flour. Pour the melted butter over them and stir until the nut mixture becomes wet and crumbly. Scrape the crust into the prepared dish, pressing down firmly with your fingers. Bake for about 15 minutes or until the crust begins to brown. Remove from the oven and let it cool completely. 4. Reduce the oven temperature to 350°F (180°C). 5. In a small saucepan over low heat, melt the 2 tablespoons of room-temperature butter. 6. Stir in the Swerve, lemon zest, and lemon juice. 7. Slowly add the egg yolks one at a time, whisking to incorporate as the filling thickens. Cook for 2 to 3 minutes, whisking. 8. Remove from the heat and whisk in the gelatin until the mixture is smooth. Pour the lemon filling over the crust and spread it evenly. Bake for 10 to 12 minutes. Remove it from the oven and let it cool. Cut into 12 squares and serve. Refrigerate, covered, for up to 1 week.
Per Serving 1 bar
Calories: 144 | fat: 13g | protein: 4g | carbs: 4g | net carbs: 4g | fiber: 0g

Nutty Shortbread Cookies

Prep time: 10 minutes | Cook time: 10 minutes | Makes 10 cookies

½ cup butter, at room temperature, plus additional for greasing the baking sheet
½ cup granulated sweetener
1 teaspoon alcohol-free pure vanilla extract
1½ cups almond flour
½ cup ground hazelnuts
Pinch sea salt

1. In a medium bowl, cream together the butter, sweetener, and vanilla until well blended. 2. Stir in the almond four, ground hazelnuts, and salt until a firm dough is formed. 3. Roll the dough into a 2-inch cylinder and wrap it in plastic wrap. Place the dough in the refrigerator for at least 30 minutes until firm. 4. Preheat the oven to 350°F. Line a baking sheet with parchment paper and lightly grease the paper with butter; set aside. 5. Unwrap the chilled cylinder, slice the dough into 18 cookies, and place the cookies on the baking sheet. 6. Bake the cookies until firm and lightly browned, about 10 minutes.

7. Allow the cookies to cool on the baking sheet for 5 minutes and then transfer them to a wire rack to cool completely.
Per Serving 1 cookie
Calories: 105 | fat: 10g | protein: 3g | carbs: 2g | net carbs: 1g | fiber: 1g

Pumpkin-Ricotta Cheesecake

Prep time: 25 minutes | Cook time: 45 minutes | Serves 10 to 12

1 cup almond flour
½ cup butter, melted
1 (14½ ounces/411 g) can pumpkin purée
8 ounces (227 g) cream cheese, at room temperature
½ cup whole-milk ricotta cheese
½ to ¾ cup sugar-free sweetener
4 large eggs
2 teaspoons vanilla extract
2 teaspoons pumpkin pie spice
Whipped cream, for garnish (optional)

1. Preheat the oven to 350°F(180°C). Line the bottom of a 9-inch springform pan with parchment paper. 2. In a small bowl, combine the almond flour and melted butter with a fork until well combined. Using your fingers, press the mixture into the bottom of the prepared pan. 3. In a large bowl, beat together the pumpkin purée, cream cheese, ricotta, and sweetener using an electric mixer on medium. 4. Add the eggs, one at a time, beating after each addition. Stir in the vanilla and pumpkin pie spice until just combined. 5. Pour the mixture over the crust and bake until set, 40 to 45 minutes. 6. Allow to cool to room temperature. Refrigerate for at least 6 hours before serving. 7. Serve chilled, garnishing with whipped cream, if desired.
Per Serving
Calories: 230 | fat: 21g | protein: 6g | carbs: 5g | fiber: 1g | sodium: 103mg

Chocolate Almond Smoothie

Prep time: 5 minutes | Cook time: 0 minutes | Serves 2

2 cups ice cubes
1 cup heavy (whipping) cream
1 cup water
¼ cup canned coconut cream
3 tablespoons almond butter
2 tablespoons cocoa powder
½ teaspoon liquid stevia

1. In a high-speed blender, combine the ice cubes, cream, water, coconut cream, almond butter, cocoa powder, and stevia. Blend on high speed until the mixture is smooth, then serve immediately.
Per Serving
Calories: 669 | fat: 68g | protein: 10g | carbs: 13g | net carbs: 8g | fiber: 5g

Stu Can't Stop Bark

Prep time: 5 minutes | Cook time: 5 minutes | Makes 24 pieces

5 bars good dark chocolate, at least 80% cacao content
3 tablespoons coconut oil
2 cups macadamia nuts, or a mixture of assorted other nuts, ground into small pieces
3 tablespoons raw almond
butter
¼ to ½ cup finely shredded coconut flakes (optional)
2 tablespoons coconut butter (optional)
Sea salt or Himalayan pink salt, to sprinkle on top

1. Break the chocolate by hand into small pieces. Melt half the chocolate in a double boiler or glass bowl fitted over a small pan of boiling water. Add the coconut oil as the chocolate is melting and stir occasionally. 2. In a big mixing bowl, combine the nuts and the remaining dark chocolate pieces. Pour the melted chocolate mixture into the bowl and stir very well. 3. In a large glass pan, spread half the mixture thinly across the bottom. Drizzle a thin layer of almond butter over the chocolate, spreading carefully so there are no thick areas. 4. Spread the rest of the chocolate evenly over the almond butter. Sprinkle on the coconut or coconut butter, if using. Sprinkle the salt lightly over the top. 5. Freeze for 1 to 2 hours or refrigerate for longer, the mixture must become rock-hard. Remove from chilling, let sit for 5 minutes, then cut into squares. 6. Store the bark in an airtight container in the fridge or freezer and serve cold (but not frozen). When serving, consume immediately because the bark will melt quickly at room temperature.

Per Serving
Calories: 236 | fat: 22g | protein: 3g | carbs: 9g | net carbs: 7g | fiber: 2g

One-Bowl Butter Cookies

Prep time: 5 minutes | Cook time: 14 minutes | Makes 12 cookies

½ cup (1 stick) salted butter, softened
1½ cups finely ground blanched almond flour
¼ teaspoon salt
½ cup granular erythritol
½ teaspoon vanilla extract
1 large egg
⅛ teaspoon liquid stevia

1. Preheat the oven to 350°F. Line a baking sheet with parchment paper. 2. Put all the ingredients in a medium-sized mixing bowl. Using a hand mixer, slowly blend on low speed, then increase the speed to medium and continue mixing until everything is well combined. 3. Using a small cookie scoop, scoop the dough onto the prepared pan, leaving 2 inches of space between the cookies. Use the back of a fork to press crisscrosses on each cookie. 4. Bake for 12 to 14 minutes, until the cookies start to turn light brown around the edges. Allow to cool completely before removing from the pan. The cookies will continue to firm up as they cool. Leftovers can be stored in an airtight container at room temperature for up to a week.

Per Serving
Calories: 297 | fat: 29g | protein: 3g | carbs: 4g | net carbs: 2g | fiber: 3g

Iced Tea Lemonade Gummies

Prep time: 10 minutes | Cook time: 5 minutes | Serves 4

¾ cup boiling water
3 tea bags
¼ cup unflavored gelatin
¾ cup fresh lemon juice
2 tablespoons confectioners'-style
erythritol or granulated xylitol
Special Equipment:
Silicone mold(s) with 36 (½ ounce/15 ml) cavities

1. Set the silicone mold(s) on a rimmed baking sheet. 2. Place the boiling water in a heat-safe mug and steep the tea according to type, following the suggested steep time on the package. Once complete, remove the tea bags and wring out as much liquid from the bags as possible. Sprinkle the gelatin over the tea and set aside. 3. Pour the lemon juice into a small saucepan. Add the erythritol and bring to a light simmer over medium heat, about 5 minutes. 4. Once at a light simmer, remove the pan from the heat. Whisk the tea mixture until the gelatin dissolves, then pour it into the hot lemon juice mixture. Whisk to combine. 5. Pour the hot mixture into the mold(s) and transfer the baking sheet to the fridge to set for at least 1 hour. Once firm, remove the gummies from the mold(s) and enjoy!

Per Serving
Calories: 48 | fat: 0g | protein: 10g | carbs: 1g | net carbs: 1g | fiber: 0g

Berry Merry

Prep time: 10 minutes | Cook time: 0 minutes | Serves 4

1½ cups blackberries
1 cup strawberries + extra for garnishing
1 cup blueberries
2 small beets, peeled and chopped
2/3 cup ice cubes
1 lime, juiced

1. For the extra strawberries for garnishing, make a single deep cut on their sides; set aside. 2. Add the blackberries, strawberries, blueberries, beet, and ice into the smoothie maker and blend the ingredients at high speed until smooth and frothy, for about 60 seconds. Add the lime juice, and puree further for 30 seconds. Pour the drink into tall smoothie glasses, fix the reserved strawberries on each glass rim, stick a straw in, and serve the drink immediately.

Per Serving
Calories: 89 | fat: 3g | protein: 3g | carbs: 13g | net carbs: 7g | fiber: 6g

Vanilla Ice Cream

Prep time: 30 minutes | Cook time: 0 minutes | Serves 6

1 (13½ ounces/400 ml) can full-fat coconut milk
6 large egg yolks
2 teaspoons vanilla extract or powder
½ cup melted (but not hot) coconut oil
2 tablespoons granulated xylitol
Pinch of finely ground gray sea salt
Optional Topping:
2 tablespoons sliced blanched almonds, roasted
Special Equipment:
Ice cream maker (optional)

1. Place an airtight, lidded 32-ounce (950-ml) or larger freezer-safe glass container, loaf pan, or bowl in the freezer. 2. Place all the ingredients in a blender and blend on high speed until smooth. 3. Transfer the mixture to an airtight container such as a mason jar and place in the fridge to chill for 2 hours. 4. Once ready to churn, add the mixture to an ice cream maker and churn following the manufacturer's instructions. 5. Transfer the churned ice cream to the chilled container (if using a loaf pan, line it with parchment paper first). Cover with the lid and place back in the freezer for at least 1½ hours before serving. 6. When ready to serve, set the ice cream on the counter to soften for 5 to 10 minutes. Garnish each serving with a teaspoon of roasted almonds, if desired.

Per Serving
Calories: 356 | fat: 36g | protein: 4g | carbs: 4g | net carbs: 4g | fiber: 0g

Vanilla Egg Custard

Prep time: 10 minutes | Cook time: 30 minutes |

Serves 2
1 cup heavy whipping cream, plus ¼ cup for topping if desired
2 large egg yolks
2 teaspoons vanilla extract
½ teaspoon liquid stevia

1. Preheat the oven to 300°F. 2. Put the 1 cup of cream, egg yolks, vanilla extract, and stevia in a medium-sized mixing bowl and beat with a hand mixer until combined. Pour into two 6 ounces/170 g ramekins. Place the ramekins in a baking dish and fill the baking dish with boiling water so that it goes two-thirds of the way up the sides of the ramekins. 3. Bake for 30 minutes, or until the edges of the custard are just starting to brown. It should not be completely baked through and firm. Place in the refrigerator to chill and set for at least 2 hours before serving. 4. If making the topping, put the ¼ cup of cream in a medium-sized mixing bowl and whip using the hand mixer until soft peaks form. Top the custard with the whipped cream prior to serving.

Per Serving
Calories: 568 | fat: 59g | protein: 5g | carbs: 4g | net carbs: 4g | fiber: 0g

Dark-Chocolate Strawberry Bark

Prep time: 10 minutes | Cook time: 1 minutes | Serves 2

½ (2.8 ounces/78 g) keto-friendly chocolate bar (I use Lily's)
1 tablespoon heavy (whipping) cream
2 tablespoons salted almonds
1 fresh strawberry, sliced

1. Line a baking sheet with parchment paper. 2. Break up the chocolate bar half into small pieces, and put them in a microwave-safe bowl with the cream. 3. Heat in the microwave for 45 seconds at 50 percent power. Stir the chocolate, and cook for 20 seconds more at 50 percent power. Stir again, making sure the mixture is fully melted and combined. If not, microwave for another 20 seconds. 4. Pour the chocolate mixture onto the parchment paper and spread it in a thin, uniform layer. 5. Sprinkle on the almonds, then add the strawberry slices. 6. Refrigerate until hardened, about 2 hours. 7. Once the bark is nice and hard, break it up into smaller pieces to nibble on. Yum! 8. The bark will keep for up to 4 days in a sealed container in the refrigerator.

Per Serving
Calories: 111 | fat: 10g | protein: 3g | carbs: 9g | net carbs: 4g | fiber: 5g

Traditional Kentucky Butter Cake

Prep time: 5 minutes | Cook time: 35 minutes | Serves 4

2 cups almond flour
¾ cup granulated erythritol
1½ teaspoons baking powder
4 eggs
1 tablespoon vanilla extract
½ cup butter, melted
Cooking spray
½ cup water

1. In a medium bowl, whisk together the almond flour, erythritol, and baking powder. Whisk well to remove any lumps. 2. Add the eggs and vanilla and whisk until combined. 3. Add the butter and whisk until the batter is mostly smooth and well combined. 4. Grease the pan with cooking spray and pour in the batter. Cover tightly with aluminum foil. 5. Add the water to the pot. Place the Bundt pan on the trivet and carefully lower it into the pot using. 6. Set the lid in place. Select the Manual mode and set the cooking time for 35 minutes on High Pressure. When the timer goes off, do a quick pressure release. Carefully open the lid. 7. Remove the pan from the pot. Let the cake cool in the pan before flipping out onto a plate.

Per Serving
Calories: 179 | fat: 16g | protein: 2g | carbs: 2g | net carbs: 2g | fiber: 0g

Rhubarb Microwave Cakes

Prep time: 5 minutes | Cook time: 0 minutes | Serves 2

1 large egg
3 tablespoons refined avocado oil or macadamia nut oil
1 tablespoon plus 1 teaspoon confectioners'-style erythritol
¼ teaspoon vanilla extract or powder
¼ cup roughly ground flax

seeds
1 teaspoon ground cinnamon
¼ teaspoon ground nutmeg
¼ teaspoon baking powder
1 (2½-in/6.5-cm) piece rhubarb, diced
1 to 2 fresh strawberries, hulled and sliced, for garnish (optional)

1. Place the egg, oil, erythritol, and vanilla in a small bowl. Whisk to combine. 2. In a separate small bowl, place the flax seeds, cinnamon, nutmeg, and baking powder. Stir to combine, then add to the bowl with the wet ingredients. 3. Add the diced rhubarb to the bowl and stir until coated. 4. Divide the mixture between two 8-ounce (240-ml) ramekins, coffee cups, or other small microwave-safe containers. Microwave for 2 to 2½ minutes, until a toothpick inserted in the middle comes out clean. Garnish with strawberry slices, if desired.

Per Serving
Calories: 303 | fat: 28g | protein: 6g | carbs: 7g | net carbs: 2g | fiber: 6g

Almond Pistachio Biscotti

Prep time: 5 minutes | Cook time: 1 hour 20 minutes | Serves 12

2 cups almond flour or hazelnut flour
½ packed cup flax meal
½ teaspoon baking soda
½ teaspoon ground nutmeg
½ teaspoon vanilla powder or 1½ teaspoons unsweetened vanilla extract
¼ teaspoon salt
1 tablespoon fresh lemon zest

2 large eggs
2 tablespoons extra-virgin olive oil
1 tablespoon unsweetened almond extract
1 teaspoon apple cider vinegar or fresh lemon juice
Low-carb sweetener, to taste (optional)
⅔ cup unsalted pistachio nuts

1. Preheat the oven to 285°F (140°C) fan assisted or 320°F (160°C) conventional. Line one or two baking trays with parchment paper. 2. In a bowl, mix the almond flour, flax meal, baking soda, nutmeg, vanilla, salt, and lemon zest. Add the eggs, olive oil, almond extract, vinegar, and optional sweetener. Mix well until a dough forms, then mix in the pistachio nuts. 3. Form the dough into a low, wide log shape, about 8 × 5 inches (20 × 13 cm). Place in the oven and bake for about 45 minutes. Remove from oven and let cool for 15 to 20 minutes. Using a sharp knife, cut into 12 slices. 4. Reduce the oven temperature to 250°F (120°C) fan assisted or 285°F (140°C) conventional. Lay the slices very carefully in a flat layer on the lined trays. Bake for 15 to 20 minutes, flip over, and bake for 15 to 20 minutes. 5. Remove from the oven and let the biscotti cool down completely to fully crisp up. Store in a sealed jar for up to 2 weeks.

Per Serving
Calories: 196 | fat: 17g | protein: 7g | carbs: 7g | fiber: 4g | sodium: 138mg

Trail Mix with Dried Coconut and Strawberries

Prep time: 15 minutes | Cook time: 3 hours 30 minutes | Makes 7 cups

10 medium strawberries, hulled and halved
2 tablespoons coconut oil
1 teaspoon ground cinnamon
½ teaspoon vanilla extract
Sweetener of choice (optional)
2 cups chopped pecans

2 cups walnut halves, chopped
1 cup unsweetened coconut flakes
½ cup macadamia nuts
½ cup sliced almonds
3 Brazil nuts, chopped
3 tablespoons hulled pumpkin seeds

1. Preheat the oven to 200ºF (93ºC). Line a baking sheet with parchment paper. 2. Arrange the strawberries cut-side up on the prepared baking sheet and bake for 3 hours, rotating the baking sheet every hour. Remove from the oven and let cool for 30 minutes. If they are still moist, cook for another 30 minutes. 3. While the strawberries are cooling, increase the oven heat to 375ºF (190ºC). 4. In a microwave-safe bowl, melt the coconut oil in the microwave. Stir in the cinnamon, vanilla, and sweetener (if using). In another bowl, combine the pecans, walnuts, coconut flakes, macadamia nuts, almonds, Brazil nuts, and pumpkin seeds. Drizzle the coconut oil mixture over the nuts until everything is lightly coated but not soaked. 5. Line two more baking sheets with parchment paper and spread the nut mixture over the sheets evenly. Bake for 15 to 30 minutes until the nuts begin to brown. Remove from the oven and pour onto a paper towel to dry. 6. Once all the ingredients have cooled, toss the nuts and strawberries together and eat right away.

Per Serving ½ cup
Calories: 388 | fat: 36g | protein: 7g | carbs: 9g | net carbs: 4g | fiber: 5g

Olive Oil Ice Cream

Prep time: 5 minutes | Cook time: 25 minutes | Serves 8

4 large egg yolks	and 1 cup whole milk
⅓ cup powdered sugar-free sweetener (such as stevia or monk fruit extract)	1 teaspoon vanilla extract
	⅛ teaspoon salt
2 cups half-and-half or 1 cup heavy whipping cream	¼ cup light fruity extra-virgin olive oil

1. Freeze the bowl of an ice cream maker for at least 12 hours or overnight. 2. In a large bowl, whisk together the egg yolks and sugar-free sweetener. 3. In a small saucepan, heat the half-and-half over medium heat until just below a boil. Remove from the heat and allow to cool slightly. 4. Slowly pour the warm half-and-half into the egg mixture, whisking constantly to avoid cooking the eggs. Return the eggs and cream to the saucepan over low heat. 5. Whisking constantly, cook over low heat until thickened, 15 to 20 minutes. Remove from the heat and stir in the vanilla extract and salt. Whisk in the olive oil and transfer to a glass bowl. Allow to cool, cover, and refrigerate for at least 6 hours. 6. Freeze custard in an ice cream maker according to manufacturer's directions.

Per Serving
Calories: 168 | fat: 15g | protein: 2g | carbs: 8g | fiber: 0g | sodium: 49mg

Lemon Coconut Cake

Prep time: 5 minutes | Cook time: 40 minutes | Serves 9

Base:	Low-carb sweetener, to taste (optional)
6 large eggs, separated	**Topping:**
⅓ cup melted ghee or virgin coconut oil	½ cup unsweetened large coconut flakes
1 tablespoon fresh lemon juice	1 cup heavy whipping cream or coconut cream
Zest of 2 lemons	¼ cup mascarpone, more heavy whipping cream, or coconut cream
2 cups almond flour	
½ cup coconut flour	
¼ cup collagen powder	½ teaspoon vanilla powder or 1½ teaspoons unsweetened vanilla extract
1 teaspoon baking soda	
1 teaspoon vanilla powder or 1 tablespoon unsweetened vanilla extract	

1. Preheat the oven to 320°F (160°C) conventional. Line a baking tray with parchment paper. A square 8 × 8–inch (20 × 20 cm) or a rectangular tray of similar size will work best. 2. **To Make the base:** Whisk the egg whites in a bowl until stiff peaks form. In a separate bowl, whisk the egg yolks, melted ghee, lemon juice, and lemon zest. In a third bowl, mix the almond flour, coconut flour, collagen, baking soda, vanilla and optional sweetener. 3. Add the whisked egg yolk–ghee mixture into the dry mixture and combine well. Gently fold in the egg whites, trying not to deflate them. 4. Pour into the baking tray. Bake for 35 to 40 minutes, until lightly golden on top and set inside. Remove from the oven and let cool completely before adding the topping. 5. **To Make the Topping:** Preheat the oven to 380°F (195°C) conventional. Place the coconut flakes on a baking tray and bake for 2 to 3 minutes. Remove from the oven and set aside to cool. 6.Whip the cream, mascarpone, and vanilla in a bowl until soft peaks form. Spread on the cake and top with coconut flakes.

Per Serving
Calories: 342 | fat: 31g | protein: 9g | carbs: 10g | fiber: 4g | sodium: 208mg

Jelly Pie Jars

Prep time: 20 minutes | Cook time: 15 minutes | Serves 8

Coconut oil, for the jars	⅓ cup water
Pie Base:	1½ teaspoons vanilla extract
1 cup blanched almond flour	3 drops liquid stevia
1 tablespoon plus 1½ teaspoons whisked egg (about ½ large egg)	¼ cup chia seeds
	1½ teaspoons balsamic vinegar
1 tablespoon lard	**Almond Butter Topping:**
2 drops liquid stevia	¾ cup unsweetened smooth almond butter
¼ teaspoon ground cinnamon	¼ cup melted coconut oil or ghee (if tolerated)
Pinch of finely ground gray sea salt	1 teaspoon ground cinnamon
Jam Filling:	2 to 4 drops liquid stevia
1½ heaping cups fresh blackberries	**For Garnish (Optional):**
	16 to 24 fresh blackberries

1. Preheat the oven to 325°F (163°C). Grease eight 4-ounce (120-ml) mason jars with a dab of coconut oil and set on a rimmed baking sheet. 2. **To prepare the base:** Place the ingredients for the base in a large bowl and mix until fully combined. 3. Divide the dough evenly among the jars, pressing it in firmly and evening it out. Place the jars back on the baking sheet and bake for 15 to 17 minutes. Remove and cool completely, at least 30 minutes. 4. **To prepare the jam filling:** Place the blackberries, water, vanilla, and stevia in a medium-sized saucepan. Cook, covered, over medium heat for 5 minutes. 5. Reduce the heat to low and add the chia seeds and balsamic vinegar. Cook, uncovered, for another 3 to 4 minutes, stirring frequently, until the mixture has thickened. Transfer the mixture to a heat-safe bowl and set aside to cool to room temperature, at least 30 minutes. 6. **To prepare the almond butter topping:** Place the topping ingredients in a small bowl and whisk to combine. 7. To assemble, divide the cooled jam filling among the jars, keep the layer as flat as possible. Then add the almond butter topping, pouring it in slowly to avoid spillover. Transfer the assembled jars to the fridge to cool for 30 minutes. 8. Before serving, top each jar with 2 or 3 blackberries, if desired.

Per Serving
Calories: 388 | fat: 32g | protein: 11g | carbs: 13g | net carbs: 4g | fiber: 9g

Coffee Fat Bombs

Prep time: 5 minutes | Cook time: 0 minutes | Serves 6

1½ cups mascarpone cheese
½ cup melted butter
3 tablespoons unsweetened cocoa powder
¼ cup erythritol
6 tablespoons brewed coffee, room temperature

1. Whisk the mascarpone cheese, butter, cocoa powder, erythritol, and coffee with a hand mixer until creamy and fluffy, for 1 minute. Fill into muffin tins and freeze for 3 hours until firm.
Per Serving
Calories: 154 | fat: 14g | protein: 4g | carbs: 3g | net carbs: 2g | fiber: 1g

Death by Chocolate Cheesecake

Prep time: 20 minutes | Cook time: 70 minutes | Makes one 9-inch cheesecake

Crust:
½ cup coconut flour
½ cup cocoa powder
½ cup powdered erythritol
½ cup (1 stick) unsalted butter, melted
Filling:
3 (8 ounces/227 g) packages cream cheese, room temperature
¼ cup plus 2 tablespoons heavy whipping cream

3 large eggs
¾ cup powdered erythritol
3 tablespoons cocoa powder
1 teaspoon vanilla extract
4 ounces (113 g) unsweetened baking chocolate (100% cacao)
1 tablespoon unsalted butter
For Garnish (Optional):
1 ounce (28 g) unsweetened baking chocolate (100% cacao)

1. **Make the Crust:** Preheat the oven to 350°F. 2. Mix the coconut flour, cocoa powder, and erythritol in a bowl. Pour the melted butter over the dry mixture and combine thoroughly. 3. Transfer the mixture to the greased pan with coconut oil spray and press into an even layer across the bottom. Par-bake the crust for 12 minutes. 4. Remove the crust from the oven and lower the oven temperature to 300°F. Allow the crust to cool for at least 20 minutes before adding the filling. 5. **Make the Filling:** beat the cream cheese and cream in a bowl until combined and smooth. Add the eggs, erythritol, cocoa powder, and vanilla extract and combine with the mixer. 6. Roughly chop the 4 ounces (113 g) of chocolate and put it in a microwave-safe bowl with the tablespoon of butter. Microwave in 20-second increments, stirring after each increment, until melted. 7. Mix the melted chocolate mixture and the rest of the filling ingredients until smooth. Pour the filling over the cooled crust and spread evenly. 8. Bake the cheesecake for 55 minutes. Set on a wire baking rack and allow to cool for 15 minutes, then place in the refrigerator until completely set, at least 3 hours. 9. Allow to sit at room temperature for 30 minutes prior to serving. 10. To serve, run a knife around the edges to loosen the cheesecake, then remove the rim of the springform pan. Cut into 12 slices.
Per Serving
Calories: 398 | fat: 37g | protein: 7g | carbs: 11g | net carbs: 5g | fiber: 6g

Blackberry Crisp

Prep time: 5 minutes | Cook time: 5 minutes | Serves 1

10 blackberries
½ teaspoon vanilla extract
2 tablespoons powdered erythritol
⅛ teaspoon xanthan gum
1 tablespoon butter
¼ cup chopped pecans
3 teaspoons almond flour
½ teaspoon cinnamon
2 teaspoons powdered erythritol
1 cup water

1. Place blackberries, vanilla, erythritol, and xanthan gum in 4-inch ramekin. Stir gently to coat blackberries. 2. In small bowl, mix remaining ingredients. Sprinkle over blackberries and cover with foil. Press the Manual button and set time for 4 minutes. When timer beeps, quick-release the pressure. Serve warm. Feel free to add scoop of whipped cream on top.
Per Serving
Calories: 346 | fat: 31g | protein: 3g | carbs: 13g | net carbs: 5g | fiber: 8g

Golden Sesame Cookies

Prep time: 10 minutes | Cook time: 15 minutes | Makes 16 cookies

1 cup almond flour
⅓ cup monk fruit sweetener, granulated form
¾ teaspoon baking powder
½ cup grass-fed butter, at
room temperature
1 egg
1 teaspoon toasted sesame oil
½ cup sesame seeds

1. Preheat the oven. Set the oven temperature to 375°F. Line a baking sheet with parchment paper and set it aside. 2. Mix the dry ingredients. In a large bowl, mix together the almond flour, sweetener, and baking powder. 3. Add the wet ingredients. Add the butter, egg, and sesame oil to the dry ingredients and mix until everything is well blended. 4. Form the cookies. Roll the dough into 1½-inch balls and roll them in the sesame seeds. Place the cookies on the baking sheet about 2 inches apart and flatten them with your fingers so they are ½ inch thick. 5. Bake the cookies. Bake for 15 minutes, or until the cookies are golden brown. Transfer them to a wire rack and let them cool. 6. Store. Store the cookies in a sealed container in the refrigerator for up to five days, or in the freezer for up to one month.
Per Serving
Calories: 173 | fat: 17g | protein: 3g | carbs: 2g | net carbs: 1g | fiber: 1g

Yellow Snow Sorbet

Prep time: 5 minutes | Cook time: 5 minutes | Serves 4

½ cup 0g net carb sweetener
4 cups water

¾ cup lemon juice, from concentrate

1. In a medium saucepan over medium heat, mix sweetener into hot water. Stir 5 minutes until all sweetener is dissolved. 2. Stir in lemon juice. 3. Remove from flame and let cool for 5 minutes. 4. Transfer mixture to a 9" × 5" × 2½" loaf pan. Place in freezer for 1½ hours. 5. Remove from freezer and whisk thoroughly. Return to the freezer and whisk every ½ hour for 3–4 more hours until desired consistency is reached. 6. Serve in four festive glasses.
Per Serving
Calories: 10 | fat: 0.4g | protein: 0.4g | carbs: 1.2g | net carbs: 1g | fiber: 0.2g

Fudgy Brownies

Prep time: 5 minutes | Cook time: 20 minutes | Makes 16 brownies

½ cup (1 stick) butter
4 ounces (113 g) unsweetened baker's chocolate
1 teaspoon vanilla extract (optional)
¾ cup (3 ounces/85 g) blanched almond flour
⅔ cup powdered erythritol

2 tablespoons unsweetened cocoa powder
¼ teaspoon sea salt (only if using unsalted butter)
2 large eggs, at room temperature, whisked
¼ cup walnuts, chopped (optional)

1. Preheat the oven to 350ºF (180ºC). Line an 8-inch square pan with parchment paper, with the edges of the paper over two of the sides. 2. In a double boiler top or heatproof bowl, combine the butter and chocolate. Bring water to a simmer in the bottom part of the double boiler or a saucepan. Place the double boiler top or bowl over the simmering water and heat gently, stirring frequently. 3. Remove the bowl from the pan as soon as the chocolate pieces have all melted and stir in the vanilla, if desired. 4. Add the almond flour, powdered erythritol, cocoa powder, sea salt, and eggs. Stir together until uniform. 5. Transfer the batter to the lined pan and smooth the top. If desired, sprinkle with the chopped walnuts. 6. Bake for 15 to 20 minutes, until an inserted toothpick comes out almost clean with just a little batter on it that balls up between your fingers. 7. Cool completely before moving or cutting. Use the overhanging pieces of parchment paper to lift the uncut brownies out of the pan and place on a cutting board. Cut into 16 brownies using a straight-down motion.
Per Serving
Calories: 163 | fat: 15g | protein: 2g | carbs: 6g | net carbs: 1g | fiber: 5g

Chocolate Protein Truffles

Prep time: 10 minutes | Cook time: 0 minutes | Makes 6 truffles

¼ cup blanched almond flour
2 tablespoons chocolate-flavored whey protein powder
1½ tablespoons cocoa powder
1 tablespoon natural almond

butter
1 tablespoon sugar-free maple syrup
1 tablespoon unsweetened almond milk
¼ cup unsweetened coconut flakes

1. Put all the ingredients, except for the coconut flakes, in a medium-sized mixing bowl and combine with a fork until uniform in texture. Cover and refrigerate until firm to the touch, at least 30 minutes. 2. Meanwhile, chop up the coconut flakes and set aside. 3. Remove the truffle mixture from the refrigerator and roll between your hands into 6 even-sized balls, about 1½ inches in diameter. Roll the balls, one at a time, in the chopped coconut and set on a plate. 4. Store in a sealed container in the refrigerator for up to a week.
Per Serving
Calories: 83 | fat: 6g | protein: 4g | carbs: 4g | net carbs: 3g | fiber: 1g

Chewy Chocolate Chip Cookies

Prep time: 10 minutes | Cook time: 20 minutes | Makes 16 cookies

1½ cups blanched almond flour
½ cup granular erythritol
1 tablespoon unflavored beef gelatin powder
1 teaspoon baking powder

½ cup (1 stick) unsalted butter, melted but not hot
1 large egg
1 teaspoon vanilla extract
½ cup sugar-free chocolate chips

1. Preheat the oven to 350°F and line 2 baking sheets with parchment paper. 2. Put the almond flour, erythritol, gelatin, and baking powder in a medium-sized bowl and whisk using a fork. Set aside. 3. Put the melted butter, egg, and vanilla extract in a large bowl and combine using a hand mixer or whisk. Add the dry mixture to wet mixture in 2 batches and combine until you have a soft dough that can easily be rolled between your hands without sticking. 4. Fold the chocolate chips into the dough with a rubber spatula. Using a cookie scoop or spoon, scoop 16 even-sized balls of the dough onto the baking sheets, leaving 2 inches of space between them. Using your hand or the spatula, flatten the cookies a little. They will spread slightly in the oven. 5. Bake for 20 minutes, or until golden brown. Allow to cool on the baking sheets for 15 minutes prior to handling. 6. Store leftovers in a sealed container in the refrigerator for up to a week or freeze for up to a month.
Per Serving
Calories: 125 | fat: 12g | protein: 3g | carbs: 3g | net carbs: 1g | fiber: 2g

Whipped Cream

Prep time: 5 minutes | Cook time: 0 minutes | Makes 2 cups

1 cup heavy whipping cream
2 tablespoons granular

erythritol
1 teaspoon vanilla extract

1. Place the ingredients in a large mixing bowl. Use a hand mixer or stand mixer to blend until stiff peaks form. Whipped cream is best if used the same day it's made, but leftovers can be stored in an airtight container in the refrigerator for up to 3 days.

Per Serving

Calories: 220 | fat: 22g | protein: 1g | carbs: 1g | net carbs: 1g | fiber: 0g

Caramelized Pumpkin Cheesecake

Prep time: 15 minutes | Cook time: 45 minutes | Serves 8

Crust:
1½ cups almond flour
4 tablespoons butter, melted
1 tablespoon Swerve
1 tablespoon granulated erythritol
½ teaspoon ground cinnamon
Cooking spray
Filling:
16 ounces (454 g) cream

cheese, softened
½ cup granulated erythritol
2 eggs
¼ cup pumpkin purée
3 tablespoons Swerve
1 teaspoon vanilla extract
¼ teaspoon pumpkin pie spice
1½ cups water

1. **To Make the Crust:** In a medium bowl, combine the almond flour, butter, Swerve, erythritol, and cinnamon and press it all together. 2. Spray the pan with cooking spray and line the bottom with parchment paper. 3. Press the crust evenly into the pan. Work the crust up the sides of the pan, about halfway from the top, and make sure there are no bare spots on the bottom. 4. Place the crust in the freezer for 20 minutes while you make the filling. 5. **To Make the Filling:** Combine the cream cheese and erythritol on medium speed . Beat until the cream cheese is light and fluffy, 2 to 3 minutes. 6. Add the eggs, pumpkin purée, Swerve, vanilla, and pumpkin pie spice. Beat until well combined. 7. Remove the crust from the freezer and pour in the filling. Cover the pan with aluminum foil and place it on the trivet. 8. Add the water to the pot and carefully lower the trivet into the pot. 9. Set the lid in place. Select the Manual mode and set the cooking time for 45 minutes on High Pressure. When the timer goes off, do a quick pressure release. Carefully open the lid. 10. Remove the trivet and cheesecake from the pot. Remove the foil from the pan. 11. Let the cheesecake cool for 30 minutes before placing it in the refrigerator to set for at least 6 hours and serve.

Per Serving

Calories: 407 | fat: 35.8g | protein: 10.3g | carbs: 6.8g | net carbs: 4.3g | fiber: 2.5g

Blueberry Panna Cotta

Prep time: 5 minutes | Cook time: 0 minutes | Serves 6

1 tablespoon gelatin powder
2 tablespoons water
2 cups goat's cream, coconut cream, or heavy whipping cream
2 cups wild blueberries, fresh

or frozen, divided
½ teaspoon vanilla powder or 1½ teaspoons unsweetened vanilla extract
Optional: low-carb sweetener, to taste

1. In a bowl, sprinkle the gelatin powder over the cold water. Set aside to let it bloom. 2. Place the goat's cream, half of the blueberries, and the vanilla in a blender and process until smooth and creamy. Alternatively, use an immersion blender. 3. Pour the blueberry cream into a saucepan. Gently heat; do not boil. Scrape the gelatin into the hot cream mixture together with the sweetener, if using. Mix well until all the gelatin has dissolved. 4. Divide among 6 (4 ounces/113 g) jars or serving glasses and fill them about two-thirds full, leaving enough space for the remaining blueberries. Place in the fridge for 3 to 4 hours, or until set. 5. When the panna cotta has set, evenly distribute the remaining blueberries among the jars. Serve immediately or store in the fridge for up to 4 days.

Per Serving

Calories: 172 | fat: 15g | protein: 2g | carbs: 8g | fiber: 2g | sodium: 19mg

Blackberry "Cheesecake" Bites

Prep time: 5 minutes | Cook time: 0 minutes | serves 4

1½ cups almonds, soaked overnight
1 cup blackberries
⅓ cup coconut oil, melted

¼ cup full-fat coconut cream
⅓ cup monk fruit sweetener
¼ cup freshly squeezed lemon juice

1. Prepare a muffin tin by lining the cups with cupcake liners. Set aside. 2. In a high-powered blender, combine the soaked almonds, blackberries, melted coconut oil, coconut cream, monk fruit sweetener, and lemon juice. 3. Blend on high until the mixture is whipped and fluffy. 4. Divide the mixture equally among the muffin cups. 5. Place the muffin tin in the freezer for 90 minutes to allow the cheesecake bites to set.

Per Serving

Calories: 514 | fat: 48g | protein: 12g | carbs: 18g | net carbs: 9g | fiber: 9g

Birthday Mug Cakes

Prep time: 5 minutes | Cook time: 2 minutes | Serves 2

Frosting:
2 ounces (57 g) full-fat cream cheese, at room temperature
1 tablespoon butter, at room temperature
2 teaspoons granulated erythritol

¼ teaspoon vanilla extract
Cake:
⅓ cup almond flour
2 tablespoons granulated erythritol
½ teaspoon baking powder
1 large egg
¼ teaspoon vanilla extract

1. **To Make the Frosting:** In a small bowl, combine the cream cheese, butter, erythritol, and vanilla. Whisk well, then place in the refrigerator to chill. 2. **To Make the Cake:** In a 12-ounce (340-g) coffee mug, combine the almond flour, erythritol, and baking powder. Using a fork, break up any clumps and mix the ingredients well. 3. Add the egg and vanilla, then beat well. Make sure you scrape the bottom edges for any unmixed flour. 4. Microwave on high power for 70 seconds. 5. Let the cake cool for 5 to 10 minutes. 6. Flip the mug onto a plate, then tap a few times. (Alternately, you can skip this step and eat it directly from the mug.). Cut the cake in half crosswise, for 2 cupcakes. 7. Frost the cupcakes before serving.

Per Serving
Calories: 279 | fat: 26g | protein: 8g | carbs: 5g | net carbs: 3g | fiber: 2g

Mixed Berry Cobbler

Prep time: 10 minutes | Cook time: 35 minutes | Serves 4

Filling:
2 cups frozen mixed berries
1 tablespoon granulated erythritol
½ teaspoon water
¼ teaspoon freshly squeezed lemon juice
¼ teaspoon vanilla extract
Crust:
½ cup coconut flour
2 tablespoons granulated

erythritol
½ teaspoon xanthan gum
½ teaspoon baking powder
6 tablespoons butter, cold
¼ cup heavy (whipping) cream
Topping:
1 teaspoon granulated erythritol
¼ teaspoon ground cinnamon

1. Preheat the oven to 350ºF (180ºC). 2. **To Make the Filling:** In a 9-inch round pie dish, combine the berries, erythritol, water, lemon juice, and vanilla. 3. **To Make the Crust:** In a food processor, pulse to combine the coconut flour, erythritol, xanthan gum, and baking powder. 4. Add the butter and cream, and pulse until pea-sized pieces of dough form. Don't overprocess. 5. Form 5 equal balls of dough, then flatten them to between ¼- and ½-inch thickness. 6. Place the dough rounds on the top of the berries so that

they are touching, but not overlapping. 7. **To Make the Topping:** In a small bowl, combine the erythritol and cinnamon. Sprinkle the mixture over the dough. 8. Bake for 30 to 35 minutes, until the topping is beginning to brown, then let cool for 10 minutes before serving.

Per Serving
Calories: 317 | fat: 25g | protein: 4g | carbs: 19g | net carbs: 12g | fiber: 7g

Peanut Butter Fat Bomb

Prep time: 10 minutes | Cook time: 0 minutes | Serves 2

1 tablespoon butter, at room temperature
1 tablespoon coconut oil
2 tablespoons all-natural peanut butter or almond

butter
2 teaspoons Swerve natural sweetener or 2 drops liquid stevia

1. In a microwave-safe medium bowl, melt the butter, coconut oil, and peanut butter in the microwave on 50 percent power. Mix in the sweetener. 2. Pour the mixture into fat bomb molds. (I use small silicone cupcake molds.) 3. Freeze for 30 minutes, unmold them, and eat! Keep some extras in your freezer so you can eat them anytime you are craving a sweet treat.

Per Serving
Calories: 196 | fat: 20g | protein: 3g | carbs: 8g | net carbs: 3g | fiber: 1g

Cake or Cookie Dough Balls

Prep time: 10 minutes | Cook time: 0 minutes | Serves 2

2 scoops keto-approved protein powder
2 tablespoons coconut flour
2 teaspoons erythritol
1 tablespoon coconut oil
4 drops cake batter flavor extract or 1½ teaspoons vanilla extract
¼ cup water or unsweetened

nondairy milk of choice
2 teaspoons sugar-free chocolate chips (optional)
2 teaspoons freeze-dried strawberries (optional)
2 teaspoons nuts of your choice (optional)
2 teaspoons cocoa powder (optional)

1. In a large mixing bowl, combine the protein powder, coconut flour, erythritol, coconut oil, cake batter extract, water or milk, and, if using, the chocolate chips, strawberries, nuts, and cocoa powder. Mix until well combined and everything is evenly distributed. 2. Roll the batter into 10 to 12 balls and put on a plate. Freeze the balls for about 1 hour, if you'd like. 3. The dough balls can be enjoyed at room temperature, or you can freeze them for about 1 hour before serving. They're delicious regardless!

Per Serving
Calories: 191 | fat: 11g | protein: 12g | carbs: 11g | net carbs: 5g | fiber: 6g

"Frosty" Chocolate Shake

Prep time: 10 minutes | Cook time: 0 minutes | Serves 2

¾ cup heavy (whipping) cream

4 ounces (113 g) coconut milk

1 tablespoon Swerve natural sweetener

¼ teaspoon vanilla extract

2 tablespoons unsweetened cocoa powder

1. Pour the cream into a medium cold metal bowl, and with your hand mixer and cold beaters, beat the cream just until it forms peaks. 2. Slowly pour in the coconut milk, and gently stir it into the cream. Add the sweetener, vanilla, and cocoa powder, and beat until fully combined. 3. Pour into two tall glasses, and chill in the freezer for 1 hour before serving. I usually stir the shakes twice during this time.

Per Serving

Calories: 444 | fat: 47g | protein: 4g | carbs: 15g | net carbs: 7g | fiber: 2g

Chocolate-Covered Coffee Bites

Prep time: 10 minutes | Cook time: 0 minutes | Serves 8

Bites:

¼ cup plus 2 tablespoons cacao butter

½ cup macadamia nuts, roasted

1 tablespoon confectioners'-style erythritol or 1 or 2 drops liquid stevia ½ teaspoon instant coffee (medium or light roast, regular or decaf)

2 tablespoons collagen peptides

Chocolate Topping:

¼ cup stevia-sweetened chocolate chips, melted

Garnish:

About ¼ teaspoon large flake sea salt

Special Equipment:

Silicone mold with eight (1 ounce/28 g) semispherical cavities

1. Place the cacao butter, macadamia nuts, erythritol, and instant coffee in a high-powered blender or food processor. Blend on high speed until the nuts have broken down quite a bit but are still chunky, about 20 seconds. 2. Add the collagen and pulse to combine. 3. Using a spoon, scoop and press the mixture into 8 cavities of a silicone mold. Place the mold in the fridge for 2 hours or in the freezer for 1 hour, until the bites are set. 4. Meanwhile, line a baking sheet with parchment paper or a silicone baking mat and set aside. 5. Remove the mold from the fridge or freezer and pop out the bites onto the prepared baking sheet. Drizzle the melted chocolate over the top, then sprinkle each bite with a pinch of salt. Return the bites to the fridge until the chocolate is set, about 10 minutes. Enjoy!

Per Serving

Calories: 213 | fat: 20g | protein: 4g | carbs: 4g | net carbs: 2g | fiber: 2g

Dark Chocolate Fudge

Prep time: 15 minutes | Cook time: 0 minutes | Makes 30 pieces

1 cup coconut oil, melted

1 cup cocoa powder

1 teaspoon vanilla extract

½ cup monk fruit sweetener, granulated form

Pinch sea salt

1. Prepare a baking dish. Line a 9-by-9-inch glass baking dish with plastic wrap and set it aside. 2. Make the fudge. Place the coconut oil, cocoa powder, vanilla, sweetener, and salt in a blender and process until the mixture is smooth and blended. Pour the mixture into the baking dish and place more plastic wrap over it. 3. Refrigerate. Place the fudge in the refrigerator for at least 4 hours, until it is set up and firm. 4. Cut and store. Remove the fudge from the baking dish, cut it into roughly 1½-inch squares and store in the freezer in a sealed container for up to one month.

Per Serving

Calories: 139 | fat: 15g | protein: 1g | carbs: 3g | net carbs: 1g | fiber: 2g

Salted Chocolate-Macadamia Nut Fat Bombs

Prep time: 10 minutes | Cook time: 10 minutes | Serves 5

½ cup coconut oil

½ cup almond butter

¼ cup unsweetened cocoa powder

1 to 2 tablespoons butter

(optional)

Pinch salt

¼ cup chopped macadamia nuts

1. In a small saucepan over low heat, melt the coconut oil. 2. Whisk in the almond butter until well combined. 3. Add the cocoa powder and butter (if using). Continue to whisk until combined. 4. Add the salt, remove the pan from the heat, and give it one more stir. Cool slightly before pouring the mixture into a mold—use silicone cupcake liners, a cocktail ice-cube tray, or even muffin tins with paper or silicone liners. Top with the macadamia nuts. 5. Freeze for 15 to 20 minutes or until they've hardened enough to handle. Refrigerate leftovers in an airtight container for up to 2 weeks.

Per Serving 1 bomb

Calories: 443 | fat: 47g | protein: 5g | carbs: 9g | net carbs: 6g | fiber: 3g

Peanut Butter Cookies

Prep time: 5 minutes | Cook time: 10 minutes | Makes 15 cookies

1 cup natural crunchy peanut butter
½ cup Swerve natural sweetener
1 egg

1. Preheat the oven to 350°F. Line a baking sheet with a silicone baking mat or parchment paper. 2. In a medium bowl, use a hand mixer to mix together the peanut butter, sweetener, and egg. 3. Roll up the batter into small balls about 1 inch in diameter. 4. Spread out the cookie-dough balls on the prepared pan. Press each dough ball down with the tines of a fork, then repeat to make a crisscross pattern. 5. Bake for about 12 minutes, or until golden. 6. Let the cookies cool for 10 minutes on the lined pan before serving. If you try to move them too soon, they will crumble. 7. Store leftover cookies covered in the refrigerator for up to 5 days.

Per Serving
Calories: 98 | fat: 8g | protein: 4g | carbs: 10g | net carbs: 3g | fiber: 1g

Coconut Chocolate Cookies

Prep time: 10 minutes | Cook time: 15 minutes | Makes 1 dozen cookies

¼ cup (½ stick) unsalted butter, room temperature
1 ounce (28 g) cream cheese (2 tablespoons), room temperature
¼ cup plus 2 tablespoons powdered erythritol
1 large egg
¼ cup heavy whipping cream
¼ cup coconut flour
¼ cup cocoa powder
½ teaspoon baking powder
¼ teaspoon pink Himalayan salt
½ cup unsweetened coconut flakes

1. Preheat the oven to 325°F and line 2 baking sheets with parchment paper. 2. In a large bowl, use a hand mixer to cream the butter, cream cheese, and erythritol until light and fluffy. Mix in the egg and cream. Set aside. 3. In a small bowl, whisk together the coconut flour, cocoa powder, baking powder, and salt. Add the dry mixture to the wet ingredients in 2 batches, mixing with the hand mixer after each addition until you achieve a soft, slightly crumbly consistency. Fold in the coconut flakes. 4. Using a cookie scoop or spoon, scoop 12 even-sized balls of the dough onto the lined baking sheets and flatten with a fork to the desired size. They will not spread in the oven. Bake for 15 minutes, or until slightly firm to touch. Allow to cool

on the baking sheets for 20 minutes prior to handling or they will fall apart. 5. Store in a sealed container or zip-top plastic bag in the refrigerator for up to a week.

Per Serving
Calories: 91 | fat: 8g | protein: 1g | carbs: 3g | net carbs: 1g | fiber: 2g

Strawberry Cheesecake Mousse

Prep time: 10 minutes | Cook time: 0 minutes | Serves 2

4 ounces (113 g) cream cheese, at room temperature
1 tablespoon heavy (whipping) cream
1 teaspoon Swerve natural
sweetener or 1 drop liquid stevia
1 teaspoon vanilla extract
4 strawberries, sliced (fresh or frozen)

1. Break up the cream cheese block into smaller pieces and distribute evenly in a food processor (or blender). Add the cream, sweetener, and vanilla. 2. Mix together on high. I usually stop and stir twice and scrape down the sides of the bowl with a small rubber scraper to make sure everything is mixed well. 3. Add the strawberries to the food processor, and mix until combined. 4. Divide the strawberry cheesecake mixture between two small dishes, and chill for 1 hour before serving.

Per Serving
Calories: 221 | fat: 21g | protein: 4g | carbs: 11g | net carbs: 4g | fiber: 1g

Spiced-Chocolate Fat Bombs

Prep time: 10 minutes | Cook time: 4 minutes | Makes 12 fat bombs

¾ cup coconut oil
¼ cup cocoa powder
¼ cup almond butter
⅛ teaspoon chili powder
3 drops liquid stevia

1. Line a mini muffin tin with paper liners and set aside. 2. Put a small saucepan over low heat and add the coconut oil, cocoa powder, almond butter, chili powder, and stevia. 3. Heat until the coconut oil is melted, then whisk to blend. 4. Spoon the mixture into the muffin cups and place the tin in the refrigerator until the bombs are firm, about 15 minutes. 5. Transfer the cups to an airtight container and store the fat bombs in the freezer until you want to serve them.

Per Serving 1 fat bomb
Calories: 117 | fat: 12g | protein: 2g | carbs: 2g | net carbs: 2g | fiber: 0g

Rich Chocolate Mug Cake

Prep time: 5 minutes | Cook time: 2 minutes | Serves 2

½ cup almond flour
2 tablespoons coconut flour
2 tablespoons cocoa powder
1¼ teaspoons baking powder
1 tablespoon monk fruit
sweetener, granulated form

¼ cup melted grass-fed butter
2 eggs
½ teaspoon vanilla extract
½ cup keto-friendly chocolate
chips like Lily's Dark
Chocolate Chips

1. Mix the dry ingredients. In a medium bowl, stir together the almond flour, coconut flour, cocoa powder, baking powder, and sweetener. 2. Finish the batter. Stir in the melted butter, eggs, and vanilla until everything is well combined. Stir in the chocolate chips. 3. Cook and serve. Divide the batter between two large mugs and microwave them on high for 90 seconds, or until the cakes are cooked. Serve them immediately.

Per Serving
Calories: 383 | fat: 35g | protein: 11g | carbs: 12g | net carbs: 5g | fiber: 7g

Cheesecake

Prep time: 10 minutes | Cook time: 40 minutes | Serves 4

Crust:
⅔ cup almond flour
2 teaspoons granulated
erythritol
¼ teaspoon psyllium husk
powder
⅛ teaspoon ground cinnamon
2 tablespoons butter, melted
1½ teaspoons heavy
(whipping) cream
Filling:
8 ounces (227 g) full-fat

cream cheese, at room
temperature
1 large egg
2 tablespoons granulated
erythritol
2 tablespoons sour
cream
¼ teaspoon freshly squeezed
lemon juice
½ teaspoon liquid stevia
Pinch of pink Himalayan sea
salt

1. Preheat the oven to 325°F (163°C). 2. **To Make the Crust:** In a small bowl, combine the almond flour, erythritol, psyllium husk powder, and cinnamon. 3. Add the butter and cream and combine with a fork. 4. Transfer the mixture to a 7-inch springform pan. 5. Using a fork or your hands, pack the mixture against the bottom of the pan to form a crust. Do not put crust up the sides. 6. **To Make the Filling:** In a large mixing bowl, using a whisk or hand mixer on medium-high speed, combine the cream cheese, egg, erythritol, sour cream, lemon juice, stevia, and salt. 7. Pour the filling directly over the crust. 8. Bake for 38 to 40 minutes, until the very edges have a hint of brown. 9.

Remove cheesecake from the oven and let cool for 1 hour. Release the springform pan and transfer the cheesecake to the refrigerator to chill for at least 1 hour. 10. Cut the cheesecake into 4 pieces and serve.

Per Serving
Calories: 373 | fat: 36g | protein: 9g | carbs: 6g | net carbs: 4g | fiber: 2g

Chia and Blackberry Pudding

Prep time: 5 minutes | Cook time: 0 minutes | Serves 2

1 cup full-fat natural yogurt
2 teaspoons swerve
2 tablespoons chia seeds

1 cup fresh blackberries
1 tablespoon lemon zest
Mint leaves, to serve

1. Mix together the yogurt and the swerve. Stir in the chia seeds. Reserve 4 blackberries for garnish and mash the remaining ones with a fork until pureed. Stir in the yogurt mixture Chill in the fridge for 30 minutes. When cooled, divide the mixture between 2 glasses. Top each with a couple of blackberries, mint leaves, lemon zest and serve.

Per Serving
Calories: 169 | fat: 10g | protein: 8g | carbs: 11g | net carbs: 4g | fiber: 7g

Coconut Cheesecake

Prep time: 5 minutes | Cook time: 25 minutes | Serves 12

Crust:
2 egg whites
¼ cup erythritol
3 cups desiccated coconut
1 teaspoon coconut oil
¼ cup melted butter Filling:
3 tablespoons lemon juice

6 ounces (170 g) raspberries
2 cups erythritol
1 cup whipped cream
Zest of 1 lemon
24 ounces (680 g) cream
cheese

1. Grease bottom and sides of a springform pan with coconut oil. Line with parchment paper. Preheat oven to 350°F and mix all crust ingredients. Pour the crust into the pan. Bake for about 25 minutes; let cool. 2. Meanwhile, beat the cream cheese with an electric mixer until soft. Add the lemon juice, zest, and erythritol. Fold the whipped cream into the cheese cream mixture. Fold in the raspberries gently. Spoon the filling into the baked and cooled crust. Place in the fridge for 4 hours.

Per Serving
Calories: 256 | fat: 25g | protein: 5g | carbs: 3g | net carbs: 2g | fiber: 1g

Strawberry Panna Cotta

Prep time: 10 minutes | Cook time: 10 minutes | Serves 4

2 tablespoons warm water
2 teaspoons gelatin powder
2 cups heavy cream
1 cup sliced strawberries, plus more for garnish
1 to 2 tablespoons sugar-free sweetener of choice (optional)
1½ teaspoons pure vanilla extract
4 to 6 fresh mint leaves, for garnish (optional)

1. Pour the warm water into a small bowl. Sprinkle the gelatin over the water and stir well to dissolve. Allow the mixture to sit for 10 minutes. 2. In a blender or a large bowl, if using an immersion blender, combine the cream, strawberries, sweetener (if using), and vanilla. Blend until the mixture is smooth and the strawberries are well puréed. 3. Transfer the mixture to a saucepan and heat over medium-low heat until just below a simmer. Remove from the heat and cool for 5 minutes. 4. Whisking constantly, add in the gelatin mixture until smooth. Divide the custard between ramekins or small glass bowls, cover and refrigerate until set, 4 to 6 hours. 5. Serve chilled, garnishing with additional sliced strawberries or mint leaves (if using).

Per Serving
Calories: 229 | fat: 22g | protein: 3g | carbs: 5g | fiber: 1g | sodium: 26mg

Coconut Whipped Cream

Prep time: 5 minutes | Cook time: 0 minutes | Serves 7

1 (13½ ounces/400 ml) can coconut cream, chilled, or cream from 2 (13½ ounces/400 ml) cans full-fat coconut milk, chilled for at least 12 hours (see Tip below)

Optional Additions:
1 tablespoon confectioners'-style erythritol
1 teaspoon vanilla extract
2 tablespoons cacao powder

1. Place the coconut cream in a blender or the bowl of a stand mixer fitted with the whisk attachment. If using a blender, cover, turn the speed to low, and slowly increase the speed until you reach medium. Stay at medium speed until the coconut milk has thickened to the consistency of whipped cream, about 30 seconds if using a high-powered blender. If using a stand mixer, whisk for 30 seconds, or until fluffy. Stop here if you want your whipped cream plain and unsweetened. Continue to Step 2 for a sweetened and flavored option. 2. To make sweetened, vanilla-flavored whipped cream, add the erythritol and vanilla. To make sweetened, chocolate-flavored whipped cream, add the erythritol, vanilla, and cacao powder. Cover and blend for another 10 seconds, until the ingredients are thoroughly combined.

Per Serving
Calories: 116 | fat: 12g | protein: 1g | carbs: 2g | net carbs: 2g | fiber: 0g

Strawberry-Lime Ice Pops

Prep time: 5 minutes | Cook time: 0 minutes | Serves 4

½ (13.5 ounces/378 g) can coconut cream, ¾ cup unsweetened full-fat coconut milk, or ¾ cup heavy (whipping) cream
2 teaspoons Swerve natural sweetener or 2 drops liquid stevia
1 tablespoon freshly squeezed lime juice
¼ cup hulled and sliced strawberries (fresh or frozen)

1. In a food processor (or blender), mix together the coconut cream, sweetener, and lime juice. 2. Add the strawberries, and pulse just a few times so the strawberries retain their texture. 3. Pour into ice pop molds, and freeze for at least 2 hours before serving.

Per Serving
Calories: 166 | fat: 17g | protein: 1g | carbs: 5g | net carbs: 3g | fiber: 1g

Southern Almond Pie

Prep time: 10 minutes | Cook time: 35 minutes | Serves 12

2 cups almond flour
1½ cups powdered erythritol
1 teaspoon baking powder
Pinch of salt
½ cup sour cream
4 tablespoons butter, melted
1 egg
1 teaspoon vanilla extract
Cooking spray
1½ teaspoons ground cinnamon
1½ teaspoons Swerve
1 cup water

1. In a large bowl, whisk together the almond flour, powdered erythritol, baking powder, and salt. 2. Add the sour cream, butter, egg, and vanilla and whisk until well combined. The batter will be very thick, almost like cookie dough. 3. Grease the baking dish with cooking spray. Line with parchment paper, if desired. 4. Transfer the batter to the dish and level with an offset spatula. 5. In a small bowl, combine the cinnamon and Swerve. Sprinkle over the top of the batter. 6. Cover the dish tightly with aluminum foil. Add the water to the pot. Set the dish on the trivet and carefully lower it into the pot. 7. Set the lid in place. Select the Manual mode and set the cooking time for 35 minutes on High Pressure. When the timer goes off, do a quick pressure release. Carefully open the lid. 8. Remove the trivet and pie from the pot. Remove the foil from the pan. The pie should be set but soft, and the top should be slightly cracked. 9. Cool completely before cutting.

Per Serving
Calories: 221 | fat: 19.0g | protein: 5.6g | carbs: 4.8g | net carbs: 2.4g | fiber: 2.4g

Raspberry Cheesecake

Prep time: 10 minutes | Cook time: 25 to 30 minutes | Serves 12

⅔ cup coconut oil, melted
½ cup cream cheese, at room temperature
6 eggs
3 tablespoons granulated

sweetener
1 teaspoon alcohol-free pure vanilla extract
½ teaspoon baking powder
¾ cup raspberries

1. Preheat the oven to 350°F. Line an 8-by-8-inch baking dish with parchment paper and set aside. 2. In a large bowl, beat together the coconut oil and cream cheese until smooth. 3. Beat in the eggs, scraping down the sides of the bowl at least once. 4. Beat in the sweetener, vanilla, and baking powder until smooth. 5. Spoon the batter into the baking dish and use a spatula to smooth out the top. Scatter the raspberries on top. 6. Bake until the center is firm, about 25 to 30 minutes. 7. Allow the cheesecake to cool completely before cutting into 12 squares.
Per Serving 1 square
Calories: 176 | fat: 18g | protein: 6g | carbs: 3g | net carbs: 2g | fiber: 1g

Chocolate Cheesecake with Toasted Almond Crust

Prep time: 15 minutes | Cook time: 1 hour 20 minutes | Serves 10

For the Crust:
1½ cups almond flour
4 tablespoons monk fruit sweetener, granulated form
1 tablespoon cocoa powder
⅓ cup melted grass-fed butter
For the Filling:
1½ pounds (680 g) cream cheese, softened
¾ cup monk fruit sweetener,

granulated form
3 eggs, beaten
1 teaspoon vanilla extract
½ teaspoon almond extract (optional)
5 ounces (142 g) keto-friendly chocolate chips like Lily's Dark Chocolate Chips, melted and cooled
1 cup sour cream

To Make the Crust: 1. Set the oven temperature to 350°F. 2. In a medium bowl, stir together the almond flour, sweetener, cocoa powder, and melted butter until the ingredients hold together when pressed. Press the crumbs into the bottom of a 10-inch springform pan and 1 inch up the sides. 3. Chill the crust in the freezer for 10 minutes. Transfer it to the oven and bake it for 10 minutes. Cool the crust completely before filling. To Make the Filling: 1. Reduce the oven temperature to 275°F. 2. In a large bowl, beat the cream cheese until very light and fluffy, scraping down the sides with a spatula at least once. Beat in the sweetener until the mixture is smooth, scraping down the sides of the bowl. 3. Beat in the eggs one at a time, scraping

down the sides of the bowl occasionally and then beat in the vanilla extract and almond extract (if using). 4. Beat in the melted chocolate and sour cream until the filling is well blended, scraping down the sides of the bowl. 5. Pour the filling into the prebaked crust and bake it for 1 hour and 10 minutes. Turn off the oven and cool the cheesecake in the closed oven until it reaches room temperature. 6. Chill the cheesecake in the refrigerator for at least 4 to 6 hours. 7. Cut the cheesecake into 10 slices and serve.
Per Serving
Calories: 408 | fat: 40g | protein: 8g | carbs: 4g | net carbs: 4g | fiber: 0g

Almond Butter Fat Bombs

Prep time: 5 minutes | Cook time: 0 minutes | Serves 4

½ cup almond butter
½ cup coconut oil
4 tablespoons unsweetened

cocoa powder
½ cup erythritol

1. Melt butter and coconut oil in the microwave for 45 seconds, stirring twice until properly melted and mixed. Mix in cocoa powder and erythritol until completely combined. Pour into muffin moulds and refrigerate for 3 hours to harden.
Per Serving
Calories: 247 | fat: 23g | protein: 6g | carbs: 4g | net carbs: 2g | fiber: 2g

Pistachio Coconut Fudge

Prep time: 10 minutes | Cook time: 0 minutes | Makes 16 pieces

½ cup coconut oil, melted
4 ounces (113 g) cream cheese (½ cup), room temperature
1 teaspoon vanilla extract
¼ teaspoon plus 10 drops of

liquid stevia
½ cup shelled raw pistachios, roughly chopped, divided
½ cup unsweetened shredded coconut, divided

1. In a medium-sized bowl, beat the coconut oil and cream cheese with a hand mixer until smooth and creamy. Add the vanilla extract and stevia and mix until combined. 2. Fold in one-third of the pistachios and one-third of the coconut flakes using a rubber spatula. Pour the fudge mixture into a 5-inch square dish or pan and top with the remaining pistachios and shredded coconut. 3. Refrigerate for at least 2 hours prior to serving. To serve, cut into 16 pieces. 4. Store leftovers in a sealed container in the refrigerator for up to a week.
Per Serving
Calories: 123 | fat: 13g | protein: 1g | carbs: 2g | net carbs: 1g | fiber: 1g

Cookies-and-Cream Fat Bomb

Prep time: 10 minutes | Cook time: 1 to 3 minutes | Serves 2

1¾ ounces (50 g) cacao butter
4 teaspoons powdered erythritol
4 teaspoons heavy cream
powder
Pinch of pink Himalayan sea salt
2 teaspoons cacao nibs

1. In a small microwave-safe bowl, heat the cacao butter on high power in 30-second increments until it is liquid. Make sure to stir between intervals of microwaving. 2. Add the powdered erythritol, heavy cream powder, and salt to the cacao butter. Whisk until the mixture is well combined. 3. Line 2 cups of a muffin pan with paper cupcake liners. Split the liquid between the cups. 4. Pour 1 teaspoon of cacao nibs into each cup, then place the muffin pan in the refrigerator to cool for about 1 hour. (The cups can be stored in the refrigerator until ready to enjoy.)

Per Serving

Calories: 242 | fat: 24g | protein: 1g | carbs: 5g | net carbs: 4g | fiber: 1g

Chocolate Hazelnut "Powerhouse" Truffles

Prep time: 5 minutes | Cook time: 50 minutes | Makes 12 truffles

Filling:
1¾ cups blanched hazelnuts, divided
½ cup coconut butter
4 tablespoons butter or ¼ cup virgin coconut oil
¼ cup collagen powder
¼ cup raw cacao powder
1 teaspoon vanilla powder
or cinnamon
Optional: low-carb sweetener, to taste
Chocolate Coating:
2½ ounces (71 g) 100% dark chocolate
1 ounce (28 g) cacao butter
Pinch of salt

1. Preheat the oven to 320°F (160°C) conventional. 2. **To Make the Filling:** Roast the hazelnuts for 40 to 50 minutes, until lightly golden. Remove and let cool for a few minutes. 3. Process the roasted hazelnuts in a food processor for 1 to 2 minutes, until chunky. Add the coconut butter, butter, collagen powder, cacao powder, vanilla, and sweetener, if using. Process again until well combined. Place the dough in the fridge for 1 hour. 4. Reserve 12 hazelnuts for filling and crumble the remaining hazelnuts unto small pieces. 5. **To Make the Chocolate Coating:** Line a baking tray with parchment. Melt the dark chocolate and cacao butter. 6. Remove the dough from the fridge and scoop about 1 ounce (28 g) of the dough. Press one whole hazelnut into the center and use your hands to wrap the dough around to create a truffle. Place in the freezer for

about 15 minutes. 7. Pierce each very cold truffle over the melted chocolate and coat the chocolate over it. Place the coated truffles on the lined tray and drizzle any remaining coating over them. Before they become completely solid, roll them in the chopped nuts. Refrigerate the coated truffles for at least 15 minutes to harden.

Per Serving

Calories: 231 | fat: 22g | protein: 4g | carbs: 8g | fiber: 4g | sodium: 3mg

Kentucky Bourbon Balls

Prep time: 20 minutes | Cook time: 3 minutes | Makes 12 balls

½ cup (1 stick) salted butter, softened
1 cup confectioners'-style erythritol
3 tablespoons bourbon
½ teaspoon vanilla extract
¼ cup chopped raw pecans
¾ cup sugar-free chocolate chips
1 tablespoon avocado oil
12 raw pecan halves, for garnish

1. Using a hand mixer on medium speed, beat the butter and erythritol until pale yellow and fluffy. Add the bourbon, vanilla extract, and pecans and stir until well combined. Place in the refrigerator for 30 minutes, until chilled and easier to shape. 2. Place the chocolate chips and oil in a small microwave-safe bowl. Microwave in 30-second increments, stirring after each increment, until melted and smooth. 3. Have on hand 12 foil candy cups or line a tray with parchment paper. Take the pecan mixture out of the refrigerator and roll 1-tablespoon scoops into 1-inch balls. Using a spoon, dip each ball into the melted chocolate to coat, then place in the candy cups or on the lined tray. Top each ball with a pecan half. 4. Place back in the refrigerator for at least 1 hour before serving. Allow the balls to sit out for 10 minutes to soften before eating. Store in an airtight container in the refrigerator for up to 2 weeks.

Per Serving

Calories: 117 | fat: 11g | protein: 0g | carbs: 3g | net carbs: 1g | fiber: 2g

Coconut Fat Bombs

Prep time: 5 minutes | Cook time: 0 minutes | Serves 4

2/3 cup coconut oil, melted
1 (14 ounces/397 g) can coconut milk
18 drops stevia liquid
1 cup unsweetened coconut flakes

1. Mix the coconut oil with the milk and stevia to combine. Stir in the coconut flakes until well distributed. Pour into silicone muffin molds and freeze for 1 hour to harden.

Per Serving

Calories: 214 | fat: 19g | protein: 4g | carbs: 7g | net carbs: 2g | fiber: 5g

Lemonade Fat Bomb

Prep time: 10 minutes | Cook time: 0 minutes | Serves 2

½ lemon
4 ounces (113 g) cream cheese, at room temperature
2 ounces (57 g) butter, at room temperature

2 teaspoons Swerve natural sweetener or 2 drops liquid stevia
Pinch pink Himalayan salt

1. Zest the lemon half with a very fine grater into a small bowl. Squeeze the juice from the lemon half into the bowl with the zest. 2. In a medium bowl, combine the cream cheese and butter. Add the sweetener, lemon zest and juice, and pink Himalayan salt. Using a hand mixer, beat until fully combined. 3. Spoon the mixture into the fat bomb molds. (I use small silicone cupcake molds. If you don't have molds, you can use cupcake paper liners that fit into the cups of a muffin tin.) 4. Freeze for at least 2 hours, unmold, and eat! Keep extras in your freezer in a zip-top bag so you and your loved ones can have them anytime you are craving a sweet treat. They will keep in the freezer for up to 3 months.

Per Serving
Calories: 404 | fat: 43g | protein: 4g | carbs: 8g | net carbs: 4g | fiber: 1g

Fresh Cream-Filled Strawberries

Prep time: 10 minutes | Cook time: 0 minutes | Serves 6

1 cup heavy (whipping) cream
Sweetener of choice

(optional)
12 large strawberries, hulled and hollowed out

1. In a large bowl, whisk the cream and sweetener (if using) until thickened into whipped cream, about 5 minutes. 2. Spoon the whipped cream into the hollowed strawberries or use a pastry tube to pipe it inside. Serve immediately. 3. Optional garnishes could include lime zest, finely chopped mint, or shaved dark chocolate.

Per Serving
Calories: 153 | fat: 15g | protein: 1g | carbs: 3g | net carbs: 3g | fiber: 0g

Bacon-Stuffed Mushrooms

Prep time: 20 minutes | Cook time: 40 minutes | Makes 16 stuffed mushrooms

16 large white mushrooms (1½ to 2 inches in diameter)
1 tablespoon avocado oil
8 slices bacon, diced
¼ cup finely chopped green onions

1 clove garlic, minced
1 (8 ounces/227 g) package cream cheese, cubed
Sliced green onions, for garnish (optional)

1. Preheat the oven to 350°F. Line a sheet pan with parchment paper. 2. Clean the mushrooms and pat them dry. Remove the stems and chop them; set aside. Set the mushroom caps on the lined sheet pan, stem side up. 3. Heat the oil in a medium-sized skillet over medium heat. Add the bacon, chopped mushroom stems, green onions, and garlic and cook until the bacon is crispy and the mushroom stems are tender. Reduce the heat to low. 4. Add the cream cheese to the skillet and stir until melted and well incorporated into the other ingredients. Remove the skillet from the heat. 5. Fill each mushroom with a spoonful of the cream cheese mixture and place on the lined sheet pan. 6. Bake the stuffed mushrooms for 30 minutes, or until tender and slightly browned on top. This could take less time depending on how large your mushrooms are. Garnish with sliced green onions before serving, if desired.

Per Serving
Calories: 305 | fat: 25g | protein: 14g | carbs: 5g | net carbs: 4g | fiber: 1g

Crispy Bacon Wrapped Onion Rings

Prep time: 15 minutes | Cook time: 40 minutes | Serves 6

1 extra-large (1 pound/454 g) onion, sliced into ½-inch-thick rings
12 slices bacon, halved

lengthwise
Avocado oil cooking spray
½ cup (2 ounces/57 g) grated Parmesan cheese

1. Preheat the oven to 400°F (205°C). Line a sheet pan with foil. If you have an ovenproof nonstick cooling rack, place it over the pan. Grease the sheet pan or rack. 2. Wrap each onion ring tightly in a thin strip of bacon, trying to cover the whole ring without overlapping. As you finish each ring, place it on a large cutting board in a single layer. 3. Spray the onion rings with avocado oil spray, then sprinkle lightly with half of the grated Parmesan. Flip and repeat on the other side. 4. Place the onion rings on the prepared baking sheet. Bake for 30 to 35 minutes, flipping halfway through, until the bacon is cooked through and starting to get a little crispy on the edges. Drain the bacon grease from the pan occasionally if not using a rack. 5. Switch the oven to broil. Broil the onion rings for 3 to 5 minutes, until crispy. To crisp up more, let the onion rings cool from hot to warm.

Per Serving
Calories: 141 | fat: 8g | protein: 9g | carbs: 7g | net carbs: 6g | fiber: 1g

Caponata Dip

Prep time: 15 minutes | Cook time: 35 minutes | Makes about 2 cups

1 large eggplant (about 1¼ pounds/567 g), cut into ½-inch pieces
1 large yellow onion, cut into ½-inch pieces
4 large cloves garlic, peeled and smashed with the side of a knife
4 tablespoons extra-virgin olive oil, divided, plus extra for garnish
½ teaspoon sea salt
¼ teaspoon ground black pepper

¼ teaspoon ground cumin
1 medium tomato, chopped into 1-inch chunks
Juice of 1 lemon
2 tablespoons chopped fresh cilantro leaves
For Garnish:
Extra-virgin olive oil
Fresh cilantro leaves
Pinch of paprika (optional)
Pine nuts (optional)
For Serving (Optional):
Low-carb flax crackers
Sliced vegetables

1. Preheat the oven to 375°F (190°C). 2. Place the eggplant, onion, garlic, 2 tablespoons of the olive oil, salt, pepper, and cumin in a large bowl and toss to combine. 3. Spread the mixture out on a rimmed baking sheet and bake for 30 to 35 minutes, until the eggplant is softened and browned, tossing halfway through. 4. Remove the eggplant mixture from the oven and transfer it to a food processor. Add the tomato, lemon juice, cilantro, and remaining 2 tablespoons of olive oil. Pulse until the mixture is just slightly chunky. Add salt and pepper to taste. 5. Scoop the dip into a serving dish and garnish with additional olive oil, cilantro, paprika (if desired), and pine nuts (optional). Serve with low-carb crackers and sliced vegetables, if desired.

Per Serving
Calories: 90 | fat: 7g | protein: 1g | carbs: 7g | net carbs: 4g | fiber: 3g

Crab Salad–Stuffed Avocado

Prep time: 20 minutes | Cook time: 0 minutes | Serves 2

1 avocado, peeled, halved lengthwise, and pitted
½ teaspoon freshly squeezed lemon juice
4½ ounces (128 g) Dungeness crabmeat
½ cup cream cheese
¼ cup chopped red bell

pepper
¼ cup chopped, peeled English cucumber
½ scallion, chopped
1 teaspoon chopped cilantro
Pinch sea salt
Freshly ground black pepper

1. Brush the cut edges of the avocado with the lemon juice and set the halves aside on a plate. 2. In a medium bowl, stir together the crabmeat, cream cheese, red pepper, cucumber, scallion, cilantro, salt, and pepper until well mixed. 3. Divide the crab mixture between the avocado halves and store them, covered with plastic wrap, in the refrigerator until you want to serve them, up to 2 days.

Per Serving

Calories: 389 | fat: 31g | protein: 19g | carbs: 10g | net carbs: 5g | fiber: 5g

Cauliflower Cheesy Garlic Bread

Prep time: 10 minutes | Cook time: 30 minutes | Serves 6

Butter, or olive oil, for the baking sheet
1 head cauliflower, roughly chopped into florets
3 cups shredded Mozzarella cheese, divided
½ cup grated Parmesan cheese
¼ cup cream cheese, at room temperature
3 teaspoons garlic powder,

plus more for sprinkling
1 teaspoon onion powder
½ teaspoon red pepper flakes
1 tablespoon salt, plus more for seasoning
Freshly ground black pepper, to taste
2 eggs, whisked
Sugar-free marinara sauce, warmed, for dipping

1. Preheat the oven to 400ºF (205ºC). 2. Grease a baking sheet with butter. Set aside. Alternatively, use a pizza stone. 3. In a food processor, pulse the cauliflower until fine. Transfer to a microwave-safe bowl and microwave on high power, uncovered, for 2 minutes. Cool slightly. Place the cauliflower in a thin cloth or piece of cheesecloth and twist to remove any water. Transfer to a large bowl. 4. Add 2 cups of Mozzarella, the Parmesan, cream cheese, garlic powder, onion powder, red pepper flakes, and salt. Season generously with black pepper. Stir well to combine. 5. Add the eggs and use your hands to mix, ensuring everything is coated with egg. Transfer to the prepared baking sheet. Spread the mixture out into a large rectangle, about 1 inch thick. Sprinkle with more salt, pepper, and garlic powder. Bake for 20 minutes or until the bread starts to turn golden brown. 6. Remove from the oven, top with the remaining 1 cup of Mozzarella, and bake for about 10 minutes more or until the cheese melts. Cool slightly and cut into breadsticks. Serve with the marinara sauce for dipping.

Per Serving

Calories: 296 | fat: 20g | protein: 21g | carbs: 10g | net carbs: 7g | fiber: 3g

Dragon Tail Jalapeño Poppahs

Prep time: 15 minutes | Cook time: 19 minutes | Serves 8

8 (2") jalapeños, halved, seeded, and deveined
4 ounces (113 g) full-fat cream cheese, softened
¼ cup full-fat mayonnaise

1 (1 ounce/28 g) package ranch powder seasoning mix
½ cup shredded Cheddar cheese

1. Preheat oven to 375ºF. Line a baking sheet with parchment paper. 2. In a medium microwave-safe bowl, microwave peppers with ¼ cup water for 3 minutes to soften. Drain and let cool. 3. Line up peppers on baking sheet, cut-side up. 4. In a separate medium microwave-safe bowl, add cream cheese, mayonnaise, ranch powder, and shredded cheese. Microwave for 30 seconds and stir. Microwave another 15 seconds and stir. 5. Carefully scoop mixture into sandwich-sized bag. Snip off one corner to make a hole (the width of a pencil). 6. Using makeshift pastry bag, fill jalapeño halves evenly with mixture. 7. Bake 15 minutes until peppers are fully softened and cheese is golden brown.

Per Serving

Calories: 137| fat: 11g | protein: 3g | carbs: 4g | net carbs: 4g | fiber: 0g

Burrata Caprese Stack

Prep time: 5 minutes | Cook time: 0 minutes | Serves 4

1 large organic tomato, preferably heirloom
½ teaspoon salt
¼ teaspoon freshly ground black pepper
1 (4 ounces/113 g) ball burrata cheese

8 fresh basil leaves, thinly sliced
2 tablespoons extra-virgin olive oil
1 tablespoon red wine or balsamic vinegar

1. Slice the tomato into 4 thick slices, removing any tough center core and sprinkle with salt and pepper. Place the tomatoes, seasoned-side up, on a plate. 2. On a separate rimmed plate, slice the burrata into 4 thick slices and place one slice on top of each tomato slice. Top each with one-quarter of the basil and pour any reserved burrata cream from the rimmed plate over top. 3. Drizzle with olive oil and vinegar and serve with a fork and knife.

Per Serving

Calories: 109 | fat: 7g | protein: 9g | carbs: 3g | fiber: 1g | sodium: 504mg

Sweet Pepper Poppers

Prep time: 10 minutes | Cook time: 20 minutes | serves 4

12 mini sweet peppers
1 (8 ounces/227 g) package
cream cheese, softened
5 slices bacon, cooked and

crumbled
1 green onion, thinly sliced
¼ teaspoon ground black
pepper

1. Preheat the oven to 400°F. Line a sheet pan with parchment paper. 2. Cut each sweet pepper in half lengthwise, then remove and discard the seeds; set the peppers aside. 3. In a small bowl, mix together the cream cheese, bacon, green onion (reserve some of the slices for garnish, if desired), and black pepper. Spoon the mixture into the sweet pepper halves. 4. Place the stuffed peppers on the lined sheet pan and bake for 20 minutes, until the peppers are tender and the tops are starting to brown. Garnish with the reserved green onion slices, if desired.

Per Serving
Calories: 163 | fat: 12g | protein: 7g | carbs: 5g | net carbs: 4g | fiber: 1g

Manchego Crackers

Prep time: 15 minutes | Cook time: 15 minutes | Makes 40 crackers

4 tablespoons butter, at
room temperature
1 cup finely shredded
Manchego cheese
1 cup almond flour

1 teaspoon salt, divided
¼ teaspoon freshly ground
black pepper
1 large egg

1. Using an electric mixer, cream together the butter and shredded cheese until well combined and smooth. 2. In a small bowl, combine the almond flour with ½ teaspoon salt and pepper. Slowly add the almond flour mixture to the cheese, mixing constantly until the dough just comes together to form a ball. 3. Transfer to a piece of parchment or plastic wrap and roll into a cylinder log about 1½ inches thick. Wrap tightly and refrigerate for at least 1 hour. 4. Preheat the oven to 350°F(180ºC). Line two baking sheets with parchment paper or silicone baking mats. 5. To make the egg wash, in a small bowl, whisk together the egg and remaining ½ teaspoon salt. 6. Slice the refrigerated dough into small rounds, about ¼ inch thick, and place on the lined baking sheets. 7. Brush the tops of the crackers with egg wash and bake until the crackers are golden and crispy, 12 to 15 minutes. Remove from the oven and allow to cool on a wire rack. 8. Serve warm or, once fully cooled, store in an airtight container in the refrigerator for up to 1 week.

Per Serving 2 crackers
Calories: 73 | fat: 7g | protein: 3g | carbs: 1g | fiber: 1g | sodium: 154mg

Sautéed Asparagus with Lemon-Tahini Sauce

Prep time: 5 minutes | Cook time: 10 minutes | Serves 4

16 asparagus spears, woody
ends snapped off
2 tablespoons avocado oil
Lemon-Tahini Sauce:
2 tablespoons tahini
1 tablespoon avocado oil

2½ teaspoons lemon juice
1 small clove garlic, minced
1/16 teaspoon finely ground
sea salt
Pinch of ground black pepper
1 to 1½ tablespoons water

1. Place the asparagus and oil in a large frying pan over medium heat. Cook, tossing the spears in the oil every once in a while, until the spears begin to brown slightly, about 10 minutes. 2. Meanwhile, **make the sauce:** Place the tahini, oil, lemon juice, garlic, salt, pepper, and 1 tablespoon of water in a medium-sized bowl. Whisk until incorporated. If the dressing is too thick, add the additional ½ tablespoon of water and whisk again. 3. Place the cooked asparagus on a serving plate and drizzle with the lemon tahini sauce.

Per Serving
Calories: 106 | fat: 8g | protein: 4g | carbs: 6g | net carbs: 3g | fiber: 3g

Savory Mackerel & Goat'S Cheese "Paradox" Balls

Prep time: 10 minutes | Cook time: 0 minutes | Makes 10 fat bombs

2 smoked or cooked
mackerel fillets, boneless,
skin removed
4.4 ounces (125 g) soft
goat's cheese
1 tablespoon fresh lemon
juice
1 teaspoon Dijon or yellow

mustard
1 small red onion, finely
diced
2 tablespoons chopped fresh
chives or herbs of choice
¾ cup pecans, crushed
10 leaves baby gem lettuce

1. In a food processor, combine the mackerel, goat's cheese, lemon juice, and mustard. Pulse until smooth. Transfer to a bowl, add the onion and herbs, and mix with a spoon. Refrigerate for 20 to 30 minutes, or until set. 2. Using a large spoon or an ice cream scoop, divide the mixture into 10 balls, about 40 g/1.4 ounces each. Roll each ball in the crushed pecans. Place each ball on a small lettuce leaf and serve. Keep the fat bombs refrigerated in a sealed container for up to 5 days.

Per Serving 1 fat bomb
Calories: 165 | fat: 12g | protein: 12g | carbs: 2g | fiber: 1g | sodium: 102mg

Marinated Feta and Artichokes

Prep time: 10 minutes | Cook time: 0 minutes | Makes 1½ cups

4 ounces (113 g) traditional Greek feta, cut into ½-inch cubes

4 ounces (113 g) drained artichoke hearts, quartered lengthwise

⅓ cup extra-virgin olive oil

Zest and juice of 1 lemon

2 tablespoons roughly chopped fresh rosemary

2 tablespoons roughly chopped fresh parsley

½ teaspoon black peppercorns

1. In a glass bowl or large glass jar, combine the feta and artichoke hearts. Add the olive oil, lemon zest and juice, rosemary, parsley, and peppercorns and toss gently to coat, being sure not to crumble the feta. 2. Cover and refrigerate for at least 4 hours, or up to 4 days. Pull out of the refrigerator 30 minutes before serving.

Per Serving

Calories: 108 | fat: 9g | protein: 3g | carbs: 4g | fiber: 1g | sodium: 294mg

Cauliflower Patties

Prep time: 10 minutes | Cook time: 10 minutes | Makes 10 patties

1 medium head cauliflower (about 1½ pounds/680 g), or 3 cups (375 g) pre-riced cauliflower

2 large eggs

⅔ cup blanched almond flour

¼ cup nutritional yeast

1 tablespoon dried chives

1 teaspoon finely ground sea salt

1 teaspoon garlic powder

½ teaspoon turmeric powder

¼ teaspoon ground black pepper

3 tablespoons coconut oil or ghee, for the pan

1. If you're using pre-riced cauliflower, skip ahead to Step 2. Otherwise, cut the base off the head of cauliflower and remove the florets. Transfer the florets to a food processor or blender and pulse 3 or 4 times to break them up into small pieces. 2. Transfer the riced cauliflower to a saucepan with enough water to completely cover the cauliflower. Cover with the lid and boil over medium heat for 3½ minutes. 3. Meanwhile, place a fine-mesh strainer over a bowl. 4. Pour the hot cauliflower into the strainer, allowing the bowl to catch the boiling water. With a spoon, press down on the cauliflower to remove as much water as possible. 5. Discard the cooking water and place the cauliflower in the bowl, then add the eggs, almond flour, nutritional yeast, chives, salt, and spices. Stir until everything is incorporated. 6. Heat a large frying pan over medium-low heat. Add the oil and allow to melt completely. 7. Scoop up a portion of the mixture and roll

to form a ball about 1¾ inches (4.5 cm) in diameter. Place in the hot oil and flatten the ball to a patty about ½ inch (1.25 cm) thick. Repeat with the remaining cauliflower mixture, making a total of 10 patties. 8. Cook the patties for 5 minutes per side, or until golden brown. Transfer to a serving plate.

Per Serving

Calories: 164 | fat: 12g | protein: 7g | carbs: 7g | net carbs: 3g | fiber: 4g

Cinnamon Bombs

Prep time: 5 minutes | Cook time: 0 minutes | Makes 8 bombs

⅓ cup smooth unsweetened nut or seed butter or coconut butter

3 tablespoons melted coconut oil, cacao butter, or ghee

¾ teaspoon ground cinnamon

2 drops liquid stevia, or 2 teaspoons confectioners'-style erythritol

Special Equipment (Optional):

Silicone mold with eight 1-tablespoon or larger cavities

1. Have on hand your favorite silicone mold. If you do not have a silicone mold, making this into a bark works well, too. Simply use an 8-inch (20-cm) square silicone or metal baking pan; if using a metal pan, line it with parchment paper, draping some over the sides for easy removal. 2. Place all the ingredients in a medium-sized bowl and stir until well mixed and smooth. 3. Divide the mixture evenly among 8 cavities of the silicone mold or pour into the baking pan. Transfer to the fridge and allow to set for 15 minutes if using cacao butter or 30 minutes if using ghee or coconut oil. If using a baking pan, break the bark into 8 pieces for serving.

Per Serving

Calories: 134 | fat: 13g | protein: 3g | carbs: 3g | net carbs: 1g | fiber: 2g

Cream Cheese and Berries

Prep time: 5 minutes | Cook time: 0 minutes | Serves 1

2 ounces (57 g) cream cheese

2 large strawberries, cut into thin slices or chunks

5 blueberries

⅛ cup chopped pecans

1. Place the cream cheese on a small plate or in a bowl. 2. Pour the berries and chopped pecans on top. Enjoy!

Per Serving

Calories: 330 | fat: 31g | protein: 6g | carbs: 7g | net carbs: 5g | fiber: 2g

Roasted Garlic Herb Nut Mix

Prep time: 5 minutes | Cook time: 15 minutes | Serves 12

2 tablespoons olive oil
1 tablespoon finely chopped fresh rosemary
½ tablespoon fresh thyme, finely chopped
½ teaspoon dried oregano
1 teaspoon sea salt
½ teaspoon garlic powder
¼ teaspoon cayenne pepper, or to taste (optional)
1 cup raw almonds
1 cup raw pecans
1 cup raw macadamia nuts

1. Preheat the oven to 375°F (190°C). Line a baking sheet with foil and grease. 2. In a large saucepan, heat the oil over medium-low heat. Add the rosemary, thyme, oregano, sea salt, garlic powder, and cayenne (if using). Continue to heat for about 2 minutes, until fragrant. 3. Remove from the heat. Add all of the nuts to the pan and stir to coat in the flavored oil and herbs. 4. Spread the nuts on the lined baking sheet in a single layer. Bake for 9 to 12 minutes, stirring about halfway through, until golden.
Per Serving
Calories: 227 | fat: 22g | protein: 4g | carbs: 4g | net carbs: 2g | fiber: 2g

Strawberry Shortcake Coconut Ice

Prep time: 5 minutes | Cook time: 0 minutes | Serves 5

9 hulled strawberries (fresh or frozen and defrosted)
⅓ cup coconut cream
1 tablespoon apple cider
vinegar
2 drops liquid stevia, or 2 teaspoons erythritol
3 cups ice cubes

1. Place the strawberries, coconut cream, vinegar, and sweetener in a blender or food processor. Blend until smooth. 2. Add the ice and pulse until crushed. 3. Divide among four ¾-cup or larger bowls and serve immediately.
Per Serving
Calories: 61 | fat: 5g | protein: 0g | carbs: 3g | net carbs: 2g | fiber: 1g

Warm Herbed Olives

Prep time: 5 minutes | Cook time: 4 minutes | Serves 4

¼ cup good-quality olive oil
4 ounces (113 g) green olives
4 ounces (113 g) Kalamata olives
½ teaspoon dried thyme
¼ teaspoon fennel seeds
Pinch red pepper flakes

1. Sauté the olives. In a large skillet over medium heat, warm the olive oil. Sauté the olives, thyme, fennel seeds, and red pepper flakes until the olives start to brown, 3 to 4 minutes. 2. Serve. Put the olives into a bowl and serve them warm.
Per Serving
Calories: 165 | fat: 17g | protein: 1g | carbs: 3g | net carbs: 2g | fiber: 1g

Baked Crab Dip

Prep time: 15 minutes | Cook time: 25 minutes | Serves 4 to 6

4 ounces (113 g) cream cheese, softened
½ cup shredded Parmesan cheese, plus ½ cup extra for topping (optional)
⅓ cup mayonnaise
¼ cup sour cream
1 tablespoon chopped fresh
parsley
2 teaspoons fresh lemon juice
1½ teaspoons Sriracha sauce
½ teaspoon garlic powder
8 ounces (227 g) fresh lump crabmeat
Salt and pepper

1. Preheat the oven to 375°F. 2. Combine all the ingredients except for the crabmeat in a mixing bowl and use a hand mixer to blend until smooth. 3. Put the crabmeat in a separate bowl, check for shells, and rinse with cold water, if needed. Pat dry or allow to rest in a strainer until most of the water has drained. 4. Add the crabmeat to the bowl with the cream cheese mixture and gently fold to combine. Taste for seasoning and add salt and pepper to taste, if needed. Pour into an 8-inch round or square baking dish and bake for 25 minutes, until the cheese has melted and the dip is warm throughout. 5. If desired, top the dip with another ½ cup of Parmesan cheese and broil for 2 to 3 minutes, until the cheese has melted and browned slightly.
Per Serving
Calories: 275 | fat: 23g | protein: 16g | carbs: 1g | net carbs: 1g | fiber: 0g

Whoops They're Gone Walnuts 'n Dark Chocolate Snack Bag

Prep time: 5 minutes | Cook time: 0 minutes | Makes about 2 cups

1 (3½ ounces/99 g) bar of dark chocolate
1½ cups shelled walnuts
6 tablespoons large coconut flakes (optional)

1. Break up the bar while it is still in the package, then pour the pieces into a zippered plastic bag. Add the walnuts and shake. 2. If desired, add the coconut flakes to the bag as well.
Per Serving
Calories: 305 | fat: 27g | protein: 7g | carbs: 9g | net carbs: 6g | fiber: 3g

Smoked Salmon Cream Cheese Rollups with Arugula and Truffle Oil Drizzle

Prep time: 10 minutes | Cook time: 0 minutes | Serves 4

½ cup cream cheese
¼ cup plain Greek-style yogurt
2 teaspoons chopped fresh dill

12 slices (½ pound/227 g) smoked salmon
¾ cup arugula
Truffle oil, for garnish

1. Mix the filling. In a small bowl, blend together the cream cheese, yogurt, and dill until the mixture is smooth. 2. Make the rollups. Spread the cream cheese mixture onto the smoked salmon slices, dividing it evenly. Place several arugula leaves at one end of each slice and roll them up. Secure them with a toothpick if they're starting to unroll. 3. Serve. Drizzle the rolls with truffle oil and place three rolls on each of four plates.

Per Serving
Calories: 234 | fat: 20g | protein: 13g | carbs: 2g | net carbs: 2g | fiber: 0g

Smoky "Hummus" and Veggies

Prep time: 15 minutes | Cook time: 20 minutes | serves 6

Nonstick coconut oil cooking spray
1 cauliflower head, cut into florets
¼ cup tahini
¼ cup cold-pressed olive oil, plus extra for drizzling
Juice of 1 lemon
1 tablespoon ground paprika

1 teaspoon sea salt
¼ cup chopped fresh parsley, for garnish
2 tablespoons pine nuts (optional)
Flax crackers, for serving
Sliced cucumbers, for serving
Celery pieces, for serving

1. Preheat the oven to 400°F and grease a baking sheet with cooking spray. 2. Spread the cauliflower florets out on the prepared baking sheet and bake for 20 minutes. 3. Remove the cauliflower from the oven and allow it to cool for 10 minutes. 4. In a food processor or high-powered blender, combine the cauliflower with the tahini, olive oil, lemon juice, paprika, and salt. Blend on high until a fluffy, creamy texture is achieved. If the mixture seems too thick, slowly add a few tablespoons of water until smooth. 5. Scoop the "hummus" into an airtight container and chill in the refrigerator for about 20 minutes. 6. Transfer the "hummus" to a serving bowl and drizzle with olive oil. Garnish with the parsley and pine nuts (if using). 7. Serve with your favorite flax crackers and sliced cucumbers and celery.

Per Serving
Calories: 169 | fat: 15g | protein: 4g | carbs: 9g | net carbs: 5g | fiber: 4g

Charlie's Energy Balls

Prep time: 10 minutes | Cook time: 20 minutes | Makes 20 balls

½ cup natural almond butter, room temperature
¼ cup coconut oil, melted
1 large egg
½ cup coconut flour

2 tablespoons unflavored beef gelatin powder
1 scoop chocolate-flavored whey protein powder

1. Preheat the oven to 350°F and grease a rimmed baking sheet with coconut oil spray. 2. In a large mixing bowl, mix together the almond butter, coconut oil, and egg using a fork. In a small bowl, whisk together the coconut flour, gelatin, and protein powder. 3. Pour the dry ingredients into the wet mixture and mash with a fork until you have a cohesive dough. It should not be too sticky. **Note:** If the dough doesn't come together well or is very sticky, add a little coconut flour until it combines well. 4. Using your hands, form the dough into 20 even-sized balls, about 1½ inches in diameter, and put them on the prepared baking sheet. 5. Bake for 20 minutes, until slightly browned and hardened. Allow to cool on the baking sheet for 10 minutes prior to serving. 6. Store in a zip-top plastic bag in the refrigerator for up to a week.

Per Serving
Calories: 91 | fat: 7g | protein: 4g | carbs: 3g | net carbs: 2g | fiber: 1g

Almond Sesame Crackers

Prep time: 15 minutes | Cook time: 15 minutes | Makes about 36 (1-inch-square) crackers

1½ cups almond flour
1 egg
3 tablespoons sesame seeds,

divided
Salt and freshly ground black pepper, to taste

1. Preheat the oven to 350ºF (180ºC). 2. Line a baking sheet with parchment paper. 3. In a large bowl, mix together the almond flour, egg, and 1½ tablespoons of sesame seeds. Transfer the dough to a sheet of parchment and pat it out flat with your clean hands. Cover with another piece of parchment paper and roll it into a large square, at least 10 inches wide. 4. Remove the top piece of parchment and use a pizza cutter or sharp knife to cut the dough into small squares, about 1 inch wide. Season with salt and pepper and sprinkle with the remaining 1½ tablespoons of sesame seeds. 5. Remove the crackers from the parchment and place them on the prepared baking sheet. Bake for about 15 minutes or until the crackers begin to brown. Cool before serving, and store any leftovers in an airtight bag or container on your counter for up to 2 weeks.

Per Serving 10 crackers
Calories: 108 | fat: 9g | protein: 5g | carbs: 3g | net carbs: 1g | fiber: 2g

Road Trip Red Pepper Edamame

Prep time: 1 minutes | Cook time: 18 minutes | Serves 4

2 cups frozen raw edamame in the shell
1 tablespoon peanut oil
2 cloves garlic, peeled and minced
⅛ teaspoon salt
½ teaspoon red pepper flakes

1. In a medium microwave-safe bowl with ½ cup water, microwave edamame 4–5 minutes. 2. In a medium saucepan over medium heat, add peanut oil. Add minced garlic and salt. Stir 3–5 minutes to soften garlic. 3. Add edamame and stir 2–3 minutes until well heated and coated. Turn off heat and cover saucepan to steam edamame for 5 additional minutes. 4. Remove lid. Add red pepper flakes and toss to coat. 5. Serve immediately for best results.

Per Serving
Calories: 139 | fat: 7g | protein: 10g | carbs: 9g | net carbs: 3g | fiber: 6g

Zucchini Cakes with Lemon Aioli

Prep time: 20 minutes | Cook time: 22 minutes | Makes 8 small cakes

Cakes:
3 lightly packed cups (450 g) shredded zucchini (about 3 medium zucchinis)
4 strips bacon (about 4 ounces/113 g)
1 teaspoon finely ground sea salt
1 large egg
1 tablespoon coconut flour
1 tablespoon arrowroot starch or tapioca starch
¾ teaspoon garlic powder
¾ teaspoon onion powder
½ teaspoon dried oregano leaves
¼ teaspoon ground black pepper
Lemon Aioli:
¼ cup mayonnaise
Grated zest of ½ lemon
1 tablespoon plus 1 teaspoon lemon juice
1 teaspoon Dijon mustard
1 clove garlic, minced
¼ teaspoon finely ground sea salt
⅛ teaspoon ground black pepper

1. Place the shredded zucchini in a strainer set over the sink. Sprinkle with the salt and allow to sit for 15 minutes. 2. Meanwhile, cook the bacon in a pan over medium heat until crispy, about 10 minutes. Remove the bacon, leaving the grease in the pan. When the bacon has cooled, crumble it. 3. While the bacon is cooking, **make the aioli:** Put the mayonnaise, lemon zest, lemon juice, mustard, garlic, salt, and pepper in a small bowl and whisk to incorporate. Set aside. 4. When the zucchini is ready, squeeze it continuously to get out water. 5. Transfer the zucchini to a large mixing bowl and add the remaining ingredients for the cakes. Stir until fully incorporated. 6. Set the frying pan with the bacon grease over medium-low heat. Scoop up 2 tablespoons of the zucchini mixture, roll it into a ball between your hands, and place in the hot pan. Repeat with the remaining mixture, making a total of 8 balls. Press each ball with the back of a fork until the cakes are about ½ inch (1.25 cm) thick. 7. Cook the cakes for 4 to 6 minutes per side, until golden. Serve with the aioli.

Per Serving
Calories: 636 | fat: 53g | protein: 28g | carbs: 12g | net carbs: 9g | fiber: 3g

Fried Cabbage Wedges

Prep time: 5 minutes | Cook time: 15 minutes | Serves 6

1 large head green or red cabbage (about 2½ pounds/1.2 kg)
2 tablespoons coconut oil or avocado oil
2 teaspoons garlic powder
½ teaspoon finely ground sea salt
¾ cup green goddess dressing
Special Equipment:
12 (4-in/10-cm) bamboo skewers

1. Cut the cabbage in half through the core, from top to bottom. Working with each half separately, remove the core by cutting a triangle around it and pulling it out. Then lay the half cut side down and cut into 6 wedges. Press a bamboo skewer into each wedge to secure the leaves. Repeat with the other half. 2. Heat the oil in a large frying pan over medium-low heat. 3. Place the cabbage wedges in the frying pan and sprinkle with the garlic powder and salt. Cook for 10 minutes on one side, or until lightly browned, then cook for 5 minutes on the other side. Serve with the dressing on the side.

Per Serving
Calories: 252 | fat: 20g | protein: 3g | carbs: 12g | net carbs: 7g | fiber: 5g

Jumbo Pickle Cuban Sandwich

Prep time: 5 minutes | Cook time: 5 minutes | Serves 2

2 deli ham slices
2 deli pork tenderloin slices
4 Swiss cheese slices
2 jumbo dill pickles, halved lengthwise
1 tablespoon yellow mustard

1. In a small sauté pan or skillet, heat the ham and tenderloin slices over medium heat until warm. 2. Using a spatula, roll the deli meats into loose rolls. Top with the Swiss cheese slices and allow the cheese to begin to melt. 3. Transfer the rolls to 2 pickle halves. 4. Top the cheese with some mustard, then close the sandwiches by topping them with the matching pickle halves. 5. Secure with toothpicks and slice in half crosswise, then serve.

Per Serving
Calories: 256 | fat: 16g | protein: 23g | carbs: 5g | net carbs: 1g | fiber: 4g

Gourmet "Cheese" Balls

Prep time: 1 hour 20 minutes | Cook time: 0 minutes | serves 6

1 cup raw hazelnuts, soaked overnight
¼ cup water
2 tablespoons nutritional yeast
1 teaspoon apple cider

vinegar
1 teaspoon miso paste
1 teaspoon mustard
½ cup almond flour
1 cup slivered almonds
1 teaspoon dried oregano

1. In a high-powered blender, combine the hazelnuts, water, nutritional yeast, vinegar, miso paste, and mustard, and blend until well combined, thick, and creamy. 2. Transfer the mixture to a medium bowl. 3. Slowly stir in the almond flour until the mixture forms a dough-like consistency. Set aside. 4. In a separate, small bowl, toss the almonds and oregano together and set aside. 5. Using a soup spoon or tablespoon, scoop some mixture into your hand and shape it into a bite-size ball. Place the ball on a baking sheet. Repeat until you have used all the mixture (about 2 dozen balls). 6. One by one, roll the hazelnut balls in the almond and oregano mixture until thoroughly coated, placing each coated ball back on the baking sheet. 7. Place the sheet in the refrigerator for 1 hour to allow the balls to set.

Per Serving
Calories: 308 | fat: 27g | protein: 10g | carbs: 11g | net carbs: 5g | fiber: 6g

Savory Broccoli Cheddar Waffles

Prep time: 15 minutes | Cook time: 20 minutes | Serves 4

1 head broccoli, florets separated, stalk reserved for another use
1 shallot, minced
3 eggs
1 teaspoon chopped fresh chives
3 garlic cloves, minced
1 teaspoon salt

Freshly ground black pepper, to taste
1 cup shredded Cheddar cheese
Nonstick olive oil cooking spray, or olive oil, for the waffle iron
Sliced scallion, for garnish

1. In a food processor, pulse the broccoli florets until roughly chopped (don't overprocess—you want it to be rough). Transfer to a microwave-safe container and microwave, uncovered, on high power for 2 minutes. Cool slightly. Place the broccoli in a thin cloth or piece of cheesecloth and twist to remove any water (not a lot will come out but the little that's there needs to be removed). Transfer to a medium bowl and add the shallot. Stir to combine. 2. In a small bowl, whisk together the eggs, chives, garlic, and salt, and season with pepper. Pour the egg mixture over the broccoli and mix together until well incorporated. 3. Add the Cheddar and continue to mix gently. 4. Turn on your waffle iron. Grease it well with cooking spray (if you don't have cooking spray, use a little olive oil on a paper towel). 5. Separate the broccoli mixture into 4 portions. Spoon the mixture onto the prepared waffle iron. Cook for 4 to 5 minutes (or follow the manufacturer's instructions if you're unsure) or until the waffle "batter" is firm and golden brown. Top with sliced scallion and serve.

Per Serving
Calories: 224 | fat: 14g | protein: 16g | carbs: 12g | net carbs: 8g | fiber: 4g

Ketone Gummies

Prep time: 10 minutes | Cook time: 5 minutes | Makes 8 gummies

½ cup lemon juice
8 hulled strawberries (fresh or frozen and defrosted)
2 tablespoons unflavored gelatin
2 teaspoons exogenous

ketones
Special Equipment (Optional):
Silicone mold with eight 2-tablespoon or larger cavities

1. Have on hand your favorite silicone mold. If you do not have a silicone mold, you can use an 8-inch (20-cm) square silicone or metal baking pan; if using a metal pan, line it with parchment paper, draping some over the sides for easy removal. 2. Place the lemon juice, strawberries, and gelatin in a blender or food processor and pulse until smooth. Transfer the mixture to a small saucepan and set over low heat for 5 minutes, or until it becomes very liquid-y and begins to simmer. 3. Remove from the heat and stir in the exogenous ketones. 4. Divide the mixture evenly among 8 cavities of the mold or pour into the baking pan. Transfer to the fridge and allow to set for 30 minutes. If using a baking pan, cut into 8 squares.

Per Serving
Calories: 19 | fat: 0g | protein: 3g | carbs: 1g | net carbs: 1g | fiber: 0g

Bacon-Wrapped Avocado Fries

Prep time: 10 minutes | Cook time: 18 minutes | Serves 4

2 medium Hass avocados, peeled and pitted (about 8 ounces/227 g of flesh)

16 strips bacon (about 1 pound/454 g), cut in half lengthwise

1. Cut each avocado into 8 fry-shaped pieces, making a total of 16 fries. 2. Wrap each avocado fry in 2 half-strips of bacon. Once complete, place in a large frying pan. 3. Set the pan over medium heat and cover with a splash guard. Fry for 6 minutes on each side and on the bottom, or until crispy, for a total of 18 minutes. 4. Remove from the heat and enjoy immediately!

Per Serving
Calories: 723 | fat: 58g | protein: 43g | carbs: 6g | net carbs: 3g | fiber: 4g

Walnut Herb-Crusted Goat Cheese

Prep time: 10 minutes | Cook time: 0 minutes | Serves 4

6 ounces (170 g) chopped walnuts
1 tablespoon chopped oregano
1 tablespoon chopped parsley
1 teaspoon chopped fresh thyme
¼ teaspoon freshly ground black pepper
1 (8 ounces/227 g) log goat cheese

1. Place the walnuts, oregano, parsley, thyme, and pepper in a food processor and pulse until finely chopped. 2. Pour the walnut mixture onto a plate and roll the goat cheese log in the nut mixture, pressing so the cheese is covered and the walnut mixture sticks to the log. 3. Wrap the cheese in plastic and store in the refrigerator for up to 1 week. 4. Slice and enjoy!

Per Serving
Calories: 304 | fat: 28g | protein: 12g | carbs: 4g | net carbs: 2g | fiber: 2g

Broccoli with Garlic-Herb Cheese Sauce

Prep time: 5 minutes | Cook time: 3 minutes | Serves 4

½ cup water
1 pound (454 g) broccoli (frozen or fresh)
½ cup heavy cream
1 tablespoon butter
½ cup shredded Cheddar
cheese
3 tablespoons garlic and herb cheese spread
Pinch of salt
Pinch of black pepper

1. Add the water to the pot and place the trivet inside. 2. Put the steamer basket on top of the trivet. Place the broccoli in the basket. 3. Close the lid and seal the vent. Cook on Low Pressure for 1 minute. Quick release the steam. Press Cancel. 4. Carefully remove the steamer basket from the pot and drain the water. If you steamed a full bunch of broccoli, pull the florets off the stem. (Chop the stem into bite-size pieces, it's surprisingly creamy.) 5. Turn the pot to Sauté mode. Add the cream and butter. Stir continuously while the butter melts and the cream warms up. 6. When the cream begins to bubble on the edges, add the Cheddar cheese, cheese spread, salt, and pepper. Whisk continuously until the cheeses are melted and a sauce consistency is reached, 1 to 2 minutes. 7. Top one-fourth of the broccoli with 2 tablespoons cheese sauce.

Per Serving
Calories: 134 | fat: 12g | protein:4 g | carbs: 5g | net carbs: 3g | fiber: 2g

Hummus Celery Boats

Prep time: 5 minutes | Cook time: 0 minutes | Serves 10

1 cup raw macadamia nuts
3 tablespoons fresh lemon juice
2 cloves garlic
2 tablespoons olive oil
2 tablespoons tahini
Pinch of cayenne pepper
Pinch of finely ground sea salt
Pinch of ground black pepper
1 bunch celery, stalks cut crosswise into 2-inch (5-cm) pieces

1. Place the macadamia nuts in a large bowl and cover with water. Cover the bowl and place in the fridge to soak for 24 hours. 2. After 24 hours, drain and rinse the macadamia nuts. Transfer to a food processor or blender. Add the lemon juice, garlic, olive oil, tahini, cayenne, salt, and pepper and blend until smooth. 3. Spread the hummus on the celery pieces and place on a plate for serving.

Per Serving
Calories: 171 | fat: 16g | protein: 2g | carbs: 5g | net carbs: 3g | fiber: 3g

Goat'S Cheese & Hazelnut Dip

Prep time: 10 minutes | Cook time: 0 minutes | Serves 8

2 heads yellow chicory or endive
Enough ice water to cover the leaves
Pinch of salt
Dip:
12 ounces (340 g) soft goat's cheese
3 tablespoons extra-virgin olive oil
1 tablespoon fresh lemon juice
1 teaspoon lemon zest (about ½ lemon)
1 clove garlic, minced
Freshly ground black pepper, to taste
Salt, if needed, to taste
Topping:
2 tablespoons chopped fresh chives
¼ cup crushed hazelnuts, pecans, or walnuts
1 tablespoon extra-virgin olive oil
Chile flakes or black pepper, to taste

1. Cut off the bottom of the chicory and trim the leaves to get rid of any that are limp or brown. Place the leaves in salted ice water for 10 minutes. This will help the chicory leaves to become crisp. Drain and leave in the strainer. 2. **To Make the Dip:** Place the dip ingredients in a bowl and use a fork or spatula to mix until smooth and creamy. 3. Stir in the chives. Transfer to a serving bowl and top with the crushed hazelnuts, olive oil, and chile flakes. Serve with the crisp chicory leaves. Store in a sealed jar in the fridge for up to 5 days.

Per Serving
Calories: 219 | fat: 18g | protein: 10g | carbs: 5g | fiber: 4g | sodium: 224mg

Sausage Balls

Prep time: 5 minutes | Cook time: 25 minutes | Makes 2 dozen

1 pound (454 g) bulk Italian sausage (not sweet)
1 cup almond flour
1½ cups finely shredded Cheddar cheese
1 large egg

2 teaspoons baking powder
1 teaspoon onion powder
1 teaspoon fennel seed (optional)
½ teaspoon cayenne pepper (optional)

1. Preheat the oven to 350°F (180°C) and line a rimmed baking sheet with aluminum foil. 2. In a large bowl, combine all the ingredients. Use a fork to mix until well blended. 3. Form the sausage mixture into 1½-inch balls and place 1 inch apart on the prepared baking sheet. 4. Bake for 20 to 25 minutes, or until browned and cooked through.

Per Serving
Calories: 241 | fat: 21g | protein: 11g | carbs: 3g | net carbs: 2g | fiber: 1g

N'Oatmeal Bars

Prep time: 25 minutes | Cook time: 0 minutes | Makes 16 bars

1 cup coconut oil
½ cup erythritol, divided
2 cups hulled hemp seeds
½ cup unsweetened shredded coconut
⅓ cup coconut flour

½ teaspoon vanilla extract
10 ounces (285 g) unsweetened baking chocolate, roughly chopped
½ cup full-fat coconut milk

1. Line a 9-inch (23-cm) square baking pan with parchment paper. 2. Melt the coconut oil and half of the erythritol in a pan over medium heat, about 2 minutes. Continue to Step 3 if using confectioners'-style erythritol; if using granulated erythritol, continue to cook until the granules can no longer be felt. 3. Add the hulled hemp seeds, shredded coconut, coconut flour, and vanilla, stirring until coated. Set aside half of the mixture for the topping. Press the remaining half of the mixture into the prepared pan. 4. Transfer the pan with the base layer to the refrigerator for at least 10 minutes, until set. 5. Meanwhile, **prepare the chocolate layer:** Place the remaining erythritol, the baking chocolate, and coconut milk in a small saucepan over low heat. Stir frequently until melted and smooth. 6. Take the base out of the fridge and spoon the chocolate mixture over the base layer, spreading it evenly with a knife or the back of a spoon. 7. Crumble the reserved hemp seed mixture over the chocolate layer, pressing in gently. Cover and refrigerate for 2 to 3 hours or overnight. 8. Cut into 16 bars and enjoy!

Per Serving
Calories: 311 | fat: 30g | protein: 8g | carbs: 10g | net carbs: 4g | fiber: 5g

Parmesan Crisps

Prep time: 5 minutes | Cook time: 5 minutes | Makes about 25 crisps

2 cups grated Parmesan cheese

1. Heat the oven to 400°F (205°C). Line a baking sheet with a silicone mat or parchment paper. Scoop a generous tablespoon of the cheese onto the sheet and flatten it slightly. Repeat with the rest of the cheese, leaving about 1 inch (2.5 cm) space in between them. 2. Bake for 3 to 5 minutes, until crisp.

Per Serving
Calories: 169 | fat: 11g | protein: 11g | carbs: 6g | net carbs: 6g | fiber: 0g

Jelly Cups

Prep time: 10 minutes | Cook time: 10 minutes | Makes 16 jelly cups

Butter Base:
⅔ cup coconut butter or smooth unsweetened nut or seed butter
⅔ cup coconut oil, ghee, or cacao butter, melted
2 teaspoons vanilla extract
7 drops liquid stevia, or 2 teaspoons confectioners'-style erythritol

Jelly Filling:
½ cup fresh raspberries
¼ cup water
3 drops liquid stevia, or 1 teaspoon confectioners'-style erythritol
1½ teaspoons unflavored gelatin

Special Equipment:
16 mini muffin cup liners, or 1 silicone mini muffin pan

1. Set 16 mini muffin cup liners on a tray or have on hand a silicone mini muffin pan. 2. **Make the Base:** Place the coconut butter, melted oil, vanilla, and sweetener in a medium-sized bowl and stir to combine. 3. Take half of the base mixture and divide it equally among the 16 mini muffin cup liners or 16 wells of the mini muffin pan, filling each about one-quarter full. Place the muffin cup liners in the fridge. Set the remaining half of the base mixture aside. 4. **Make the Jelly Filling:** Place the raspberries, water, and sweetener in a small saucepan and bring to a simmer over medium heat. Simmer for 5 minutes, then sprinkle with the gelatin and mash with a fork. Transfer to the fridge to set for 15 minutes. 5. Pull the muffin cup liners and jelly filling out of the fridge. Roll a portion of the jelly into a ball, then flatten it into a disc about 1 inch (2.5 cm) in diameter. Press into a chilled butter base cup. Repeat with the remaining jelly filling and cups. Then spoon the remaining butter base mixture over the tops. 6. Place in the fridge for another 15 minutes before serving.

Per Serving
Calories: 151 | fat: 15g | protein: 1g | carbs: 3g | net carbs: 1g | fiber: 2g

Macadamia Nut Cream Cheese Log

Prep time: 10 minutes | Cook time: 0 minutes | Serves 8

1 (8 ounces/227 g) brick cream cheese, cold	1 cup finely chopped macadamia nuts

1. Place the cream cheese on a piece of parchment paper or wax paper. 2. Roll the paper around the cream cheese, then roll the wrapped cream cheese with the palm of your hands lengthwise on the cream cheese, using the paper to help you roll the cream cheese into an 8-inch log. 3. Open the paper and sprinkle the macadamia nuts all over the top and sides of the cream cheese until the log is entirely covered in nuts. 4. Chill in the refrigerator for 30 minutes before serving. 5. Serve on a small plate, cut into 8 even slices.

Per Serving ⅛ roll
Calories: 285 | fat: 29g | protein: 4g | carbs: 4g | net carbs: 3g | fiber: 1g

Bar Side Mozzarella Sticks

Prep time: 20 minutes | Cook time: 20 minutes | Makes 16 sticks

3 ounces (85 g) pork rinds, finely ground	½ teaspoon ground black pepper
¼ cup grated Parmesan cheese, plus extra for garnish	2 large eggs
	1 tablespoon heavy whipping cream
½ teaspoon dried oregano leaves	8 sticks mozzarella string cheese
½ teaspoon red pepper flakes	2 cups coconut oil, for deep-frying
½ teaspoon pink Himalayan salt	Low-carb marinara sauce, for serving (optional)

1. Place the pork rinds, Parmesan, oregano, red pepper flakes, salt, and pepper in a shallow dish and combine with a fork. 2. Place the eggs and cream in a separate shallow dish and lightly beat with a fork. 3. Cut each stick of string cheese in half crosswise. Dip each piece in the egg mixture and then in the pork rind mixture. Make sure that each piece has a thick coating. You may have to press the breading into the cheese to ensure an even coat. Place on a plate and freeze for 2 hours. 4. In a 2-quart saucepan, heat the oil over medium-high heat until it reaches between 330°F and 345°F on a deep-fry thermometer. 5. Remove the breaded cheese sticks from the freezer. Fry in batches for 3 to 5 minutes per batch, until golden brown. Use a slotted spoon to remove the sticks from the oil and place on a paper towel–lined plate to drain. Allow to cool for 5 minutes, then garnish with grated Parmesan. Serve with marinara sauce, if desired. 6. Store leftovers in a sealed container in the refrigerator for up to 4 days. Reheat in a preheated 350°F oven for 10 minutes.

Per Serving
Calories: 356 | fat: 25g | protein: 32g | carbs: 2g | net carbs: 2g | fiber: 0g

Ultimate Nut Butter

Prep time: 5 minutes | Cook time: 30 minutes | Makes about 2 cups

1½ cups macadamia nuts	1 teaspoon vanilla powder or 1 tablespoon unsweetened vanilla extract
1 cup pecans	
½ cup coconut butter	
5 tablespoons light tahini	¼ teaspoon salt
2 teaspoons cinnamon	

1. Preheat the oven to 285°F (140°C) fan assisted or 320°F (160°C) conventional. Line a baking tray with parchment. 2. Place the macadamias and pecans on the baking tray, transfer to the oven, and bake for about 30 minutes. Remove the nuts from the oven, let cool for about 10 minutes, and then transfer to a food processor while still warm. 3. Add the remaining ingredients. Blend until smooth and creamy, 2 to 3 minutes, scraping down the sides as needed with a spatula. Transfer to a jar and store at room temperature for up to 1 week or in the fridge for up to 1 month.

Per Serving ¼ cup
Calories: 374 | fat: 39g | protein: 3g | carbs: 6g | fiber: 4g | sodium: 76mg

Classy Crudités and Dip

Prep time: 15 minutes | Cook time: 0 minutes | Serves 8

Vegetables	Sour Cream Dip
1 cup whole cherry tomatoes	2 cups full-fat sour cream
	3 tablespoons dry chives
1 cup green beans, trimmed	1 tablespoon lemon juice
2 cups broccoli florets	½ cup dried parsley
2 cups cauliflower florets	½ teaspoon garlic powder
1 bunch asparagus, trimmed	⅛ teaspoon salt
1 large green bell pepper, seeded and chopped	⅛ teaspoon black pepper

1. Cut vegetables into bite-sized uniform pieces. Arrange in like groups around outside edge of a large serving platter, leaving room in middle for dip. 2. Make dip by combining dip ingredients in a medium-sized decorative bowl and mixing well. 3. Place dip bowl in the center of platter and serve.

Per Serving
Calories: 146 | fat: 10g | protein: 4g | carbs: 9g | net carbs: 6g | fiber: 3g

Cheese Chips and Guacamole

Prep time: 10 minutes | Cook time: 10 minutes | Serves 2

For the Cheese Chips:
1 cup shredded cheese (I use Mexican blend)
For the Guacamole:
1 avocado, mashed
Juice of ½ lime

1 teaspoon diced jalapeño
2 tablespoons chopped fresh cilantro leaves
Pink Himalayan salt
Freshly ground black pepper

To Make the Cheese Chips: 1. Preheat the oven to 350°F. Line a baking sheet with parchment paper or a silicone baking mat. 2. Add ¼-cup mounds of shredded cheese to the pan, leaving plenty of space between them, and bake until the edges are brown and the middles have fully melted, about 7 minutes. 3. Set the pan on a cooling rack, and let the cheese chips cool for 5 minutes. The chips will be floppy when they first come out of the oven but will crisp as they cool. **To Make the Guacamole:** 1. In a medium bowl, mix together the avocado, lime juice, jalapeño, and cilantro, and season with pink Himalayan salt and pepper. 2. Top the cheese chips with the guacamole, and serve.

Per Serving
Calories: 323 | fat: 27g | protein: 15g | carbs: 8g | net carbs: 3g | fiber: 5g

Snappy Bacon Asparagus

Prep time: 20 minutes | Cook time: 25 minutes | Serves 6

24 asparagus spears
6 strips no-sugar-added bacon, uncooked

2 tablespoons olive oil
⅛ teaspoon salt

1. My favorite part of preparing asparagus is the SNAP. Grab the "nonpointed" end of stalk and bend until it breaks. This usually happens about an inch from the end with the cut. Now, line up asparagus and cut entire bunch at "snapping" point, making all of your stalks uniform in length. Fancy, right? 2. On a microwave-safe plate, microwave asparagus 2 minutes to soften. Let cool 5 minutes. 3. Lay strip of bacon on a cutting board at 45-degree angle. Lay four asparagus spears centered on bacon in an "up and down" position. 4. Pick up bacon and asparagus where they meet and wrap two ends of bacon around asparagus in opposite directions. 5. Wrap bacon tightly and secure, pinning bacon to asparagus at ends with toothpicks. Don't worry if bacon doesn't cover entire spears. 6. Brush asparagus with olive oil and sprinkle with salt. 7. Heat a medium nonstick skillet over medium heat. Cook asparagus/bacon 3–5 minutes per side while turning to cook thoroughly. Continue flipping until bacon is brown and crispy.

Per Serving
Calories: 104 | fat: 8g | protein: 5g | carbs: 3g | net carbs: 2g | fiber: 1g

Peanut Butter Keto Fudge

Prep time: 5 minutes | Cook time: 10 minutes | Serves 12

½ cup (1 stick) butter
8 ounces (227 g) cream cheese
1 cup unsweetened peanut butter

1 teaspoon vanilla extract (or the seeds from 1 vanilla bean)
1 teaspoon liquid stevia (optional)

1. Line an 8- or 9-inch square or 9-by-13-inch rectangular baking dish with parchment paper. Set aside. 2. In a saucepan over medium heat, melt the butter and cream cheese together, stirring frequently, for about 5 minutes. 3. Add the peanut butter and continue to stir until smooth. Remove from the heat. 4. Stir in the vanilla and stevia (if using). Pour the mixture into the prepared dish and spread into an even layer. Refrigerate for about 1 hour until thickened and set enough to cut and handle. Cut into small squares and enjoy! Refrigerate, covered, for up to 1 week.

Per Serving 1 fudge square
Calories: 261 | fat: 24g | protein: 8g | carbs: 5g | net carbs: 4g | fiber: 1g

Cubed Tofu Fries

Prep time: 25 minutes | Cook time: 20 minutes | Serves 4

1 (12 ounces/340 g) package extra-firm tofu
2 tablespoons sesame oil
⅛ teaspoon salt, divided

⅛ teaspoon black pepper, divided
⅛ teaspoon creole seasoning, divided

1. Remove tofu from packaging and wrap in paper towel. Set on a clean plate. Place a second plate on top and put a 3- to 5-pound weight on top. Let sit 20 minutes. Drain excess water. 2. Unwrap tofu and slice into small cubes no larger than ½" square (a little larger than sugar cubes). 3. In a large skillet over medium heat, heat oil. 4. Combine salt, pepper, and creole seasoning in a small bowl. Sprinkle one-third of spice mixture evenly into skillet and add tofu evenly. 5. Sprinkle one-third of spices on top and let fry 5 minutes on each side, flipping three times (for the four sides), browning all four sides. 6. Dust tofu with remaining spice mixture. 7. Remove from heat. Enjoy while hot!

Per Serving
Calories: 126 | fat: 10g | protein: 7g | carbs: 2g | net carbs: 1g | fiber: 1g

Keto Trail Mix

Prep time: 5 minutes | Cook time: 0 minutes | Serves 4

¼ cup pumpkin seeds
¼ cup salted almonds
¼ cup salted macadamia nuts

¼ cup salted walnuts
1 cup crunchy cheese snack
¼ cup sugar-free chocolate chips

1. In a resealable 1-quart plastic bag, combine the pumpkin seeds, almonds, macadamia nuts, walnuts, cheese snack, and chocolate chips. Seal the bag and shake to mix.

Per Serving
Calories: 253 | fat: 23g | protein: 7g | carbs: 5g | net carbs: 2g | fiber: 3g

Pecan Ranch Cheese Ball.

Prep time: 15 minutes | Cook time: 0 minutes | serves 8

2 (8 ounces/227 g) packages cream cheese, softened
1 cup shredded sharp cheddar cheese
2 tablespoons ranch seasoning

1 cup chopped raw pecans
Serving Suggestions:
Celery sticks
Mini sweet peppers
Pork rinds

1. Put the cream cheese, cheddar cheese, and ranch seasoning in a medium-sized bowl. Using a spoon, mix the ingredients together until well blended. 2. Shape the mixture into a ball or disc shape and roll it in the pecans. Wrap and refrigerate overnight before serving. 3. Serve with the scoopers of your choice. Leftovers can be stored in an airtight container in the refrigerator for up to 5 days.

Per Serving
Calories: 303 | fat: 27g | protein: 9g | carbs: 11g | net carbs: 5g | fiber: 2g

Breaded Mushroom Nuggets

Prep time: 15 minutes | Cook time: 50 minutes | Serves 4

24 cremini mushrooms (about 1 pound/454 g)
2 large eggs
½ cup blanched almond flour
1 teaspoon garlic powder
1 teaspoon paprika
½ teaspoon finely ground

sea salt
2 tablespoons avocado oil
½ cup honey mustard dressing, for serving (optional)
Special Equipment (Optional):
Toothpicks

1. Preheat the oven to 350°F (177°C). Line a rimmed baking sheet with parchment paper or a silicone baking mat. 2. Break the stems off the mushrooms or cut them short so that the stems are level with the caps. 3. Crack the eggs into a small bowl and whisk. 4. Place the almond flour, garlic powder, paprika, and salt in a medium-sized bowl and whisk to combine. 5. Dip one mushroom at a time into the eggs, then use the same hand to drop it into the flour mixture, being careful not to get the flour mixture on that hand. Rotate the mushroom in the flour mixture with a fork to coat on all sides, then transfer it to the lined baking sheet. Repeat with the remaining mushrooms. 6. Drizzle the coated mushrooms with the oil. Bake for 50 minutes, or until the tops begin to turn golden. 7. Remove from the oven and serve with the dressing, if using. If serving to friends and family, provide toothpicks.

Per Serving
Calories: 332 | fat: 29g | protein: 8g | carbs: 9g | net carbs: 7g | fiber: 2g

Pickled Herring

Prep time: 4 minutes | Cook time: 5 minutes | Serves 12

4 pounds (1.8 kg) herring or skinned Northern Pike fillets, cut into 2-inch pieces
Saltwater Brine:
10 cups water
½ cup fine sea salt
Pickling Brine:
½ cup thinly sliced red onions
Handful of fresh dill
2 cups water
2½ cups coconut vinegar
½ cup Swerve confectioners'-style sweetener or equivalent amount of liquid or powdered sweetener

2 teaspoons ground allspice
1 teaspoon dry mustard or mustard seeds
½ teaspoon grated fresh ginger
½ teaspoon prepared horseradish
½ teaspoon peppercorns
For Serving:
Hard-boiled eggs, halved or quartered
Pickled ginger
Capers
Fermented pickles
Sliced red onions
Fresh dill sprigs

1. Place the fish in a large bowl with the 10 cups of water. Add the salt and stir. Cover and refrigerate for 24 hours, then drain the fish and rinse it well. 2. Place the drained and rinsed fish in a clean 2-liter glass jar, layering it with the sliced onions and dill. 3. In a large pot over medium heat, heat the 2 cups of water, coconut vinegar, sweetener, allspice, mustard, ginger, horseradish, and peppercorns. Once the sweetener has dissolved, about 5 minutes, allow the brine to cool a little, then pour over the fish packed in the jar. Cover and refrigerate overnight to allow the flavors to meld; the longer the better for stronger flavors. If you let it sit for 5 days, the bones will dissolve. The pickled fish will keep in an airtight container in the fridge for up to 1 month. 4. To serve, arrange the pickled fish on a platter with hard-boiled eggs, pickled ginger, capers, fermented pickles, sliced red onions, and fresh dill.

Per Serving
Calories: 240 | fat: 14g | protein: 27g | carbs: 2g | net carbs: 2g | fiber: 0g

Crispy Parmesan Crackers

Prep time: 10 minutes | Cook time: 5 minutes | Makes 8 crackers

1 teaspoon butter
8 ounces full-fat Parmesan

cheese, shredded or freshly grated

1. Preheat the oven to 400°F. 2. Line a baking sheet with parchment paper and lightly grease the paper with the butter. 3. Spoon the Parmesan cheese onto the baking sheet in mounds, spread evenly apart. 4. Spread out the mounds with the back of a spoon until they are flat. 5. Bake the crackers until the edges are browned and the centers are still pale, about 5 minutes. 6. Remove the sheet from the oven, and remove the crackers with a spatula to paper towels. Lightly blot the tops with additional paper towels and let them completely cool. 7. Store in a sealed container in the refrigerator for up to 4 days.
Per Serving 1 cracker
Calories: 133 | fat: 11g | protein: 11g | carbs: 1g | net carbs: 1g | fiber: 0g

Cheese Almond Crackers

Prep time: 10 minutes | Cook time: 20 minutes | Serves 4

Olive oil cooking spray
1 cup almond flour
½ cup finely shredded Cheddar cheese
1 tablespoon nutritional yeast

¼ teaspoon baking soda
¼ teaspoon garlic powder
¼ teaspoon sea salt
1 egg
2 teaspoons good-quality olive oil

1. Preheat the oven temperature to 350°F. Line a baking sheet with parchment paper. Lightly grease two sheets of parchment paper with olive oil cooking spray. 2. In a large bowl, stir together the almond flour, Cheddar, nutritional yeast, baking soda, garlic powder, and salt until well blended. 3. In a small bowl, whisk together the egg and olive oil. Mix the wet ingredients into the dry until the dough sticks together to form a ball. Gather the ball together and knead it firmly a few times. 4. Place the ball on one of the lightly greased parchment paper pieces and press it down to form a disk. Place the other piece of greased parchment paper on top and roll the dough into a 9-by-12-inch rectangle about ⅛ inch thick. 5. Use a pizza cutter and a ruler to cut the edges of the dough into an even rectangle and cut the dough into 1½-by-1½-inch columns and rows. Transfer the crackers to the baking sheet. 6. Bake the crackers for 15 to 20 minutes until they're crisp. Transfer them to a wire rack and let them cool completely. 7. Eat the crackers immediately or store them in an airtight container in the refrigerator for up to one week.
Per Serving
Calories: 146 | fat: 12g | protein: 7g | carbs: 1g | net carbs: 0g | fiber: 1g

Finger Tacos

Prep time: 15 minutes | Cook time: 0 minutes | serves 4

2 avocados, peeled and pitted
1 lime
1 tablespoon tamari
1 teaspoon sesame oil
1 teaspoon ginger powder
1 teaspoon togarashi (optional)

½ cup kale chiffonade
½ cup cabbage chiffonade
10 fresh mint leaves chiffonade
⅓ cup cauliflower rice
1 (0.18 ounce/5 g) package nori squares or seaweed snack sheets

1. Put the avocados into a large mixing bowl, and squeeze the lime over them. 2. Roughly mash the avocados with a fork, leaving the mixture fairly chunky. 3. Gently stir in the tamari, sesame oil, ginger powder, and togarashi (if using). 4. Gently fold in the kale, cabbage, mint, and cauliflower rice. 5. Arrange some nori squares on a plate. 6. Use a nori or seaweed sheet to pick up a portion of the avocado mixture and pop it into your mouth.
Per Serving
Calories: 180 | fat: 15g | protein: 4g | carbs: 13g | net carbs: 5g | fiber: 8g

Lemon Pepper Wings

Prep time: 5 minutes | Cook time: 16 minutes | Serves 6

1 to 2 cups coconut oil or other Paleo fat, for frying
1 pound (454 g) chicken wings (about 12 wings)
½ teaspoon fine sea salt, divided
1 teaspoon freshly ground

black pepper, divided
Sauce:
¼ cup MCT oil or extra-virgin olive oil
Grated zest of 1 lemon
Juice of 1 lemon

1. Preheat the oil to 350ºF (180ºC) in a deep-fryer or in a 4-inch-deep (or deeper) cast-iron skillet over medium heat. The oil should be at least 3 inches deep; add more oil if needed. 2. While the oil is heating, make the sauce: Place the MCT oil in a small dish. Add the lemon zest and juice and whisk to combine. 3. Fry the wings in the hot oil, about six at a time, until golden brown on all sides and cooked through, about 8 minutes. Remove the wings from the oil and sprinkle with half of the salt and pepper. Repeat with the remaining wings, salt, and pepper. 4. Place the wings on a serving platter and serve with the sauce. They are best served fresh. Store extra wings and sauce separately in airtight containers in the fridge for up to 3 days. To reheat, place the wings on a rimmed baking sheet and heat in a preheated 400ºF (205ºC) oven for 4 minutes, or until the chicken is warm.
Per Serving
Calories: 286 | fat: 24g | protein: 16g | carbs: 1g | net carbs: 1g | fiber: 0g

Blueberry Crumble with Cream Topping

Prep time: 5 minutes | Cook time: 25 minutes | Serves 6

18 ounces (504 g) fresh or frozen blueberries
1 cup blanched almond flour
⅓ cup coconut oil or ghee, room temperature
⅓ cup erythritol

2 tablespoons coconut flour
1 teaspoon ground cinnamon
1 cup coconut cream, or 1 cup full-fat coconut milk, for serving

1. Preheat the oven to 350°F (177°C). 2. Place the blueberries in an 8-inch (20-cm) square baking pan. 3. Place the almond flour, oil, erythritol, coconut flour, and cinnamon in a medium-sized bowl and mix with a fork until crumbly. Crumble over the top of the blueberries. 4. Bake for 22 to 25 minutes, until the top is golden. 5. Remove from the oven and let sit for 10 minutes before dividing among 6 serving bowls. Top each bowl with 2 to 3 tablespoons of coconut cream.

Per Serving
Calories: 388 | fat: 33g | protein: 5g | carbs: 17g | net carbs: 13g | fiber: 4g

Sweet and Spicy Beef Jerky

Prep time: 15 minutes | Cook time: 4 to 6 hours | Serves 16

3 pounds flat-iron steak
Marinade:
½ cup soy sauce
½ cup apple cider vinegar
¼ cup Frank's RedHot sauce
½ teaspoon liquid stevia

2 teaspoons liquid smoke
2 teaspoons ground black pepper
1½ teaspoons garlic powder
1 teaspoon onion powder
Special Equipment:
10 (12-inch) bamboo skewers

1. **Marinate the Steak:** Slice the steak into thin jerky-sized strips, about ¼ inch thick, and put them in a gallon-sized ziptop plastic bag. Add the marinade ingredients, seal the bag, and shake to fully coat the meat. 2. Seal the bag tightly (removing any excess air) and place it in a bowl to catch any leakage. Place the bowl in the refrigerator for at least 4 hours or up to 24 hours. 3. **Make the Jerky:** Adjust the racks in your oven so that one is in the highest position and one is in the lowest position. Preheat the oven to 190°F. 4. Remove the steak strips from the marinade and pat them as dry as possible using paper towels; discard the remaining marinade. 5. Using bamboo skewers, pierce the tip of each meat strip so that there are anywhere from 5 to 7 strips hanging on each skewer. Be sure to leave space between the strips so that air can circulate around them. Hang the skewers from the top oven rack and place a rimmed baking sheet on the lowest rack to catch any drippings. 6. Bake for 4 to 6 hours, until the jerky is dry to the touch. 7. Store in a zip-top plastic bag in the refrigerator for up to 10 days.

Per Serving
Calories: 150 | fat: 10g | protein: 16g | carbs: 1g | net carbs: 1g | fiber: 0g

Pecan Sandy Fat Bombs

Prep time: 15 minutes | Cook time: 0 minutes | Makes 8 fat bombs

½ cup (1 stick) unsalted butter, room temperature
¼ cup granulated sugar-free sweetener

½ teaspoon vanilla extract
1 cup almond flour
¾ cup chopped roasted unsalted pecans, divided

1. In a large bowl, use an electric mixer on medium speed to cream together the butter and sweetener until smooth. Add the vanilla and beat well. 2. Add the almond flour and ½ cup of chopped pecans, and stir until well incorporated. Place the mixture in the refrigerator for 30 minutes, or until slightly hardened. Meanwhile, very finely chop the remaining ¼ cup of pecans. 3. Using a spoon or your hands, form the chilled mixture into 8 (1-inch) round balls and place on a baking sheet lined with parchment paper. Roll each ball in the finely chopped pecans, and refrigerate for at least 30 minutes before serving. Store in an airtight container in the refrigerator for up to 1 week or in the freezer for up to 2 months.

Per Serving
Calories: 242 | fat: 25g | protein: 4g | carbs: 4g | net carbs: 1g | fiber: 3g

The Best Deviled Eggs

Prep time: 15 minutes | Cook time: 0 minutes | Serves 4

1 tablespoon mayonnaise
1 tablespoon extra-virgin olive oil
1 teaspoon Dijon mustard
1 teaspoon anchovy paste
¼ teaspoon freshly ground black pepper
4 large hard-boiled eggs,

shelled
8 pitted green olives, chopped
1 tablespoon red onion, minced
1 tablespoon fresh parsley, minced

1. In a small bowl, whisk together the mayonnaise, olive oil, mustard, anchovy paste, and pepper. Set aside. 2. Slice the hard-boiled eggs in half lengthwise, remove the yolks, and place the yolks in a medium bowl. Reserve the egg white halves and set aside. 3. Smash the yolks well with a fork and stir in the mayonnaise mixture. Add the olives, onion, and parsley and stir to combine. 4. Spoon the filling into each egg white half. Cover and chill for 30 minutes or up to 24 hours before serving cold.

Per Serving
Calories: 137 | fat: 12g | protein: 7g | carbs: 1g | net carbs: 1g | fiber: 0g

Chicken-Pecan Salad Cucumber Bites

Prep time: 15 minutes | Cook time: 0 minutes | Serves 2

1 cup diced cooked chicken breast
2 tablespoons mayonnaise
¼ cup chopped pecans
¼ cup diced celery
Pink Himalayan salt
Freshly ground black pepper
1 cucumber, peeled and cut into ¼-inch slices

1. In a medium bowl, mix together the chicken, mayonnaise, pecans, and celery. Season with pink Himalayan salt and pepper. 2. Lay the cucumber slices out on a plate, and add a pinch of pink Himalayan salt to each. 3. Top each cucumber slice with a spoonful of the chicken-salad mixture and serve.

Per Serving
Calories: 323 | fat: 24g | protein: 23g | carbs: 6g | net carbs: 4g | fiber: 3g

Salami Chips with Pesto

Prep time: 10 minutes | Cook time: 12 minutes | Serves 6

Chips:
6 ounces (170 g) sliced Genoa salami
Pesto:
1 cup fresh basil leaves
3 cloves garlic
¼ cup grated Parmesan
cheese
¼ cup raw walnuts
¼ teaspoon pink Himalayan salt
¼ teaspoon ground black pepper
½ cup extra-virgin olive oil

1. **Make the Chips:** Preheat the oven to 375°F and line 2 rimmed baking sheets with parchment paper. 2. Arrange the salami in a single layer on the lined baking sheets. Bake for 10 to 12 minutes, until crisp. Transfer to a paper towel–lined plate to absorb the excess oil. Allow to cool and crisp up further. 3. **Make the Pesto:** Put all the pesto ingredients, except for the olive oil, in a food processor and pulse until everything is roughly chopped and a coarse paste has formed. 4. With the food processor running, slowly pour in the olive oil. Process until all of the oil has been added and the ingredients are fully incorporated. Taste and season with additional salt and pepper, if desired. 5. Pour the pesto into a small serving bowl and serve the salami chips alongside. Store leftover pesto in a sealed container in the refrigerator for up to 2 weeks; store the chips in a zip-top plastic bag in the refrigerator for up to 5 days.

Per Serving
Calories: 202 | fat: 9g | protein: 8g | carbs: 1g | net carbs: 1g | fiber: 0g

Herbed Cashew Cheese

Prep time: 10 minutes | Cook time: 0 minutes | Makes 1½ cups

1 cup raw cashews
1 cup warm water
¼ cup extra-virgin olive oil
¼ cup water
2 tablespoons fresh lemon juice
1 clove garlic, minced or grated
2 tablespoons minced fresh chives
Sea salt and ground black pepper, to taste

1. Place the cashews in a small container and add the warm water. (If it doesn't cover the cashews completely, just add more warm water.) Soak for 1 to 4 hours unrefrigerated or up to overnight in the refrigerator. 2. Drain and rinse the cashews, then place them in a blender or food processor. Add the olive oil, the ¼ cup water, the lemon juice, and the garlic. Process until smooth and creamy, stopping occasionally to scrape down the sides of the processor, about 5 minutes total. Mix in the chives and add salt and pepper to taste. 3. If you'd like a lighter texture, add warm water, 1 tablespoon at a time, until you achieve the desired consistency.

Per Serving
Calories: 288 | fat: 25g | protein: 7g | carbs: 13g | net carbs: 12g | fiber: 1g

Easy Baked Zucchini Chips

Prep time: 5 minutes | Cook time: 2½ hours | Serves 4

2 medium zucchini (10 ounces/283 g total)
1 tablespoon olive oil or
avocado oil
½ teaspoon sea salt

1. Preheat the oven to 200°F (93°C). 2. Use a mandoline or a sharp knife to slice the zucchini into ⅛-inch-thick slices. 3. Place the zucchini in a large bowl. Add the olive oil and toss to thoroughly coat. Sprinkle lightly with sea salt. Toss to coat again. 4. Place ovenproof wire cooling racks on top of two baking sheets, then top those with parchment paper. (The cooling rack method allows for better air circulation.) Arrange the zucchini slices in a single layer. It's fine if they touch, but make sure they don't overlap. 5. Bake side by side for about 2½ hours, rotating the pans front to back halfway through, until the chips are golden and just starting to get crispy. 6. Allow the chips to cool in the oven with the heat off and the door propped slightly open. This is a crucial step, as they will be soft initially and crisp up when they cool using this method.

Per Serving
Calories: 46 | fat: 4g | protein: 2g | carbs: 4g | net carbs: 2g | fiber: 2g

Taste of the Mediterranean Fat Bombs

Prep time: 15 minutes | Cook time: 0 minutes | Makes 6 fat bombs

1 cup crumbled goat cheese
4 tablespoons jarred pesto
12 pitted Kalamata olives, finely chopped
½ cup finely chopped walnuts
1 tablespoon chopped fresh rosemary

1. In a medium bowl, combine the goat cheese, pesto, and olives and mix well using a fork. Place in the refrigerator for at least 4 hours to harden. 2. Using your hands, form the mixture into 6 balls, about ¾-inch diameter. The mixture will be sticky. 3. In a small bowl, place the walnuts and rosemary and roll the goat cheese balls in the nut mixture to coat. 4. Store the fat bombs in the refrigerator for up to 1 week or in the freezer for up to 1 month.
Per Serving 1 fat bomb
Calories: 235 | fat: 22g | protein: 10g | carbs: 2g | fiber: 1g | sodium: 365mg

Sweet Pepper Nacho Bites

Prep time: 5 minutes | Cook time: 5 minutes | Makes 24 bites

12 mini sweet peppers (approximately 8 ounces/227 g)
½ cup shredded Monterey
Jack cheese
½ cup guacamole
Juice of 1 lime

1. Preheat the oven to 400ºF (205ºC). 2. Carefully cut each pepper in half lengthwise and remove the seeds. Place them cut side up on a rimmed baking sheet so they aren't touching. Place 1 teaspoon of shredded cheese inside each. Bake 3 to 5 minutes, until the cheese starts to melt. 3. Remove from the oven and top each with 1 teaspoon of guacamole. Squeeze the lime juice over top. Serve immediately.
Per Serving
Calories: 137 | fat: 12g | protein: 4g | carbs: 5g | net carbs: 3g | fiber: 2g

Cookie Fat Bombs

Prep time: 10 minutes | Cook time: 0 minutes | serves 6

1 cup almond butter
½ cup coconut flour
1 teaspoon ground
cinnamon
¼ cup cacao nibs or vegan keto chocolate chips

1. Line a baking sheet with parchment paper. If you don't have parchment paper, use aluminum foil or a greased pan.
2. In a mixing bowl, whisk together the almond butter, coconut flour, and cinnamon. 3. Fold in the cacao nibs. 4. Cover the bowl and put it in the freezer for 15 to 20 minutes. 5. Remove the bowl from the freezer and, using a spoon or cookie scoop, scoop out a dollop of mixture and roll it between your palms to form a ball. Repeat to use all the mixture. 6. Place the fat bombs on a baking sheet and put the sheet in the freezer to chill for 20 minutes until firm.
Per Serving
Calories: 319 | fat: 26g | protein: 8g | carbs: 18g | net carbs: 8g | fiber: 10g

Everything Bagel Cream Cheese Dip

Prep time: 10 minutes | Cook time: 0 minutes | Serves 4

1 (8 ounces/227 g) package cream cheese, at room temperature
½ cup sour cream
1 tablespoon garlic powder
1 tablespoon dried onion, or onion powder
1 tablespoon sesame seeds
1 tablespoon kosher salt

1. In a small bowl, combine the cream cheese, sour cream, garlic powder, dried onion, sesame seeds, and salt. Stir well to incorporate everything together. Serve immediately or cover and refrigerate for up to 6 days.
Per Serving
Calories: 291 | fat: 27g | protein: 6g | carbs: 6g | net carbs: 5g | fiber: 1g

Cucumber Salmon Coins

Prep time: 5 minutes | Cook time: 0 minutes | Serves 2

¼ cup mayonnaise
Grated zest of ½ lemon
1 tablespoon plus 1 teaspoon lemon juice
1 teaspoon Dijon mustard
1 clove garlic, minced
¼ teaspoon finely ground sea salt
⅛ teaspoon ground black
pepper
1 English cucumber (about 12 in/30.5 cm long), sliced crosswise into coins
8 ounces (227 g) smoked salmon, separated into small pieces
2 fresh chives, sliced

1. Place the mayonnaise, lemon zest, lemon juice, mustard, garlic, salt, and pepper in a small bowl and whisk to combine. 2. Divide the cucumber coins between 2 plates. Top each coin with a piece of smoked salmon, then drizzle with the mayonnaise mixture and sprinkle with sliced chives. 3. Serve right away or store in the fridge for up to 1 day.
Per Serving
Calories: 337 | fat: 25g | protein: 22g | carbs: 5g | net carbs: 4g | fiber: 2g

Southern Pimento Cheese Dip

Prep time: 5 minutes | Cook time: 0 minutes | Serves 10

8 ounces (227 g) cream cheese, at room temperature
1 cup shredded sharp Cheddar cheese
1 cup shredded Pepper Jack cheese
⅓ cup mayonnaise
1 (4 ounces/113 g) jar

pimentos, diced
1 teaspoon garlic powder
1 teaspoon onion powder
¼ teaspoon cayenne pepper
Pinch sea salt
Pinch freshly ground black pepper

1. In a large bowl, combine the cream cheese, Cheddar, Pepper Jack, mayonnaise, pimentos, garlic powder, onion powder, and cayenne. Beat together using an electric mixer. Season with salt and pepper and beat again until well combined. 2. Chill in the refrigerator for a few hours (or overnight) to let the flavors set.
Per Serving ⅓ cup:
Calories: 225 | fat: 21g | protein: 7g | carbs: 2g | net carbs: 2g | fiber: 0g

Cucumber Finger Sandwiches

Prep time: 10 minutes | Cook time: 0 minutes | serves 4

1 medium English cucumber
2 ounces (57 g) cream cheese (¼ cup), softened
2 to 3 slices sharp cheddar

cheese, cut into 1-inch pieces
4 slices bacon, cooked and cut crosswise into 1-inch pieces

1. Slice the cucumber crosswise into rounds about ¼ inch thick. Spread the cream cheese on half of the cucumber slices, then top each with a piece of cheese and a piece of bacon. Place the remainder of the cucumber slices on top to make sandwiches. Serve immediately or cover and refrigerate before serving. These sandwiches should be eaten the day they are made or they will become soggy.
Per Serving
Calories: 187 | fat: 14g | protein: 10g | carbs: 3g | net carbs: 3g | fiber: 0g

Bacon Avocado Mousse Cups

Prep time: 10 minutes | Cook time: 20 minutes | Serves 6

12 bacon slices
2 or 3 ripe avocados, halved and pitted
½ cup plain Greek yogurt

Juice of ½ lime
Salt and freshly ground black pepper, to taste

1. Preheat the oven to 425ºF (220ºC). 2. Wrap each piece of bacon around the sides and bottom of the wells of a mini muffin tin to create little bacon cups. Bake for 15 to 20 minutes or until the bacon is cooked through and crisp. 3. While the bacon cooks, in a medium bowl, combine the avocado flesh, yogurt, and lime juice. Mix well until combined and smooth. Season with salt and pepper and transfer to a piping bag (or a plastic bag with the tip cut off). 4. Remove the bacon from the oven and cool slightly. Pipe each bacon cup full of avocado mousse. Serve immediately.
Per Serving 2 filled cups: Calories: 530 | fat: 38g | protein: 31g | carbs: 16g | net carbs: 9g | fiber: 7g

Hangover Bacon-Wrapped Pickles

Prep time: 5 minutes | Cook time: 20 minutes | Serves 4

3 large pickles
6 strips uncooked no-sugar-added bacon, cut in half

lengthwise
¼ cup ranch dressing

1. Preheat oven to 425°F. Line a baking sheet with foil. 2. Quarter each pickle lengthwise (yielding twelve spears). 3. Wrap each spear with a half strip bacon. Place on baking sheet. 4. Bake 20 minutes or until crispy, flipping at the midpoint. 5. Serve your crispy bacon-wrapped pickles while still hot with a side of the ranch dipping sauce.
Per Serving
Calories: 96| fat: 6g | protein: 6g | carbs: 3g | net carbs: 2g | fiber: 1g

Bacon-Wrapped Avocados

Prep time: 10 minutes | Cook time: 15 minutes | Serves 4

8 bacon slices
1 ripe avocado, peeled and cut into 8 wedges
Salt and freshly ground

black pepper, to taste
1 or 2 lime wedges
Ground cayenne pepper

1. Wrap 1 bacon slice around each avocado wedge. If needed, use a toothpick to secure them. 2. Heat a nonstick skillet over medium-high heat. Evenly space the bacon-wrapped wedges around the skillet. If you aren't using a toothpick, place the loose end of the bacon facing down to create a seal as it cooks. Cook for 6 to 8 minutes, turning every couple of minutes until the bacon is cooked. 3. Remove from the heat and finish with a sprinkle of salt, pepper, lime juice, and cayenne. Serve warm.
Per Serving
Calories: 314 | fat: 26g | protein: 15g | carbs: 5g | net carbs: 2g | fiber: 3g

Brazilian Moqueca (Shrimp Stew)

Prep time: 15 minutes | Cook time: 10 minutes | Serves 6

1 cup coconut milk	14 ounces (397 g) diced
2 tablespoons lime juice	tomatoes
¼ cup diced roasted peppers	2 tablespoons sriracha sauce
1½ pounds shrimp, peeled	1 chopped onion
and deveined	¼ cup chopped cilantro
¼ cup olive oil	Fresh dill, chopped to garnish
1 garlic clove, minced	Salt and black pepper, to taste

1. Heat the olive oil in a pot over medium heat. Add onion and cook for 3 minutes or until translucent. Add the garlic and cook for another minute, until soft. Add tomatoes, shrimp, and cilantro. Cook until the shrimp becomes opaque, about 3-4 minutes. 2. Stir in sriracha sauce and coconut milk, and cook for 2 minutes. Do not bring to a boil. Stir in the lime juice and season with salt and pepper. Spoon the stew in bowls, garnish with fresh dill to serve.

Per Serving
Calories: 313 | fat: 21g | protein: 23g | carbs: 8g | net carbs: 5g | fiber: 3g

Cauliflower Rice and Chicken Thigh Soup

Prep time: 15 minutes | Cook time: 13 minutes | Serves 5

2 cups cauliflower florets	pepper
1 pound (454 g) boneless,	½ cup sliced zucchini
skinless chicken thighs	⅓ cup sliced turnips
4½ cups chicken broth	1 teaspoon dried parsley
½ yellow onion, chopped	3 celery stalks, chopped
2 garlic cloves, minced	1 teaspoon ground turmeric
1 tablespoon unflavored	½ teaspoon dried marjoram
gelatin powder	1 teaspoon dried thyme
2 teaspoons sea salt	½ teaspoon dried oregano
½ teaspoon ground black	

1. Add the cauliflower florets to a food processor and pulse until a ricelike consistency is achieved. Set aside. 2. Add the chicken thighs, chicken broth, onions, garlic, gelatin powder, sea salt, and black pepper to the pot. Gently stir to combine. 3. Lock the lid. Select Manual mode and set cooking time for 10 minutes on High Pressure. 4. When cooking is complete, quick release the pressure and open the lid. 5. Transfer the chicken thighs to a cutting board. Chop the chicken into bite-sized pieces and then return

the chopped chicken to the pot. 6. Add the cauliflower rice, zucchini, turnips, parsley, celery, turmeric, marjoram, thyme, and oregano to the pot. Stir to combine. 7. Lock the lid. Select Manual mode and set cooking time for 3 minutes on High Pressure. 8. When cooking is complete, quick release the pressure. 9. Open the lid. Ladle the soup into serving bowls. Serve hot.

Per Serving
Calories: 247 | fat: 10.4g | protein: 30.2g | carbs: 8.3g | net carbs: 6.1g | fiber: 2.2g

Slow Cooker Taco Bell Soup

Prep time: 20 minutes | Cook time: 2 hours 20 minutes | Serves 8

2 pounds (907 g) lean	2 cups water
ground beef	8 ounces (227 g) full-fat
1 medium onion, peeled and	cream cheese, cubed
chopped	½ cup finely chopped cilantro
2 cloves garlic, peeled and	2 (4 ounces/113 g) cans diced
minced	green chilies, drained
6 cups beef broth	2 tablespoons taco seasoning

1. In a medium skillet over medium heat, brown ground beef 10–15 minutes while stirring. Drain fat. Add onion and garlic. Sauté 5 minutes. 2. Add meat mixture to slow cooker along with rest of ingredients. 3. Cover with lid and cook 2 hours on high or 4 hours on low. 4. Let cool 10 minutes and then serve.

Per Serving
Calories: 307| fat: 16g | protein: 26g | carbs: 6g | net carbs: 4g | fiber: 2g

Miso Magic

Prep time: 5 minutes | Cook time: 10 minutes | serves 8

8 cups water	mushrooms
6 to 7 tablespoons miso	1 cup drained and cubed
paste	sprouted tofu
3 sheets dried seaweed	1 cup chopped scallions
2 cups thinly sliced shiitake	1 teaspoon sesame oil

1. In a large stockpot over medium heat, add the miso paste and seaweed to the water and bring to a low boil. 2. Toss in the mushrooms, tofu, scallions, and sesame oil. 3. Allow to simmer for about 5 minutes and serve.

Per Serving
Calories: 80 | fat: 2g | protein: 4g | carbs: 12g | net carbs: 10g | fiber: 2g

Loaded Fauxtato Soup

Prep time: 5 minutes | Cook time: 20 minutes | serves 4

3 tablespoons salted butter
½ cup chopped white onions
2 cloves garlic, minced
1 (16 ounces/170 g) bag frozen cauliflower florets
2 cups vegetable broth
2 cups shredded sharp

cheddar cheese, plus extra for garnish
1 cup heavy whipping cream
Salt and ground black pepper
8 slices bacon, cooked and cut into small pieces, for garnish

1. Melt the butter in a stockpot over medium heat. Sauté the onions and garlic in the butter until the onions are tender and translucent. 2. Add the cauliflower and broth to the pot. Bring to a gentle boil over high heat, then reduce the heat to maintain a simmer and continue cooking until the cauliflower is tender, stirring occasionally, about 15 minutes. 3. Turn the heat down to the lowest setting and add the cheese and cream to the pot. Stir until the cheese is melted and well combined with the rest of the soup. 4. Season to taste with salt and pepper. Serve garnished with extra cheese and bacon pieces. Leftovers can be stored in an airtight container in the refrigerator for up to 5 days.
Per Serving
Calories: 560 | fat: 45g | protein: 5g | carbs: 9g | net carbs: 6g | fiber: 3g

✗ Chili-Infused Lamb Soup

Prep time: 5 minutes | Cook time: 25 minutes | Serves 6

1 tablespoon coconut oil
¾ pound ground lamb
2 cups shredded cabbage
½ onion, chopped
2 teaspoons minced garlic
4 cups chicken broth

2 cups coconut milk
1½ tablespoons red chili paste or as much as you want
Zest and juice of 1 lime
1 cup shredded kale

1. Cook the lamb. In a medium stockpot over medium-high heat, warm the coconut oil. Add the lamb and cook it, stirring it often, until it has browned, about 6 minutes. 2. Cook the vegetables. Add the cabbage, onion, and garlic and sauté until they've softened, about 5 minutes. 3. Simmer the soup. Stir in the chicken broth, coconut milk, red chili paste, lime zest, and lime juice. Bring it to a boil, then reduce the heat to low and simmer until the cabbage is tender, about 10 minutes. 4. Add the kale. Stir in the kale and simmer the soup for 3 more minutes. 5. Serve. Spoon the soup into six bowls and serve.
Per Serving
Calories: 380 | fat: 32g | protein: 17g | carbs: 7g | net carbs: 6g | fiber: 1g

Cioppino Seafood Soup

Prep time: 10 minutes | Cook time: 30 minutes | Serves 6

2 tablespoons olive oil
½ onion, chopped
2 celery stalks, sliced
1 red bell pepper, chopped
1 tablespoon minced garlic
2 cups fish stock
1 (15 ounces/425 g) can coconut milk
1 cup crushed tomatoes
2 tablespoons tomato paste
1 tablespoon chopped fresh basil

2 teaspoons chopped fresh oregano
½ teaspoon sea salt
½ teaspoon freshly ground black pepper
¼ teaspoon red pepper flakes
10 ounces (283 g) salmon, cut into 1-inch pieces
½ pound (227 g) shrimp, peeled and deveined
12 clams or mussels, cleaned and debearded but in the shell

1. Sauté the vegetables. In a large stockpot over medium-high heat, warm the olive oil. Add the onion, celery, red bell pepper, and garlic and sauté until they've softened, about 4 minutes. 2. Make the soup base. Stir in the fish stock, coconut milk, crushed tomatoes, tomato paste, basil, oregano, salt, pepper, and red pepper flakes. Bring the soup to a boil, then reduce the heat to low and simmer the soup for 10 minutes. 3. Add the seafood. Stir in the salmon and simmer until it goes opaque, about 5 minutes. Add the shrimp and simmer until they're almost cooked through, about 3 minutes. Add the mussels and let them simmer until they open, about 3 minutes. Throw out any mussels that don't open. 4. Serve. Ladle the soup into bowls and serve it hot.
Per Serving
Calories: 377 | fat: 29g | protein: 24g | carbs: 9g | net carbs: 7g | fiber: 2g

"Dolla Store" Pumpkin Soup

Prep time: 15 minutes | Cook time: 25 minutes | Serves 8

2 (9 ounces/255 g) packages soy chorizo
6 cups chicken bone broth
½ (15 ounces/425 g) can pure pumpkin
2 cups cooked riced cauliflower
1 cup unsweetened coconut

milk
1 teaspoon garlic powder
1 teaspoon ground cinnamon
1 teaspoon ground ginger
1 teaspoon ground nutmeg
1 teaspoon paprika
⅛ teaspoon salt
⅛ teaspoon black pepper

1. Place a medium soup pot over medium heat and add all ingredients. Bring to boil while stirring regularly (5–10 minutes). 2. Reduce heat. Let simmer 15 minutes, stirring regularly until desired consistency achieved. 3. Remove from heat, let cool 5 minutes, and serve.
Per Serving
Calories: 237| fat: 15g | protein: 17g | carbs: 13g | net carbs: 8g | fiber: 5g

Green Minestrone Soup

Prep time: 10 minutes | Cook time: 20 minutes | Serves 4

2 tablespoons ghee
2 tablespoons onion-garlic puree
2 heads broccoli, cut in florets
2 stalks celery, chopped
5 cups vegetable broth
1 cup baby spinach
Salt and black pepper to taste
2 tablespoons Gruyere cheese, grated

1. Melt the ghee in a saucepan over medium heat and sauté the onion-garlic puree for 3 minutes until softened. Mix in the broccoli and celery, and cook for 4 minutes until slightly tender. Pour in the broth, bring to a boil, then reduce the heat to medium-low and simmer covered for about 5 minutes. 2. Drop in the spinach to wilt, adjust the seasonings, and cook for 4 minutes. Ladle soup into serving bowls. Serve with a sprinkle of grated Gruyere cheese.

Per Serving
Calories: 227 | fat: 20g | protein: 8g | carbs: 4g | net carbs: 2g | fiber: 2g

Fennel and Cod Chowder with Fried Mushrooms

Prep time: 20 minutes | Cook time: 35 minutes | Serves 4

1 cup extra-virgin olive oil, divided
1 small head cauliflower, core removed and broken into florets (about 2 cups)
1 small white onion, thinly sliced
1 fennel bulb, white part only, trimmed and thinly sliced
½ cup dry white wine (optional)
2 garlic cloves, minced
1 teaspoon salt
¼ teaspoon freshly ground
black pepper
4 cups fish stock, plus more if needed
1 pound (454 g) thick cod fillet, cut into ¾-inch cubes
4 ounces (113 g) shiitake mushrooms, stems trimmed and thinly sliced (⅛-inch slices)
¼ cup chopped Italian parsley, for garnish (optional)
¼ cup plain whole-milk Greek yogurt, for garnish (optional)

1. In a stockpot, heat ¼ cup olive oil over medium-high heat. Add the cauliflower florets, onion, and fennel and sauté for 10 to 12 minutes. Add the white wine (if using), garlic, salt, and pepper and sauté for another 1 to 2 minutes. 2. Add 4 cups fish stock and bring to a boil. Cover, reduce the heat to medium-low, and simmer until vegetables are very tender, another 8 to 10 minutes. Remove from the heat and allow to cool slightly. 3. Purée the vegetable mixture, slowly drizzling in ½ cup olive oil, until very smooth and silky, adding additional fish stock if the mixture is too thick. 4. Turn the heat back to medium-high and bring the soup to a low simmer. Add the cod pieces and cook, covered, until the fish is cooked through, about 5 minutes. Remove from the heat and keep covered. 5. In a skillet, heat the remaining ¼ cup olive oil over medium-high heat. When very hot, add the mushrooms and fry until crispy. Transfer them to a plate, reserving the frying oil. Toss the mushrooms with a sprinkle of salt. 6. Serve the chowder hot, topped with fried mushrooms and drizzled with 1 tablespoon reserved frying oil. Garnish with chopped fresh parsley and 1 tablespoon of Greek yogurt (if using).

Per Serving
Calories: 663 | fat: 57g | protein: 28g | carbs: 57g | fiber: 4g | sodium: 700mg

✗ Cream of Cauliflower Gazpacho

Prep time: 15 minutes | Cook time: 25 minutes | Serves 4 to 6

1 cup raw almonds
½ teaspoon salt
½ cup extra-virgin olive oil, plus 1 tablespoon, divided
1 small white onion, minced
1 small head cauliflower, stalk removed and broken into florets (about 3 cups)
2 garlic cloves, finely
minced
2 cups chicken or vegetable stock or broth, plus more if needed
1 tablespoon red wine vinegar
¼ teaspoon freshly ground black pepper

1. Boil a small pot of water and add the almonds. Then boil again for 1 minute. Drain in a colander and run under cold water. Pat dry and, using your fingers, squeeze the meat of each almond out of its skin. Discard the skins. 2. In a food processor or blender, blend together the almonds and salt. With the processor running, drizzle in ½ cup extra-virgin olive oil, scraping down the sides as needed. Set the almond paste aside. 3. In a large stockpot, heat the remaining 1 tablespoon olive oil over medium-high heat. Add the onion and sauté until golden, 3 to 4 minutes. Add the cauliflower florets and sauté for another 3 to 4 minutes. Add the garlic and sauté for 1 minute more. 4. Add 2 cups stock and bring to a boil. Cover, reduce the heat to medium-low, and simmer the vegetables until tender, 8 to 10 minutes. Remove from the heat and allow to cool slightly. 5. Add the vinegar and pepper. Using an immersion blender, blend until smooth. With the blender running, add the almond paste and blend until smooth, adding extra stock if the soup is too thick. 6. Serve warm, or chill in refrigerator at least 4 to 6 hours to serve a cold gazpacho.

Per Serving
Calories: 328 | fat: 31g | protein: 8g | carbs: 10g | fiber: 4g | sodium: 232mg

Tomato Bisque

Prep time: 10 minutes | Cook time: 40 minutes | serves 8

Nonstick coconut oil cooking spray
1 pound (454 g) heirloom cherry tomatoes, coarsely chopped
1 yellow onion, coarsely chopped
2 garlic cloves, coarsely chopped
¼ cup cold-pressed olive oil, plus more for drizzling
2 thyme sprigs
Sea salt
Freshly ground black pepper
1 lemon, halved
1 cup coconut cream
⅓ cup chopped fresh basil, for garnish

1. Preheat the oven to 400°F. Grease a baking dish with cooking spray and set aside. 2. Combine the tomatoes, onion, and garlic in the baking dish. Drizzle with the olive oil and toss in the thyme. Season with salt and pepper. Top with the lemon halves and roast for 20 minutes or until the tomatoes start to blister. 3. Remove from the oven and transfer the mixture to a large saucepan over low heat. 4. Stir in the coconut cream and bring the soup to a simmer. Cook for 20 minutes to allow the flavors to meld together. 5. Remove and discard the lemon halves. 6. Turn off the heat and blend the soup with an immersion blender until it is silky smooth (adding warm water if necessary to reach desired texture). 7. Finish with cracked black pepper, olive oil drizzle, the basil, and additional salt, if desired.
Per Serving
Calories: 142 | fat: 14g | protein: 1g | carbs: 7g | net carbs: 5g | fiber: 2g

Cream of Mushroom Soup

Prep time: 10 minutes | Cook time: 10 minutes | Serves 4

1 pound (454 g) sliced button mushrooms
3 tablespoons butter
2 tablespoons diced onion
2 cloves garlic, minced
2 cups chicken broth
½ teaspoon salt
¼ teaspoon pepper
½ cup heavy cream
¼ teaspoon xanthan gum

1. Press the Sauté button and then press the Adjust button to set heat to Less. Add mushrooms, butter, and onion to pot. Sauté for 5 to 8 minutes or until onions and mushrooms begin to brown. Add garlic and sauté until fragrant. Press the Cancel button. 2. Add broth, salt, and pepper. Click lid closed. Press the Manual button and adjust time for 3 minutes. When timer beeps, quick-release the pressure. Stir in heavy cream and xanthan gum. Allow a few minutes to thicken and serve warm.
Per Serving
Calories: 220 | fat: 19g | protein: 5g | carbs: 6g | net carbs: 5g | fiber: 1g

No-Guilt Vegetable Soup

Prep time: 20 minutes | Cook time: 35 minutes | Serves 12

2 tablespoons vegetable oil
1 cup diced celery
1 small carrot, peeled and diced
1 medium head cauliflower, chopped into bite-sized florets
1 small eggplant, diced
2 cups finely cut broccoli florets
2 (64 ounces/1.8 kg) cans chicken bone broth
1 cup cut green beans (cut into 1" sections)
2 medium zucchini, diced
1½ teaspoons dried basil
¼ teaspoon dried thyme leaves
1 teaspoon black pepper
¼ teaspoon dried sage
¼ teaspoon garlic salt
4 ounces (113 g) full-fat cream cheese

1. In a large soup pot over medium heat, add oil and then sauté celery, carrot, cauliflower, eggplant, and broccoli until lightly softened (about 3–5 minutes), stirring regularly. 2. Add bone broth and remaining vegetables and spices. 3. Cover pot and bring to boil. Reduce heat and simmer 30 minutes until vegetables reach desired level of softness. Stir every 5 minutes. 4. Stir in cream cheese until fully blended. 5. Let cool 10 minutes and then serve.
Per Serving
Calories: 153 | fat: 5g | protein: 16g | carbs: 10g | net carbs: 6g | fiber: 4g

Creamy Cauliflower Soup with Bacon Chips

Prep time: 10 minutes | Cook time: 20 minutes | Serves 4

2 tablespoons ghee
1 onion, chopped
2 head cauliflower, cut into florets
2 cups water
Salt and black pepper to
taste
3 cups almond milk
1 cup shredded white cheddar cheese
3 bacon strips

1. Melt the ghee in a saucepan over medium heat and sauté the onion for 3 minutes until fragrant. 2. Include the cauli florets, sauté for 3 minutes to slightly soften, add the water, and season with salt and black pepper. Bring to a boil, and then reduce the heat to low. Cover and cook for 10 minutes. Puree cauliflower with an immersion blender until the ingredients are evenly combined and stir in the almond milk and cheese until the cheese melts. Adjust taste with salt and black pepper. 3. In a non-stick skillet over high heat, fry the bacon, until crispy. Divide soup between serving bowls, top with crispy bacon, and serve hot.
Per Serving
Calories: 401 | fat: 37g | protein: 8g | carbs: 9g | net carbs: 6g | fiber: 3g

Cauliflower & Blue Cheese Soup

Prep time: 15 minutes | Cook time: 20 minutes | Serves 5

2 tablespoons extra-virgin avocado oil
1 small red onion, diced
1 medium celery stalk, sliced
1 medium cauliflower, cut into small florets
2 cups vegetable or chicken stock
¼ cup goat's cream or

heavy whipping cream
Salt and black pepper, to taste
1 cup crumbled goat's or sheep's blue cheese, such as Roquefort
2 tablespoons chopped fresh chives
5 tablespoons extra-virgin olive oil

1. Heat a medium saucepan greased with the avocado oil over medium heat. Sweat the onion and celery for 3 to 5 minutes, until soft and fragrant. Add the cauliflower florets and cook for 5 minutes. Add the vegetable stock and bring to a boil. Cook for about 10 minutes, or until the cauliflower is tender. Remove from the heat and let cool for a few minutes. 2. Add the cream. Use an immersion blender, or pour into a blender, to process until smooth and creamy. Season with salt and pepper to taste. Divide the soup between serving bowls and top with the crumbled blue cheese, chives, and olive oil. To store, let cool and refrigerate in a sealed container for up to 5 days.

Per Serving
Calories: 337 | fat: 30g | protein: 10g | carbs: 9g | fiber: 3g | sodium: 383mg

Coconut and Cauliflower Curry Shrimp Soup

Prep time: 5 minutes | Cook time: 2 hours 15 minutes | Serves 4

8 ounces (227 g) water
1 (13.5 ounces/378 g) can unsweetened full-fat coconut milk
2 cups riced/shredded cauliflower (I buy it pre-riced at Trader Joe's)
2 tablespoons red curry paste

2 tablespoons chopped fresh cilantro leaves, divided
Pink Himalayan salt
Freshly ground black pepper
1 cup shrimp (I use defrosted Trader Joe's Frozen Medium Cooked Shrimp, which are peeled and deveined, with tail off)

1. With the crock insert in place, preheat the slow cooker to high. 2. Add the water, coconut milk, riced cauliflower, red curry paste, and 1 tablespoon of chopped cilantro, and season with pink Himalayan salt and pepper. Stir to combine. 3. Cover and cook on high for 2 hours. 4. Season the shrimp with pink Himalayan salt and pepper, add them to the slow cooker, and stir. Cook for an additional 15

minutes. 5. Ladle the soup into four bowls, top each with half of the remaining 1 tablespoon of chopped cilantro, and serve.
Per Serving
Calories: 269 | fat: 21g | protein: 16g | carbs: 8g | net carbs: 5g | fiber: 3g

Bone Marrow Chili Con Keto

Prep time: 12 minutes | Cook time: 2 hours | Serves 12

4 slices bacon, diced
1 pound (454 g) 80% lean ground beef
1 pound (454 g) Mexican-style fresh (raw) chorizo, removed from casings
1 (26½ ounces/751 g) box diced tomatoes with juices
1 cup tomato sauce
¼ cup chopped onions
1 red bell pepper, chopped
2 green chiles, chopped
½ cup beef bone broth, homemade or store-bought
2 tablespoons chili powder
2 teaspoons minced garlic
2 teaspoons dried oregano

leaves
1 teaspoon ground cumin
½ teaspoon cayenne pepper
½ teaspoon paprika
½ teaspoon fine sea salt
½ teaspoon freshly ground black pepper
2 bay leaves
Bone Marrow:
8 (2-inch) cross-cut beef or veal marrow bones, split lengthwise
1 teaspoon fine sea salt
½ teaspoon freshly ground black pepper
For Garnish:
Chopped fresh cilantro

1. Fry the bacon until crisp over medium-high heat, then remove it and set aside, leaving the fat in the pot. Cook the ground beef and chorizo into the hot fat until evenly browned, about 5 minutes. 2. Pour in the diced tomatoes and tomato sauce. Add the onions, bell pepper, chiles, beef broth, and half of the cooked bacon. Season with the chili powder, garlic, oregano, cumin, cayenne, paprika, salt, pepper and the bay leaves and stir. Cover and simmer over low heat for at least 2 hours, stirring occasionally. 3. After 2 hours, taste the chili and add more salt, pepper, or chili powder, if desired. Remove the bay leaves before serving. 4. While the chili is simmering, make the bone marrow. Preheat the oven to 450ºF (235ºC). Rinse and drain the bones and pat dry, then season them with the salt and pepper. 5. Roast the bones in a pan for 15 to 25 minutes, until the marrow in the center has puffed slightly and is warm. 6. To test for doneness, insert a metal skewer into the center of the bone. There should be no resistance when it is inserted, and some of the marrow will have started to leak from the bones. Scoop the marrow out of the bones into each bowl of chili. Garnish with chopped cilantro before serving.
Per Serving
Calories: 366 | fat: 32g | protein: 13g | carbs: 6g | net carbs: 4g | fiber: 2g

New England Clam Chowder

Prep time: 10 minutes | Cook time: 30 minutes | Serves 8

¼ pound (113 g) uncured bacon, chopped
2 tablespoons grass-fed butter
½ onion, finely chopped
1 celery stalk, chopped
2 teaspoons minced garlic
2 tablespoons arrowroot
4 cups fish or chicken stock
1 teaspoon chopped fresh thyme

2 bay leaves
3 (6½ ounces/184 g) cans clams, drained
1½ cups heavy (whipping) cream
Sea salt, for seasoning
Freshly ground black pepper, for seasoning
2 tablespoons chopped fresh parsley

1. Cook the bacon. In a medium stockpot over medium-high heat, fry the bacon until it's crispy. Transfer the bacon with a slotted spoon to a plate and set it aside. 2. Sauté the vegetables. Melt the butter in the stockpot, add the onion, celery, and garlic and sauté them until they've softened, about 3 minutes. Whisk in the arrowroot and cook for 1 minute. Add the stock, thyme, and bay leaves and bring the soup to just before it boils. Then reduce the heat to medium-low and simmer until the soup thickens, about 10 minutes. 3. Finish the soup. Stir in the clams and cream and simmer the soup until it's heated through, about 5 minutes. Find and throw out the bay leaves. 4. Serve. Season the chowder with salt and pepper. Ladle it into bowls, garnish with the parsley, and crumbles of the bacon, then serve.

Per Serving
Calories: 384 | fat: 28g | protein: 23g | carbs: 6g | net carbs: 6g | fiber: 2g

⚡ Bacon Cheddar Cauliflower Soup

Prep time: 15 minutes | Cook time: 30 minutes | Serves 6

1 large head cauliflower, chopped into florets
¼ cup olive oil
Salt and freshly ground black pepper, to taste
12 ounces (340 g) bacon, chopped
½ onion, roughly chopped
2 garlic cloves, minced
2 cups chicken broth, or

vegetable broth, plus more as needed
2 cups heavy (whipping) cream, plus more as needed
½ cup shredded Cheddar cheese, plus more for topping
Sliced scallion, green parts only, or fresh chives, for garnish

1. Preheat the oven to 400°F (205°C). 2. On a large rimmed baking sheet, toss the cauliflower with the olive oil and season with salt and pepper. Bake for 25 to 30 minutes or until slightly browned. 3. While the cauliflower roasts, in a large saucepan over medium heat, cook the bacon for 5 to 7 minutes until crispy. Transfer the bacon to a paper towel-lined plate to drain; leave the bacon fat in the pan.

4. Return the pan to medium heat and add the onion and garlic. Stir well to combine and sauté for 5 to 7 minutes until the onion is softened and translucent. Season with salt and pepper. 5. Remove the cauliflower from the oven and add it to the pan with the onion and garlic. Stir in the broth and bring the liquid to a simmer. Reduce the heat to low. Cook for 5 to 7 minutes. Remove from the heat. With an immersion blender, carefully blend the soup. Alternatively, transfer the soup to a regular blender (working in batches if necessary), blend until smooth, and return the soup to the pan. 6. Stir in the cream. Add the Cheddar and stir until melted and combined. Spoon the soup into bowls and top with bacon and more Cheddar. Garnish with scallion.

Per Serving 1 cup
Calories: 545 | fat: 49g | protein: 15g | carbs: 11g | net carbs: 7g | fiber: 4g

Coconut Shrimp Saffron Soup

Prep time: 5 minutes | Cook time: 15 minutes | Serves 4

1 tablespoon coconut oil
1 red bell pepper, chopped
2 teaspoons minced garlic
2 teaspoons grated fresh ginger
4 cups chicken stock
1 (15 ounces/425 g) can coconut milk
1 pound (454 g) shrimp,

peeled, deveined, and chopped
1 cup shredded kale
Juice of 1 lime
½ cup warm water
Pinch saffron threads
Sea salt, for seasoning
2 tablespoons chopped fresh cilantro

1. Sauté the vegetables. In a large saucepan over medium heat, warm the coconut oil. Add the red pepper, garlic, and ginger and sauté until they've softened, about 5 minutes. 2. Simmer the soup. Add the chicken stock and coconut milk and bring the soup to a boil, then reduce the heat to low and stir in the shrimp, kale, and lime juice. Simmer the soup until the shrimp is cooked through, about 5 minutes. 3. Mix in the saffron. While the soup is simmering, stir the saffron and the warm water together in a small bowl and let it sit for 5 minutes. Stir the saffron mixture into the soup when the shrimp is cooked, and simmer the soup for 3 minutes more. 4. Season and serve. Season with salt. Ladle the soup into bowls, garnish it with the cilantro, and serve it hot.

Tip: As mentioned above, there's a reason that saffron is expensive, so if you come across some that is cheap, take a close look to make sure it's the real deal. Take a look at the threads, and if the saffron is a uniform color on the whole strand (instead of having a lighter tip), it is probably not real saffron.

Per Serving
Calories: 504 | fat: 36g | protein: 32g | carbs: 15g | net carbs: 12g | fiber: 3g

Cheesy Cauliflower Soup

Prep time: 5 minutes | Cook time: 20 minutes | Serves 4

1 tablespoon butter
½ onion, chopped
2 cups riced/shredded cauliflower (I buy it pre-riced at Trader Joe's)
1 cup chicken broth
2 ounces (57 g) cream

cheese
1 cup heavy (whipping) cream
Pink Himalayan salt
Freshly ground pepper
½ cup shredded Cheddar cheese (I use sharp Cheddar)

1. In a medium saucepan over medium heat, melt the butter. Add the onion and cook, stirring occasionally, until softened, about 5 minutes. 2. Add the cauliflower and chicken broth, and allow the mixture to come to a boil, stirring occasionally. 3. Lower the heat to medium-low and simmer until the cauliflower is soft enough to mash, about 10 minutes. 4. Add the cream cheese, and mash the mixture. 5. Add the cream and purée the mixture with an immersion blender (or you can pour the soup into the blender, blend it, and then pour it back into the pan and reheat it a bit). 6. Season the soup with pink Himalayan salt and pepper. 7. Pour the soup into four bowls, top each with the shredded Cheddar cheese, and serve.

Per Serving
Calories: 372 | fat: 35g | protein: 9g | carbs: 9g | net carbs: 6g | fiber: 3g

Broccoli Ginger Soup

Prep time: 5 minutes | Cook time: 25 minutes | Serves 4

3 tablespoons coconut oil or avocado oil
1 small white onion, sliced
2 cloves garlic, minced
5 cups broccoli florets
1 (13½ ounces/400 ml) can full-fat coconut milk
1½ cups chicken bone broth
1 (2-in/5-cm) piece fresh

ginger root, peeled and minced
1½ teaspoons turmeric powder
¾ teaspoon finely ground sea salt
⅓ cup collagen peptides (optional)
¼ cup sesame seeds

1. Melt the oil in a large frying pan over medium heat. Add the onion and garlic and cook until translucent, about 10 minutes. 2. Add the broccoli, coconut milk, broth, ginger, turmeric, and salt. Cover and cook for 15 minutes, or until the broccoli is tender. 3. Transfer the broccoli mixture to a blender or food processor. Add the collagen, if using, and blend until smooth. 4. Divide among 4 bowls, top each bowl with 1 tablespoon of sesame seeds, and enjoy!

Per Serving
Calories: 344 | fat: 26g | protein: 13g | carbs: 12g | net carbs: 7g | fiber: 5g

Broc Obama Cheese Soup

Prep time: 25 minutes | Cook time: 25 minutes | Serves 8

8 cups chicken broth
2 large heads broccoli, chopped into bite-sized florets
1 clove garlic, peeled and minced

¼ cup heavy whipping cream
¼ cup shredded Cheddar cheese
⅛ teaspoon salt
⅛ teaspoon black pepper

1. In a medium pot over medium heat, add broth and bring to boil (about 5 minutes). Add broccoli and garlic. Reduce heat to low, cover pot, and simmer until vegetables are fully softened, about 15 minutes. 2. Remove from heat and blend using a hand immersion blender to desired consistency while still in pot. Leave some chunks of varying sizes for variety. 3. Return pot to medium heat and add cream and cheese. Stir 3–5 minutes until fully blended. Add salt and pepper. 4. Remove from heat, let cool 10 minutes, and serve.

Per Serving
Calories: 104 | fat: 4g | protein: 7g | carbs: 10g | net carbs: 7g | fiber: 3g

McDonald'S Cheeseburger Soup

Prep time: 20 minutes | Cook time: 25 minutes | Serves 4

1 pound (454 g) lean ground beef
3 cups beef broth
4 ounces (113 g) full-fat cream cheese, cubed
1½ cups shredded Cheddar cheese
4 strips no-sugar-added bacon, cooked and crumbled

¼ cup heavy whipping cream
2 tablespoons unsalted butter
2 tablespoons tomato paste
1 tablespoon yellow mustard
½ teaspoon garlic powder
¼ teaspoon paprika
⅛ teaspoon salt
⅛ teaspoon black pepper

1. In a large pot over medium heat, brown ground beef 5–10 minutes. Drain fat. 2. Stir in broth and cream cheese and cook 3–5 minutes until fully melted. Mix thoroughly. 3. Add in remaining ingredients, stirring 10 minutes until creamy and all cheese is melted. 4. Remove from heat. Let cool 10 minutes and then serve.

Per Serving
Calories: 627 | fat: 44g | protein: 41g | carbs: 5g | net carbs: 4g | fiber: 1g

Vegan Pho

Prep time: 10 minutes | Cook time: 20 minutes | serves 8

8 cups vegetable broth
1-inch knob fresh ginger, peeled and chopped
2 tablespoons tamari
3 cups shredded fresh spinach
2 cups chopped broccoli
1 cup sliced mushrooms
½ cup chopped carrots
⅓ cup chopped scallions
1 (8 ounces/227 g) package

shirataki noodles
2 cups shredded cabbage
2 cups mung bean sprouts
Fresh Thai basil leaves, for garnish
Fresh cilantro leaves, for garnish
Fresh mint leaves, for garnish
1 lime, cut into 8 wedges, for garnish

1. In a large stockpot over medium-high heat, bring the vegetable broth to a simmer with the ginger and tamari. 2. Once the broth is hot, add the spinach, broccoli, mushrooms, carrots, and scallions, and simmer for a few minutes, just until the vegetables start to become tender. 3. Stir in the shirataki noodles, then remove the pot from the heat and divide the soup among serving bowls. 4. Top each bowl with cabbage, sprouts, basil, cilantro, mint, and a lime wedge.

Per Serving
Calories: 47 | fat: 0g | protein: 3g | carbs: 10g | net carbs: 7g | fiber: 3g

Salsa Verde Chicken Soup

Prep time: 5 minutes | Cook time: 10 minutes | Serves 4

½ cup salsa verde
2 cups cooked and shredded chicken
2 cups chicken broth
1 cup shredded cheddar cheese
4 ounces (113 g) cream

cheese
½ teaspoon chili powder
½ teaspoon ground cumin
½ teaspoon fresh cilantro, chopped
Salt and black pepper, to taste

1. Combine the cream cheese, salsa verde, and broth, in a food processor; pulse until smooth. Transfer the mixture to a pot and place over medium heat. Cook until hot, but do not bring to a boil. Add chicken, chili powder, and cumin and cook for about 3-5 minutes, or until it is heated through. 2. Stir in cheddar cheese and season with salt and pepper to taste. If it is very thick, add a few tablespoons of water and boil for 1-3 more minutes. Serve hot in bowls sprinkled with fresh cilantro.

Per Serving
Calories: 346 | fat: 23g | protein: 25g | carbs: 4g | net carbs: 3g | fiber: 1g

Chicken Soup

Prep time: 15 minutes | Cook time: 45 minutes | Serves 4

3 tablespoons olive oil
1 (14 ounces/397 g) bag frozen peppers and onions
1 pound (454 g) chicken thigh meat, diced
1 tablespoon dried thyme
½ tablespoon garlic powder
1 teaspoon salt

1 teaspoon freshly ground black pepper
1 (32 ounces/907 g) container chicken or vegetable broth, or bone broth
½ pound (227 g) spinach
1 teaspoon dried basil (optional)

1. Heat the oil in a large pot over medium heat. 2. Add the peppers and onions and cook until no longer frozen, 8 to 10 minutes. 3. Add the chicken and cook, stirring occasionally. 4. Stir in the thyme, garlic powder, salt, and pepper. Add the broth and cook for about 25 minutes. 5. Add the spinach and cook for another 5 minutes. 6. Serve the soup in bowls, sprinkled with the basil (if using).

Per Serving
Calories: 323 | fat: 19g | protein: 28g | carbs: 10g | net carbs: 7g | fiber: 3g

Tootin' Chili

Prep time: 20 minutes | Cook time: 50 minutes | Serves 10

2 pounds (907 g) lean ground turkey
1 medium onion, peeled and diced
1 medium green bell pepper, seeded and chopped
6 cloves garlic, peeled and minced
2 tablespoons tomato paste
1 (28 ounces/784 g) can

crushed tomatoes
1 (15 ounces/425 g) can black soybeans
1 cup water
2 tablespoons chili powder
2 tablespoons paprika
1 tablespoon garlic powder
1 tablespoon onion powder
1 tablespoon ground cumin
½ teaspoon salt

1. In a large pot over medium heat, add turkey and cook 10–15 minutes, stirring regularly until browned. Transfer meat from pot to a large bowl. 2. To the pot, add onion, bell pepper, and garlic. Sauté 3–5 minutes until translucent. 3. Add ground meat, tomato paste, crushed tomatoes, black soybeans, water, and dry spices, stirring regularly. 4. Cover pot and reduce heat. Let simmer 30 minutes until meat is tender. 5. Let cool 10 minutes and then serve.

Per Serving
Calories: 242 | fat: 10g | protein: 24g | carbs: 14g | net carbs: 9g | fiber: 5g

Power Green Soup

Prep time: 10 minutes | Cook time: 15 minutes | Serves 6

1 broccoli head, chopped
1 cup spinach
1 onion, chopped
2 garlic cloves, minced
½ cup watercress
5 cups veggie stock
1 cup coconut milk
1 tablespoon ghee
1 bay leaf
Salt and black pepper, to taste

1. Melt the ghee in a large pot over medium heat. Add onion and garlic, and cook for 3 minutes. Add broccoli and cook for an additional 5 minutes. Pour the stock over and add the bay leaf. Close the lid, bring to a boil, and reduce the heat. Simmer for about 3 minutes. 2. At the end, add spinach and watercress, and cook for 3 more minutes. Stir in the coconut cream, salt and black pepper. Discard the bay leaf, and blend the soup with a hand blender.

Per Serving
Calories: 392 | fat: 38g | protein: 5g | carbs: 7g | net carbs: 6g | fiber: 1g

Sausage Zoodle Soup

Prep time: 10 minutes | Cook time: 25 minutes | Serves 8

1 tablespoon olive oil
4 cloves garlic, minced
1 pound (454 g) pork sausage (no sugar added)
½ tablespoon Italian seasoning
3 cups regular beef broth
3 cups beef bone broth
2 medium zucchini (6 ounces/170 g each), spiralized

1. In a large soup pot, heat the oil over medium heat. Add the garlic and cook for about 1 minute, until fragrant. 2. Add the sausage, increase the heat to medium-high, and cook for about 10 minutes, stirring occasionally and breaking apart into small pieces, until browned. 3. Add the seasoning, regular broth, and bone broth, and simmer for 10 minutes. 4. Add the zucchini. Bring to a simmer again, then simmer for about 2 minutes, until the zucchini is soft. (Don't overcook or the zoodles will be mushy.)

Per Serving
Calories: 216 | fat: 17g | protein: 12g | carbs: 2g | net carbs: 2g | fiber: 0g

Chapter 10 Vegetables and Sides

Zoodles and Doodles

Prep time: 5 minutes | Cook time: 0 minutes | Serves 4

For Zoodles:
2 medium zucchinis (about 7 ounces/198 g each), green or yellow

For Doodles:
1 medium daikon (about 14 ounces/397 g)

1. If you have a spiral slicer, slice a zucchini or daikon into noodles, following the manufacturer's instructions. To make noodles using a vegetable peeler, take a zucchini or daikon in your non-dominant hand. Hold it over a bowl and, with the opposite hand, begin peeling the zucchini or daikon. How far you go down the zucchini/daikon will determine the length of the ribbons. If you want shorter ribbons, simply drag the vegetable peeler across a shorter section of the zucchini/daikon. Repeat until most of the zucchini/daikon has been peeled and only a small, long core remains in your hand. 2. If making Zoodles, repeat with the second zucchini. 3. Use immediately or store as directed at left.
Per Serving
Calories: 16 | fat: 0g | protein: 1g | carbs: 3g | net carbs: 2g | fiber: 1g

Garlicky Broccoli Rabe with Artichokes

Prep time: 5 minutes | Cook time: 10 minutes | Serves 4

2 pounds (907 g) fresh broccoli rabe
½ cup extra-virgin olive oil, divided
3 garlic cloves, finely minced
1 teaspoon salt
1 teaspoon red pepper flakes

1 (13¾ ounces/390 g) can artichoke hearts, drained and quartered
1 tablespoon water
2 tablespoons red wine vinegar
Freshly ground black pepper

1. Trim away any thick lower stems and yellow leaves from the broccoli rabe and discard. Cut into individual florets with a couple inches of thin stem attached. 2. In a large skillet, heat ¼ cup olive oil over medium-high heat. Add the trimmed broccoli, garlic, salt, and red pepper flakes and sauté for 5 minutes, until the broccoli begins to soften. Add the artichoke hearts and sauté for another 2 minutes. 3. Add the water and reduce the heat to low. Cover and simmer until the broccoli stems are tender, 3 to 5 minutes. 4. In a small bowl, whisk together remaining ¼ cup olive oil and the vinegar. Drizzle over the broccoli and artichokes. Season with ground black pepper, if desired.
Per Serving
Calories: 341 | fat: 28g | protein: 11g | carbs: 18g | fiber: 12g | sodium: 750mg

Sautéed Spinach with Garlic

Prep time: 5 minutes | Cook time: 10 minutes | Serves 4

2 tablespoons butter, or olive oil
¼ white onion, diced
3 garlic cloves, sliced

12 ounces (340 g) fresh spinach
Salt and freshly ground black pepper, to taste

1. In a large skillet over medium heat, melt the butter. 2. Add the onion and garlic. Cook for 5 to 7 minutes until the onion is softened and translucent. 3. Add the spinach and reduce the heat to medium low. Season well with salt and pepper. Cook for 3 to 4 minutes or until the spinach wilts. Serve immediately.
Per Serving
Calories: 75 | fat: 6g | protein: 3g | carbs: 4g | net carbs: 2g | fiber: 2g

Pan-Roasted Green Beans

Prep time: 5 minutes | Cook time: 15 minutes | Serves 4

3 tablespoons extra-virgin olive oil
1 (12 ounces/340 g) bag frozen green beans, rinsed and patted dry
1 teaspoon garlic salt

1 teaspoon freshly ground black pepper
¼ cup sliced almonds
¼ cup grated Parmesan cheese

1. In a skillet over medium heat, heat the oil. 2. Add the green beans, garlic salt, and pepper to the skillet and cook, stirring frequently and tossing to coat, for 10 to 12 minutes. 3. Increase the heat to high and keep moving the beans around until they begin to brown. 4. Sprinkle in the almonds and stir to combine. 5. Remove from the heat, sprinkle the Parmesan cheese on top, and serve.
Per Serving ¼ recipe: Calories: 193 | fat: 16g | protein: 6g | carbs: 8g | net carbs: 5g | fiber: 3g

Cauliflower Fritters

Prep time: 5 minutes | Cook time: 15 minutes | Serves 4

1 large head cauliflower, chopped into florets
1 or 2 garlic cloves, chopped
¼ cup almond flour
¼ cup shredded Mozzarella cheese

2 eggs, whisked
Salt and freshly ground black pepper, to taste
2 tablespoons butter
2 tablespoons sliced scallion, green parts only

1. In a large saucepan of boiling water, quickly cook the cauliflower for 5 to 6 minutes or until just fork-tender. Drain and cool slightly. Transfer to a food processor and process until it almost has the consistency of mashed potato. Transfer to a large bowl. 2. Add the garlic, almond flour, Mozzarella, and eggs. Season with salt and pepper. Stir until well incorporated. 3. In a large skillet over medium-high heat, melt the butter. Spoon about 2 heaping tablespoons of the cauliflower mixture into your hand and create a patty about half the size of your palm. Repeat with the remaining mixture. Carefully add the patties to the butter (you may have to do this in batches). Cook for about 3 minutes until browned. Flip and cook the other side for about 3 minutes until browned. Serve garnished with the sliced scallion. Refrigerate leftovers in an airtight container for up to 1 week.

Per Serving
Calories: 170 | fat: 11g | protein: 9g | carbs: 12g | net carbs: 7g | fiber: 5g

Roasted Delicata Squash and Kale Salad

Prep time: 5 minutes | Cook time: 20 minutes | Serves 8

1 cup slivered delicata squash half-moons, about ¼ inch thick
6 tablespoons extra-virgin olive oil, divided
1 teaspoon salt, divided
4 cups baby kale or baby spinach leaves

¼ cup roasted pumpkin seeds (or pecans or walnuts)
1 tablespoon balsamic vinegar
¼ teaspoon freshly ground black pepper
4 ounces (113 g) goat cheese, crumbled

1. Preheat the oven to 400ºF (205ºC) and line a rimmed baking sheet with aluminum foil. 2. In a medium bowl, toss together the squash, 2 tablespoons of olive oil, and ½ teaspoon of salt. Spread the squash in a single layer on the prepared baking sheet, reserving the bowl, and roast until golden and tender, 15 to 20 minutes. 3. Meanwhile, place the kale in the reserved bowl. Add the pumpkin seeds. Set aside. 4. In a small bowl, whisk together the remaining 4 tablespoons of olive oil, the remaining ½ teaspoon of salt, the vinegar, and pepper and set aside. 5. When the squash has cooked, remove from the oven and add the warm squash to the greens. Drizzle with the dressing and toss to coat well. Top with goat cheese and serve warm.

Per Serving
Calories: 162 | fat: 15g | protein: 4g | carbs: 4g | net carbs: 3g | fiber: 1g

Faux-tato Salad

Prep time: 20 minutes | Cook time: 10 minutes | Serves 4

½ head cauliflower, cut into florets
⅓ cup mayonnaise
2 tablespoons stone-ground mustard
1 tablespoon red wine vinegar
¼ teaspoon pink Himalayan sea salt
¼ teaspoon freshly ground black pepper

4 ounces (113 g) bacon, cooked until crisp and chopped
1 large egg, hard-boiled, peeled, and chopped
¼ medium red onion, thinly sliced
2 tablespoons grated Cheddar cheese
2 scallions, white and green parts, chopped

1. Set a steamer basket in a small pot and add a couple inches of water. Place the cauliflower in the steamer, cover the pot, and steam for 7 to 10 minutes, until tender but not mushy. Let cool. 2. In a small bowl, combine the mayonnaise, mustard, vinegar, salt, and pepper. 3. In a large bowl, combine the cauliflower, bacon, chopped egg, red onion, cheese, and scallions. 4. Pour the dressing over the salad, then give it one final mix before serving. If desired, place the bowl in the refrigerator to chill the salad for about 1 hour before serving.

Per Serving
Calories: 287 | fat: 27g | protein: 7g | carbs: 3g | net carbs: 2g | fiber: 1g

Grandma-Mah's Creamed Spinach

Prep time: 5 minutes | Cook time: 15 minutes | Serves 6

20 ounces (567 g) fresh spinach, finely chopped
⅓ cup grated Parmesan cheese
6 ounces (170 g) full-fat cream cheese, softened

4 tablespoons full-fat sour cream
½ teaspoon garlic powder
½ teaspoon onion powder
¼ teaspoon salt
¼ teaspoon black pepper

1. In a large nonstick saucepan over medium heat, add spinach. Cook 3–5 minutes while stirring until wilted and excess water is removed. 2. Add remaining ingredients and stir 5–10 minutes until cheeses are melted and ingredients are blended. Serve.

Per Serving
Calories: 148 | fat: 11g | protein: 6g | carbs: 6g | net carbs: 4g | fiber: 2g

Spicy Roasted Asparagus with Lemon

Prep time: 5 minutes | Cook time: 15 minutes | Serves 4

1 pound (454 g) asparagus, trimmed and rinsed
1 tablespoon cooking fat of choice, melted
½ teaspoon granulated garlic
Sea salt and ground black pepper, to taste

1 tablespoon extra-virgin olive oil
Juice of ½ lemon
¼ cup shaved Parmesan cheese (optional)
Grated zest of 1 lemon
1 teaspoon red pepper flakes

1. Preheat the oven to 375°F (190°C). 2. Place the asparagus on a rimmed baking sheet and toss with the melted cooking fat. Sprinkle it with the granulated garlic and lightly season with salt and pepper. Roast for 10 to 15 minutes, until bright green and fork-tender. You'll need less time for very thin asparagus, more time for very thick asparagus. 3. Remove the asparagus from the oven and drizzle it with the olive oil and lemon juice, then top with the cheese (if using), lemon zest, and red pepper flakes.
Per Serving
Calories: 83 | fat: 7g | protein: 3g | carbs: 5g | net carbs: 3g | fiber: 2g

Keto Vegetable Pad Thai

Prep time: 10 minutes | Cook time: 20 minutes | Serves 4

Sauce:
2 tablespoons peanut butter (or almond butter)
2 garlic cloves, minced (or 1 teaspoon garlic powder)
2 tablespoons fish sauce
1 tablespoon coconut aminos
1 tablespoon coconut vinegar or apple cider vinegar
1 teaspoon chili paste
¼ teaspoon ground ginger (optional)
Dash sweetener

Noodles:
2 tablespoons coconut oil
2 cups chopped broccoli
3 (7 ounces/198 g) packages shirataki noodles, rinsed and thoroughly drained
2 cups bean sprouts
2 scallions, chopped
Sea salt and freshly ground black pepper, to taste
½ cup chopped fresh basil (optional)
¼ cup chopped roasted peanuts (optional)
Lime wedges for serving (optional)

Make the Sauce: 1. In a small microwave-safe bowl, heat the peanut butter in the microwave for 20 to 30 seconds until melted. Add the garlic, fish sauce, coconut aminos, vinegar, chili paste, ginger (if using), and sweetener. Whisk to combine, taste, and adjust the sweetness or spiciness depending on your preference.
Make the Noodles: 2. In a large wok or skillet, melt the coconut oil over medium-high heat. Add the broccoli and cook, stirring occasionally, for 5 minutes. Add the noodles, bean sprouts, and scallions and pour in the sauce. Toss to mix well and sauté for 10 to 15 minutes until the broccoli is cooked through. Taste and season with salt and pepper. 3. Remove from the heat and toss in the basil (if using). Serve garnished with peanuts and lime wedges (if using).
Per Serving
Calories: 211 | fat: 15g | protein: 8g | carbs: 11g | net carbs: 6g | fiber: 5g

Tender Grilled Asparagus Spears

Prep time: 5 minutes | Cook time: 5 minutes | Serves 4

1 pound (454 g) fresh asparagus spears, woody ends snapped off
2 tablespoons good-quality

olive oil
Sea salt, for seasoning
Freshly ground black pepper, for seasoning

1. Preheat the grill. Set the grill to high heat. 2. Prepare the asparagus. In a medium bowl, toss the asparagus spears with the olive oil and season them with salt and pepper. 3. Grill and serve. Grill the asparagus until tender, 2 to 4 minutes. Arrange them on a platter and serve.
Per Serving
Calories: 82 | fat: 7g | protein: 3g | carbs: 4g | net carbs: 2g | fiber: 2g

Keto Refried "Beans"

Prep time: 20 minutes | Cook time: 55 minutes | Makes 8 cups

1 pound (454 g) bacon
3 eggplants, peeled and chopped
3 zucchini, chopped
1 onion, chopped
1 jalapeño pepper, finely chopped
6 garlic cloves, minced
2 tablespoons ground cumin

1 tablespoon dried oregano
1 tablespoon dried parsley
1 teaspoon chili powder
½ teaspoon cayenne pepper
Sea salt and freshly ground black pepper, to taste
1 cup shredded sharp Cheddar cheese

1. Cook the bacon over medium-high heat in two to three batches, for 5-7 minutes each. Remove the cooked bacon to a paper towel, leaving the grease in the skillet. 2. Add the eggplant and zucchini to the skillet and cook about 15 minutes. Transfer the eggplant and zucchini to a food processor, leaving bacon grease in the pan. Add the bacon to the food processor and pulse 4-5 times. 3. Add the onion, jalapeño, garlic, cumin, oregano, parsley, chili powder, cayenne, salt, and pepper to the skillet. Cook 8-10 minutes. Add the eggplant mixture to the skillet and stir to combine. 4. Stir in the cheese, reduce the heat to low, and simmer for 10-15 minutes. Transfer to a plate and serve.
Per Serving ½ cup
Calories: 179 | fat: 13g | protein: 7g | carbs: 8g | net carbs: 5g | fiber: 3g

Get Loaded Smashed Cauliflower

Prep time: 10 minutes | Cook time: 18 minutes | Serves 6

1 pound (454 g) cauliflower florets
3 tablespoons unsalted butter
¼ teaspoon garlic powder
½ cup fat-free sour cream

2 tablespoons chopped green onion, divided
1 cup shredded Cheddar cheese, divided
¼ teaspoon salt

1. Steam florets 10–15 minutes until very soft. Remove from heat and let sit in metal colander for 10–15 minutes to release water. 2. Pulse florets in a food processor 2–3 minutes until fluffy. Add butter, garlic powder, and sour cream and process 2–3 more minutes until it resembles mashed potatoes. 3. Scoop cauliflower into a medium microwave-safe bowl and mix in two-thirds of the green onion and ½ cup cheese and salt. Microwave 2–3 minutes. 4. Serve and sprinkle remaining cheese and green onion on top.

Per Serving
Calories: 183| fat: 14g | protein: 6g | carbs: 5g | net carbs: 3g | fiber: 2g

Turnip Fries with Dipping Sauce

Prep time: 15 minutes | Cook time: 30 minutes | serves 6

Fries:
4 medium turnips
2 tablespoons avocado oil
½ cup grated Parmesan cheese
1 teaspoon paprika
½ teaspoon chili powder
½ teaspoon garlic powder

Dipping Sauce:
½ cup mayonnaise
¼ cup sugar-free ketchup
2 tablespoons dill relish
1½ teaspoons white vinegar
¼ teaspoon ground black pepper
⅛ teaspoon salt

1. Preheat the oven to 425°F. Line a sheet pan with parchment paper. 2. **Make the Fries:** Peel the turnips and cut them into 3 by ¼-inch sticks. In a large bowl, toss the fries in the oil to coat. 3. Put the Parmesan cheese, paprika, chili powder, and garlic powder in a separate bowl and stir to combine. Add the oiled fries to the seasoning mixture and toss to coat evenly. Spread the fries on the prepared pan. 4. Bake for 30 minutes or until the fries are brown and crisp around the edges, turning them halfway through for even browning. 5. Meanwhile, **make the dipping sauce:** Place all the sauce ingredients in a small bowl and stir to combine. 6. When the fries are done, remove from the oven and serve immediately with the dipping sauce.
Per Serving
Calories: 224 | fat: 21g | protein: 3g | carbs: 7g | net carbs: 5g | fiber: 2g

 ## Spiralized Broccoli Noodles

Prep time: 10 minutes | Cook time: 10 minutes | Serves 4

2 tablespoons butter
1 garlic clove, minced
2 heads broccoli, florets removed, stalks spiralized, or peeled with a vegetable

peeler into strips and cut into noodles
Salt and freshly ground black pepper, to taste
¼ cup grated Parmesan cheese

1. In a medium skillet over medium heat, melt the butter and add the garlic. Cook for 2 to 3 minutes. 2. Add the broccoli florets. Cook for 3 to 4 minutes. 3. Add the broccoli noodles. Cook for 4 to 5 minutes more. Season with salt and pepper and top with the Parmesan. Refrigerate leftovers in an airtight container for up to 1 week.
Per Serving
Calories: 104 | fat: 8g | protein: 5g | carbs: 6g | net carbs: 4g | fiber: 2g

Braised Greens with Olives and Walnuts

Prep time: 5 minutes | Cook time: 20 minutes | Serves 4

8 cups fresh greens (such as kale, mustard greens, spinach, or chard)
2 to 4 garlic cloves, finely minced
½ cup roughly chopped pitted green or black olives
½ cup roughly chopped

shelled walnuts
¼ cup extra-virgin olive oil
2 tablespoons red wine vinegar
1 to 2 teaspoons freshly chopped herbs such as oregano, basil, rosemary, or thyme

1. Remove the tough stems from the greens and chop into bite-size pieces. Place in a large rimmed skillet or pot. 2. Turn the heat to high and add the minced garlic and enough water to just cover the greens. Bring to a boil, reduce the heat to low, and simmer until the greens are wilted and tender and most of the liquid has evaporated, adding more if the greens start to burn. For more tender greens such as spinach, this may only take 5 minutes, while tougher greens such as chard may need up to 20 minutes. Once cooked, remove from the heat and add the chopped olives and walnuts. 3. In a small bowl, whisk together olive oil, vinegar, and herbs. Drizzle over the cooked greens and toss to coat. Serve warm.
Per Serving
Calories: 254 | fat: 25g | protein: 4g | carbs: 6g | fiber: 3g | sodium: 137mg

Loaded Roasted Cauliflower

Prep time: 10 minutes | Cook time: 30 minutes | serves 4

1 medium head cauliflower
2 tablespoons avocado oil
Salt
2 slices bacon, chopped

2 green onions, sliced
1 cup shredded sharp cheddar cheese

1. Preheat the oven to 400°F. Line a sheet pan with parchment paper. 2. Core the cauliflower and cut the florets into bite-sized pieces. Toss the cauliflower with the oil, then spread it on the lined sheet pan and sprinkle lightly with salt. Top the cauliflower evenly with the bacon and green onions. 3. Bake for 25 minutes, then remove from the oven and top with the cheese. Bake for 2 to 4 more minutes, until the cheese is melted.

Per Serving

Calories: 242 | fat: 19g | protein: 11g | carbs: 9g | net carbs: 6g | fiber: 3g

Roasted Brussels Sprouts with Tahini-Yogurt Sauce

Prep time: 10 minutes | Cook time: 35 minutes | Serves 4

1 pound (454 g) Brussels sprouts, trimmed and halved lengthwise
6 tablespoons extra-virgin olive oil, divided
1 teaspoon salt, divided
½ teaspoon garlic powder

¼ teaspoon freshly ground black pepper
¼ cup plain whole-milk Greek yogurt
¼ cup tahini
Zest and juice of 1 lemon

1. Preheat the oven to 425°F (220°C). Line a baking sheet with aluminum foil or parchment paper and set aside. 2. Place the Brussels sprouts in a large bowl. Drizzle with 4 tablespoons olive oil, ½ teaspoon salt, the garlic powder, and pepper and toss well to coat. 3. Place the Brussels sprouts in a single layer on the baking sheet, reserving the bowl, and roast for 20 minutes. Remove from the oven and give the sprouts a toss to flip. Return to the oven and continue to roast until browned and crispy, another 10 to 15 minutes. Remove from the oven and return to the reserved bowl. 4. In a small bowl, whisk together the yogurt, tahini, lemon zest and juice, remaining 2 tablespoons olive oil, and remaining ½ teaspoon salt. Drizzle over the roasted sprouts and toss to coat. Serve warm.

Per Serving

Calories: 330 | fat: 29g | protein: 7g | carbs: 15g | fiber: 6g | sodium: 635mg

Easy Peanut Zoodles

Prep time: 10 minutes | Cook time: 5 minutes | Serves 2

2 large zucchini, spiralized or peeled into thin strips
Salt, to taste
1 teaspoon sesame oil
1 garlic clove, minced
1 teaspoon red pepper flakes
1 tablespoon gluten-free soy sauce
3 tablespoons unsweetened peanut butter

2 to 3 tablespoons chicken broth (optional)
Freshly ground black pepper, to taste
2 tablespoons crushed peanuts
2 tablespoons chopped fresh cilantro leaves
2 lime wedges

1. Place the zucchini noodles in a colander and sprinkle liberally with salt. Let sit in the sink for 15 to 20 minutes before rinsing and patting dry with a paper towel. 2. While the zucchini is draining, in a large skillet over medium-low heat, heat the sesame oil. 3. Add the garlic and red pepper flakes. Cook for 2 to 3 minutes until fragrant. 4. Stir in the soy sauce and peanut butter. 5. Add the zucchini noodles and toss to combine, ensuring that sauce coats all of the noodles. (If the sauce is too thick, add some chicken broth to thin it.) Season with salt and pepper and transfer to two bowls to serve. 6. Top with the crushed peanuts and cilantro and serve with the lime wedges.

Per Serving

Calories: 221 | fat: 18g | protein: 10g | carbs: 8g | net carbs: 6g | fiber: 2g

Easy Cheesy Caulirice

Prep time: 5 minutes | Cook time: 20 minutes | serves 4

2 tablespoons salted butter
1 (12 ounces/340 g) bag frozen riced cauliflower
½ cup shredded cheddar

cheese
2 tablespoons heavy whipping cream
Salt and ground black pepper

1. Melt the butter in a medium-sized skillet over medium heat. 2. Put the cauliflower in the skillet and cook, stirring occasionally, until tender, about 15 minutes. 3. Turn off the heat. Add the cheese and cream to the skillet and stir until the cheese is completely melted and the ingredients are fully combined. 4. Season to taste with salt and pepper. Serve immediately.

Per Serving

Calories: 156 | fat: 14g | protein: 5g | carbs: 5g | net carbs: 3g | fiber: 2g

Cheesy Broccoli and Bacon

Prep time: 10 minutes | Cook time: 25 minutes | Serves 4

4 slices bacon
5 cups fresh broccoli florets
1 teaspoon minced garlic
Sauce:
1 tablespoon unsalted butter

2 tablespoons heavy whipping cream
1 cup shredded cheddar cheese (about 4 ounces/113 g), divided

1. Preheat the oven to 400°F. 2. Cook bite-sized bacon pieces over medium heat for 3 to 5 minutes. Take out one-quarter of the bacon pieces to a plate. 3. Add broccoli and garlic and stir-fry for 5 to 7 minutes and transfer the broccoli mixture to an 8-inch round or square baking pan or dish. 4. **Make the sauce:** Put the butter and cream in a small saucepan over low heat. Allow the butter to melt, stirring often. 5. Once the butter is fully melted, add ½ cup of the shredded cheese and continue to stir until the cheese has melted and formed a thick sauce. 6. Pour the sauce over the broccoli and toss to coat using a spoon. Layer the remaining ½ cup of shredded cheese and the reserved bacon over the entire mixture. 7. Bake for 10 minutes, or until the cheese has melted and slightly browned. Serve immediately. 8. Store leftovers in a sealed container in the refrigerator for up to 4 days. Reheat in the microwave for a couple minutes, until the cheese has melted.
Per Serving
Calories: 241 | fat: 19g | protein: 13g | carbs: 9g | net carbs: 6g | fiber: 3g

Sautéed Wild Mushrooms with Bacon

Prep time: 10 minutes | Cook time: 15 minutes | Serves 4

6 strips uncured bacon, chopped
4 cups sliced wild mushrooms

2 teaspoons minced garlic
2 tablespoons chicken stock
1 tablespoon chopped fresh thyme

1. Cook the bacon. In a large skillet over medium-high heat, cook the bacon until it's crispy and cooked through, about 7 minutes. 2. Cook the mushrooms. Add the mushrooms and garlic and sauté until the mushrooms are tender, about 7 minutes. 3. Deglaze the pan. Add the chicken stock and stir to scrape up any browned bits in the bottom of the pan. 4. Garnish and serve. Put the mushrooms in a bowl, sprinkle them with the thyme, and serve.
Per Serving
Calories: 214 | fat: 19g | protein: 7g | carbs: 4g | net carbs: 4g | fiber: 0g

Cheesy Cauliflower Gratin

Prep time: 10 minutes | Cook time: 30 minutes | Serves 4

1 head cauliflower, cut into florets
2 tablespoons butter
2 garlic cloves
2 cups heavy (whipping) cream

¼ cup cream cheese
Salt and freshly ground black pepper, to taste
½ cup grated white Cheddar cheese

1. Preheat the oven to 400°F (205°C). 2. Bring a large saucepan of water to a boil over high heat and add the cauliflower. Boil for 2 to 3 minutes and drain. Transfer the cauliflower to an 8-by-8-inch baking dish. 3. Return the pan to medium heat and add the butter to melt. 4. Add the garlic. Cook for about 2 minutes until fragrant. Reduce the heat to low and, while stirring, add the cream. Simmer for about 2 minutes. 5. Add the cream cheese. Season with salt and pepper. Stir until smooth. Pour the sauce over the cauliflower and top with the Cheddar. Bake for about 20 minutes or until the cheese melts and is golden brown. Refrigerate leftovers in an airtight container for up to 4 days.
Per Serving
Calories: 622 | fat: 60g | protein: 11g | carbs: 16g | net carbs: 11g | fiber: 5g

Herbed Radishes

Prep time: 10 minutes | Cook time: 15 minutes | Serves 2

3 tablespoons lard
14 ounces (397 g) radishes (about 2 bunches), quartered
⅛ teaspoon finely ground gray sea salt
⅛ teaspoon ground black

pepper
2 tablespoons sliced fresh chives
1 tablespoon chopped fresh herbs, such as thyme and/or rosemary

1. Heat the lard in a large frying pan over medium heat until melted. Add the quartered radishes, salt, and pepper. Cover and cook for 5 minutes, or until softened. 2. Remove the lid and cook for another 7 minutes, stirring frequently, or until the pieces begin to brown. 3. Add the chives and fresh herbs and toss to combine. Reduce the heat to medium-low and continue to cook for 2 minutes. 4. Remove from the heat, divide among 4 small bowls, and serve.
Per Serving
Calories: 223 | fat: 19g | protein: 6g | carbs: 7g | net carbs: 6g | fiber: 1g

Academy Parmesan Cauliflower

Prep time: 10 minutes | Cook time: 35 minutes | Serves 4

16 ounces (454 g) cauliflower, cut into bite-sized florets
4 tablespoons melted unsalted butter

2 tablespoons olive oil
¼ teaspoon salt
¼ teaspoon black pepper
1 cup grated Parmesan cheese
2 teaspoons parsley flakes

1. Preheat oven to 400°F. Line a baking sheet with parchment paper. 2. In a large mixing bowl, toss cauliflower, melted butter, and olive oil. Add salt and pepper. 3. Place coated cauliflower on the baking sheet. Keep cauliflower in a single layer so it cooks evenly. Bake 25–30 minutes or until soft. 4. Remove from oven and dust with Parmesan cheese and parsley. Return to oven for 5 minutes to melt cheese. 5. Remove from the oven and serve warm.
Per Serving
Calories: 279 | fat: 23g | protein: 9g | carbs: 9g | net carbs: 7g | fiber: 2g

Classic Butter Biscuits

Prep time: 15 minutes | Cook time: 25 minutes | Serves 12

¾ cup water
3 tablespoons unflavored gelatin
1½ cups coconut flour
¾ teaspoon baking powder
¾ teaspoon finely ground gray sea salt

½ cup full-fat coconut milk
6 tablespoons coconut oil
1 tablespoon apple cider vinegar
¾ cup coconut oil, for serving

1. Preheat the oven to 375°F (190°C) and line a baking sheet with parchment paper or a silicone baking mat. 2. Sprinkle the gelatin on top of the water in a small saucepan. Do not stir. After 5 minutes, bring the mixture to a light boil over medium heat, stirring occasionally. Set aside once smooth. If it begins to solidify, reheat to liquid form. 3. Meanwhile, place the coconut flour, baking powder, and salt in a stand mixer or in a mixing bowl (if using a hand mixer). Mix until combined. 4. Add the coconut milk, coconut oil, vinegar, and gelatin mixture and mix until the batter is combined and sticky. 5. Working quickly, divide the batter into 12 balls, about ¼ cup in size. Pressing and rotating the balls with the your palm into biscuits of the desired shape. 6. Place the biscuits on the prepared baking sheet, leaving ½ inch (1.25 cm) of space between them. 7. Bake the biscuits for 20 to 25 minutes, until the tops crack and begin to turn golden. 8. Allow the biscuits to cool on the baking sheet for 1 hour. Enjoy each biscuit with 1 tablespoon of coconut oil.
Per Serving
Calories: 266 | fat: 24g | protein: 4g | carbs: 8g | net carbs: 3g | fiber: 5g

Bacon-y Caramelized Onions

Prep time: 10 minutes | Cook time: 45 minutes | Makes about 1 cup

2 tablespoons bacon fat
4 small yellow onions, thinly sliced
½ teaspoon sea salt

½ teaspoon dried rosemary leaves or thyme leaves (optional)

1. In a large sauté pan or skillet over medium heat, melt the bacon fat, then add the onions. Cook for 8 to 10 minutes, until the onions begin to become translucent. Add the salt and dried rosemary (if using). 2. Turn the heat down to medium-low and slowly cook the onions, stirring occasionally, for 45 minutes, allowing them to brown just slightly before stirring each time. If you find that the onions are browning too quickly or are sticking too much, reduce the heat slightly, add 1 to 2 tablespoons of warm water at a time to the pan, and stir it into the onions to keep them cooking evenly. 3. As they cook, the onions will become more and more browned and softened, and eventually they will look as they do in the photo. They will be rich-tasting and richly colored at the end of cooking. This process requires low, slow heat; faster, hotter heat will not yield the same results.
Per Serving
Calories: 85 | fat: 6g | protein: 1g | carbs: 7g | net carbs: 6g | fiber: 1g

Loaded Cauliflower Mash

Prep time: 10 minutes | Cook time: 10 minutes | Serves 8

1 head cauliflower, cut into florets (4 cups or 2 pounds/907 g florets)
2 tablespoons butter
¼ cup sour cream
2 tablespoons heavy cream

3 cloves garlic, minced
1 teaspoon sea salt
1½ cups shredded Cheddar cheese
⅓ cup cooked bacon bits
¼ cup chopped green onions

1. Bring a large pot of water to a boil on the stove top. Add the cauliflower florets and cook for 8 to 10 minutes, until very soft. Drain well and pat dry. 2. Meanwhile, in a microwave-safe bowl or in a saucepan, combine the butter, sour cream, heavy cream, garlic, and sea salt, and heat in the microwave or on the stove until hot and melted. 3. Transfer the cauliflower florets to a food processor. Add the butter-cream mixture and purée until smooth. 4. Transfer the cauliflower to a serving dish. Immediately stir in most of the Cheddar, bacon bits, and green onions, reserving a little of each for the topping. To serve, garnish with the reserved Cheddar, bacon, and green onions.
Per Serving
Calories: 180 | fat: 13g | protein: 9g | carbs: 5g | net carbs: 3g | fiber: 2g

Southern Fried Cabbage

Prep time: 10 minutes | Cook time: 15 minutes | Serves 4

3 bacon slices, diced
1 small white onion, diced
1 garlic clove, minced
1 head cabbage, chopped
Salt and freshly ground black pepper, to taste

1. In a large saucepan over medium-high heat, sauté the bacon for 5 to 7 minutes until it begins to crisp. 2. Add the onion and garlic and sauté for 5 to 7 minutes until the onion is softened and translucent. 3. Add the cabbage, tossing it in the bacon fat. Season with salt and pepper and cook for about 5 minutes or until the cabbage softens and begins to brown and get a little crispy around the edges. Refrigerate leftovers in an airtight container for up to 3 days.
Per Serving
Calories: 161 | fat: 10g | protein: 6g | carbs: 15g | net carbs: 9g | fiber: 6g

Green Veg & Macadamia Smash

Prep time: 25 minutes | Cook time: 15 minutes | Serves 6

⅔ cup macadamia nuts
Enough water to cover and soak the macadamias
7 ounces (198 g) cavolo nero or kale, stalks removed and chopped
1 medium head broccoli, cut into florets, or broccolini
2 cloves garlic, crushed
¼ cup extra-virgin olive oil
2 tablespoons fresh lemon juice
4 medium spring onions, sliced
¼ cup chopped fresh herbs, such as parsley, dill, basil, or mint
Salt and black pepper, to taste

1. Place the macadamias in a small bowl and add enough water to cover them. Soak for about 2 hours, then drain. Discard the water. 2. Fill a large pot with about 1½ cups (360 ml) of water, then insert a steamer colander. Bring to a boil over high heat, then reduce to medium-high. Add the cavolo nero and cook for 6 minutes. Add the broccoli and cook for 8 minutes or until fork-tender. Remove the lid, let the steam escape, and let cool slightly. 3. Place the cooked vegetables in a blender or a food processor. Add the soaked macadamias, garlic, olive oil, lemon juice, spring onions, and fresh herbs (you can reserve some for topping). 4. Process to the desired consistency (smooth or chunky). Season with salt and pepper to taste and serve. To store, let cool completely and store in a sealed container in the fridge for up to 5 days.
Per Serving
Calories: 250 | fat: 22g | protein: 5g | carbs: 12g | fiber: 5g | sodium: 44mg

Citrus Asparagus with Pistachios

Prep time: 10 minutes | Cook time: 15 minutes | Serves 4

5 tablespoons extra-virgin olive oil, divided
Zest and juice of 2 clementines or 1 orange (about ¼ cup juice and 1 tablespoon zest)
Zest and juice of 1 lemon
1 tablespoon red wine
vinegar
1 teaspoon salt, divided
¼ teaspoon freshly ground black pepper
½ cup shelled pistachios
1 pound (454 g) fresh asparagus
1 tablespoon water

1. In a small bowl, whisk together 4 tablespoons olive oil, the clementine and lemon juices and zests, vinegar, ½ teaspoon salt, and pepper. Set aside. 2. In a medium dry skillet, toast the pistachios over medium-high heat until lightly browned, 2 to 3 minutes, being careful not to let them burn. Transfer to a cutting board and coarsely chop. Set aside. 3. Trim the rough ends off the asparagus, usually the last 1 to 2 inches of each spear. In a skillet, heat the remaining 1 tablespoon olive oil over medium-high heat. Add the asparagus and sauté for 2 to 3 minutes. Sprinkle with the remaining ½ teaspoon salt and add the water. Reduce the heat to medium-low, cover, and cook until tender, another 2 to 4 minutes, depending on the thickness of the spears. 4. Transfer the cooked asparagus to a serving dish. Add the pistachios to the dressing and whisk to combine. Pour the dressing over the warm asparagus and toss to coat.
Per Serving
Calories: 271 | fat: 24g | protein: 6g | carbs: 12g | fiber: 4g | sodium: 585mg

Old-Fashioned Green Beans

Prep time: 10 minutes | Cook time: 1 hour 30 minutes | serves 4

1 pound (454 g) fresh green beans
1½ cups vegetable broth
4 slices bacon, chopped
1 tablespoon dried minced onions, or ¼ cup chopped
raw onions
½ teaspoon ground black pepper
½ teaspoon garlic powder
1 tablespoon salted butter
Salt

1. Snap the ends off the green beans and break them in half or in thirds. Place the beans in a medium-sized saucepan and add the broth, bacon, onions, pepper, and garlic powder. 2. Bring the bean mixture to a boil over medium-high heat. Continue to boil for 10 minutes, then reduce the heat to low. Cover the pot and simmer for 1 hour 20 minutes or until the beans have cooked down and the juices have reduced but aren't completely gone. 3. Stir in the butter and season to taste with salt before serving.
Per Serving
Calories: 123 | fat: 6g | protein: 6g | carbs: 9g | net carbs: 6g | fiber: 3g

Radish Potatoes in Drag

Prep time: 5 minutes | Cook time: 50 minutes | Serves 4

20 medium radishes, trimmed and halved
2 tablespoons olive oil
2 teaspoons Italian seasoning, divided

¼ teaspoon salt
¼ teaspoon black pepper
¼ cup grated Parmesan cheese

1. Preheat oven to 400°F. Grease a large baking dish with olive oil. 2. Add halved radishes to baking dish, brush with olive oil, and dust with half of the Italian seasoning, salt, and pepper. 3. Bake 45 minutes until light brown and crisp. Toss and re-season halfway through. 4. Add Parmesan on top and bake 5 more minutes. Remove from the oven and your golden radishes are ready to serve.

Per Serving
Calories: 89 | fat: 8g | protein: 2g | carbs: 2g | net carbs: 2g | fiber: 0g

Hush Puppies

Prep time: 10 minutes | Cook time: 30 minutes | Serves 4

½ cup coconut flour
¼ cup psyllium husk powder
1 teaspoon baking powder
½ teaspoon onion powder
½ teaspoon pink Himalayan salt

4 large eggs
⅓ cup extra-virgin olive oil
⅓ cup water
2 tablespoons diced white onions
Coconut oil, for deep-frying

1. Mix and whisk the coconut flour, psyllium husk powder, baking powder, onion powder, and salt in a small bowl. 2. Whisk together the eggs, olive oil, and water in a large bowl. Mix the two bowl and stir with a wooden spoon to form a thick, slightly sticky, and pliable dough. Fold in the diced onions. 3. Shape the dough into 20 evenly sized balls and place on a parchment-lined plate. 4. Pour enough coconut oil into a medium-sized saucepan over medium-high heat to completely submerge the deviled eggs, but no more than halfway up the saucepan. Place a deep-fry thermometer into the heating oil. 5. When the oil temperature reaches anywhere from 330°F to 350°F, drop some of the hush puppies into the oil and fry until dark brown on the outside, about 8 minutes. Once cooked through, remove the hush puppies from the oil using a slotted spoon and place on the paper towel–lined plate to absorb the excess oil. 6. Repeat until all the hush puppies are fried. Serve immediately. 7. Store leftovers in a zip-top plastic bag. Reheat in the microwave for 30 to 60 seconds.

Per Serving
Calories: 322 | fat: 25g | protein: 8g | carbs: 17g | net carbs: 5g | fiber: 12g

Zesty Roasted Broccoli

Prep time: 5 minutes | Cook time: 30 minutes | Serves 4

4 cups broccoli florets (about 10 ounces/283 g)
2 tablespoons melted lard, tallow, coconut oil, or other preferred fat
2 tablespoons freshly squeezed lemon juice
1 teaspoon garlic powder

1 teaspoon sea salt
½ teaspoon freshly ground black pepper
1 teaspoon lemon zest
½ teaspoon red pepper flakes
½ cup freshly grated Parmesan cheese

1. Preheat the oven to 400°F (205°C). Line a large baking sheet with parchment paper or a silicone mat. 2. Arrange the broccoli in a single layer on the prepared baking sheet and drizzle with the lard or oil. Toss with your hands so all the pieces are coated. 3. Drizzle the lemon juice on top of the broccoli and then sprinkle with the garlic powder, salt, pepper, lemon zest, and red pepper flakes. 4. Bake for 20 to 25 minutes until fork-tender. 5. Sprinkle with the Parmesan and bake for another 5 minutes or until the cheese is melted.

Per Serving
Calories: 147 | fat: 11g | protein: 7g | carbs: 5g | net carbs: 3g | fiber: 2g

Crunchy Pork Rind Zucchini Sticks

Prep time: 5 minutes | Cook time: 25 minutes | Serves 2

2 medium zucchini, halved lengthwise and seeded
¼ cup crushed pork rinds
¼ cup grated Parmesan cheese

2 garlic cloves, minced
2 tablespoons melted butter
Pink Himalayan salt
Freshly ground black pepper
Olive oil, for drizzling

1. Preheat the oven to 400°F. Line a baking sheet with aluminum foil or a silicone baking mat. 2. Place the zucchini halves cut-side up on the prepared baking sheet. 3. In a medium bowl, combine the pork rinds, Parmesan cheese, garlic, and melted butter, and season with pink Himalayan salt and pepper. Mix until well combined. 4. Spoon the pork-rind mixture onto each zucchini stick, and drizzle each with a little olive oil. 5. Bake for about 20 minutes, or until the topping is golden brown. 6. Turn on the broiler to finish browning the zucchini sticks, 3 to 5 minutes, and serve.

Per Serving
Calories: 231 | fat: 20g | protein: 9g | carbs: 8g | net carbs: 6g | fiber: 2g

Asparagus with Goat Cheese and Sunflower Seeds

Prep time: 5 minutes | Cook time: 12 minutes | Serves 4

1 bunch asparagus (about 1 pound/454 g), tough ends removed
1 tablespoon extra-virgin olive oil
½ teaspoon pink Himalayan

salt
¼ teaspoon ground black pepper
2 ounces (57 g) fresh (soft) goat cheese
¼ cup raw sunflower kernels

1. Preheat the oven to 400°F. 2. Line a rimmed baking sheet with a single layer of asparagus. Brush the asparagus with the olive oil and season with the salt and pepper. 3. Bake for 10 to 12 minutes, until bright green and fork-tender. 4. Crumble the goat cheese down the center of the asparagus and top with the sunflower kernels. Serve immediately.
Per Serving
Calories: 148 | fat: 10g | protein: 8g | carbs: 6g | net carbs: 3g | fiber: 3g

Crispy Chicken Skin Croutons

Prep time: 5 minutes | Cook time: 45 minutes | Serves 12

1 pound (454 g) chicken skin and fat
¼ cup diced onions
Minced garlic (optional)

Chopped fresh basil or other herbs of choice (optional)
Fine sea salt and freshly ground black pepper, to taste

1. Rinse the chicken skin and fat, pat dry, then cut it into ¼-inch pieces. Cover and cook the pieces in a large greased skillet set over low heat for about 15 minutes. Uncover and raise the heat to medium-low when liquid fat accumulates. Cook for another 15 to 20 minutes, breaking the pieces apart with a spatula and stirring until the skin starts to brown and curl at the edges. Remove the pan from the heat. 2. Collect the fat of small pieces of skin from the skillet in a container for later use. 3. Return the cooked chicken skin and fat to the skillet. Add the onions, garlic and herbs (if using) to the skillet. Season to taste with salt and pepper. 4. Stir-fry the mixture for 15 to 20 minutes over medium heat, until the pieces are dark brown (not black!) and crispy. Remove from the skillet and drain on a paper towel. Season again with salt and pepper to taste. Store the croutons in an airtight container in the fridge for up to 3 days. Reheat in a preheated 400°F (205°C) oven or toaster oven for 3 minutes.
Per Serving
Calories: 169 | fat: 15g | protein: 8g | carbs: 0g | net carbs: 0g | fiber: 0g

Mashed Cauliflower

Prep time: 10 minutes | Cook time: 15 minutes | Serves 4

8 cups water
1 head cauliflower, washed and chopped
2 to 3 tablespoons butter
1 garlic clove, minced

¼ cup heavy (whipping) cream, plus more as needed
Salt and freshly ground black pepper, to taste

1. In a large saucepan over high heat, bring the water to a boil. 2. Add the cauliflower and cook for about 10 minutes or until fork-tender. Remove from the heat, drain, and set aside. 3. Return the pan to medium heat and add the butter and garlic. Sauté for 2 to 3 minutes until the garlic browns slightly. 4. Return the cauliflower to the pan. Use an immersion blender to purée the mixture. If you don't have an immersion blender, carefully transfer everything to a regular blender and purée. 5. Add the cream. Continue to blend until the mashed cauliflower is as smooth as you like it. Season with salt and pepper. If necessary, add another splash of cream (or some chicken broth) to thin it a bit. Serve immediately, or keep warm until ready to serve. Refrigerate leftovers in an airtight container for up to 5 days.
Per Serving
Calories: 180 | fat: 14g | protein: 5g | carbs: 12g | net carbs: 7g | fiber: 5g

Green "Potato" Boats

Prep time: 10 minutes | Cook time: 30 minutes | Serves 4

2 medium zucchini
½ cup grated Cheddar cheese
2 ounces (57 g) full-fat cream cheese, softened
¼ cup diced onion
¼ cup full-fat sour cream
2 tablespoons melted

unsalted butter
¼ teaspoon salt
4 strips no-sugar-added bacon, cooked and crumbled
1 medium jalapeño pepper, deveined, seeded, and finely chopped

1. Preheat oven to 350°F. 2. Cut the zucchini in half lengthwise. Cut in half again at the midpoint to create eight "boats" 3"–4" long to be hollowed out. 3. With a spoon, scoop out each boat; try to get most out but leave enough so the sides aren't too thin (about ¼" max). Chop the removed flesh finely and put in a medium bowl. 4. Place eight scooped-out boats in a large greased baking dish. 5. Add remaining ingredients except bacon and jalapeños to bowl with zucchini flesh and mix well. Divide mixture evenly and scoop into the boats. 6. Top with crumbled bacon and jalapeño. 7. Bake 30 minutes until filling bubbles and zucchini boats are softened. 8. Remove from oven and let cool 5 minutes. Serve.
Per Serving
Calories: 259 | fat: 20g | protein: 10g | carbs: 6g | net carbs: 5g | fiber: 1g

Green Bean Bacon Bundles

Prep time: 15 minutes | Cook time: 25 minutes | serves 4

12 ounces (340 g) fresh green beans (about 2 cups), trimmed
2 tablespoons avocado oil
8 slices bacon, cut in half

crosswise
½ teaspoon salt
¼ teaspoon ground black pepper

1. Preheat the oven to 400°F. Line a sheet pan with parchment paper. 2. Toss the green beans in the oil. 3. Using the bacon slices, wrap the green beans into bundles of 4 or 5 beans each. The number per bundle will depend on the length of the bacon and thickness of the beans. Place each bundle on the prepared pan with the seam of the bacon facedown. Sprinkle evenly with the salt and pepper. 4. Bake for 25 minutes or until the bacon reaches the desired crispness and the green beans are tender.

Per Serving
Calories: 186 | fat: 16g | protein: 8g | carbs: 4g | net carbs: 2g | fiber: 1g

Cheesy Broccoli and Cauliflower Casserole

Prep time: 5 minutes | Cook time: 40 minutes | Serves 4

4 cups broccoli florets
4 cups cauliflower florets
2 tablespoons butter
1 cup sour cream
1 cup grated Gruyère cheese
1 tablespoon Dijon mustard
1 tablespoon dried thyme

1 teaspoon kosher salt
1 teaspoon black pepper
½ cup grated Parmesan cheese
2 cups crushed pork rinds or pork rind crumbs

1. Preheat the oven to 375ºF (190ºC). 2. Chop the broccoli and cauliflower florets into smaller pieces. Melt the butter in a skillet over medium-high heat. Add the broccoli and cauliflower, and let sit undisturbed about 2 minutes. Stir and let sit undisturbed another couple minutes. When the brown bits begin to form, remove from the heat. 3. In a medium bowl, mix the sour cream, Gruyère, mustard, thyme, salt, and pepper. Stir in the veggies. Transfer the mixture to a casserole dish and sprinkle the Parmesan on top. 4. Bake for 20 minutes. Remove from the oven and sprinkle the pork rinds evenly over top. Return to the oven and bake another 10 to 15 minutes, until the top is crunchy and the casserole is bubbling around the edges.

Per Serving
Calories: 461 | fat: 37g | protein: 20g | carbs: 12g | net carbs: 9g | fiber: 3g

Simple Butter-Sautéed Vegetables

Prep time: 10 minutes | Cook time: 10 minutes | Serves 4

2 tablespoons grass-fed butter
1 tablespoon good-quality olive oil
2 teaspoons minced garlic
2 zucchini, cut into ¼-inch rounds

1 red bell pepper, cut into thick slices
1 yellow bell pepper, cut into thick slices
Sea salt, for seasoning
Freshly ground black pepper, for seasoning

1. Cook the vegetables. In a large skillet over medium-high heat, warm the butter and olive oil. Add the garlic and sauté it for 2 minutes. Add the zucchini and the red and yellow bell peppers to the skillet and sauté, stirring from time to time, for 7 minutes. 2. Serve. Season the vegetables with salt and pepper, spoon them into a bowl, and serve.

Per Serving
Calories: 100 | fat: 9g | protein: 1g | carbs: 4g | net carbs: 3g | fiber: 1g

Pesto Cauliflower Steaks

Prep time: 5 minutes | Cook time: 20 minutes | Serves 2

2 tablespoons olive oil, plus more for brushing
½ head cauliflower
Pink Himalayan salt
Freshly ground black pepper

2 cups fresh basil leaves
½ cup grated Parmesan cheese
¼ cup almonds
½ cup shredded mozzarella cheese

1. Preheat the oven to 425°F. Brush a baking sheet with olive oil or line with a silicone baking mat. 2. To prep the cauliflower steaks, remove and discard the leaves and cut the cauliflower into 1-inch-thick slices. You can roast the extra floret crumbles that fall off with the steaks. 3. Place the cauliflower steaks on the prepared baking sheet, and brush them with the olive oil. You want the surface just lightly coated so it gets caramelized. Season with pink Himalayan salt and pepper. 4. Roast the cauliflower steaks for 20 minutes. 5. Meanwhile, put the basil, Parmesan cheese, almonds, and 2 tablespoons of olive oil in a food processor (or blender), and season with pink Himalayan salt and pepper. Mix until combined. 6. Spread some pesto on top of each cauliflower steak, and top with the mozzarella cheese. Return to the oven and bake until the cheese melts, about 2 minutes. 7. Place the cauliflower steaks on two plates, and serve hot.

Per Serving
Calories: 448 | fat: 34g | protein: 24g | carbs: 17g | net carbs: 10g | fiber: 7g

Curried Coconut Cauliflower

Prep time: 10 minutes | Cook time: 20 minutes | Serves 4

1 tablespoon ghee
½ onion, diced
2 garlic cloves
½ serrano chile pepper, seeded and finely diced
1 head cauliflower, washed
and trimmed into florets
Salt and freshly ground black pepper, to taste
1 (13½ ounces/383 g) can full-fat coconut milk
3 tablespoons curry powder

1. In a large skillet over medium heat, melt the ghee. 2. Add the onion and garlic. Sauté for 5 to 7 minutes until the onion is softened and translucent. 3. Add the serrano and cauliflower. Cook for 4 to 5 minutes more. Season with salt and pepper. 4. Pour the coconut milk over the cauliflower and add the curry powder. Stir to combine. Simmer for 5 minutes to allow the flavors to combine. Serve hot. Refrigerate leftovers in an airtight container for up to 1 week.

Per Serving
Calories: 310 | fat: 28g | protein: 6g | carbs: 15g | net carbs: 10g | fiber: 5g

Roasted Greek Cauliflower

Prep time: 10 minutes | Cook time: 35 minutes | Serves 6

6 cups cauliflower florets (1 medium head cauliflower)
½ cup extra-virgin olive oil, divided
1 teaspoon dried oregano
½ teaspoon salt
¼ teaspoon freshly ground black pepper
10 pitted Kalamata olives,
coarsely chopped
2 cups baby spinach leaves, coarsely chopped
¼ cup fresh parsley leaves, coarsely chopped
8 ounces (227 g) crumbled feta cheese, divided
4 ounces (113 g) goat cheese
½ cup heavy cream

1. Preheat the oven to 425ºF (220ºC). 2. In a large bowl, combine the cauliflower florets, ¼ cup of olive oil, oregano, salt, and pepper and toss to coat well. Transfer to a 9-by-13-inch glass baking dish, reserving the oiled bowl. Roast the cauliflower for 15 to 20 minutes, or until just starting to turn golden brown. 3. Meanwhile, in the same large bowl, combine the olives, spinach, parsley, half the feta, the goat cheese, and the remaining ¼ cup of olive oil. Stir to combine well and incorporate the goat cheese into the mixture. 4. Transfer the hot cauliflower to the large bowl with the olive-and-cheese mixture and toss to coat well. Add the heavy cream and toss again. Transfer back to the baking dish and sprinkle the remaining 4 ounces (113 g) of feta on top of the vegetables. Return to the oven and roast until bubbly, 10 to 12 minutes. Serve warm.

Per Serving
Calories: 414 | fat: 38g | protein: 12g | carbs: 8g | net carbs: 5g | fiber: 3g

Zia's Spinach Torta

Prep time: 10 minutes | Cook time: 1 hour | Serves 4

2 (10 ounces/283 g) packages fresh spinach
3 tablespoons butter
½ white onion, finely chopped
3 garlic cloves, minced
8 ounces (227 g) ricotta cheese
1 cup shredded Monterey Jack cheese
¼ cup grated Parmesan cheese
Salt, to taste
Freshly ground black pepper, to taste
2 eggs, whisked

1. Preheat the oven to 350ºF (180ºC). 2. In a medium saucepan of boiling water, boil the spinach for 2 minutes. Drain and let cool before squeezing out as much excess liquid as possible. Chop it finely. 3. In a large skillet over medium heat, melt the butter. 4. Add the onion and garlic. Sauté for 5 to 7 minutes until the onion is softened and translucent. 5. Stir in the spinach. Cook for 1 minute then remove from the heat. 6. Stir in the ricotta, Monterey Jack, and Parmesan. Season with salt and pepper. Mix well to combine. 7. Add the eggs and stir to combine. Transfer the mixture to a pie dish and bake for 45 minutes or until set. Cool slightly and cut into slices or squares.

Per Serving
Calories: 380 | fat: 29g | protein: 23g | carbs: 9g | net carbs: 6g | fiber: 3g

Wraps

Prep time: 4 minutes | Cook time: 8 minutes | Makes 2 wraps

2 large eggs
2 hard-boiled eggs, peeled
2 tablespoons chopped fresh cilantro or other fresh herbs
of choice or green onions
½ teaspoon fine sea salt
1½ teaspoons coconut oil

1. Place the raw eggs, peeled hard-boiled eggs, herbs, and salt in a blender and combine until very smooth, without lumps. 2. Heat an 8-inch crepe pan or nonstick pan over medium-low heat, then add the oil. When the oil is hot, pour half of the egg mixture into the pan and tilt the pan to spread the eggs into a very large, thin wrap. Let the eggs set for 3 to 4 minutes, until cooked through. (Do not flip the wrap.) Slide the wrap onto a plate to cool. Repeat with the remaining half of the egg mixture. 3. Once cool, drizzle the wraps with the keto dressing of your choice (drizzling is easier than spreading, which often breaks the wrap) and fill with lettuce and other fillings of your choice. Wrap up like a burrito and enjoy! Store extras in an airtight container in the fridge for up to 3 days.

Per Serving
Calories: 172 | fat: 13g | protein: 13g | carbs: 1g | net carbs: 1g | fiber: 0g

Sheet-Pan Green Bean Casserole

Prep time: 10 minutes | Cook time: 20 minutes | Serves 6

3 cups (about 1 pound/454 g) green beans, trimmed
1 (12 ounces/340 g) package bacon (about 14 slices), chopped
¼ white onion, cut into thin rings

2 tablespoons extra-virgin olive oil
¼ cup slivered almonds
1 teaspoon garlic powder
1 teaspoon sea salt
1 teaspoon freshly ground black pepper

1. Preheat the oven to 425°F (220°C). Line a baking sheet (or two, so that the veggies don't overlap too much) with parchment paper or aluminum foil. 2. In a large bowl, combine the green beans, bacon, onion, oil, almonds, and garlic powder and toss to coat. Spread the mixture out in an even layer on the baking sheet(s). Sprinkle the salt and pepper generously over everything. 3. Bake for about 20 minutes. Serve immediately.
Per Serving
Calories: 199 | fat: 15g | protein: 9g | carbs: 7g | net carbs: 4g | fiber: 3g

Brussels Sprouts with Pancetta and Walnuts

Prep time: 10 minutes | Cook time: 40 minutes | Serves 4

½ cup walnuts
1 pound (454 g) Brussels sprouts, trimmed and halved
6 tablespoons extra-virgin olive oil, divided
½ teaspoon salt
½ teaspoon garlic powder

¼ teaspoon freshly ground black pepper
4 ounces (113 g) pancetta, cut into ½-inch strips
2 tablespoons balsamic vinegar

1. Preheat the oven to 425°F (220°C). Place the walnuts on a large baking sheet lined with aluminum foil. 2. Toast the walnuts until just browned and fragrant, but not burned, 3 to 4 minutes. Remove from the oven, roughly chop, and set aside, reserving the foil on the baking sheet. 3. In a large bowl, combine the Brussels sprouts, 4 tablespoons of olive oil, the salt, garlic powder, and pepper and toss to coat well. 4. Transfer the Brussels sprouts to the prepared baking sheet. Do not rinse the bowl. Roast the sprouts for 20 minutes. Remove from the oven, sprinkle with the pancetta, and toss to blend. Return to the oven and roast until the sprouts are golden brown and pancetta is crispy, another 10 to 15 minutes. Remove from the oven and return to the reserved bowl. 5. Add the chopped toasted walnuts to the warm Brussels sprouts and pancetta, and toss to coat. 6. In a small bowl, whisk together the remaining 2 tablespoons of olive oil and the vinegar and drizzle over the mixture. Toss to coat and serve warm.

Per Serving
Calories: 450 | fat: 41g | protein: 10g | carbs: 14g | net carbs: 9g | fiber: 5g

Garlicky Green Beans

Prep time: 10 minutes | Cook time: 10 minutes | Serves 4

1 pound (454 g) green beans, stemmed
2 tablespoons olive oil
1 teaspoon minced garlic

Sea salt
Freshly ground black pepper
¼ cup freshly grated Parmesan cheese

1. Preheat the oven to 425°F. Line a baking sheet with aluminum foil and set aside. 2. In a large bowl, toss together the green beans, olive oil, and garlic until well mixed. 3. Season the beans lightly with salt and pepper. 4. Spread the beans on the baking sheet and roast them until they are tender and lightly browned, stirring them once, about 10 minutes. 5. Serve topped with the Parmesan cheese.
Per Serving
Calories: 104 | fat: 9g | protein: 4g | carbs: 2g | net carbs: 1g | fiber: 1g

Superflax Tortillas

Prep time: 5 minutes | Cook time: 10 minutes | Serves 6

1 packed cup flax meal
⅓ cup coconut flour
¼ cup ground chia seeds
2 tablespoons whole psyllium husks

1 teaspoon salt, or to taste
1 cup lukewarm water
2 tablespoons extra-virgin avocado oil or ghee

1. Place all the dry ingredients and water in a bowl. Mix until well combined. (For ground chia seeds, pulse them in a coffee grinder or food processor until smooth.) Place the dough in the refrigerator for about 30 minutes. 2. When ready, take out the dough and equally cut it into 4. Place one piece of dough between two pieces of parchment paper and roll it out until very thin. Remove the top piece of parchment paper. Press a 8-inch (20 cm) lid into the dough or trace around it with your knife to cut out the tortilla. 3. Repeat for the remaining pieces of dough. Add the cut-off excess dough to the last piece and create the remaining 2 tortillas from it. 4. Grease a large pan with the avocado oil and cook 1 tortilla at a time for 2 to 3 minutes on each side over medium heat until lightly browned. Don't overcook as the tortillas should be flexible, not too crispy. 5. Once cool, store the tortillas in a sealed container for up to 1 week and reheat them in a dry pan, if needed.
Per Serving
Calories: 182 | fat: 16g | protein: 4g | carbs: 8g | fiber: 7g | sodium: 396mg

Garlic Butter Baby Bok Choy

Prep time: 5 minutes | Cook time: 20 minutes | Serves 4

3 tablespoons butter or ghee
4 garlic cloves, minced
1½ pounds (680 g) baby bok choy (about 12 small heads), ends trimmed off and halved lengthwise

1 cup bone broth
1 teaspoon sea salt
½ teaspoon freshly ground black pepper
½ teaspoon ground ginger
Pinch red pepper flakes

1. In a large skillet over medium heat, melt the butter. Add the garlic and cook until fragrant, 3 to 5 minutes. 2. Add the bok choy to the garlic butter and stir to evenly coat. Add the bone broth, salt, pepper, and ginger. Simmer for 10 to 15 minutes until the bok choy is fork-tender. 3. Sprinkle with red pepper flakes and serve.
Per Serving6 halves: Calories: 113 | fat: 9g | protein: 3g | carbs: 5g | net carbs: 3g | fiber: 2g

Creamy Mashed Turnips

Prep time: 45 minutes | Cook time: 30 minutes | Serves 10

4 large turnips (about 2¼ pounds/1 kg), cubed
2 tablespoons refined avocado oil, melted tallow, or ghee (if tolerated) 6 small cloves garlic, peeled
2 teaspoons dried thyme leaves

1 teaspoon finely ground gray sea salt
⅔ cup heated full-fat coconut milk

For Garnish (Optional):
Freshly ground black pepper
Chopped fresh parsley

1. Preheat the oven to 375°F (190°C). 2. Place the cubed turnips, avocado oil, garlic cloves, thyme, and salt on an unlined rimmed baking sheet. Toss with your hands to coat the turnips. 3. Roast the turnips for 25 to 30 minutes, flipping them every 10 minutes, until they are soft and browned. 4. Transfer the roasted turnips to a blender or food processor. Add the hot coconut milk and pulse 5 to 10 times, until the desired consistency is reached. 5. Transfer to a 1-quart (950-ml) serving dish and serve sprinkled with freshly ground pepper and chopped parsley. If not serving immediately, cover to keep warm.
Per Serving
Calories: 93 | fat: 6g | protein: 1g | carbs: 8g | net carbs: 6g | fiber: 2g

Bacony Green Beans

Prep time: 5 minutes | Cook time: 40 minutes | Serves 3

¼ pound (113 g) uncooked bacon, cut into 1-inch pieces
1 teaspoon seasoned salt

1 teaspoon freshly ground black pepper
1 teaspoon garlic powder

1 (14½ ounces/411 g) can green beans, undrained

¼ medium red onion, chopped

1. In a medium skillet over medium heat, cook the bacon. 2. Once the bacon is cooked, add the seasoned salt, pepper, and garlic powder, and stir. 3. Add the green beans and their juices, then the onion, mixing to combine. 4. Reduce the heat to low and simmer for 30 minutes, stirring occasionally.
Per Serving½ cup: Calories: 150 | fat: 13g | protein: 4g | carbs: 5g | net carbs: 3g | fiber: 2g

Creamy Baked Asparagus

Prep time: 5 minutes | Cook time: 20 minutes | Serves 4

1 pound (455 g) asparagus, tough ends removed
1 cup Ranch dressing
½ cup pork dust or roughly ground pork rinds

Pinch of finely ground gray sea salt
Chopped fresh parsley, for garnish (optional)

1. Preheat the oven to 375°F (190°C). Place the asparagus spears in a medium-sized casserole dish. 2. Evenly distribute the ranch dressing over the top of the asparagus, then coat them with the pork dust. Sprinkle with the salt. 3. Bake for 18 to 20 minutes, until the top is lightly golden. 4. Serve immediately, garnished with fresh parsley, if desired.
Per Serving
Calories: 292 | fat: 25g | protein: 10g | carbs: 6g | net carbs: 3g | fiber: 3g

Creamy Cauliflower Purée

Prep time: 10 minutes | Cook time: 15 minutes | Serves 4

1 medium head cauliflower, roughly chopped into 2- to 3-inch pieces (about 4 cups)

¼ cup butter or ghee
Sea salt and ground black pepper, to taste

1. Fill a large pot with 2 inches of water and place a steamer basket in the pot. Cover and bring to a boil over high heat. Add the cauliflower pieces to the basket and steam until fork-tender, about 15 minutes. 2. Place the cauliflower in a food processor. Add the butter and a few pinches of salt and pepper to taste. Purée until smooth and creamy.
Per Serving
Calories: 136 | fat: 12g | protein: 3g | carbs: 8g | net carbs: 4g | fiber: 4g

MEASUREMENT CONVERSION CHART

VOLUME EQUIVALENTS(DRY)

US STANDARD	METRIC (APPROXIMATE)
1/8 teaspoon	0.5 mL
1/4 teaspoon	1 mL
1/2 teaspoon	2 mL
3/4 teaspoon	4 mL
1 teaspoon	5 mL
1 tablespoon	15 mL
1/4 cup	59 mL
1/2 cup	118 mL
3/4 cup	177 mL
1 cup	235 mL
2 cups	475 mL
3 cups	700 mL
4 cups	1 L

WEIGHT EQUIVALENTS

US STANDARD	METRIC (APPROXIMATE)
1 ounce	28 g
2 ounces	57 g
5 ounces	142 g
10 ounces	284 g
15 ounces	425 g
16 ounces (1 pound)	455 g
1.5 pounds	680 g
2 pounds	907 g

VOLUME EQUIVALENTS(LIQUID)

US STANDARD	US STANDARD (OUNCES)	METRIC (APPROXIMATE)
2 tablespoons	1 fl.oz.	30 mL
1/4 cup	2 fl.oz.	60 mL
1/2 cup	4 fl.oz.	120 mL
1 cup	8 fl.oz.	240 mL
1 1/2 cup	12 fl.oz.	355 mL
2 cups or 1 pint	16 fl.oz.	475 mL
4 cups or 1 quart	32 fl.oz.	1 L
1 gallon	128 fl.oz.	4 L

TEMPERATURES EQUIVALENTS

FAHRENHEIT(F)	CELSIUS(C) (APPROXIMATE)
225 °F	107 °C
250 °F	120 °C
275 °F	135 °C
300 °F	150 °C
325 °F	160 °C
350 °F	180 °C
375 °F	190 °C
400 °F	205 °C
425 °F	220 °C
450 °F	235 °C
475 °F	245 °C
500 °F	260 °C

The Dirty Dozen and Clean Fifteen

The Environmental Working Group (EWG) is a nonprofit, nonpartisan organization dedicated to protecting human health and the environment Its mission is to empower people to live healthier lives in a healthier environment. This organization publishes an annual list of the twelve kinds of produce, in sequence, that have the highest amount of pesticide residue-the Dirty Dozen-as well as a list of the fifteen kinds ofproduce that have the least amount of pesticide residue-the Clean Fifteen.

THE DIRTY DOZEN

- The 2016 Dirty Dozen includes the following produce. These are considered among the year's most important produce to buy organic:

Strawberries	Spinach
Apples	Tomatoes
Nectarines	Bell peppers
Peaches	Cherry tomatoes
Celery	Cucumbers
Grapes	Kale/collard greens
Cherries	Hot peppers

- *The Dirty Dozen list contains two additional itemskale/collard greens and hot peppers-because they tend to contain trace levels of highly hazardous pesticides.*

THE CLEAN FIFTEEN

- The least critical to buy organically are the Clean Fifteen list. The following are on the 2016 list:

Avocados	Papayas
Corn	Kiw
Pineapples	Eggplant
Cabbage	Honeydew
Sweet peas	Grapefruit
Onions	Cantaloupe
Asparagus	Cauliflower
Mangos	

- *Some of the sweet corn sold in the United States are made from genetically engineered (GE) seedstock. Buy organic varieties of these crops to avoid GE produce.*

Appendix 3 Recipes Index

Printed in Great Britain
by Amazon

85023879R00106